# principles & practice of medical computing

# principles & practice of medical computing

edited by L G Whitby and W Lutz

foreword by J H F Brotherston

Churchill Livingstone    Edinburgh and London    1971

ISBN 0 443 00778 0

*Filmset in Plantin by Typesetting Services Ltd., Glasgow and Edinburgh and Printed Offset by T. & A. Constable Ltd., Edinburgh*

# Foreword

'Computers, with all their implications in terms of equipment, procedures and ways of thinking, will play too large a part in the work of all doctors in the future to be left entirely to the expert; every doctor should at least learn to understand their basic principles and potentialities.'

This passage from the Report of the Royal Commission on Medical Education (1968) sums up admirably the justification for the publication of this book. It is written, not for the computer specialist, but for the medical undergraduate and graduate, no matter in what field his medical interests lie.

The authors make the point that computer science is essentially a practical discipline. This book, the contributors to which include both pioneers and experts in their own fields, attempts firstly to ensure awareness of the broad principles. It stresses that to obtain a true understanding, both of the potential of the computer and of its limitations, it is necessary to become involved at a practical level in the programming and in the use of computer equipment. While the majority of doctors will be content to obtain a grasp of the basic principles, it is to be hoped that an increasing proportion of our younger generation of doctors will actively seek to adapt this powerful tool to their everyday work. Computers will only influence and advance the boundaries of medical science if both clinicians and medical administrators actively accept and involve themselves in their use.

The contributors illustrate, over a broad field covering medical administration, patient care, research and education, some of the applications of this new technology. An objective assessment is also made of the constraints that may hinder development, such as high costs, lack of highly skilled computer specialists and fears relating to the confidentiality of medical data held on computer files. These are problems which will have to be solved but can be overcome.

I hope this book will obtain the wide circulation it deserves. Those who read it will be stimulated by the descriptions of a new technology which, if properly harnessed, could greatly influence the quality of medical care in our present day society.

1971

J. H. F. BROTHERSTON
Chief Medical Officer,
Scottish Home and Health Department

# Preface

IN 1967, the President of the United States' Science Advisory Committee on 'Computers in Higher Education' recorded its belief 'that the computer and computing are rapidly coming to have an impact on the life of practically every member of our society. Most people educated beyond the high school level will have occasion to make use of these tools, and all will need sufficient understanding of their possibilities and limitations realistically to appraise the new opportunities now available for information processing'. This American Report—commonly called the Pierce Report—was followed in 1970 in Britain by the Report of a Joint Working Party of the University Grants Committee and of the Computer Board for Universities and Research Councils on the subject of 'Teaching Computing in Universities'. Broadly speaking, the British Report agreed with the conclusions of the Pierce Report and estimated the requirements for implementing its recommendations.

In the context of medical practice and administration, medical education and research, there is already a considerable amount of experience and a wide range of interest in the application and exploitation of computer technology. To appreciate the possibilities and limitations it is necessary to have a basic knowledge of the principles underlying computing techniques, in their various forms, and an understanding of the extent to which these principles have been successfully applied to the specific field of medicine.

This book sets out to meet the requirements of the many groups of people nowadays interested in the field of medical computing. It has been written with a view to stimulating the interest of all medical undergraduates. We also believe that the book will provide a useful review of medical computing both for doctors and for administrators in the National Health Service. While mainly written on the basis of British experience, some of the lessons learned undoubtedly have wider origin and application. Two things should be made clear: the book has not been written for the computer specialist, nor does it set out to teach its readers how to write computer programs, although some features of program writing are discussed.

As editors, we would like to thank our contributors for having submitted their chapters remarkably promptly, and for having by and large accepted uncomplainingly the editorial revisions undertaken with a view to producing a degree of uniformity in presentation. We should also like to express our gratitude to our Secretaries, Miss D. A. Fisher, Mrs E. A. Welsh and Mrs S. H. Haston for having typed the manuscript, and to the Department of Medical Photography, University of Edinburgh for preparing many of the illustrations. Other acknowledgements for the reproduction of figures are cited in the relevant figure legends.

In conclusion, we would like to draw attention to two facts relating to the production of this book. Firstly, a comment is called for on the variable quality of reproduction of the Figures and Tables. This arises out of the fact that we decided to include examples of computer-printed documents, and the quality of their reproduction has been considerably influenced by the typing operation and by the nature of the paper on which the original document was produced. For instance, Figure 26 (p. 147) was produced by a teletype printing on to plain white paper, whereas, Table XIII (p. 119) was produced by a line-printer printing on to a form of stationery that is commonly used; this has a fine horizontally lined background alternating (with each vertical spacing) with segments of unlined paper. Secondly, and finally, we would like to thank our publishers, E. & S. Livingstone, for having recognised that computers are a fast moving field and for having done everything to ensure rapidity of publication while at the same time maintaining high standards of production.

Edinburgh, April, 1971                                          L. G. WHITBY
                                                               W. LUTZ

# List of Authors

H. P. Dinwoodie, General Practitioner, Edinburgh.

F. T. de Dombal, Senior Lecturer in Surgery, University of Leeds.

A. S. Duncan, Professor of Medical Education and Executive Dean of the Faculty of Medicine, University of Edinburgh.

D. C. Flenley, Senior Lecturer in Medicine, University of Edinburgh.

J. C. Gray, Principal Assistant Treasurer, South-Eastern Regional Hospital Board, Scotland.

J. D. Grene, General Practitioner, Warwick.

A. J. Harley, Principal Scientific Officer, National Lending Library for Science and Technology.

M. A. Heasman, Co-director of the Research and Intelligence Unit, Scottish Home and Health Department.

A. Iggo, Professor of Veterinary Physiology, University of Edinburgh.

W. Lutz, Senior Lecturer in Social Medicine, University of Edinburgh.

B. P. Marmion, Professor of Bacteriology, University of Edinburgh.

C. H. Nicholas, System Analyst, Edinburgh Regional Computing Centre.

J. H. Ottaway, Senior Lecturer in Biochemistry, University of Edinburgh.

R. J. Prescott, Lecturer in Social Medicine, University of Edinburgh.

R. W. Prince, Data Processing Officer, University of Edinburgh.

J. C. A. Raison, Senior Medical Officer, Department of Health and Social Security, and previously Senior Clinical Physiologist, Presbyterian Medical Center, San Francisco.

D. E. M. Taylor, Senior Lecturer in Physiology, University of Edinburgh and Honorary Consultant in Thoracic Surgery, Royal Infirmary of Edinburgh.

G. E. Thomas, Director, Edinburgh Regional Computing Centre.

H. R. A. Townsend, Consultant in Clinical Neurophysiology to the South-Eastern Regional Hospital Board, Scotland and Senior Lecturer in Surgical Neurology and in Machine Intelligence and Perception, University of Edinburgh.

L. G. Whitby, Professor of Clinical Chemistry and Dean of the Faculty of Medicine, University of Edinburgh.

Elizabeth D. Whittle, Information Officer to the Faculty of Medicine, University of Edinburgh and MEDLARS Liaison Officer for Scotland.

L. M. Williams, Treasurer, South-Eastern Regional Hospital Board, Scotland.

# Contents

## Section IV

## Some examples of the use of computers in research and medical education

## Section V

## Future developments and outstanding problems

# Glossary of computer terms

## Introduction: the term 'computer'

THE definitions in this glossary frequently refer to terms that are themselves explained elsewhere in the glossary. When cross-references apply within the glossary, such terms are printed in italics on first occurrence in a definition, the only exception to this rule being the term computer whenever it appears without a qualifying adjective. A computer is a generic term for all devices that can automatically accept data or signals, operate on these according to an internally stored set of previously defined rules or instructions, and proceed to supply the results of obeying these rules. It is usually understood that these rules can easily be altered to cope with a wide range of problems or tasks, and that it is possible to impose conditions such that alternate sets of rules are obeyed whenever these conditions are encountered. Computers vary considerably in their size and functions, and their cost may range from a few thousand pounds to several million pounds. Instruments covering such a wide spectrum of prices cannot be adequately described in a single definition, and the purpose of the book as a whole is to give a better understanding of computers and their capabilities. The interrelationships of many of the terms used in working with computers and defined in the glossary form the main subject matter of Chapters 1 and 2.

**Abbreviations:** The following abbreviations are used in the glossary:

adj = adjective
n = noun
syn = synonymous with
v = verb

**Access:** to find a piece of information (data) in a *store* and transmit it elsewhere or replace it.

**Access time:** the time taken to locate a piece of data, measured from the moment when the execution of the *instruction* began up to the time when the transfer of the data to the specified *location* has been completed.

**Accumulator:** a *register* in which the results of arithmetic and *logical operations* are formed.

**A D converter** (ADC): syn, *analog digital converter*.

**Address:** a label that identifies for the computer a specific *location* in *memory* where certain information is stored.

**ALGOL,** n: a *language* designed to simplify the programming of *digital computers* for scientific problems. It is an acronym for ALGOrithmic Language.

**Alphanumeric,** adj: a contraction of the words 'alphabetic' and 'numeric', applied to any *coding* system that provides for letters, numbers, and special symbols such as punctuation.

**Analog:** the representation and measurement of the performance or behaviour of a system by continuously variable physical entities (e.g. currents, voltages, etc.)

**Analog computer:** a computer which operates on continuous variable signals. Also, see introduction to glossary.

**Analog digital converter:** an instrument for expressing a continuous signal, current or wave in digital form (i.e. in numerical form), usually by sampling the analog signal at frequent intervals and converting the instantaneous sample reading from the continuous signal into a number.

**Analogue:** used synonymously with *analog*.

**Arithmetic unit:** the part of the *central processor* that performs arithmetic and *logical operations*.

**Array:** an arrangement of individual items of data, each specifically identifiable, and so constructed that a *program* can examine the whole arrangement and extract a specific item of data.

**Assembly language:** a *language* coded so as to have a simple and usually also a one-to-one correspondence with the structure of a *machine language,* but intended to be more readily intelligible to the *programmer.*

**Assembly program** (syn, assembler): a *program* which takes sequential *instructions* written in an *assembly language* and changes these into *machine language.*

**Autocode,** n: any computer (programming) *language* using a *mnemonic code.*

**Automation:** a term of convenience, for which the definition tends to vary according to the context. The concept of automation can include the design, development and application of methods or techniques so as to render a process or group of instruments self-actuating (e.g. automatic alarms), self-operating (e.g. automatic chemical analysis) and self-adjusting (i.e. there must be feed-back control for full automation to be present).

**Auxiliary store:** syn, *backing store.*

**Backing store:** *peripheral equipment* providing facilities for storing information in addition to the storage space available in the *memory* of the *central processor* of the computer.

**Batch processing:** the organisation of the work of a computer in such a way that the work is collected and fed into the computer in batches, for processing as a single unit.

**Baud,** n: a measure of the speed of transmission of information along a telegraph or telephone line, or other type of signal channel. Unit of measurement, *bits* per second.

**BCD:** syn, *binary coded decimal representation.*

**Binary:** syn, *binary representation*.

**Binary coded decimal representation** (BCD): a system of representing decimal numbers, each digit position of a decimal number being allocated four binary digits (*bits*) and the decimal number itself being represented as follows:

| Decimal code | | Binary representation | Decimal code | | Binary representation |
|---|---|---|---|---|---|
| 0 | = | 0000 | 5 | = | 0101 |
| 1 | = | 0001 | 6 | = | 0110 |
| 2 | = | 0010 | 7 | = | 0111 |
| 3 | = | 0011 | 8 | = | 1000 |
| 4 | = | 0100 | 9 | = | 1001 |

**Binary digit:** syn, *bit*.

**Binary number:** any number expressed in *binary representation* (i.e. as a string of *bits*), and thus easily represented in a digital computer.

**Binary representation:** a notation by which *alphanumeric* symbols are represented by the two digits 0 and 1 in an agreed sequence. In this system, the displacement of one digit position to the left denotes multiplication by a power of 2. Thus 1 means one, 10 means two, 100 means 4, etc. Also see *binary coded decimal representation*.

**Bit,** n: one of the two digits, 0 or 1, used in *binary representation* to build up strings of bits and thereby represent any number or *alphanumeric* code.

**Block:** a self-contained section of a *program*. Also, a short section of *magnetic tape*, usually of fixed length.

**Block diagram:** syn, *flow chart*.

**Boolean algebra:** a mathematical system devised in the 19th century by George Boole to express the relationships and results of logical operations such as AND and OR, and used in the preparation of the *logic design* of a *program* for any type of computer or mixed system.

**Bootstrap,** n: the technique whereby a *program* is *loaded* into a computer by means of preliminary *instructions* which in their turn call in further instructions to read in programs or data.

**Buffer:** a local *store*, restricted in its siting to a *peripheral* and serving that peripheral by temporarily holding data (*input* or *output*) so as to match the high speed of the *central processor* with the slower speeds of devices such as *teletypes, card readers,* etc.

**Bug:** an error in a *program,* or a troublesome aspect in the operation of a system.

**Byte,** n: a group of eight (very occasionally nine) *bits,* handled as a single unit by a *digital computer*.

**Capacity:** syn, *store capacity*.

**Card:** syn, *punched card*.

**Card field:** a number of consecutive columns assigned on a *punched card* and devoted to a unit of coded information.

**Card punch:** a device for punching holes on to *punched cards* in *alphanumeric* or in *binary* code. Also see *verifier*.

**Card reader:** a device for *reading* information from *punched cards* into a computer.

**Card sorter:** an instrument for sorting a deck of *punched cards* into subsets of cards according to which row has been punched. Sorting is carried out on one column at a time, on whichever column is set on the sorter.

**Central processor:** the unit of a *digital computer* installation that controls and performs the *execution* of *instructions*. It includes the *control unit*, the *memory* and the *arithmetic unit*.

**Character:** an *alphanumeric* symbol which constitutes, in some computers, the basic unit of information occupying one storage *location* and being manipulated as a single entity. Also, see *word*.

**COBOL,** n: a business *language* developed by the data processing industry and designed for manipulating *files* controlled by *digital computers*. It is an acronym for COmmon Business Oriented Language.

**Code:** (1), n: a system of *characters* and rules for representing information in a form that can be understood and handled by the computer; (2), v: the act of listing the possible answers or responses to a question and assigning a special character or code (n) to each of these answers. Also, see *precoded*.

**Coding,** n: the act of using a *code*.

**Collate:** to combine two *files*.

**Collator:** a device which combines two or more ordered decks of *cards* to produce a single ordered *file*.

**Comparator:** (1) an *analog* unit or *analog digital converter* in which two analog signals are compared and used to control logical operations governed by 'greater than' or 'less than' *conditional statements*; (2) a device for comparing two items and producing a signal which depends on the result of the comparison (e.g. when comparing two copies of punched paper tape by passing them through a comparator).

**Compile time:** the time required by a computer to translate a *program* into *machine language* and to perform any associated operations of data transfer prior to the *execution* of the *instructions*.

**Compiled program:** syn, *object program*. Also, see *compiler*.

**Compiler:** a *program* which translates a *source language* into the *machine language* of a particular computer.

**Computer:** see the introduction to this glossary. Also, see *analog computer, digital computer* and *hybrid computer*.

**Computer program:** syn, *program*.

**Computing amplifier:** syn, *operational amplifier*.

**Conditional statement:** a step in a program describing the conditions under which one of several alternative further paths will be followed and usually written in the form 'IF . . . THEN . . . '.

**Configuration:** the collection of equipment connected directly *on-line* to a computer or serving to put *peripheral equipment* on-line. The term includes the computer itself and any *backing store,* but generally excludes *off-line data preparation equipment.*

**Console:** a device through which the operator supervises and controls the *central processor* and the attached *peripheral equipment* during the operation of a *program.*

**Continuous number:** a system of numbers in which there is no step between successive numbers; no matter how close two numbers may approximate, it is always possible to interpose an intermediate number. Also, see *discrete number.*

**Control unit:** the section of the *central processor* which controls all information transfers and arithmetic *operations* in a *digital computer* and which, in most computers, also controls the sequence of operations and initiates the proper commands to the computer circuits after decoding each *instruction.*

**Conversational mode:** a method of controlling and using a computer from an *on-line terminal* whereby the appropriate *instruction* entered by an operator generates a response from the computer that indicates the next action to be taken by the operator.

**Core:** the fast *access memory* of the computer.

**Core memory:** syn, *memory.*

**Core store:** syn, *core.*

**CRAM:** acronym for Card Random Access Memory units which provide *file* storage for high-speed processing of data recorded on magnetic cards.

**Cycle:** the interval in which a set of events is completed. Also, see *loop, memory cycle.*

**Cycle time:** syn, *memory cycle.*

**Cylinder:** the set of data tracks passing at a given instant under the *read/write* heads of a *magnetic disc* that possesses more than one recording surface.

**D A converter:** syn, *digital analog converter.*

**Data acquisition:** syn, *data capture.*

**Data acquisition unit** (DAU): a *peripheral* used particularly in *real-time* systems for acquiring signals from equipment, sometimes situated remotely, and for transmitting these to the computer under *program* control.

**Data bank:** a *file* of data usually held on fast *access* storage devices (e.g. *magnetic disc*), and usually accessible for updating in *real time* via a number of remote *terminals.* Reels of magnetic tape can constitute an effective data bank, if fast access and real time working are not essential.

**Data base:** a *file* of data organised in such a way that a number of different applications can *access* and can *update* the file without constraining its design.

**Data capture:** the collection of data for *input* to a computer by some automatic means, usually by equipment connected *on-line* to a computer.

**Data preparation:** this expression is used to cover all the activities required to prepare information for *input* to a computer, including the clerical work which often precedes the operations of *card punching, verifying* and *sorting*.

**Data preparation equipment:** a comprehensive term which includes *card punches, card sorters* and *teletypes*; some of this equipment may be operated *on-line* to a computer.

**Data processing:** a general term for any sequence of *operations* which is carried out on data, such as *sorting, collating,* etc., and used to distinguish the wide range of procedures involving computers that cannot properly be called calculation.

**Debug:** (1), v: to isolate and remove all errors from a *program*; (2) as a noun, referring to the operation of debugging.

**Dedicated computer:** a computer installed for a special purpose or group of purposes, and restricted in its application to this one set of tasks.

**Diagnostics** (syn, diagnostic aids): a procedure whereby a computer *program* tests, during *compile time,* whether each *instruction* in another program that is being read in satisfies the rules of the program *language,* and which prints out a list of errors detected indicating their type and position in the program. It is also possible for a program that has been satisfactorily compiled to fault during its *execution,* if incorrect data preventing its execution are submitted, and diagnostics can help to define this type of fault as well.

**Digital analog converter:** an instrument that performs the reverse of the operations carried out by an *analog digital converter*.

**Digital computer:** a computer which can only operate at discrete signal levels. Only two levels of signal are normally used, resulting in *binary* operations. Also, see introduction to glossary.

**Diode:** A device used to permit the flow of current in one direction only, and thus used as a switching device to control current flow in an associated circuit.

**Diode function generator** (DFG): an *analog* unit which simulates a complex curve by dividing it into a series of straight lines, *diodes* being used to determine the switching point between lines and *operational amplifiers* so as to produce each linear segment. In a fixed diode function generator (FDFG) the function is pre-set (e.g. $x^2$, log x, etc.) whereas in a variable diode function generator (VDFG) the function is set by the operator to simulate any curve.

**Disc:** syn, *magnetic disc.*

**Disc drive:** the power mechanism rotating a *magnetic disc* or *drum*; it includes a driving motor and magnetic *read* and *write* heads.

**Disc pack:** a *disc storage* unit consisting of one or more *magnetic discs* mounted coaxially on a spindle, and fitted on to a *disc drive* where it is rotated continuously at high speed while in use; the disc pack may be either fixed or interchangeable (movable).

**Discrete number:** a system of numbers in which there is a fixed step between one number and the next (e.g. the *binary* scale). Also, see *continuous number.*

**Document reader:** syn, *optical character reader* (OCR).

**Document mark reader:** an instrument which detects marks made on specific areas of *coded* documents and forms, and interprets these marks as digits or *characters.*

**Double precision arithmetic:** a process in which two computer *words* are used to represent one number so as to obtain more accuracy than a single word of computer storage will provide.

**Down time:** an expression for the time when a computer or any *peripheral* vital to its operation is out of working order during the period scheduled for computer use.

**Drum:** syn, *magnetic drum.*

**Edit:** (1) to correct, modify or re-arrange *instructions* or data on *files*; (2) to correct errors in a deck of *cards* or on a reel of *paper tape.*

**Elapsed time:** the sum of *input* time PLUS *compile time* PLUS the time needed for *access* to *peripherals* PLUS the time required for actual computation PLUS *output* time. Computer costs are often based on elapsed time, but with complex computer systems this equation may no longer be valid.

**Erase:** to eradicate information *stored* on a storage device (e.g. *magnetic tape*).

**Execute:** to carry out an *instruction,* a *routine* or a *program.*

**External memory:** syn, *backing store.*

**Fail safe:** a term used to describe the situation where *hardware* provision has been made to incorporate duplicate or alternative devices, or *files,* to be available in the event of failure of the system, especially due to machine breakdown.

**Fail soft:** a term used to describe the organisation of a total computer system so that partial failure of the system still allows the operations of highest priority to continue, usually by suitable design of the *software.*

**Fast time:** a method of operation that is quicker than *real time.*

**Feedback loop:** the components and processes which are together involved in controlling or correcting a system by using part of the system's output to modify the input, thereby achieving self-correction.

**Ferrite core:** a magnetizable piece of material shaped into a core; it can be magnetized in one of two directions and is very stable in either state. It is a two-state device capable of representing one or other of the two *binary* states.

**Ferrite core store:** a collection of registers, each of which is a linear arrangement of a number of *ferrite cores*, and therefore has a correspondingly large capacity for storing data.

**Field:** a *character* or group of characters constituting one unit of information (e.g. the *bits* needed to encode a person's name). Sometimes used for a set of consecutive columns on *cards*, used as a fixed area for holding specified items of information.

**File:** any system of ordered or organised information. Also, see *record*.

**First generation computer:** a term used to refer to computers built between about 1946 and 1958, and which depended mainly on thermionic valves in their design.

**Fixed diode function generator** (FDFG): see *diode function generator*.

**Fixed word length:** a term which refers to computers that have a *word* which always contains the same number of *bits*. Also, see *variable word length*.

**Flow chart** (syn, flow diagram): a graphic representation that outlines sequentially the more important steps in a process, using symbols to represent computer (or machine) actions, but without detailing how the work is to be performed.

**FORTRAN,** n: a *language* especially suited for *programming digital computers* to undertake scientific (mathematical) work. It is an acronym for FORmula TRANslation.

**Full hybrid computer system:** see *hybrid computer*.

**Gate:** the basic type of logical component which carries out the *operations* of AND and OR. Combinations of gates are used to carry out parts of a *program* expressed in *Boolean algebra,* and are components in many types of digital computing units. Syn, *logic element*.

**Graph plotter:** a *peripheral* which draws graphs and pictures as *hard copy*.

**Hard copy:** visual or readable *output* from a computer in a form which can be stored, usually as printed results obtained with a *line printer* or *teletype,* or as graphical output on a *graph plotter*.

**Hardware:** the mechanical and electrical components of a computer system.

**High level language:** a *language* in which each *instruction* corresponds to several instructions when written in *machine code*.

**Hold mode:** see *mode*.

**Hybrid computer:** a computer containing both *analog* and *digital computing* elements, and one in which both types of element play an essential and significant role in the solution of problems. In a parallel hybrid computer the digital component is known as *parallel logic*; it has the functions both of a digital *control unit* and of a *central processor* but has no *memory* store. A full hybrid computer system consists of a parallel hybrid computer interfaced with a *digital computer*.

**Immediate access:** syn, *random access*.

**Indirect addressing:** a term that expresses the need to split a single *address* between two computer *words*, a procedure rendered necessary in computers with a short *word length* in which it may be impossible to address all parts of the *internal memory* with a single word.

**Initial condition:** the value possessed by each unit of an *analog computer* at zero time in the solution of a problem.

**Initial condition mode:** see *mode*.

**Input,** n: (1) the transfer of external information into the *central processor* or temporarily into a storage device; (2) used to describe the external information itself; also (3) sometimes used as a verb.

**Input/output terminal** (I/O terminal): see *terminal*.

**Instruction:** a *word* or sequence of *characters* which directs a computer to perform some *operation*.

**Instruction repertoire:** the collection of basic *instructions* which can be interpreted directly by a particular computer; all other instructions are combinations or arrangements of this basic repertoire. Also see *vocabulary*.

**Integrator:** see *operational amplifier*.

**Interactive:** syn, *conversational mode*.

**Interface,** n: (1) the connection between basic types of computers (e.g. the junction between the components of a *parallel hybrid computer*); (2) the connection between major computing components in a system of modular design; also (3) used as a verb.

**Internal memory:** syn, *immediate access store*: the main *memory* situated inside the *central processor* of the computer, and able to be *accessed* directly by *instructions*.

**Internally stored program:** a sequence of *instructions* stored inside the *central processor* and executed automatically, rather than having to be entered into the computer one at a time; the ability to hold an internally stored program is one of the principal differences between a computer and a calculating machine.

**Interrupt:** a temporary break in a *program* or *routine* caused by an event which is described by *instructions* that are rated as having higher priority for being processed than the program or routine that is currently being handled; such breaks may be achieved immediately or at the next predetermined step that permits interrupts in the program that is being processed, the interrupted program later being resumed from the point at which the break occurred.

**Interrupt levels:** the *hardware* provision which permits *programs* or *routines* to be ranked in orders of priority for processing by a computer.

**Iteration:** the repetitive running of a series of equations on any type of computer, during which a small change is made under the control of *program instructions* or of *parallel logic* in one *initial condition* on each successive run, the final solution to the problem being obtained by successive approximations. Also see *repetitive operation*.

**K,** n: the symbol is an abbreviation for $2^{10}$, or 1024; it is used as a basic unit to denote the number of *locations* or *words* in a computer's *memory*. For instance, a computer described as having a 16K *core store* has a memory that contains $16 \times 2^{10}$ or 16,384 locations.

**Language:** a term used to describe a *coding* system by which *instructions* may be given to a computer. Also, see *ALGOL, assembly language, COBOL, FORTRAN, high level language, machine language*, etc.

**Library:** this term has three main connotations when used in connection with computing: (1) a collection of books and periodicals on computers and computing; (2) a collection of proven *programs* and *routines*; and (3) a collection of data *files*. The first meaning is self-explanatory. With the two other meanings, the collection may be stored *off-line* (as *hard copy*, *paper tape*, etc.) or *on-line* where it can be called directly into a program during *execution*.

**Light pen:** a device used with a *visual display unit* (VDU) to identify to the computer a precise point on the cathode ray screen.

**Limiter:** see *operational amplifier*.

**Line printer:** a fast computer-controlled printing device which prints whole lines of *characters* in one *operation* rather than character by character.

**Load:** to move a *program* from *external memory* or any other *peripheral* device into the proper *location* in *internal memory*; the same term applies to movements of data.

**Location:** a place in *store* where a unit of data or an *instruction* may be stored.

**Logic design:** a description of the working relationships between the parts of a computer system, but one which does not take into account the detailed nature of the equipment that could be used.

**Logic diagram:** a graphical representation of the *logic design*.

**Loop:** a *coding* technique whereby a group of *instructions* is repeated, possibly with modification of some of the instructions within the group or with modification of the data being operated on, or with modification of both instructions and data.

**Low level language:** (syn, *basic language*). A language in which each *instruction* has a single equivalent in *machine code*.

**Machine equation:** a mathematical statement which has been scaled in terms of *machine units* and *machine time* so as to be acceptable in an *analog program* and to be capable of being *simulated* by a single unit or module.

**Machine language:** a form of coded *instruction* upon which a computer can act directly without any further setting or translation. Different types of computers have their own particular machine languages.

**Machine time:** the representation of time used by an *analog* or *hybrid computer* when solving a problem involving time as one of the variables. It is usually expressed in terms of *machine units* and is related to actual time by the *time scaler*.

**Machine unit** (MU): the basic unit used in writing *programs* for an *analog computer*. The *reference voltage* of the computer is normally equivalent to 1 MU, giving a range for each module in the computer of from $-1$ MU to $+1$ MU. The use of machine units allows an analog program to be independent of the machine.

**Magnetic core memory:** a common *internal memory* device usually consisting of thousands of magnetic cores arranged in layers to make a stack. Each individual core element may be magnetized in one of two directions, depending on the direction of current flow, so as to *store* the value of one *bit*. One magnetic direction represents a *binary* one, the other a binary zero.

**Magnetic disc:** a fast random *access* bulk *store* in the form of *discs* coated with a magnetic layer, and which resemble gramophone records on which information is stored in *binary* form on concentric tracks.

**Magnetic drum:** a fast random *access* bulk *store,* in the form of a rotating cylinder coated with a magnetic layer, for holding information in *binary* form.

**Magnetic tape:** a slow (relative to *magnetic disc* or *magnetic drum*) *access* but high capacity cheap bulk *store*. Information in *binary* form is held sequentially on tape which is made of film or plastic coated with a magnetic material.

**Mark sense documents:** documents of which parts are divided into columns that are usually two or three times the width of normal punching columns, so as to facilitate *mark sensing*.

**Mark sensing:** a system in which marks made in fixed positions on a document are *read* optically or electrically and *coded*.

**Matrix:** a term which has two particularly common meanings in relation to computers: (1) in mathematics, an *array* of quantities in prescribed form, usually capable of being subjected to mathematical operations; (2) an array of coupled circuit elements (e.g. *diodes, magnetic cores*).

**Memory:** a general term for the equipment that *stores* information in *binary code*, in electrical or in magnetic form.

**Memory bank:** a term which usually implies a large *store capacity*, applied to a collection of devices for storing information external to the computer (e.g. *magnetic discs, drums* or *tapes*).

**Memory cycle:** the time required to complete the processes of making a copy of a *character* held in *core store* and placing this copy into the *arithmetic* or *control unit*.

**Merge:** to combine two or more *files* into a single file, usually in a specified sequence.

**Microsecond** ($\mu$s): one millionth of a second.

**Millisecond** (ms): one thousandth of a second.

**Mnemonic code:** *instructions* for a computer written in a form which is easier for the *programmer* to remember and to follow, but which must later be converted into *machine language*.

**Mode:** (1) for a *digital computer*, a term used to describe the method of operation (e.g. *batch processing* mode, *on-line* processing mode); (2) for *analog* and *hybrid computers*, or any of their computing modules, a term used to describe their state, the mode usually being controlled by switches between or within modules which can be either under manual control of the operator, or controlled by *parallel logic* or by an interfaced digital computer, the common modes being set-pot mode (where equation constants are set up on potentiometers), initial condition mode (where initial conditions are set and the *debug* carried out), operate mode (where the problem solution is carried out), hold mode (where a problem solution can be stopped and held at a given point), and rep-op mode (where problem solution is performed repetitively and usually at high speed).

**Modem,** n: a device which enables data to be transmitted over long distances. An acronym for MOdulator/DEModulator.

**Module:** a part of the circuits in a computer or a *peripheral* device, manufactured as a sub-unit so that it can be easily detached from, or attached to, the system. It is common practice for different modules to be designed to certain standard specifications, so that they can be more readily interchanged or interconnected so as to construct a larger unit.

**Monitor:** (1) a type of *program* used to supervise and verify the correct *operation* of other programs during their *execution*; (2) a term applied to the supervision of the functioning of certain biological systems, to give warning of undesirable levels or patterns and in some instances to initiate remedial action. Also see *patient monitoring*.

**Multi-access system:** a system connecting several (up to several hundred) *input/output terminals on-line* to a single central computer in such a way that the terminals can be used independently and simultaneously for completely unrelated tasks. It is usual to operate a multi-access system under a *time sharing* arrangement so that none of the on-line terminals need wait for any significant length of time before signals are accepted and responded to by the computer.

**Multiplexor:** a connecting device interfaced between a computer and two or more *peripheral* devices (e.g. *teletypes*), and which samples these devices in a serial manner (not necessarily consecutively); as a result these peripherals can all effectively operate simultaneously on a single *input* channel.

**Multiplier:** a class of composite *diode function generators* which carry out the procedures of multiplication, division, squaring and taking a square root.

**Multiprocessing:** a term loosely used to refer to the *execution* of over-lapping *programs*. Also see *multiprogramming*.

**Multiprocessor:** a term used to describe a *central processor* which has two or more independent *arithmetic units* and their associated *control units*.

**Multiprogramming:** a technique for handling numerous *routines* or *programs*, while simultaneously held in core, by overlapping or inter-leaving their *execution* (thereby permitting *time sharing* of machine components by two or more programs). Also see *multithreading*.

**Multithreading:** a term which is almost synonymous with *multi-programming*, but the operations are all carried out in *real time*.

**Nanosecond** (ns): one thousand-millionth ($10^{-9}$) of a second.

**Noise:** a term that describes the occurrence of random variations in a signal either during recording or during transmission; it is usually un-wanted, and the use of the term implies that the true signal has in some way been obscured.

**Object program** (syn, *compiled program*): a *program* that has been translated into *machine language*. Also, see *compiler*.

**Off-line:** a part of a computer system is described as off-line if it acts independently of the control exerted by the *central processor*.

**Off-line operation:** the performance of an *operation* (e.g. *in data processing*) using equipment that is not connected to and therefore not controlled by the *central processor*.

**On-line:** a part of a computer system is described as on-line if it is directly under the control of the *central processor*. Also, see *peripherals*.

**On-line operation:** the performance of *operations* (e.g. in *data processing*) under *program* control exerted by the *central processor* of the computer system.

**Operate mode:** see *mode*.

**Operation:** a specific action which the computer performs automatically whenever an *instruction* calls for it (e.g. addition, subtraction, comparison).

**Operational amplifier:** these are *analog* computing units that consist of high gain amplifiers with input and feed-back impedance networks arranged so that the output bears an assigned relation to the input, the ratio of output to input being known as the *transfer function*. The commonest types are the summer-inverter (which adds inputs and reverses the sign), integrator (where the output is the time integral of the input), and limiter (where output equals input, only with limits applied). In this definition, the words input and output refer to voltages and are not being used as specific computer terms.

**Optical character reader** (OCR): an instrument designed to recognise *characters* by analysis of their detailed shape and to read this information into a computer system.

**Optical scanner:** a device that scans any light-reflecting surface, and converts the degree of light reflection into *binary* form for *input* to a computer. Can also be used with light-transmitting surfaces.

**Output,** n: (1) information that has been processed by the *central processor* and issued to an external device (e.g. *line-printer, tape punch*); (2) the act of transferring such information to an external device; also (3) sometimes used as a verb.

**Paper tape:** a punched (*coded*) ribbon of paper used both as computer *input* and as *output* medium.

**Parallel hybrid computer:** see *hybrid computer*.

**Parallel logic:** see *hybrid computer*.

**Parallel working:** a phase during the introduction of a computer-based system when it is necessary that some or all the processes in which the computer is to be involved should continue to be operated by the methods used hitherto as well as in the new computer-dependent manner, usually for reasons of security and validation.

**Parity check:** a technique which checks the *binary* coding of a *character*, by counting digits, so that an error in the *code* representing the character can in most cases be automatically detected, the convention being that the number of digits is always even, or always odd.

**Patch:** to set up a *program* for an *analog* or *hybrid computer* on the *patch panel* of a computer by means of external cables or plugs that interconnect the units of the computer.

**Patch panel:** the component of an *analog* or *hybrid computer* on which the *input, output* and feed-back connections of the computing units terminate, and on which the *program* is *patched*. Patch panels are frequently removable, enabling programs which have been patched to be stored until required.

**Patient monitoring:** monitoring applied to patients; computer surveillance of some biological function of a patient. Also, see *monitor*.

**Peripherals** (syn, *peripheral devices or peripheral equipment*): These are physically independent auxiliary units which work under the direct control or supervision of the *central processor* (e.g. *line printer, card reader, tape punch, magnetic disc,* etc.).

**PL/1:** a *language* designed to combine and extend the features provided by both *COBOL* and *FORTRAN*. It is an acronym for Programming Language 1.

**Plotter:** syn, *graph plotter*.

**Precoded:** used to describe a document (e.g. a questionnaire) which has been divided into sub-sections, each sub-section being designated by a *code*.

**Printer:** syn, *line printer*.

**Program:** the term is spelled as shown and has two meanings: (1), n: a sequence of steps to be *executed* by the computer to solve a given problem; (2), v: to prepare a program (i.e. to plan the steps necessary for the computer to solve part of a problem).

**Programmer:** a person who plans the sequence of events that a computer must follow in order to solve a problem and who describes them by using a *language* in order to write a *program*.

**Punch:** (1), n: a device for punching patterns of holes on *cards* or *paper tape* to represent a *code* that can be read by the computer or by a *peripheral* device; (2), v: the act of punching holes to represent coded information.

**Punched card:** a common means of entering data into a computer. Each *card* usually consists of 80 columns with 12 positions in each column. Also see *card punch*.

**Punched tape:** see *paper tape*.

**Radix:** the base of a numbering system, equal to the total number of distinct values or symbols used in the numbering system. In the *binary scale* there are only two marks or symbols (0 and 1); the radix is therefore two.

**Random access store:** a form of *memory* so constructed that the time taken to *access* any part of the store is largely independent of its position within the store. Also, see *sequential access*.

**Read:** (1), v: to acquire information, usually from some form of storage; (2), v: to scan a document (as part of a *coding* operation—e.g. *mark sensing*); (3), n: the process of transmitting *instructions* or data from *paper tape* or *cards* into a computer.

**Reader:** an instrument for reading *coded* information into a computer. Usually a *paper tape reader* or *card reader*. Also see *document mark reader, optical character reader*.

**Readout:** the manner in which a computer displays information that has been processed (e.g. in the form of *punched tape, punched cards,* printed reports, etc.).

**Read/write head:** an electromagnetic component of magnetic storage equipment (e.g. *magnetic discs, tape*) that can *write* on to the magnetic surface by converting incoming pulses into magnetic spots, or *read* off the surface by generating electrical pulses when it passes over magnetic spots.

**Real time:** *operations* performed by a *data processing* system that occur fast enough to analyse and control external events (i.e. the operations proceed sufficiently quickly for the information output from the computer to affect and influence actions and decisions repeatedly within the overall system).

**Record:** (1), v: to put data into some form of *store* (e.g. *magnetic tape*); (2), n: one or more items of information usually pertaining to a recognisable entity (e.g. a patient, an experiment, or a transaction); used in this way the term often implies some ordering or arrangement of the information on a *file*.

**Record linkage:** the bringing together of *records* relating to one individual (or to one family), the records originating at different times or places, under circumstances where identification data are often incomplete.

**Reference supply:** a voltage supply from a single source in an *analog computer*, this supply being used as the *machine unit* in terms of which all other voltages are measured.

**Register:** (1) with *digital computers,* a device within the *central processor* used for storing a piece of information while it is being used or until it is used, each register usually storing no more than one *word* or one *field* at a time; (2) with *hybrid computers,* a *parallel logic* unit which can be used for storing digital information until required.

**Reliability:** the ability of a component, device, unit of equipment or functional section of a system to perform to a specified standard when required, without remedial action apart from routine servicing. Reliability is measured in terms of probability that no failure will occur within a specified period, or as the mean time that elapses between failures.

**Repetitive operation:** the repeated solution of the same equation without change in the *initial conditions*; this technique can be used at high rates of repetition to display a solution as an apparently steady graph on an oscilloscope. Also, see *iteration*.

**Rep-op mode:** see *mode*.

**Reproducer:** an instrument for duplicating a pack of *punched cards*. Most reproducers have facilities for adding, deleting or interchanging columns on the duplicated pack as compared with the original card pack.

**Reset mode** (syn, *initial condition mode*): see mode.

**Response time:** the time interval between *input* to a computer and the corresponding *output*. A term frequently used in connection with *on-line* and *real time* computer systems.

**Routine:** (1) a set of *instructions* arranged in the correct sequence so as to direct the computer to perform a common *operation* or series of operations; (2) a small *program* or portion of a program. Also, see *subroutine*.

**Satellite computer**: a computer which forms part of a larger *data processing* system, usually situated at a distance from the main *central processor* which *supervises* and controls the flow of information within the overall system.

**Scale**: to multiply equations capable of simulation by a single *analog* unit by a scaling factor, so that the equations are acceptable for solution by an *analog computer* in terms of *machine units* (MU). With a correctly scaled *machine equation*, neither side of the equation will exceed the limits $\pm 1$ MU during problem solution. Also, see *time scaling*.

**Scaler**: an *analog* unit in which the *output* is a fixed proportion of the *input*, and one which carries out the mathematical procedure $y = kx$. (The commonest example is a variable potentiometer.)

**Search**: to examine (or search) *files* for items with particular properties or conforming to specified criteria (e.g. a selected diagnosis).

**Second generation computer**: a term used to refer to computers built between about 1958 and 1965, and in which the thermionic valve of the *first generation computers* was replaced by the transistor, a *solid state* device which made them more compact, more reliable, faster, and less productive of heat than the first generation machines.

**Sequential access**: the characteristic method of operation of a storage device on which *access* to any section of *memory* is not possible without having to pass through all the sections physically intervening between the required section and the present position of the *read* or *write head* (e.g. *magnetic tape*). Also, see *random access store*.

**Serial processing**: a type of *data processing* occurring within a *digital computer*, whereby all *programs* are handled sequentially rather than simultaneously.

**Set-pot mode**: see *mode*.

**Simulate** (simulation): to represent a system in a computer by a model which will react to changes in a manner similar to those observed in the system that is being simulated.

**Slave**: to control the *operation* or *mode* of a computer from another computer with which the slave computer is *interfaced*.

**Software,** n: a generic term for all *programs, routines, compilers,* etc., that set the *hardware* of the computer to perform the required tasks or to solve specified problems.

**Solid state devices**: electronic devices (e.g. transistors) which utilise the properties of semi-conducting materials. See *second generation computer*.

**Sort,** n: a *program* which arranges a *file* of *items* in a logical sequence, according to a designated key *word* or *field* contained within each item (e.g. the arranging of items according to date, serial number, etc.).

**Sorter**: see *card sorter*.

**Source language:** the *language* in which a *program* is initially written; this is usually some type of *mnemonic code* or procedure-orientated notation, but is not *machine language*.

**Source program:** a *program* that is not written in *machine language*. See *source language*.

**Static check:** the *debug* of an *analog computer program*.

**Store:** (1), v: to hold in *memory*; (2), n: see *memory*.

**Store capacity:** the amount of data that can be retained in the *memory* of a computer; usually expressed as the number of *words* or *characters* that can be retained and often quoted in terms of *K* words or K *bytes*.

**Subroutine:** part of a *routine*; the *operations* constitute self-contained sections of a *program*, and *software* systems are often designed to permit frequently required subroutines to be called from a random access *library* into a program as and when required during *execution*.

**Summer-inverter:** see *operational amplifier*.

**Supervise:** see *monitor*.

**Symbolic code:** see *mnemonic code*.

**Systems analysis:** the analysis of an activity to determine precisely what is required of the system, how this can best be accomplished, and in what ways a computer can be useful; a vital preliminary to the preparation of any computer *programs* for the task.

**Tape:** a term used to refer loosely to *paper tape* or to *magnetic tape*.

**Tape punch:** (1) a device for punching holes in *paper tape,* usually a keyboard operated unit. The term can also be used (2) to describe an *output* device which generates *punched tape* under the control of the *central processor*.

**Telecommunications:** (1) a general term that includes the transmission of data between a computing system and remotely located devices, via a unit that performs the necessary formal conversion and controls the rate of transmission; also (2) the reception of data by similar means.

**Teletype:** a slow keyboard device similar to an electric typewriter, used for *input* of *instructions* or data into a computer, either when attached directly *on-line* or, as an *off-line* device, with the intermediate production of *punched tape* in which case the equipment includes a *paper tape reader* and *punch*. Teletypes are being increasingly used as the simplest on-line device, where they can also serve as a slow *output* device, for the production of *hard copy* or paper tape.

**Terminal:** a device at the end of a communication line, usually as an *input/output* instrument capable of *on-line* communication with a computer. Typical examples of on-line terminals are *teletypes* and *visual display units*.

**Test routine:** a routine designed to test whether or not a computer is functioning properly.

**Third generation computer:** a term used to refer to computers that have only been commercially available since 1965; their configurations are built up from compatible modular parts which enable configurations to be extended and modified with considerable flexibility.

**Throughput:** the amount of data that is processed by a computer within a given period of time. Computers with 'high throughput rates' in general have a large *core store*, a rapid *memory cycle*, and are provided with fast *access backing stores*.

**Time scaling:** when an equation contains time as its variable, the process of scaling this equation (see *scale*) is called time scaling. When the time scaling factor is 1, problem solution is said to occur in *real time*, if less than 1, in fast time and if greater than 1, in extended time.

**Time sharing:** (1) a system whereby a single *program* is processed in the *central processor* for a short period (or until *access* to a slower device is necessary) this program then being dumped to permit *execution* of another program; time sharing will, in general, permit a variable allocation of time according to an agreed system of job priorities, carried out under the control of the *monitor*; (2) a system of allocating certain *hardware* features or devices in sequence to concurrently running work, with one of the programs receiving a short period of access (or use) of the device before the concurrently running program receives a similar short period of access; (3) the term is sometimes loosely used synonymously with *multiprogramming*.

**Time slicing:** a special form of *time sharing* in which time is allocated to different users in fixed slices (e.g. a stated number of seconds). If the *program* or sub-program is not completed during its slice of time, it is temporarily dumped and another program is given its turn. This system of time sharing favours the processing of short jobs.

**Track store:** an *operational amplifier* which can either follow (track) or hold (store) the value of a variable during problem solution under the control of *parallel logic*. It can be used to give a limited short term *analog memory* to a *parallel hybrid computer* complementary to the digital memory provided by *registers*.

**Transducer:** a sensing element which transforms the variable being measured (e.g. temperature, pressure) into an electrical signal proportional to its value.

**Transfer function:** a concise mathematical notation for the relationship of the output of an *operational amplifier* or group of operational amplifiers to the input to the amplifier(s).

**Transfer time:** The time required to complete the process of making a copy of a *block* of information from an *external memory* and bringing this into *core store*.

**Translate:** this describes the process of converting one computer *language* into another. Also, see *compiler*.

**Updating:** the act of processing changes in the contents of a data *file* by adding, deleting or modifying information.

**Up time:** the time during which a computer is operating or is able to be operated without malfunction; usually expressed as a percentage of the scheduled operating time. Also, see *down time*.

**Variable diode function generator** (VDFG): see *diode function generator*.

**Variable word length:** a term applied to computers where the number of *bits* comprising a computer *word* is not fixed, thus allowing the *programmer* some flexibility in the *word length* he uses, and permitting better use of *core* space. Also, see *fixed word length*.

**Verifier:** a piece of equipment used for checking the accuracy of *punched cards* or *paper tape,* by comparing the pattern of holes already punched with the pattern associated with the key that has been depressed on the verifier's keyboard; if the patterns differ an error signal is given.

**Visual display unit** (VDU): an *input/output* device on which information is displayed visually by means of a cathode ray tube or screen. Some devices permit both graphical display and the display of text, and some permit graphical input by means of a *light pen*.

**Vocabulary:** a list of operating *codes* or *instructions* available to the *programmer* for the writing of other *programs,* and *routines*. The size of the vocabulary varies with the make and size of the computer and with the available *software*. Generally, the larger the vocabulary the easier it is to program the computer. Also, see *instruction repertoire*.

**Word:** in computer terminology, this is used to represent a collection of *bits* treated as a single entity by the computer and having a single *location* and *address*. A word constitutes the basic item of information; it is treated by the *control unit* as an *instruction*, and by the *arithmetic unit* as a quantity.

**Word length:** the number of *bits* constituting a *word*. The word length in the earlier computers was set by the manufacturer but varied with the type of computer (12, 18, 36 and 48 bit words were common). More recently manufactured computers have a *variable word length*. A distinction needs to be drawn between a computer word, which may have a fixed length of *bits*, and an *instruction* word or a *program* word which may give rise to a variable length of *characters*.

**Write:** in computer terminology, this means (1) to impart or introduce information, usually into some form of storage device (e.g. *magnetic tape*), and (2) to transfer information from *internal store* to an *output* device or to a *backing store*.

**X-Y plotter:** a *graph plotter* which continuously draws a graph of the relationship between two variables in response to digital or *analog* signals.

## Suggestions for further reading or consultation

Cawthorn, J. I. (1970). *Data Trend: Data EDP Manual*, 3rd ed. Sydney, New South Wales: Rydge Publications.

Chandor, A., Graham, J. & Williamson, R. (1970). *A Dictionary of Computers*. Harmondsworth, Middlesex: Penguin Books.

Weik, M. H. (1969). *Standard Dictionary of Computers and Information Processing*. New York: Hayden Book Co.

# Symbols Used in Flow Charts and Program Descriptions

## Symbols used particularly in digital computer systems

The flow or direction of successive stages of a system or program is indicated by connecting the various symbols by lines, usually marked with arrow heads to indicate the direction of movement. Explanatory legends are written within the symbols, the size of which may be varied according to the instruction requirements.

| Symbol | Name | Definition |
|---|---|---|
| | Connector | The start or end of a computer system or program. Points of entry and of exit on a flow chart. |
| | Terminal, interrupt | A terminal point in a flow chart, often an on-line interrupt to start or stop a program. |
| | Process | A section of a system or a program executing a defined operation. |
| | Decision | A decision or switching operation as a result of which one of a number of alternative paths is followed. |
| | Input/output (I/O) | Input/output, or read/write instructions. |
| | Punched card | An I/O function in which the medium is a machine-readable card (e.g. punched card, mark sense card). |
| | Document | An I/O function in which the medium is a document. |
| | Display | An I/O function in which the information is often shown in visible form (e.g. visual display unit). |
| | Magnetic tape | An I/O function in which the medium is magnetic tape. |
| | Magnetic disc | An I/O function in which the medium is a magnetic disc. |
| | Communication link | A symbol indicating transfer of information by a telecommunications link (from left to right for a horizontal symbol; from top to bottom for a vertical symbol). |

| Symbol | Name | Definition |
|---|---|---|
| | Auxiliary operation | An off-line operation, performed on equipment not directly under control of the central processor. |
| | Manual operation | Any off-line process geared to the speed of a human being, without using mechanical aid. |

## Symbols used in analog computer systems

The descriptions of the modules represented by the following commonly used analog computing symbols are to be found in the glossary or in Chapter 2, as indicated by the page reference numbers.

| Symbol | Name | Page references |
|---|---|---|
| | Resistor | 38–41 |
| | Capacitor | 40–41 |
| | Diode | xvi |
| | Grounded potentiometer | 42–43 |
| | Ungrounded potentiometer | 42–43 |
| | High gain amplifier | 38–41 |
| | Summer-inverter | 40 |
| | Integrator | 40 |
| | Function generator (The class of function is indicated in the small box: e.g. log x, sin x). | 42 |
| | Comparator and associated switch | xiv |

### REFERENCE
BRITISH STANDARD 4058: Part 1 (1966). *Specification for data processing problem definition and analysis*. Part 1: Flow chart symbols. London: British Standards Institution.

# A General Introduction to Computers

# CHAPTER ONE

# Digital Computers and the Basis of Their Operation

## By W. LUTZ

### SUMMARY

THIS chapter describes the main features of digital computers and the peripheral equipment that can be used with them. The various categories of programming languages and the different modes of operation are described. Some of the more detailed concepts relating to the operations performed by computers are considered in a very elementary form in an Appendix to the chapter; the fundamental requirement of the digital computer is for it to receive its information in a highly precise, ordered and structured manner.

The importance of defining the nature of each project before deciding on the type of computing facility is stressed; the very flexibility of the digital computer rules out a single best or unique solution. Consideration needs to be given to the various possible modes of operation, and whether to select off-line batch mode, on-line, or real time operation or some variation of these. For a particular task, some methods of operation may prove cheaper, faster or more convenient than others.

### INTRODUCTION

The digital computer is a generic term for all devices that can automatically accept binary data or signals, operate on these according to an internally stored set of rules or instructions, and then proceed to supply the results of obeying these rules. The digital computer is often described as the most versatile machine yet invented, but it must operate under constraints and limitations; these can largely be understood in non-technical terms. The rules governing the computer's operation can be altered to cope with a wide range of problems or tasks, and it is possible to impose certain conditions which cause an alternative set of rules to be obeyed whenever these conditions are met.

This chapter outlines the basic features of hardware and software common to most present day digital computers. It draws attention to the fact that, while computers are not manufactured to users' specifications, there is now available a sufficient range of hardware options and peripherals, and the organisation of these in relation to one another is so flexible that the larger computer installations are effectively assembled to meet the customer's requirements. This generalisation has immediately to be qualified by a cautionary reference to cost, which is nearly always a limiting factor when defining the required computer configuration.

Computers have achieved their importance mainly due to the following reasons:

1. The accuracy and speed with which they perform operations analogous to logical and arithmetical steps.

2. Their ability to store and retrieve large quantities of data.

3. The development of on-line techniques so that a single computer can serve, apparently simultaneously, an increasing number of users working on unrelated problems.

4. The relative ease with which they can be programmed to perform, within the limitations of the configuration selected, a seemingly unending variety of tasks.

The first three of these factors chiefly represent engineering and hardware achievements, and the fourth factor has depended on software development. Despite the intricacy of the computer's hardware, all installations conform to a single basic configuration.

## THE BASIC CONFIGURATION OF A DIGITAL COMPUTER

Figure 1 provides a simple representation of a digital computer installation. All must contain equipment designated in Figure 1 by the letters A, B, and C, and all but the smallest configurations also include category D equipment in one form or another. These components will now be briefly described, and then some of their more important features discussed in greater detail.

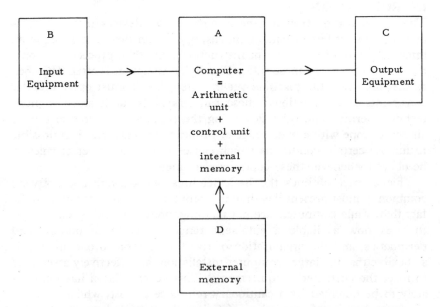

Fig. 1. The basic components of a digital computer configuration. Some systems do not include an external memory (D).

The digital computer itself (A, Fig. 1) consists of three essential sub-units, as follows: (1) the arithmetic unit, which does all the calculations in binary arithmetic; (2) the control unit, which governs the sequence and logic of the operations within the computer; and (3) the internal storage unit (often referred to as core or memory) for storing instructions and data both before, during and after the completion of a particular task. Each of these units may vary in size and complexity, and with the physical principles according to which the computer has been constructed.

The input equipment (B, Fig. 1) includes devices such as an electric typewriter and a paper tape or punched card reader. It provides a means of sending discrete electrical impulses into the digital computer, the order and pattern of these signals constituting a program of instructions for the computer to follow, or data for it to act upon. Nearly all computers, except the very smallest, can accept several different input modes on the same installation.

The output equipment (C, Fig. 1) displays, prints, or in some other way makes available the results of the computations. Electric typewriters, fast line printers, cathode ray display tubes and graph plotters are frequently used, and many computer installations can operate with at least three different types of output device; this makes such installations better able to meet the varying requirements of different jobs.

External storage (D, Fig. 1) usually consists of magnetic tape, disc, or drum units. Its purpose is to augment the storage capacity of the internal storage unit, but at comparatively low cost. Bulk storage requirements can only be satisfied economically, at present, by devices external to the computer.

## Peripheral devices

Input to a digital computer requires the generation of discrete electrical impulses. These can be produced with instruments connected directly to the computer, for instance by depressing a key and closing the corresponding circuit on the keyboard of an on-line teletype. Data can also be prepared for input as an off-line operation, for instance as punched cards or tape. The coded patterns on these documents can then be read into the computer by suitable readers which generate patterns of electrical signals corresponding to the coded representations on the input documents; these electrical patterns are produced by photo-electric detection of light shining through the punched tape or cards or, in the case of document mark readers, by differential reflection off the surface of the marked documents.

Output is essentially the reverse of the input process, the computer itself generating patterns of electrical impulses. When led on to suitable devices, these impulses set off printing or display mechanisms, or

TABLE I

A summary of the common peripherals (excluding storage units), together with some of their chief characteristics

| | Off-line operation | On-line operation | Speed range | Character set limitations | Computer input device | Computer output device |
|---|---|---|---|---|---|---|
| Teletype (without paper tape reader/punch) | — | ✓ | 10–15 characters per second | Usually 64 alphanumeric character set | Keyboard only | Typed hardcopy |
| Teletype with paper tape reader/punch | ✓ | ✓ | 10–15 characters per second | Same as above | Keyboard and paper tape input | Typed hardcopy plus punched paper tape |
| Visual Display Unit (VDU) (without a light pen) | — | ✓ | Keyboard at manual speeds. Screen display speeds from 1/10 sec. to 30 sec. for full renewal | Same as above | Keyboard only | Visual display only (no hardcopy) |
| Visual Display Unit (fitted with a light pen) | — | ✓ | Same as above | Same as above plus graphical input facilities | Keyboard plus graphical input | Visual display only (no hardcopy) |
| Mark (Sense) Reader | (Only if attached to an off-line recording device) | ✓ | Up to 200 cards/min. | No | ✓ | — |
| Card Reader | — | ✓ | From 100 to 2,000 cards/min. | Some models restricted to 64 alphanumeric character set | ✓ | — |

TABLE I (continued)

| | Off-line operation | On-line operation | Speed range | Character set limitations | Computer input device | Computer output device |
|---|---|---|---|---|---|---|
| Paper Tape Reader | (Only as a unit attached to a teletype) ✓ | ✓ | *Off-line:* 10–15 characters/sec. *On-line:* up to 2,000 chars./sec. | Alphanumeric | ✓ | — |
| Card Punch | ✓ | (Special on-line models only) | *Off-line:* Manual speed *On-line:* 100–500 cards/min. | No restrictions | — | ✓ |
| Paper Tape Punch | (Only as a unit attached to a teletype) ✓ | ✓ | *Off-line:* 10–15 characters/sec. *On-line:* up to 150 chars./sec. | Alphanumeric | — | ✓ |
| Line Printers | (Under special circumstances only) | ✓ | 80 to 2,000 lines/minute | Alphanumeric | — | ✓ |
| Graph Plotters | (Only with special attachments) | ✓ | Incremental plotters in speeds up to at least 3''/sec. (Non-incremental plotters attain faster speeds with less precision) | No limitations | — | ✓ |

**Note** Peripherals are undergoing a period of very intense development. Printers in particular are now available as line or serial printers employing electro-mechanical principles, photographic and sensitised paper methods and also ink-squirting techniques.

magnetise precise areas on magnetic media (e.g. discs or tapes) if the program stipulates that the information is to be stored in this way.

Peripheral devices perform tasks that can be conveniently considered under a limited number of headings. These include the ability to be used as off-line or on-line devices, their speed of operation, and whether they can serve as input or output devices, and the type of output they provide and the range of characters in the printing set. Table I lists these characteristics for some of the commoner peripheral devices, apart from external storage units (p. 11). While some peripherals (e.g. readers, punches and line printers) are clearly single function instruments, any of the consoles (on-line keyboard-operated input/output, or I/O, devices) are designed to be multi-functional.

The teletype is the cheapest and most flexible of the peripherals. If provided with a paper tape reader/punch unit, it can be used as an off-line device for preparing and checking programs and data punched on paper tape, while at the same time providing typed hard copy. The same instrument, slightly modified, can be used as an on-line console; if the paper tape unit is attached, the teletype can also serve as a slow paper tape I/O device. In whatever form it is used, the teletype is always restricted to a limited character set.

**The preparation of computer input: punched cards and tape**
Off-line devices are used almost entirely for the preparation or editing (correcting) of the input medium, which is usually in the form of paper tape or cards. The preparation of programs and data for computer input is unfortunately very liable to errors. These can occur at all stages, both in the preparation of programs and in the recording of data for computer input. Errors in programming will normally be discovered during preliminary test runs, but errors in data preparation may be much more difficult to eliminate. Mistakes in the data may occur at the time this is collected and recorded, or there may be errors at the time of coding and preparing for input to the computer (e.g. punching an 80-column card), or occasionally there may be instrumental failure such as misreading by a card reader. It is important, therefore, to verify and edit any mistakes detected in the input before running the program.

For editing paper tape the hard copy produced during the punching can be compared with the original data sheet. This visual checking should preferably be performed by another operator but even then is not entirely satisfactory. With punched cards it is best to have another operator check the complete pack with a verifier, in effect repeating the whole card-punching process.

The controversy over the relative merits of punched cards and paper tape has largely subsided. A pack of cards is relatively easily corrected by the replacement of incorrectly punched cards, whereas manually editing a large reel of tape is very tedious and requires skill. However, availability of on-line high speed paper tape punches has simplified the editing of paper tape, since corrections can now be effected by an on-line teletype using an editing program. Coding on paper tape is limited to a restricted character set. With cards on the other hand, there is the opportunity to use binary punching; this gives multiple-punched cards that bear codes not necessarily corresponding to any of the standard codes. This feature of punched cards can be particularly useful in recording multiple responses (e.g. answers to questions such as 'Which of the following drugs were administered?'). Some of the principal disadvantages of cards are their comparative bulk, and their sensitivity to dust, humidity and temperature. Moreover, the sequence of cards in a pack is vital to the operation of a program; this sequence may be disturbed without the fact being noticed or reported.

On balance, for work that needs versatile coding, or in investigations requiring the collection of data from a wide area (e.g. survey data, hospital records systems, etc.), punched cards have in general been found to be more convenient than paper tape as computer input medium. At computer installations catering for numerous small computing jobs entered by many users, however, paper tape may be the preferred input medium although such installations can often accept both tapes and cards. Efforts are in fact being made to eliminate the need for punched tape or cards altogether. Document readers capable of reading type or standard print have recently become available but are still very expensive. Simple devices (document mark sense readers) that detect marks on specified areas of coded documents and translate these marks into the equivalent coded electrical impulses are now being offered at moderately competitive prices, although they are still considerably more expensive than teletype units.

## Bits, bytes, words and blocks

The program of instructions on which a computer acts, and the data it is required to process, are composed of discrete units of information or 'bits'. A bit, which is short for binary digit, can take on one of two possible values, either 0 or 1; these correspond to the two possible physical states of 'off' and 'on' in the case of electrical circuits, or to the demagnetised as against the magnetised state of magnetic components. Symbols other than 0 or 1 are represented by a string or pattern of bits, and a byte has been found the most useful working unit of information. Bytes usually consist of eight successive bits.

The byte allows unique representation of a 64 character set, by making use of the first six bits, each of which can take on two possible values ($2^6 = 64$). This character set can include the 26 upper case letters of the alphabet, the digits 0 to 9, the usual punctuation marks, and a number of special algebraic and programming symbols. This leaves two bits in each byte uncommitted. The seventh bit is used frequently for parity checking, and the eighth bit is available for other checks or signals useful in the transmission of information (Fig. 2).

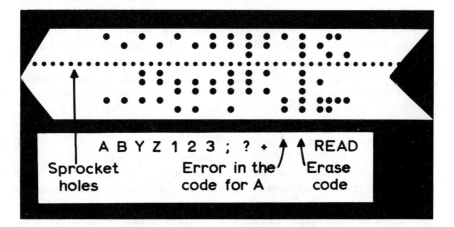

FIG. 2. Example of a strip of punched paper tape. The sprocket holes serve as a guide in the tape punch or tape reader, but play no part in codings. With this particular example, acceptable codings have an even number of holes punched, each of the 64 standard symbols being represented uniquely by a code containing an even number of holes. Several acceptable codings are shown, but the eleventh symbol punched, which should have been an A, shows three holes and a computer operating on even parity would immediately sense this error because of the odd number of holes punched. Errors such as the mispunched A can be corrected by over-punching with the erase code, which is here shown separately; this consists of eight holes and the erase code is ignored by the computer.

The unit of information for storing and manipulating information within the computer itself is the 'word'. First and second generation computers work with a fixed word length; this is an unalterable hardware feature of each computer model. Words of 12, 16, 18, 32, 36 and 48 bits in length are common. Third generation computers work with a variable word length of 1, 2, 4 and 8 bytes. To avoid unnecessary complication the word length of the third generation computer is taken as the byte, it being understood that bytes can be doubled up to form larger words as and when necessary.

On external memory devices, the smallest unit for purposes of updating or retrieval is the block, this being a number of successive words located on adjacent spaces on the magnetic surface. On most of these devices the size of the block (the number of successive words) has been fixed by the manufacturer, but on the most recent magnetic storage units the block size can to some extent be varied by program instructions.

## Memory: the internal storage unit (internal memory or core store)

The internal memory, apart from holding instructions and data, also stores all intermediate results arising during a computer's operations. The performance of the computer will be quite unacceptable unless the internal storage unit is extremely reliable and can be accessed at very high speeds. It is very expensive meeting such stringent engineering requirements and the size of a computer's internal memory is therefore limited, even in the most recent and the largest computers.

The size of the internal memory is usually expressed in units of K words ($1K = 2^{10} = 1024$). For instance, an 8K word computer has a core store of $8 \times 2^{10} = 8192$ separate and individually identifiable words. This measure of internal memory size is misleading unless the word size (e.g. 12-bit word or 18-bit word) of the computer is also quoted. This source of confusion does not arise with the large third generation computers, where the size is expressed in the number of bytes of memory (e.g. 256K bytes).

## Memory: external memory devices

The relatively high cost of core store and its consequently limited size means that external memory devices are needed. Fortunately, these can be attached as peripherals to a computer installation. There are three main types of external memory devices, namely magnetic tapes, magnetic drums and magnetic discs. These data storage devices are themselves I/O instruments in the sense that they can supply information as signals to the computer, and can store signals that are output from the computer.

The computer cannot act directly on any information held on external storage devices. It is necessary first to copy the information (referred to as reading from store) and transfer it to the internal memory of the computer. The computer can then manipulate this copied information according to programmed instructions and can, if required, transfer the results back to external storage (referred to as writing to store). Reading from a storage device, whether the internal memory or an external memory unit of a computer installation, is always non-destructive (i.e. taking a copy of stored information leaves the original stored data unaltered). Writing to store, however, is always destructive since the 'write head' always demagnetises the magnetic surface immediately prior to magnetically imprinting the new data; similarly an instruction to 'write' to a location in the core store automatically first erases any data held in that location. Most programming languages require write instructions to be preceded by instructions designed to reduce the likelihood of writing to a file in error and thereby destroying the original record.

Information stored on external devices cannot be read or written in single words. To locate and change a single word of information it is first necessary to read the corresponding block into core. The specified word is changed and the whole block, now suitably updated, is then written back into the same section from which it was read. The speed with which data can be located, copied from and transferred back to a storage device effectively determines the speed at which the computer operates in situations requiring frequent access to memory devices.

External memory devices extend the limited internal memory capacity of the computer. They have the additional attraction that some units (e.g. reels of magnetic tape) are interchangeable. Such units can be demounted and stored 'off-line', to be remounted when required.

### External memory: magnetic tape storage

Magnetic tape stores information in a serial manner along its length. This means that the tape has to be wound to the required section in order to give access to the information stored there. This is a very slow process in computer terms, sometimes taking seconds or even minutes. However, if the information can be accessed or written serially, then the time spent in moving from one block of information to the next is measured in milliseconds, which is much more acceptable. To reduce the number of long, frustrating searches on magnetic tape, if the computer installation can accept a fast access backing store (e.g. disc or drum), then it is often cheaper to read data held on magnetic tape on to the fast access store before proceeding to act upon it.

The principal advantage of magnetic tape is its relatively low cost. The storage capacity is easily and cheaply extended by acquiring additional reels which can be mounted by hand as and when required. Full utilisation of tape capacity is not usually possible, however, because of the need to store the information in 'blocks'; this means that spaces have to be left between blocks for recording details such as the block number which help with the location of blocks during updating and retrieval operations. The capacity for storing information is nevertheless very high—one reel of tape can store up to 29 million bytes of information. Storage on magnetic tape can thus provide 'fail-safe' storage relatively cheaply for data already stored on a faster access device.

### External memory: magnetic disc and drum storage

Magnetic discs consist of one or more rapidly rotating horizontal metal discs, stacked one above the other, each with magnetic tracks on their surfaces (except for the top and bottom discs, where only the inner surface is used). Arms which move horizontally carry the read/write heads. To locate a specified area on a disc, the arm moves to the required track and the disc then needs to spin at most through one complete revolution before the required block passes the read/write head. Some disc units are now available with fixed read/write heads; they have arms extending the full depth of the disc unit with a separate read/write head for each magnetic track, thereby eliminating arm movement. Both fixed head and replaceable disc units are available; the replaceable unit can be disconnected from the computer while another disc is connected in a manner somewhat analogous to replacing a reel of magnetic tape. The larger discs presently available are all of the fixed (i.e. non-replaceable) kind, but it may be possible to attach several of these units to the same computer.

Magnetic drums consist of rapidly revolving drums with magnetic tracks on their surface. Fixed multiple read/write heads are usually fitted, and so far drums have been of the fixed type only. As with disc units, however, it is possible to attach more than one fixed drum to a single computer.

Both discs and drums provide high speed access to stored data. However, these units are all relatively very expensive, when compared with a magnetic tape unit. Costs are beginning to fall, particularly for the larger units, in so far as the price of discs and drums does not increase in proportion with the storage capacity. Disc capacities range from 32K 12-bit words up to 688 million bytes.

## OPERATING A DIGITAL COMPUTER: PROGRAMMING

It is not possible to give a detailed description of the operation of a digital computer in a book of this size and scope. In summary, the operations are carried out within the computer itself, by the arithmetic unit acting under the direction of the control unit, which in turn has its operations determined by the program or section of the program of instructions held in the internal storage unit and relevant to the computer's operation at that point in time. The program held in the core store is called by the control unit, instruction by instruction, and the computer performs each instruction in turn as it is called. The data on which the computer has to act is also held, at least temporarily, in the internal storage unit from which it is called by the control unit to be acted upon according to the program.

The arithmetic and control units in different computers vary greatly as regards performance and construction. The arithmetic units always incorporate registers that perform certain operations such as addition or subtraction on any numbers (in binary pattern) placed in these registers. A description of how these units function is given in the Appendix to this chapter (p. 30). Computer programs consist of sets of rules or instructions, stored in the computer or held on its backing store until required, and which exercise control over the computer by setting it to execute an ordered sequence of instructions that solve problems or control other instruments or systems. If the sequence or actions to be carried out by a computer is likely to be complex and involved, the first step in writing a program is usually to draw a flow chart that describes the principal stages, and thereby clarify the problem.

### Programming: flow charts

Flow charts represent graphically the successive stages and principal operations occurring in an organised system or program. The amount of detail varies from flow charts which are no more than outline sketches of a system (Fig. 7) to those which are almost as detailed as the program of instructions (Figs. 79 and 80).

Flow charts allow the systems analysts and programmers to plan the most important stages of an involved procedure without immediately immersing themselves in excessive and distracting detail. They are primarily planning tools to be used during the early stages of arranging for a computer to perform some task. Any important stages or objectives that are not indicated in such flow charts are unlikely to be incorporated in the program, and the need to include them at a later stage may involve extensive reprogramming, frustration and additional cost.

### Computer codes, languages and compilers

After planning the set of instructions which will make up the computer's program, it is necessary to write these out in detail. The program is then punched up off-line on to paper tape or cards, to be used as input to the computer, unless the keypunching can be performed on an on-line console.

Data needed by the computer for the execution of a program may be incorporated with the original program, but is more generally prepared and read into the computer separately, on punched tape or cards, or from an external storage device.

Programs may be written in languages belonging to any one of three distinct language groups. These are machine code, assembly code, and a 'high level language' (sometimes called an autocode).

### Languages: machine codes

Machine codes are conventions, determined by the manufacturers and differing for each make of computer. By these codes, the limited repertoire of computer operations, such as add, clear all bits of a word (i.e. set a location to zero) etc. are represented in binary code. Each machine code instruction corresponds to a single computer operation, and sets this operation in motion.

A machine code program, if well written, requires less space in the core store and less time for its execution by the central processor of the computer than the same program written in some other computer language. This is because instructions in machine code correspond directly to machine operations designed to exploit optimally the particular hardware features of different computer models. Machine code is tedious to use, however, especially for long programs, since it demands the careful checking of patterns of octal or hexadecimal numbers used to represent the binary notation. It also requires a precise understanding of the way a particular computer model functions, and this effectively limits its use to professional programmers.

Small programs that are frequently used are often written in machine code and incorporated into larger programs written in a more convenient language. One example is given by the computer random number generating routine (sub-program), used in simulation problems, in which random numbers may be called repeatedly many thousands of times so that the efficiency of the machine code may effect an appreciable saving in run time.

## Programming: assembly codes

The tedium of machine code has led manufacturers to provide an assortment of assembly codes or languages. These consist of mnemonic terms, one for each of the basic machine instructions. Translation of an assembly language into machine code is done by the 'assembler'. Effective use of the core space in small (8K or less) computers requires the use of an assembly language. On computers with larger core size, the need to utilise every part of the available core efficiently is less critical, and it is then often more convenient to use a high level language.

## Programming: high level languages

The most commonly used high level languages are ALGOL, BASIC, COBOL, FORTRAN and more recently PL/1, but there are many others including locally developed languages. Examples of this last group include IMP and POP2, which are extensively used in Edinburgh. High level languages use terms similar to ordinary language, and their written structure somewhat resembles simple algebraic equations. An example of a program written in BASIC is shown in Figure 7, and discussed in greater detail in the Appendix (p. 33).

High level languages are designed for specific areas of application. ALGOL and FORTRAN, for example, are particularly convenient for mathematical purposes and are now being modified so as to extend their use to cope more readily with file handling. On the other hand, COBOL was designed as a file handling language, but its arithmetical facilities are poor. No single language can so far satisfy all application needs. Ideally the problem, and the computer system on which it is to be run, should dictate the language to be used, but in practice this is not always possible.

### Programming: compilers

All languages must first be transcribed into machine code in order to be able to run on a computer. Transcription is done by a compiler, itself a program in machine code that will translate (compile) a program in another language (the source program) into machine code. The existence of compilers allows a programmer to write in the much more convenient high level languages, and to leave to the computer and its compiler the task of translating the program as written into the corresponding machine code program (the object program). The efficiency with which a compiler performs this task is very important since it materially affects the performance of the computer.

Each language requires its own compiler. In larger computers the compiler, or sometimes a whole set of compilers, is stored permanently on a fast access disc or drum; the source program calls the appropriate compiler into core. An additional function of the more advanced compilers is to check the source program, while in the process of compiling it, for errors such as undeclared variables, incomplete or illegal instructions, etc., and to print out helpful error messages (diagnostics). If no errors are encountered in the source program, compilation is completed and the program is ready to be run.

Assemblers (p. 15) resemble compilers in some respects, but differ in that they only provide a term by term translation without taking into account the program structure; diagnostics are thus much more limited.

As already indicated, the specific problem to be handled by the computer will determine whether certain deficiencies in a language are likely to prove troublesome or not. For instance, COBOL compiles slowly and prints slowly, but is perhaps superior to other languages in its retrieval and updating facilities. At an installation where long searches for data and retrieval from files are the commonest type of job, COBOL may be a very suitable language. On the other hand, in an environment where numerous small computational jobs are required, as is the case in many research institutions, the slow compile time and the inadequate arithmetical facilities of COBOL become serious disadvantages. Similar lists of advantages and disadvantages could be drawn up for other presently available languages, and note should be taken of the fact that increasing use of real time and on-line computing, and developments in respect of in-core compilers, will undoubtedly affect requirements to be met by computer languages and their performance. An over-hasty declaration in favour of a single language is likely to rebound to the detriment of the user.

### Program execution

When executing a program each line (instruction) is called one at a time and acted upon step by step in the order in which instructions occur, unless the computer encounters an instruction directing execution to some other part of the program. Such directions can lead on to a later part of the program or back to an earlier part, or they may call for and execute another complete section of the program (calling a routine) before proceeding to the next line. More complex operations must be derived from the proper combination and sequence of the elementary machine instructions. Frequently recurring 'instruction complexes', consisting in effect of a complete machine code program, are then referred to by a single mnemonic term or abbreviation (e.g. PRINT and READ in Figure 7); in this lies some of the power and convenience of high level languages.

Certain other features are common to all the high level languages. Flexibility in the execution of programs written in these languages is achieved by four important programming features of the digital computer. These are cyclic operations (or loops), conditional instructions, jump (or skip) instructions, and the calling or insertion of a routine (or sub-program).

A cyclic instruction helps in the programming of repetitive operations. For instance, summing a series of figures is equivalent to the repetitive performance of additions, and one way of programming this is to place the adding instruction within a cycle instruction. Conditional instructions always specify a test that has to be applied. If the criteria of the test are not met, some alternative action is automatically executed. These alternative actions may be a direction to proceed to some other part of the program, in which case the direction is used in conjunction with a 'jump' instruction, or consist of directions to alter to pre-set values the numbers stored in certain locations. Examples of cyclic, conditional and jump instructions are shown in Figure 7 and are discussed further in the Appendix (p. 35).

In a lengthy program certain operations constituting self-contained sub-programs may be repeatedly required (called) within the main program. To avoid writing out the full instructions each time, the sub-program is written as a routine and given a 'name' by which it can be called when needed. The calling of a routine is a powerful and elegant tool but its skilful use requires practice, since excessive use of this facility may significantly increase the time needed for a computer run. Because a correctly programmed routine may be inserted into other programs, fully tested routines and the necessary documentation are kept in 'program libraries' from which copies of the routines and related documentation can be obtained. In some computer applications programs may consist of little more than a sequence of routines. Frequently required routines (e.g. certain matrix and statistical procedures) may be held on a fast access backing store (e.g. magnetic disc or drum) and called as needed by program instructions.

It is not difficult to learn the elements of programming in a high level language and this is made even easier if on-line training facilities are provided. However, to program effectively (i.e. so as to minimise the core space required and the run time for a program) is both an art and a skill. Anyone who has not actually tried to program is unlikely to appreciate the care and attention to detail required before a program will run and produce correct results. Even fully tested programs, used successfully over many months, may still reveal unsuspected defects.

**Operating systems**

An operating system is a master program permanently resident in core. It controls or supervises the functioning of all other programs, including the compilers. Its function is to exploit as efficiently as possible the speed of the central processor in relation to I/O devices and human operators. The operating system is also responsible for arranging any queueing or time-sharing between different jobs. Operating systems were introduced with some of the more advanced second generation computers, but they are indispensable for large third generation machines; the design of operating systems differs from one computer to another.

Before a program can be presented to a computer controlled by an operating system, it is preceded by a 'job-heading' which indicates a number of features. For instance, it specifies the I/O devices that the program needs, the type of external storage required and the programming language. These 'parameters' are responded to by the operating system, and the operating system then arranges that these facilities are made available at the time the program requires them, or halts further work on this program (often by temporarily 'dumping' it while other work of higher priority is proceeded with) until the facilities again become free and work on the program can continue. In particular, the operating system calls into core the compiler corresponding to the language stated in the job heading. Since the operating system is designed to organise the work within the computer, as well as to control all communication schedules between the computer and its peripherals, the efficiency of a computer installation is in large measure dependent on its operating system.

## OPERATING MODES FOR COMPUTERS

Computing can be considered as a progression of modes, with some installations offering more than one mode, the choice of the most suitable operating mode being determined by cost, by the type of work and its degree of urgency, and by personal preference. The modes, not necessarily listed in order of complexity, are as follows:

1. Batch processing mode.

2. On-line processing modes: (a) on-line consoles,

　　　　　　　　　　　　　　　(b) remote access immediate response (RAIR) stations,

　　　　　　　　　　　　　　　(c) satellite computers,

　　　　　　　　　　　　　　　(d) real time computing.

3. Dedicated computing.

## Batch processing operations

In batch mode the work is organised for subsequent running on the computer, and job queueing (or priority scheduling) is done manually during the preparation of each batch. With this system of operation, the computer can be easily and economically run for more than an 8-hour shift, since a comparatively small number of operators can supervise the input and output of the various batches. Duplication of expensive peripheral equipment is also kept to a minimum, since it is rare for more than three card or tape readers or two line printers to be required at even the largest batch processing installations, and this in turn leads to the fuller utilisation of these peripheral devices. Batch processing systems have major advantages, therefore, whenever the bulk of the work consists of standard computations using proven software, with the more time-consuming jobs being put on the night shift as a rule, as long as there is no urgency attaching to the majority of jobs. These conditions are likely to apply at large data processing installations where most of the work involves routine storage of data on file followed by standard statistical analysis, and repetitive accounting procedures.

Batch processing usually entails a relatively long 'turn-round' time, the interval between sending in a job and receiving the output; in this respect it compares unfavourably with other modes of operating. The turn-round time may be over 24 hours, even though the time needed to run the job on the computer may be no more than a few seconds. Turn-round time is affected by the distance each user's place of work is from the computer, and by the system of communication adopted for collecting jobs and delivering the results.

The acceptability of slow turn-round depends largely on the nature of the work. Much managerial, administrative and routine work is not adversely affected by a few hours' delay due to the computer's method of operating, but such delays can be quite unacceptable for staff involved in the development of programs. This is because errors and short-comings in the program are only detected with the help of error messages (diagnostics) or by faulty output from the computer. Debugging a program involves successive elimination of faults and usually needs several computer runs. Slow turn-round may, therefore, seriously delay program development, and the additional working strain on the pro-gramming staff is severe, especially if they are not working close to the computer. Unless program development constitutes only a small proportion of the work, it is desirable to augment batch processing by some kind of on-line system. Despite these limitations, because of its cheapness, technical robustness and organisational simplicity, batch mode is likely to remain the preferred operational mode at most computing centres.

### On-line processing modes: general points

On-line operating requires electrical contact or connection of a device to the computer, by cable, telephone or satellite. The device is to some extent under the control or guidance of the computer.

Communication between each device and the computer requires the introduction of certain commands, and recognisable responses to the commands which order and control the flow of signals, to prevent their superimposition. It is necessary to prevent a signal entering the computer directly and thereby interrupting work already in progress. As a minimum it is necessary to have commands and computer responses covering the following aspects:

1. A signal to request access to the computer.

2. A reply from the computer, indicating whether it is free to deal with the device requesting access.

3. A command relaying the input, when permission has been given to enter it.

4. A signal indicating the termination of transmission.

Output may be on the same on-line device as the input (I/O devices), or on a separate peripheral. As with input a minimum set of messages and commands is needed to establish whether the receiving device is free (ready) to receive output, followed by the actual relaying of the output and finally a terminating signal which releases the output device for use by another program.

The software, and the organisation of work in progress within a computer, are influenced by the basic requirements inseparable from on-line computing. Each incoming request for access must receive a response even though the computer is at that instant engaged on other work. The uncommitted space in core may be sufficient to allow the simultaneous processing, on a time-sharing basis, of the incoming program and data alongside work already in progress. However, if there is insufficient core space available at that moment, queueing arrangements come into play; these either store the incoming request while waiting for access, or arrange for ongoing work to be dumped and for the incoming request to be processed in its place, because it has higher priority of access.

A major problem with on-line working is to decide the amount of core space to allocate to an incoming program since initially the computer may have no exact indication of the extent of core store required. There are various ways of catering for this but one of the most commonly adopted methods is for the system to allow each on-line user a fixed maximum number of bytes per program; if programs exceed this allocation they have to be segmented. Segmentation means the breaking up of a program into separately and independently working sub-programs; these are stored externally until the relevant segment is required when it is transferred to the core store.

Because of their ability to operate on programs at different levels of priority, coupled with the facility to dump programs of low priority temporarily during their execution, there need be little serious competition of interest between batch processing and on-line operation at a computer installation which can simultaneously handle both types of operation. The principal exception to this generalisation is the dedicated computer system serving a process control function, where batch processing operations may suffer long delays. On most installations, however, the batch process is operated in effect as if it represented one terminal, with its own I/O characteristics, situated in the immediate vicinity of the computer. It is accorded a low degree of priority in the queueing system relative to the on-line devices, some or all of which may be situated at a distance, the details of the queueing system being adjusted to meet the requirements of the various users.

It should be noted that the request and response signals between the computer and the on-line devices are not always directly under the control of the user. With on-line teletypes and with visual display units (VDUs), the user issues the commands and decides upon the next step to be taken following the response from the computer; this is interactive computing, in which the human processes of decision and judgment can be reinforced by the computing power and the facilities for storing and retrieving information offered by a digital computer. With automatic laboratory instruments, however, analyses continue and signals are transmitted automatically (pp. 167 and 263); if the computer is not immediately free to accept such signals the voltages are buffered (stored peripherally) for a fraction of a second and then resubmitted to the computer.

## On-line processing: on-line consoles

The on-line teletype is very useful for the development of programs and for running programs involving the input and output of small amounts of data (e.g. certain small mathematical/statistical programs). If the teletype is provided with a paper tape unit, this can be used to punch out the developed program on paper tape, and the program held in this form can later be used in connection with batch processing work. On-line VDUs are also useful for program development and are suitable for recalling, displaying and amending records stored in readable form. However, they do not themselves provide hard copy so are less suitable for computational work.

### On-line processing: remote access immediate response (RAIR) stations

These stations, also called remote job entry terminals, consist of moderately fast I/O devices on-line to a computer, either directly or via a multiplexor, in general making use of the Post Office network for transmission of their signals. The devices usually include card, document, and fast paper tape readers as input devices, and line printers for output. A RAIR station can be used for input of data in bulk, as well as for the development of programs and it is often run in conjunction with a data preparation pool. For example, a new program can be punched up off-line and read in on the appropriate reader; within minutes, output and any diagnostics can be available from the line printer. With the help of these diagnostics, program errors are corrected and the revised program read in to check for other errors. A RAIR station may only require one or two operators, and its equipment can be used very effectively so as to offer a flexible service that can be adjusted to the needs of the various users of the station. These stations can be used as I/O devices for batch processing operations.

### On-line processing: satellite computers

Peripheral devices can be connected to a satellite computer, itself linked to a central installation; this type of configuration makes faster and more efficient communication possible. The satellite computer can be used to perform locally tasks that fall within the capacity of this machine, and larger tasks can be shared between the satellite and the central computer. Many of the special facilities often available only at the larger computer centres become available remotely on-line via the satellite computer. For instance, some graph plotters and display screens cannot function effectively when receiving signals at the transmission rates operated by the Post Office network, but a satellite computer can be used to augment the control of the central computer over these devices.

### On-line processing: real time computing

With real time computing the interval between the input of a signal and the output of the response must be short enough for the response to affect the next stage of the total process or system within which the computer is working. With some computer applications a time-interval of several hours may be acceptable, but in others only a few milliseconds. Depending on the time-scale, therefore, real time computing may sometimes be possible with a computer operating in batch mode, and certainly it must be stressed that on-line computing represents a concept that is distinct from real time operations. However, having separated these concepts, it must be pointed out that real time computing nearly always makes use of on-line computing facilities.

The monitoring and controlling of vital physiological processes, for instance with patients needing intensive care, require warning signals to be emitted within seconds of emergencies such as cardiac arrest. The response interval clearly needs to be very short, and is unattainable with a computer operating in the batch processing mode. In this type of situation, the monitoring and control systems generally demand prolonged surveillance, and human involvement in this fatiguing task should be eliminated as far as possible; this again spells on-line operation. It should be noted, however, that analog computers may sometimes be less expensive and better suited for monitoring and process control operations than real time digital computer systems.

## Dedicated computing

This term applies to computer facilities reserved for special functions or tasks. Strictly speaking, dedicated computing constitutes a subcategory of the batch processing mode or of one of the four on-line processing modes already discussed. For instance, a dedicated computer may serve as a satellite to a larger computer and periodically transmit data arising from this process to the files controlled by the central computer. Frequently, only limited aspects of the work or process require constant surveillance and control by a computer, with responses in real time. In such instances a small computer may be able to fulfil the functions that require a dedicated machine, and the more intermittent tasks (e.g. storing the results of the process) may be able to be dealt with remotely by another, larger installation.

Locally sited computers, operating entirely independently of any central installation, have the advantage to the user that a computer system can be designed to meet his specific requirements, and the programming may be easier as a result. In the majority of instances, however, this approach can mean that the installation becomes unduly expensive, since a larger range of peripherals, or more extensive peripherals, may be required on site than can be kept fully occupied by work arising from the special function or task that needed the dedicated computer in the first place. The association of small locally sited computers, dedicated to process control functions, together with remotely situated large computer systems providing file-handling facilities and a fuller range of fast output devices, are relatively more attractive in financial terms than independent dedicated installations. As long as these combined systems can still provide satisfactory local control, dedicated computing is likely to find increasing application in medicine, in systems where the dedicated computer operates as a satellite to a central computer installation offering on-line facilities.

## THE CHOICE OF DIGITAL COMPUTER FOR A SPECIFIC APPLICATION

Some computing requirements can be satisfactorily met without the need to contemplate the purchase or rental of a computer. For other applications, however, a remotely situated computer may not be suitable and purchase or rental of a computer for local installation may be essential. The advantages and disadvantages of outright purchase, as against the rental of computers, their peripherals and off-line devices, need to be carefully considered in relation to each item of the total installation, but the present discussion is concerned with the choice of the computer itself.

On the basis of the objectives to be met by introducing a computer, several possible options may theoretically be available for consideration, but in practice financial considerations usually curtail the range of choice, and the question arises whether a sufficiently large computer can be obtained with the money available. The nature of the application itself will probably suggest the type of peripherals required, and the cost of these peripherals may serve to limit the money available for the purchase of the computer. It is important not to reach a hasty decision under these circumstances, as there is nothing more frustrating than an inadequate computer system. On the other hand, an unduly large installation could well be equally wasteful of resources.

The choice of computer should not be finalised until two problems have been considered. The first is to decide whether a particular computer, of given size and performance and equipped with specified peripherals, is in fact capable of performing the required task in an acceptable manner. This problem reduces itself to a careful consideration of whether the computer's internal memory is sufficiently large to accept the program, or the largest segment of the program, necessary for the application.

Having resolved the first problem, it is then necessary to consider what operating constraints will be imposed by the fact that a computer of only limited size can be installed. This second problem can be much more difficult to assess. A potentially serious difficulty is the extent of restrictions imposed on the software by a small internal memory. The specific programming difficulties that arise with a small computer (8K or less) include the fact that the full range of high level language commands will not be available, and the use of a less convenient assembly language is necessary to exploit the limited core space more effectively. Another disadvantage derives from the fact that small computers frequently have a short word of fixed length, commonly a 12, 16 or 18 bit word, as a result of which arithmetical operations are either imprecise or double precision arithmetic must be employed (this making further demands on the limited core space). Other programming constraints, with many small computers, include the need to employ indirect addressing, which is often inconvenient and which places additional demands on the core space. Further demands on the limited core derive from the need to use software to overcome certain hardware deficiencies often encountered in small computers, such as the inability to perform multiplication and division automatically.

None of these constraints is critical in applications where programs are small in relation to the available core space, or where the computer is dedicated to a limited number of tasks so that the initial programming difficulties, once successfully overcome, are unlikely to recur.

For certain process control and real time applications, speed is crucial, and many small computers have speeds similar to much larger computers for basic computing operations such as adding, subtracting, and access time to core. Where the response rate in a small computer is unsatisfactory, it is more likely to arise from software problems than from an inadequate memory cycle.

Small computers (up to 8K) are often well suited to act as satellites for larger installations, or as dedicated machines supervising a limited range of tasks. On the other hand, an 8K word computer can only with difficulty, and under special circumstances, become the central computer for a system with several on-line consoles; it would need a very fast memory cycle, a word length of at least 24 bits (i.e. effectively a 24K byte computer) and adequate support by fast random access storage devices (e.g. discs). In addition, the on-line devices could only make limited demands to the computer in respect of the range of commands it could accept and the type of work to be transmitted.

In the foreseeable future it seems unlikely, at least in Britain, that a doctor drawing up a computer specification for his own particular application will find himself having to consider the purchase of a computer with core size larger than 16K, because of financial restrictions. Even with a computer limited in size to 8K the financial allocation may be inadequate for the purposes envisaged, and the possibility of renting equipment or the availability for purchase of reliable second-hand computers deserves careful consideration. For medical computing applications requiring much larger facilities, for instance a hospital computer, the decisions in respect of systems specification and the choice of computer hardware will probably remain the responsibility of the health departments of the government and the potential user will have to consult these authorities as well as the computer manufacturers. The uninitiated should beware of the almost incurable optimism of computer salesmen, and would be well advised to visit a computer installation that is said to be able to meet his requirements, so as to see it in operation. There are, of course, many problems in medicine requiring access to computing facilities which can be handled entirely by access to one of the existing bureau installations, assuming that the requisite programs are available or can be written.

## THE COLLECTION AND PREPARATION OF DATA FOR INPUT TO A DIGITAL COMPUTER

The foregoing description of the various components of a digital computer installation, the short account of programming languages and review of operating modes, touched only briefly on the problems of data collection. Reference will be made to the importance of reliable input data in several of the later chapters, but the subject is so important that it merits consideration here also, even at the expense of possible repetition. If the input data are faulty, inadequate or substantially incomplete, a computer cannot be expected to provide reliable information on which to base decisions. It may nevertheless be able to manipulate the data and provide impressive printouts which can give a misleading impression of reliability in respect of both data collection and data processing.

Data collection is a big subject and the introduction of instruments capable of recording data automatically has made this a very specialised field. To illustrate the principal procedures adopted at many data processing installations, the example selected is the collection of information based on interviews or forms completed by the person answering the questions; this still constitutes one of the most widely used methods of collecting data.

### Data collection: free text and coded information

Interviews and reports, including the results of medical examinations, are often taken down in free text (narrative form), sometimes using readily understood abbreviations. The information can be used as computer input in this form, although this is unlikely. The main advantage of free text is the ease with which it can be read and understood, requiring the minimum of preparation before being used as input. The disadvantages of free text are very great, however, since its use demands a large amount of storage space and problems arise during updating, tabulation and analysis of information within the record. Narrative recording does not assign a fixed position or standard way of representing items of information, and it is therefore necessary to 'search' through the record until the required item is located; if it is absent, the entire record is searched before this absence is confirmed. Narrative form also implies the unrestricted use of synonyms and alternative forms of phrasing, so a 'dictionary' is needed for the computer to be able to decide logically whether certain alternative expressions refer to the required type of information. Because of these objections, the use of free text recording for computer input is usually restricted to recording in full the name and address of a patient. The shortcomings of free text point to the need for a definite structure and the drawing up of coding systems for recording information and preparing it as input for a computer. Coding is largely an arbitrary process, representing categories of information by symbols and numbers; for some purposes, standard coding conventions are widely accepted (e.g. the International Classification of Disease). More important than the codes adopted are the definitions, divisions and groupings of the information on the input data sheet, and these should be agreed prior to devising a code.

Coding inventions can be divided into two groups; alphanumeric codes and more general codes referred to as binary codes or multipunching. The term multi-punching derives from the fact that the patterns of holes on the input card may involve several holes per column without these necessarily representing any of the alphanumeric symbols (Fig. 4). Alphanumeric codes have advantages in that keyboard instruments (typewriters and consoles) can accept them and they are more quickly processed by a computer. On the other hand, the binary codes are easier and more natural to use in the initial recording stages, especially where there may be several responses to the same question (Examples of codings are shown in Figures 2 to 4).

If the information to be collected is standard and follows a definite sequence, use should be made of precoded forms as much as possible. The design of the forms can greatly influence the ease with which an interview with a patient is conducted, and good design may eliminate the need for tiresome 'transcription sheets'. Transcription implies the need to extract information and enter it on to another document before the data can be used to prepare the input to the computer; this extra process increases the chances of errors in the input. Figure 3 shows one page from a precoded medical questionnaire. The doctor fills in the left-hand side of the page, by marking the appropriate response to a question, and an assistant copies this information on to the detachable strip (which incidentally does not contain the patient's name or address). This strip is then sent to a data preparation office where the card punching is done directly (i.e. without the need for further preparation) from these strips. The left-hand portion is retained as part of the patient's case notes.

## Data preparation for computer input

Large data processing installations often organise extensive data preparation 'pools' in which as many as 100 operators prepare the information from questionnaires and forms for computer input. The work may involve coding and transcription prior to punching cards or

- 9 -

CLINICAL FINDINGS on Admission
(Please tick appropriate box)

| 3 | 4 | 8 | 0 |

COL.

| 3 | 4 | 8 | 0 |

|  | Present | Absent | N.R. |
|---|---|---|---|
| Pallor | ✓ y | ☐ x | ☐ 0 |
| Sweating | ✓ 1 | ☐ 2 | ☐ 3 |
| Cold skin | ☐ 4 | ✓ 5 | ☐ 6 |
| Cyanosis | ✓ 7 | ☐ 8 | ☐ 9 |

39

| Y |
| I |
| 5 |
| 7 |

| Confusion | ☐ y | ✓ x | ☐ 0 |
|---|---|---|---|
| Restlessness | ☐ 1 | ✓ 2 | ☐ 3 |
| J.V.P. greater than 2 cms. (J.V.P. height  / cms.) | ☐ 4 | ✓ 5 | ☐ 6 |
| Basal crepitations persisting after coughing | ✓ 7 | ☐ 8 | ☐ 9 |

40

| X |
| 2 |
| 5 |
| 7 |

| Dyspnoea at rest | ☐ y | ✓ x | ☐ 0 |
|---|---|---|---|
| Oedema | ☐ 1 | ✓ 2 | ☐ 3 |
| 3rd or 4th H.S. or unspecified triple rhythm | ☐ 4 | ✓ 5 | ☐ 6 |

41

| X |
| 2 |
| 5 |

Pulse rate per minute          *110*

42-44

| I | I | O |

Blood pressure in mm. Hg.      *90/60*

45-47

| 0 | 9 | 0 |
systolic

48-50

| 0 | 6 | 0 |
diastolic

Other significant findings

0  Yes

①  No

X  Not Recorded

Specify on next page

N.R. = XXX

51

| I |

FIG. 3. Part of a set of hospital case notes, recorded on to a precoded form. The right-hand portion of the form is used by the punch-card operator and columns 39–41 are examples of columns which will be multi-punched. Columns 42–51 will each be punched with a single figure. Permission to reproduce this form was kindly given by Dr P. Mary Fulton.

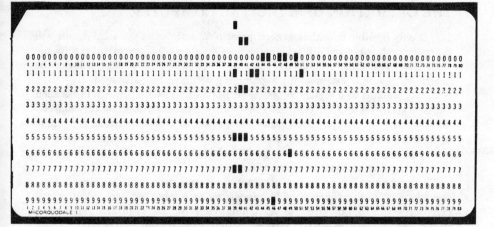

FIG. 4. An 80-column card coded with the data entered on the form shown in Figure 3. The patient's serial number shown on the top of the form has not yet been punched; this number will be punched later in columns 73–76 in each of the cards relating to this patient's records.

paper tape, although the use of precoded forms has reduced this aspect of the work. Errors may be introduced both during the transcription and the punching stages.

To minimise errors in data preparation, coding and transcription errors are checked by assistants working independently while punch operations can be repeated on a verifier (at extra cost). Punch operators can work very fast (e.g. 100 to 200 cards either punched or verified per hour), but the processes of data preparation nevertheless add significantly to the cost of electronic data processing by computer. Document readers, including full optical character readers and the technologically simpler and cheaper mark sense readers, have been developed and their use has reduced the need for manual keypunching and verifying of input in some computer applications.

At computer installations offering dynamic file systems, which permit rapid access to individual records and the ability to update them, the standard procedures for handling input at data preparation centres need to be augmented by on-line consoles. Checking of amendments and additions to records is still very important, but with dynamic file systems this cannot be completely centralised in a data preparation office. Computer assisted checking can be provided if the data to be handled is sufficiently standard; these checks may appear on a VDU screen, or as printout on a teletype, and the record is only accepted (i.e. stored) when the errors stated in the output have been satisfied. Even these checks cannot eliminate all errors, however, but they do prevent gross mistakes and serve to raise the general level of care taken over the reliability of input data.

# THE OPERATION OF A DIGITAL COMPUTER

It is only possible to outline general principles, since exact technical details will differ for each make and size of computer. The operations are carried out by the control and arithmetic units in the computer itself, and their working will now be described. A simple example of programming will then be considered.

The operations of a digital computer rest upon the careful distinction between a memory address and the contents stored, always in binary form, at this address. The contents can be interpreted either as a number or as an instruction, depending upon the unit into which the contents are placed. The control unit interprets a binary pattern as an instruction or part of an instruction, whereas the arithmetic unit treats the same binary pattern as a number.

The arithmetic unit consists of a series of sub-units that perform distinct operations upon the contents of locations read into these registers. Most digital computers can be pictured as executing eight or more distinct arithmetic operations, special hardware devices (often referred to as registers) being responsible for each of these. All but the smallest computers have separate hardware units for addition, subtraction, multiplication and division; subtraction may also involve the addition unit, while multiplication and division can be performed by repeated addition and subtraction.

TABLE II

An example of a possible simple correspondence table set up by a computer

| Program symbol in order encountered | Corresponding compiler-allocated core address |
|:---:|:---:|
| — | Preceding address allocation |
| — | Preceding address allocation |
| A | 1037 |
| B | 1038 |
| C | 1039 |
| X | 1040 |
| S | 1041 |
| Y | 1042 |
| — | Subsequent address allocation |
| — | Subsequent address allocation |

Before considering the functioning of the control unit, the operations which occur under the guidance of the computer during compile time need to be considered. In general, the compiler stores the program of instructions in binary form in a specially allocated area of core, in adjacent locations; the program area of the core does not differ in its physical characteristics from other memory areas, however, and the exact area and amount set aside for the program may differ from one occasion to the next. During compilation, three distinct but related operations occur:

1. Complex instructions, containing two or more arithmetic unit operations (e.g. addition and multiplication) are segmented into simple instructions involving only a single arithmetic unit operation. For example, LET $X = A + B$ is a simple instruction, involving only one 'add' operation, whereas LET $Y = A + \dfrac{X}{C}$ contains two separate arithmetic operations, 'add' and 'divide', and is a complex instruction. The latter is rewritten by the compiler as two simple instructions: (a) LET $S = \dfrac{X}{C}$, and (b) LET $Y = A + S$, where S is a temporary symbol assigned by the compiler.

2. The compiler sets up a one-to-one correspondence between the program symbols and the locations in core where the values of these symbols are stored, usually in the order in which these symbols (and temporary symbols) occur in the program. A 'correspondence table' such as Table II might be set up.

TABLE III

An example of a possible simple coding scheme used by a computer

| Arithmetic unit operation | Numerical code | Binary equivalent code |
|---|---|---|
| No operation | 0 | 0000 |
| Clear the accumulator (addition register) | 1 | 0001 |
| Add second operand to first operand | 2 | 0010 |
| Complement a register (set all zeros to one and vice versa) | 3 | 0011 |
| Multiply second operand by the first operand | 4 | 0100 |
| Divide first operand by the second operand | 5 | 0101 |
| etc. | 6 | 0110 |
| etc. | etc. | etc. |

3. The compiler translates each instruction symbol, apart from the 'equal' sign which serves to separate the two sides of the instruction, into its binary equivalent; this includes translating location numbers and the operation codes of the arithmetic unit. A possible coding scheme is shown in Table III.

The effect of the compile operations is that the simple instruction LET $X = A + B$ can be carried out, on the basis of Tables II and III, if the information shown in Figure 5 is placed in the control unit; the symbols equivalent to the information are also shown in Figure 5.

| Operation Code | Result Storage Address | First Operand Address | Second Operand Address | Next Simple Instruction Address |
|:---:|:---:|:---:|:---:|:---:|
| 2 | 1040 | 1037 | 1038 | |
| + (addition) | X | A | B | |

FIG. 5. Information to be placed in the control unit corresponding to the simple instruction LET $X = A + B$ (see text).

If the program is to continue, the control unit must also receive information about the location of the next instruction and the last cell in the above diagram is used for this purpose. To illustrate this, the example LET $Y = A + \dfrac{X}{C}$ will be considered, assuming that this complex instruction comes immediately after LET $X = A + B$ and that the necessary simple instructions are held in core at the following locations:

| | |
|---|---|
| LET $X = A + B$ | location 103 |
| LET $S = \dfrac{X}{C}$ | location 106 |
| LET $Y = A + S$ | location 110 |
| Next simple instruction | location 124. |

These instructions are coded in strict sequence into the control unit using Tables II and III, while Figure 6 (omitting binary representation for convenience) shows the pattern of codings.

The control unit acts (operates) on this information (beginning with the instruction LET $X = A + B$) by placing the contents at location 1037 (A) into the addition unit, which is within the arithmetic unit, in response to the operating code 2. Next the control unit places the contents at location 1038 (B) into the addition unit. On completion of the automatic (hardware) addition operation, it places the result into location 1040 (X), and it then calls in from location 106 the next simple instruction, which includes the address for the subsequent simple instruction. This sequence of operations by the control unit is repeated until the end of the program is reached.

This schematic description should not be taken to represent in detail the operation of arithmetic or control units. Although the principles will be widely applicable, the detailed steps are constantly changing as the design of computers

| Operation Code | Result Address | First Operand Address | Second Operand Address | Next Simple Instruction Address |
|---|---|---|---|---|
| (previous instruction code here) | | | | 103 |
| 2 | 1040 | 1037 | 1038 | 106 |
| + | X | A | B | |
| 5 | 1041 | 1040 | 1039 | 110 |
| / (division) | S | X | C | |
| 2 | 1042 | 1037 | 1041 | 124 |
| + | Y | A | S | |

FIG. 6. Information to be placed in sequence in the control unit corresponding to the complex instruction LET $Y = A + \dfrac{X}{C}$.

develops. The speed and effective core capacity of the computer depends on the detailed arrangement of information within the control unit. The simple example considered here assumes that a simple instruction, as well as the location of the next instruction, can be coded within a single word; this may be possible for computers with a large word length and small core, but more often several words are required to store the various addresses and the operation code. Considerable skill and ingenuity is devoted to designing methods and procedures that minimise the requirements for storage space in the control unit and that maximise the speeds of operation for simple instructions. The manufacturers' literature should be consulted for details relating to any particular computer.

## An example of on-line programming

Figure 7 illustrates the writing and editing of a program using a console on-line to a computer situated 45 miles away, and using the Post Office telephone network as the communication link. After dialling the telephone number of the computer installation, a short interval occurs before a whistling noise signifies that connection has been established. The console has then come under the control of the computer and the first line of Figure 7 records the time and date when contact was effected (this information is required for charging purposes). In the subsequent six lines of 'dialogue' at the top left of Figure 7, type appearing to the left and including the '–' symbols represent the computer's requests for specific information, and the user's response to these requests is given on the right of these symbols. The explanation of these answers is given on Figure 7; the user has to give his code number so as to establish that he is a bona fide user of the on-line system. Full programming facilities are established when the computer responds with the word READY.

ON-LINE PROGRAMMING

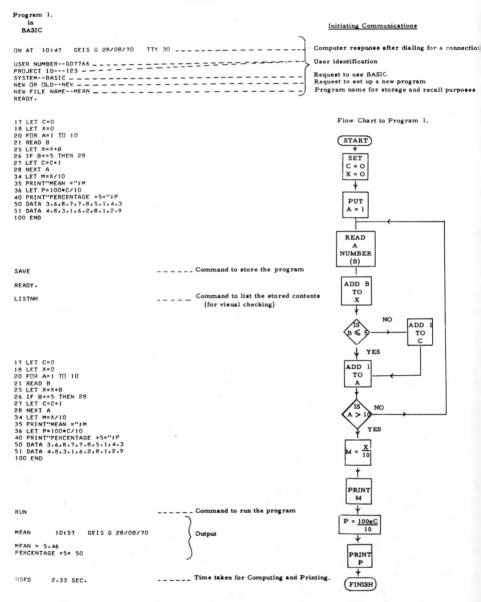

Program 1.
in
BASIC

Initiating Communications

```
ON AT  10:47    GEIS G 28/08/70    TTY 30 ------------------
```
Computer response after dialing for a connection
```
USER NUMBER--G07766 ------------------------------------
PROJECT ID---123 -------------------------------------
SYSTEM--BASIC --------------------------------------
NEW OR OLD--NEW -----------------------------------
NEW FILE NAME--MEAN -------------------------------
READY.
```
User identification

Request to use BASIC
Request to set up a new program
Program name for storage and recall purposes

```
17 LET C=0
18 LET X=0
20 FOR A=1 TO 10
21 READ B
25 LET X=X+B
26 IF B<=5 THEN 28
27 LET C=C+1
28 NEXT A
34 LET M=X/10
35 PRINT"MEAN ="+M
36 LET P=100*C/10
40 PRINT"PERCENTAGE >5="+P
50 DATA 3.6,8.7,7.8,5.1,4.3
51 DATA 4.8,3.1,6.2,8.1,2.9
100 END
```

Flow Chart to Program 1.

```
SAVE                    ------- Command to store the program

READY.

LISTNH                  ------ Command to list the stored contents
                                (for visual checking)
```

```
17 LET C=0
18 LET X=0
20 FOR A=1 TO 10
21 READ B
25 LET X=X+B
26 IF B<=5 THEN 28
27 LET C=C+1
28 NEXT A
34 LET M=X/10
35 PRINT"MEAN ="+M
36 LET P=100*C/10
40 PRINT"PERCENTAGE >5="+P
50 DATA 3.6,8.7,7.8,5.1,4.3
51 DATA 4.8,3.1,6.2,8.1,2.9
100 END
```

```
RUN                     ------ Command to run the program

MEAN       10:57    GEIS G 28/08/70       Output

MEAN = 5.46
PERCENTAGE >5= 50

USED     2.33 SEC.      ------ Time taken for Computing and Printing.
```

FIG. 7. A program written in BASIC for computing the mean of 10 numbers and calculating the percentage of numbers with values greater than 5.

The program is next typed in on the teletype, and the flow chart with accompanying comments will be used later to explain the various program instructions. Typing in the program is completed where the line 100 END appears first in Figure 7. As long as work continues under the program name MEAN, the program as written remains immediately accessible and any further commands or amendments refer to this immediately accessible program without further reference to its name. A copy of the current program is stored on disc by using the command SAVE, and the program can then be recalled from disc on subsequent occasions, by responding with the word OLD (instead of NEW) and quoting the name of the program, MEAN, when re-establishing an on-line connection. After the computer has responded READY to the command SAVE, it is possible to run this program, but it is in practice useful to list the in-core program for visual checking before doing so. The listing is shown in Figure 7, and appears in response to the command LISTNH (the letters NH denote 'no heading' and suppress unwanted titles). The user command RUN sets the actual program in motion resulting in the output, which includes the name of the program, the time and date. The computer then indicates the time used for running the program and printing its output.

Figure 7 illustrates several simple programming rules and conventions. During its execution the program always follows the line numbers in sequence unless a jump or conditional jump instruction (e.g. line 26) transfers execution to another part of the program. No two lines can have the same line number since the computer will automatically replace the first of these lines by the second. The line number plays a vital role when programming in BASIC, since all jump instructions are in effect instructions to proceed to a particular line number. The line number serves to identify each instruction and the program execution order follows the number sequence, unless a jump instruction transfers execution to another program section. It is normal practice not to start at line 1 (Fig. 7) and to avoid using consecutive numbers, since it is then easier to insert additional lines at later stages of program development if amendments should become necessary.

Line 17 illustrates another simple rule. It states LET C = 0. The computer executes this instruction by taking the value on the right hand side and storing it in binary form in the internal memory location called C. The symbol C is not the actual value but the location in which some value is to be stored. Line 27 is an example of a more general and flexible instruction. It states LET C = C + 1, and this instructs the computer to increment the value held in C by 1. The full sequence of operations followed by the computer starts with an evaluation of the right hand side, by taking the value stored in C. This value is then increased by adding 1 to it, and the result of this operation is stored in the location given on the left hand side (i.e. the new value is stored in location C). The final operation in line 27 is equivalent to a write instruction, so that the previous value in location C is erased in putting the new value into that location.

Line 25 resembles the instruction in line 27, except that the value stored in location B is added to the value in location X and the result is then stored in the location on the left-hand side (i.e. in X) when the value previously held in X is lost.

Lines 20 to 28 together constitute a cyclic operation. All instructions within this cycle are carried out repeatedly until the cycle has run its course. The cycling variable used here (A) is set to 1 in this program when line 20 is first encountered.

It will then be set at 2 when the program reaches NEXT A (line 28). This operation will repeat itself, with A being incremented by 1 each time, until the last repetition occurs when A is set to 10, the uppermost limit stated in line 20. If a cyclic operation includes repeated summation, it is good practice (and in some languages this is mandatory) initially to set the summation variables (X and C) to zero; this was done in lines 17 and 18.

Line 26 is a conditional jump instruction which tests whether the value of the observation B (which was read in at line 21) exceeds 5. If B is less than or equal to 5, execution of the program is transferred to line 28, thereby missing out line 27; as a consequence, C is not incremented on this occasion. When an observation (B) exceeds 5, the condition in line 26 is not satisfied so the jump instruction is ignored and execution goes on line by line; at line 27, C is increased by 1. The instruction in line 26 means that the value of C is increased when B exceeds 5, but not otherwise.

In this example the data are inserted into the program itself (lines 50 and 51) and read in strict sequence. The first time line 21 (READ B) is executed, the value placed in location B is 3.6. When the second cycle is executed, the value 8.7 is stored (written) in B and the previous value (3.6) is erased, and so on.

If the programming rules and conventions explained above are borne in mind, the program shown in Figure 7 can be read almost as easily as ordinary text. The summation variables, C and X, are first set to zero. Observations are then repeatedly (10 times) read in, added to the sum of readings so far obtained (X), and an increment of 1 occurs with C whenever the value stored in B exceeds 5. Having completed these operations, the program computes the mean (line 34) and prints out the result (line 35). The percentage of values exceeding 5 is calculated (line 36) and the instruction to print this result is given in line 40. Lines 50 and 51 give the data and when the instruction END (line 100) is reached this halts all further operations on the program.

The program in Figure 7 is very restrictive, since it will only work for samples of 10 observations and will always compute the percentage of values in excess of 5, a fixed value in this program. This example has been deliberately chosen for its simplicity in presentation, but it should be noted that relatively minor alterations to the program shown in Figure 7 remove these restrictions.

SUGGESTIONS FOR FURTHER READING

DAVIDSON, C. H. & KOENIG, E. C. (1967). *Computers: Introduction to Computers and Applied Computing Concepts.* New York: Wiley.

HOLLINGDALE, S. H. & TOOTILL, G. C. (1970). *Electronic Computers,* 2nd ed. Harmondsworth, Middlesex: Penguin Books.

LAVER, F. J. M. (1965). *Introducing Computers.* London: Her Majesty's Stationery Office.

LEVISON, M. & SENTANCE, W. A. (1968). *Introduction to Computer Science.* London: Oldbourne.

MALEY, G. A. & HEILWELL, M. (1968). *Introduction to Digital Computers.* New York: Prentice-Hall.

ROSEN, S. (1969). Electronic Computers: A historical survey. *Computing Surveys,* **1**, 7–36.

# CHAPTER TWO

# An Introduction to Analog and Hybrid Computers

## By D. E. M. TAYLOR

## SUMMARY

ANALOG computers use a continuously varying electrical voltage (an analog signal) to represent numbers. These machines are composed of several computing elements, in each of which the relationship of output to input is represented by the expression $y = f(x)$. The solution of problems is carried out by interconnecting computing elements so as to simulate the required equations. Greater power and flexibility can be given to analog computers by adding digital computing elements capable of control and logic functions, such composite configurations being known as hybrid computers. Analog and hybrid computers have a wide application in processing continuous information and in the mathematical simulation of dynamic systems.

## INTRODUCTION

Discussions about electronic computers usually refer only to digital machines, but such discussions overlook the other basic category, the analog computer. The fundamental difference between digital and analog computers is in their method of counting. Digital machines use a binary system and count only in discrete numbers, whereas analog computers represent numbers by voltages which can be varied infinitely between positive and negative maxima and therefore work with continuous numbers. The digital computer is like an abacus, whereas the analog computer is like a slide rule. There are also functional differences between these two categories of computer in their method of programming and operation and in the ease with which certain types of mathematical procedure are carried out, particularly those of calculus.

Because of these major differences, the two basic types of computer should in no way be considered as competitive, but rather as complementary. Each has specific advantages and disadvantages, and the choice of computer for the solution of a given problem must depend on which type is best able to produce a solution of the required degree of accuracy, taking account of time and cost-effectiveness.

In many biomedical applications it is being increasingly found that neither a purely digital nor a purely analog computer can provide the best configuration. Instead, a computer system containing both digital and analog elements may be required; these mixed computers are called hybrid computers.

This chapter is principally concerned with general purpose analog and hybrid computers. It should be noted, however, that small dedicated analog and hybrid systems are frequently used for clinical and experimental work. They form a part of much automatic patient monitoring equipment, in the control and alarm systems of equipment supporting vital functions (e.g. artificial ventilators, artificial kidneys) and in the diagnostic equipment used by clinical physiologists (e.g. cardiac output estimators, E.E.G. frequency analysers).

## THE COMPONENTS OF AN ANALOG COMPUTER

To assess the relative advantages and disadvantages of analog computers it is necessary to consider first how they are organised and operated. They consist of three main sections:

1. Control console or panel; this includes the sources of input.
2. Central processor: (a) Computing modules,
   (b) Patch panel.
3. Read-out.

In the central processor of an analog computer, the computing modules correspond to the arithmetic unit, and the patch panel to the control unit of a digital computer. There is no analog equivalent to the digital computer's memory store, and this represents one of the principal limitations of a purely analog computer.

### The computing modules

The arithmetic unit in an analog computer consists of a number of computing modules each of which can perform a limited number of specific mathematical procedures. As a result each module, or any combination of computing modules, can only carry out mathematical procedures of the general form $y = f(x)$, where x is the input and y the output. Provided that the modules are connected and controlled satisfactorily, all stages of problem solution can occur simultaneously in an analog computer. This contrasts sharply with digital computers, where mathematical procedures are carried out in a serial manner with intermediate values being stored in registers. Figure 8 illustrates the difference between the main categories of computer, in terms of the time required to carry out computations for problems of progressively increasing complexity.

The basic analog computing unit is the operational amplifier. This consists of an electronic high gain amplifier (e.g. a gain factor of $10^7 - 10^8$), in which the output is fed back to the input; both the input and the feed-back signals pass through some type of impedance before reaching the input side of the amplifier. In the simplest arrangement, a single input $V_I$ is fed through a resistance $R_I$ and the output $V_O$ is fed back through a resistance $R_F$ (Fig. 9).

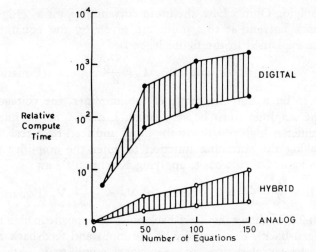

FIG. 8. The relative time taken for computing problems which require different numbers of machine equations. The time taken for an analog computer solution is taken as unity. The figure shows that the hybrid computer is not much slower than the analog but the digital computer is slower by two orders of magnitude when more than 50 simultaneous equations are involved. The figure does not indicate the comparative accuracy of the different solutions provided.

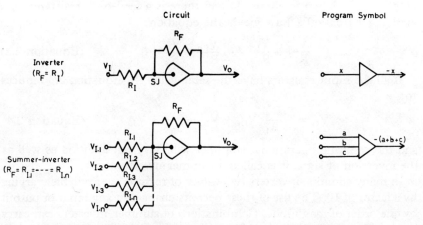

FIG. 9. The basic circuit program symbols for an analog inverter and for a summer-inverter. In the circuit diagrams, $V_I$, $V_{I.1}$, ..., $V_{I.n}$ are the input voltages and $V_O$ the output voltage; $R_I$, $R_{I.1}$, ..., $R_{I.n}$ are the input resistors and $R_F$ the feed-back resistor; and SJ is the summing junction. In the corresponding program symbols, a, b, c and x represent voltages.

The relationship between output and input can be determined by applying Kirchhoff's Law, which states that the algebraic sum of the currents at a point is zero. The point where input and feed-back currents meet and pass on into the amplifier is known as the summing junction

(SJ). By applying Ohm's Law, the input current at point SJ (Fig. 9) and the feed-back current at this point are given by the equations (the symbols are explained in the figure legend):

$$\text{(a)} \quad I_I = \frac{V_I}{R_I} \quad \text{and} \quad \text{(b)} \quad I_F = \frac{V_O}{R_F} \qquad \text{(Equations 2.1)}$$

If $V_O$ is to be within the range of the amplifier, the voltage at the input of the amplifier must be very small. Likewise, as the impedance of the amplifier is high relative to the input and feed-back resistors, the current leaving the summing junction to enter the amplifier may be regarded as zero. On this basis, applying Kirchhoff's Law:

$$\text{(a)} \quad I_I + I_F = \frac{V_I}{R_I} + \frac{V_O}{R_F} = 0; \quad \text{hence (b)} \quad V_O = -\frac{R_F}{R_I} \cdot V_I \quad \text{(Equations 2.2)}$$

Equation 2.2(b) shows that feed-back must be opposite in sign to input (negative feed-back). Furthermore, if the input and feed-back resistors are equal, the simplest type of operational amplifier is obtained, an inverter with a gain of one. In this special case, the general relationship $y = f(x)$ becomes $y = -x$. The ratio of output to input is often referred to as the transfer function of a module or group of modules; in the case of a summer-inverter the transfer function is $-1$.

If several inputs are fed into the summing junction of an operational amplifier, as shown in Figure 9, and there is a feed-back resistance $R_F$, applying Kirchhoff's Law yields the equation:

$$\frac{V_{I.1}}{R_{I.1}} + \frac{V_{I.2}}{R_{I.2}} \cdots \frac{V_{I.n}}{R_{I.n}} + \frac{V_O}{R_F} = 0 \qquad \text{(Equation 2.3)}$$

If all the input resistors have the same value $R_I$, Equation 2.3 reduces to:

$$V_O = -\frac{R_F}{R_I}(V_{I.1} + V_{I.2} + \cdots + V_{I.n}) \qquad \text{(Equation 2.4)}$$

and the resulting operational amplifier will carry out addition as well as the inversion of sign; it is called a summer-inverter.

In many summer-inverters two values of resistor are available, varying by a factor of 10. The use of these permits changes in any input or output by one order of magnitude. Combinations of summer-inverters can carry out a wide range of simple arithmetic, as shown in Figure 10.

By using a capacitor in place of one of the resistors the basic procedures of calculus can be simulated. Applying the type of analysis outlined above, and using input resistors and a feed-back capacitor it can be shown that an operational amplifier results in which the output is the integral of the input with respect to time. This type of operational amplifier is called an integrator (Fig. 11). Integrators also have an additional input known as the initial condition; this corresponds to the constant of integration and is the same as the value of the output function at zero time. The converse

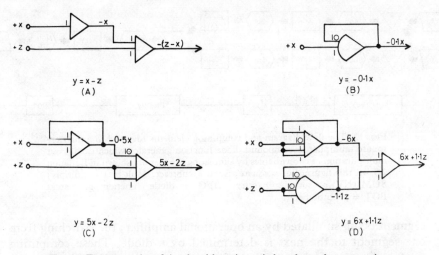

FIG. 10. Four examples of simple arithmetic carried out by analog computing techniques using only summer-inverters.

arrangement of impedance, an input capacitor and a feed-back resistor, theoretically produces an operational amplifier in which the output is the differential of the input with respect to time (Fig. 11). However, this arrangement is seldom employed in practice as it is prone to high noise levels and it is more usual to carry out differentiation indirectly. Compound input and feed-back impedance can be used for the simulation of more complex transfer functions.

Simulations that use a single operational amplifier all produce a linear type of function. To simulate a non-linear function, the output function must be divided into a series of approximately linear segments, each

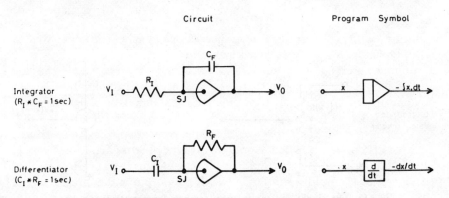

FIG. 11. The circuits and the program symbols for operational amplifiers capable of carrying out the basic operations of calculus, namely integration and differentiation. $C_I$ = Input capacitor; $C_F$ = Feed back capacitor; $*$ = multiply. For other symbols, see Figure 9.

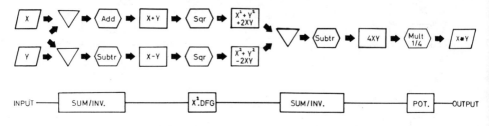

FIG. 12. The flow diagram and computing elements involved in a quarter-square multiplier, a compound diode function generator which carries out multiplication of two variables by simulating the identity shown in Equation 2.5. In this figure, Sqr = square; Subtr = subtract; Mult or $\star$ = multiply; SUM/INV = summer/inverter; DFG = diode function generator; POT = potentiometer.

segment being simulated by an operational amplifier; the switching from one segment to the next is determined by a diode. These computing modules are referred to as diode function generators (DFG); they may either be fixed in function (e.g. sin $x$ or log $x$) or capable of being programmed to perform any variable function.

A special but common type of complex fixed function generator is the multiplier. This is needed in analog computing whenever it is necessary

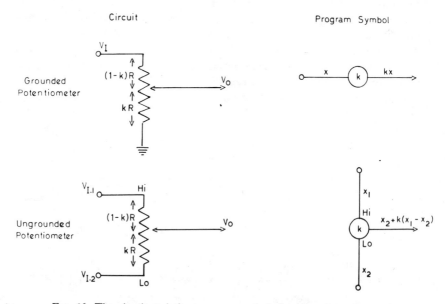

FIG. 13. The circuit and the program symbols for potentiometers, used either grounded or ungrounded, to produce multiplication by constants. R = Total resistance of potentiometer: k = proportional setting of wiper on potentiometer from grounded or low voltage end; Hi = high; Lo = low voltage end.

to multiply or to divide two variables. Multiplication and division cannot be done directly by analog means. Instead, a complex function is used which gives the required function when it is solved. One example (Fig. 12) is the quarter-square multiplier which simulates the identity:

$$xy = \tfrac{1}{4} ( (x + y)^2 - (x - y)^2 ) \qquad \text{(Equation 2.5)}$$

The last, and incidentally the simplest, analog computing unit is the variable potentiometer. Potentiometers may be grounded or un-grounded (Fig. 13). If a potentiometer is grounded and a voltage applied at one end, the voltage at an intermediate point is a fraction of the total voltage applied, the fraction being related to the position of read off; grounded potentiometers are used to multiply by a simple constant, and $y = f(x)$ becomes $y = kx$. A variable potentiometer, with a voltage applied to each end, is used where a factor involving two variables is required (Fig. 13).

To function efficiently, an analog computer must have a stabilised voltage supply; this also serves as the reference level against which other voltages in the machine are measured. To make analog computing programs independent of the type of machine, the reference voltage is taken as representing one 'machine unit' (1 MU), and all other outputs are expressed in terms of machine units. The voltage at which operational amplifiers overload is usually just above 1 MU, so this value also represents the maximum voltage allowed at any stage of an analog solution.

### The patch panel, and programming an analog computer

The front of an analog computer carries a panel, the patch panel, on which the terminals of all the computing modules end as sockets. The operator programs the computer directly on to the patch panel, by connecting the appropriate modules (Figs. 14 and 15). Once the program is set, and the computer switched to operate mode, computation proceeds continuously. This means that an analog computer can deal only with continuous data, and does not have the ability to accept discrete or discontinuous data but, within these limitations, analog programming and patching is not difficult. This can be illustrated by a simple example.

The equation for simple harmonic motion states that acceleration is proportional, but of opposite sign, to displacement. This can be stated mathematically as:

$$\frac{d^2x}{dt^2} = -kx \qquad \text{(Equation 2.6)}$$

A flow diagram (Fig. 16A) can be drawn for a closed loop solution of Equation 2.6 since the following equations also hold:

$$\frac{d^2x}{dt^2} = \frac{d}{dt} \cdot \frac{dx}{dt} \qquad \text{(Equation 2.7)}$$

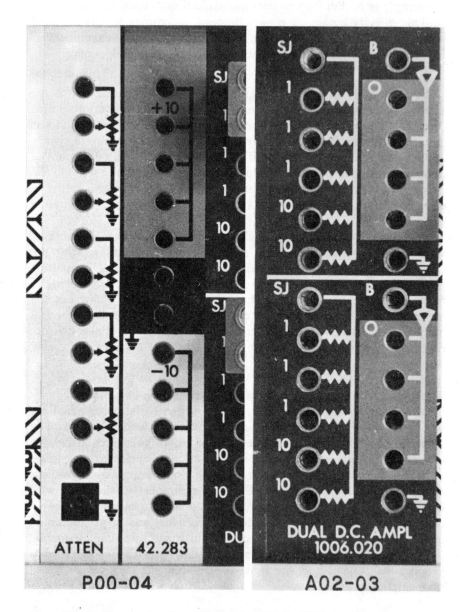

FIG. 14. Photographs of components of an E.A.L., TR48 general purpose analog computer, showing the termination of patch panels corresponding to (A) potentiometers and reference voltage supplies; (B) a dual amplifier with resistors. The symbols on the patch panel correspond to those used in circuit diagrams (See Figs. 9 and 11).

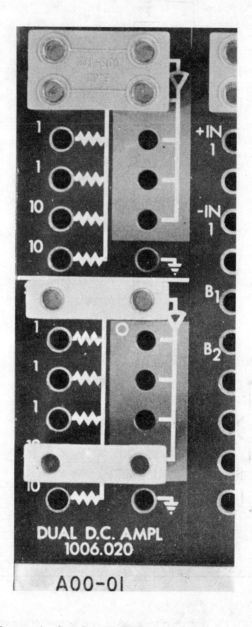

Fig. 15. Photograph of an E.A.L., TR48 analog computer showing the modules patched, but without input or output cabling shown, for a dual summer-inverter with output = − 1.0 input at the top and output = − 0.1 input at the bottom.

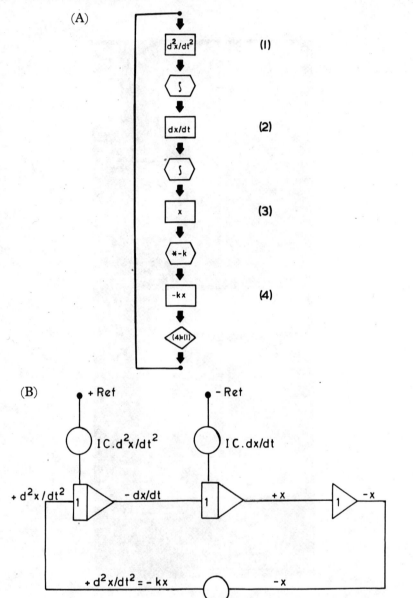

Fig. 16. (A). The flow chart for a closed loop solution of the equation for simple harmonic motion expressed in the form $\frac{d^2x}{dt^2} = -kx$. The symbol $\star$ signifies multiply.

(B). The analog computer diagram for the simulation of simple harmonic motion by the closed loop solution of the equation $\frac{d^2x}{dt^2} = -kx$.

$$\text{and} \quad \frac{dx}{dt} = \frac{d}{dt}(x) \qquad \text{(Equation 2.8)}$$

As shown in Figure 11, an integrator carries out the function:

Output $= -\int(\text{Input}) \cdot dt$, and this function may be restated as:

$$\text{Input} = -\frac{d}{dt}(\text{Output})$$

This last form of statement is analogous to Equations 2.7 and 2.8, and integrators and an inverter can therefore be used to simulate the closed loop solution represented in the flow chart (Fig. 16A). The computer diagram that is produced (Fig. 16B) is an analog program, and can be transferred directly to the patch panel by cords or plugs which link the appropriate input and output sockets of the computing modules (Fig. 17); this process is referred to as patching. With many analog computers, the programs can be stored since the patch panel is removable, this enabling extensive or frequently used programs to be kept patched up and fitted to the computer when required. However, the smallest patch panel occupies considerably more space than, for instance, magnetic or paper tape on which programs for a digital computer may be stored.

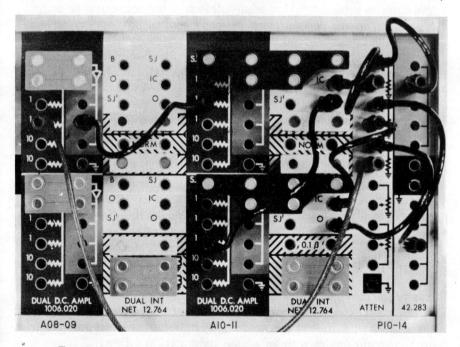

Fig. 17. A patch panel on an E.A.L., TR48 analog computer set up for the simulation of simple harmonic motion by solution of the equation:

$$\frac{d^2x}{dt^2} = -kx.$$

This system of linear programming is similar to the system used in preparing digital programs, but the transformation of a flow chart into a machine language program for use with an analog computer is much simpler. The same basic procedure is followed for the programming of an analog solution to most problems. The problem solution is first broken down into a series of machine equations, each capable of simulation by a single computing module. These equations are then converted, sometimes with the aid of a flow chart, into an analog program. The main difficulty at this stage is that the machine equations must, whenever necessary, be multiplied by constants which ensure that at no stage in the solution of a problem will the output of a computing module exceed 1.0000 machine units; these constants are known as scaling factors. In addition, as a general rule for maintaining accuracy, no module must remain at a value close to zero. This process is called scaling; it is often the most critical point in analog programming.

### Input and output: control panel and read-out

The analog control panel consists of two main components, an address system and a mode control system. To function fully, the control system also requires some method of read-out. Part of the read-out is an integral component in the control panel of many general purpose analog computers, and consists of either a continuous scale needle voltmeter (VM) or a digital voltmeter (DVM), or of both types of voltmeter. Additional peripheral read-out equipment may be used, the most common peripherals being display oscilloscopes and X–Y plotters. The final component, usually incorporated in the control panel, is the overload indicator which gives a visual warning when any computing module exceeds its maximum value.

The address system consists of a series of push buttons by which a given computing element can be called, using an alphanumeric code (e.g. potentiometer address—P:07; operational amplifier address—A:24) and connected to a selector outlet on the patch panel. The outlet can be patched to a read-out element, most commonly the digital voltmeter, so that the value held by the selected module can be read. The address system is used while setting up the program, for setting equation constants on potentiometers, during the static check or debug of the program, and for observing the results of particular stages in the solution of a problem while the program is being run.

The mode control system also consists of a series of push buttons; these select and control the mode of operation of the computer. There are four main modes with an analog computer, as follows:

*Modes used during setting-up procedures*

1. Set-pot mode, for setting potentiometers.
2. Initial condition mode.

*Modes used during the solution of a problem*
   3. Operate mode.
   4. Hold mode.

Some analog computers have an additional mode, the rep-op (repetitive operation) mode, which is used during problem solution. The functions of these different modes are best considered in a discussion of the general method of solving problems by an analog computer.

## THE SOLUTION OF PROBLEMS USING AN ANALOG COMPUTER

The steps in solving a problem with an analog computer follow a fairly standard pattern (Fig. 18). There are critical considerations at several stages if the computer is to be used in an accurate and efficient manner. Some of these considerations have already been mentioned, but they have such an important bearing on the use and limitations of analog computers that they will be re-iterated in the description which follows.

### The need to define the equations which express a problem

Analog computing modules, either alone or in combination, can only simulate the general mathematical identity $y = f(x)$, where x is the input and y the output. It is only possible, therefore, to solve with an analog computer problems which can eventually be reduced to a series of simultaneous equations of this form. The problem must be capable of being stated in precise mathematical form, as one or more simultaneous identities. This consideration is common to all types of computing, but with an analog computer additional restrictions are imposed since the system can only accept a few simple logical constraints. Two further deficiencies of analog computers must also be remembered—their relative inability to accept anything other than a continuous form of input, and the absence of any form of bulk memory store.

### The production of machine equations

The basic principle of reducing a problem to a set of machine equations is to produce a number of equations each of which is capable of simulation by a single computing module; each equation must be in the form $y = f(x)$. To do this, each part of every equation is reduced to a series of equations in which the right hand side is the function of a single analog module. The skill with which the initial problem is reduced to machine equations determines the number and type of computing modules required, and this skill therefore influences both the cost of the computing operation, in terms of the hardware required, and the accuracy of the solution. Since all parts of a problem are solved simultaneously, however, these considerations do not have any effect on the time needed to perform the computing operations in the way that they would when using a digital computer.

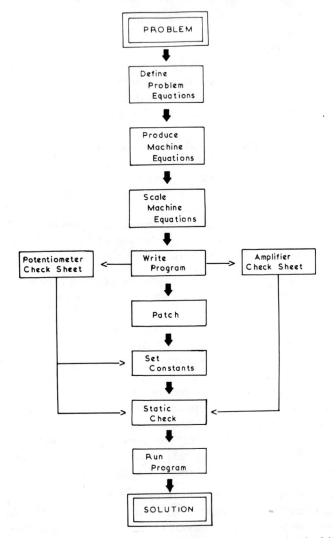

Fig. 18. A schematic diagram summarising the routine steps involved in preparing equations for solving a problem, using either an analog or a hybrid computer, and the steps involved in carrying out the solution of the problem.

## The scaling of machine equations

Although machine equations permit a flow chart and a program for the interconnections of computing modules to be drawn up (Fig. 16), the full program cannot immediately be written. The machine equations must first be scaled in terms of machine units before quantitative values can be assigned in the program. In digital computing scaling is not usually required since, over a wide range, no quantitative limits are imposed. In analog computing, however, scaling is almost always required, because the output of each computing module must lie within the range of $-1.0000$ MU to $+1.0000$ MU; this means that machine equations must be scaled so that, during solution of a problem, all outputs remain within these machine limits.

Again, with analog computing, outputs must remain at as high a value as possible if accuracy is to be maintained. For example, a computing module with an accuracy of 0.1 per cent has a reliability in the range $\pm 0.0010$ MU. If a module has an output which varies between 1.0000 and 0.5000 MU, these figures give a maximum error of $\pm 0.2$ per cent, which is an acceptable margin for most biomedical work. However, if the output were to vary between 0.0100 and 0.0050 MU, the range of error would be increased to $\pm 20$ per cent, which would in general be unacceptable. Where the problem solution is to be performed other than in real time, time-scaling of the machine equations is also required. Scaling is the most critical stage in program writing, for these reasons, since the accuracy of the final solution depends upon it. Unfortunately, scaling is the skill which many analog programmers find the most difficult one to master.

## The writing of an analog program

When the critical stages of producing and scaling machine equations have been accomplished, program writing is comparatively simple, at least when compared to the equivalent stage in digital computing. A complete analog computer program consists of four sheets, which are all used in the set-up and static check of the program on the computer.

The first of these sheets is the patching diagram (e.g. Fig. 16), which gives a graphical translation of the machine equations in terms of computing modules and their interconnections, and the allocation of alphanumeric addresses for individual modules. The only difficulty experienced at this stage is in taking account of the sign inversion which occurs at many computing modules. The next sheet is the potentiometer check sheet, which gives the allocation and scaled values for all the potentiometers used in the program; the potentiometers are used to represent the constants in the scaled machine equations. The other sheets are the amplifier static check sheet and the amplifier derivative check sheet, which give the allocation and output values for all the operational amplifiers at zero time in the solution of the problem.

## The set-up and static check (debug) of an analog computer program

The computer is first placed in set-pot mode, which isolates all amplifiers from their summing junctions, and connects the input to earth, isolates all potentiometers from their inputs, and attaches 1 MU to the input end. The basic program is then patched up and each potentiometer on the check sheet is addressed in turn, and set to its required value (manually or, in more modern machines, automatically), the output being monitored on the digital voltmeter. This procedure sets all the constants in the scaled machine equations, and the program can now be debugged by the static check.

The static check is carried out by placing the computer in initial condition mode. In this mode, all the computing modules except the integrators are connected to their inputs, the integrators being disconnected from their summing junctions and connected internally so that the values occurring at their outputs represent the initial conditions. The operational amplifiers are now addressed in turn and their outputs checked against the calculated values listed on the amplifier static check sheet or the amplifier derivative check sheet; the values are read off from the digital voltmeter.

This completes the set-up and static check, the whole procedure being much simpler and carried out much more rapidly than the equivalent debug of a digital computer program. The analog program is now ready to run.

### The running of an analog computer program

Placing the computer in initial condition mode sets all the computing modules to their values at the start of the solution of a problem. To run the program, the computer is placed in operate mode; this starts all the computing modules operating and all the stages in the solution of the problem then proceed simultaneously regardless of the complexity of the problem. The solution is observed on an output device, the nature of which depends on the type of solution that is being produced.

If the solution is in the form of a unique value, this can be read off from the digital voltmeter after a stable state has been reached, the required operational amplifiers being addressed in turn. For other types of problem, where a continuously variable solution occurs, other output devices are employed, and either the hold or the rep-op mode of the computer may be required. Continuous solutions are usually displayed on an oscilloscope or on an X-Y plotter.

Rep-op mode is used where the shape of the solution is to be observed continuously, particularly if the operator wants to watch the effect upon the solution of altering an equation parameter. When placed in rep-op mode, the computer continuously and automatically alternates between initial condition and operate mode; this means that the problem is repeatedly solved from the same initial conditions. In many machines this mode contains a facility for automatic time-scaling and the program then runs in fast time, the solution being displayed on an oscilloscope apparently as a standing wave.

Hold mode is used where the solution needs to be read either at a given time or when one variable has reached a stated value. As its name implies, this mode holds all the computing modules at the stage which they have reached in the solution of the problem at the time this condition is fulfilled. The relevant amplifiers are now addressed in turn and their values read, after which the solution can be allowed to proceed by returning the computer to operate mode.

## ADVANTAGES AND LIMITATIONS OF ANALOG COMPUTERS

The main advantages and limitations of analog computers have been mentioned while considering the composition and the operation of these machines. These factors need to be brought together and compared with the corresponding advantages and limitations of digital computers, as a preliminary to considering the most appropriate spheres of application for the two main types of computer configuration that are at present used in biomedical work. Examples of these applications form the main subject matter of this book. Another reason for making this comparison at this stage is for it to serve as an introduction to the subject of mixed computer configurations, otherwise known as hybrid computers.

The advantages of analog computers derive from the fact that the time they take to solve a problem is independent of the complexity of that problem, since all stages of the solution occur simultaneously. This is particularly helpful in the solution of multiple differential equations, analog machines being considerably faster than digital when solving problems which required approximately more than 20 machine equations for their description (Fig. 8). The ease of programming and debugging analog computers has been stressed, as has their ability to cope with continuous data without any preliminary conversion; this feature is particularly useful in the biomedical field, where much of the raw data that has to be handled is in the form of a continuous analog output from a variety of transducers or amplifiers (e.g. blood pressure from an indwelling catheter). Furthermore, processes such as integration are carried out directly and continuously with an analog computer, a factor that is particularly relevant to biomedical work where rates of change and cumulative values are frequently of interest.

On the other hand, analog computers have several serious limitations. In the first place, their precision is limited, the degree of precision obtainable being very dependent on the skill of the programmer in producing and scaling the machine equations. In addition, an analog computer is unable to cope with logical constraints, apart from a minor capacity to handle simple conditional or limiting statements, nor can it have its operation appreciably determined by logical statements. Other important disadvantages include the absence of a memory, the inability to undertake automatic programming, the bulk of the programmed patch panels, the expense involved in storing patched panels, and the fact that the hardware required is directly proportional to the complexity of a problem.

In contrast to analog computers, the main advantages of digital computers are their great precision, which can be set to any desired level; their dependence upon logic and their possession of a memory; their ability to cope with discontinuous and tabulated data; and the existence of an automatic programming facility which does not require additional hardware.

Digital computers, however, have important limitations. These include the fact that speed of operation and the precision of operation are approximately related in inverse proportion, so that increased precision is achieved in terms of extra computing time, which is expensive. Again, the time needed for performing computations is proportional to the complexity of a problem (Fig. 8), which is not only a disadvantage in terms of cost-effectiveness (Fig. 19) but can prevent their use for the on-line study of rapid dynamic systems. Digital computers cannot handle continuous data without preliminary conversion into digital form, and this can represent a problem when studying rapidly changing inputs

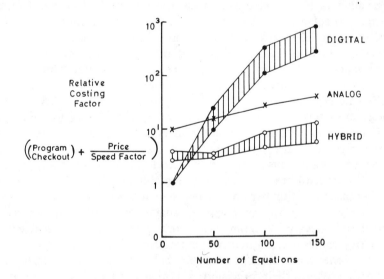

Fig. 19. The relative costing factors for operating the three main categories of computer, depending on the complexity of the problem. This factor takes into account the cost of programming, the time needed to debug and the time required for the actual solution of the problem by the computer. The factor therefore includes components for staff time, for the complexity of the hardware and for the operating time. Figures 8 and 19 are based on data supplied by the Systems Analysis Division, U.K. Computing Centre, Electronic Associates Ltd, Victoria Road, Burgess Hill, Sussex.

such as action potentials where a very high rate of sampling is required. Another limitation is their inability to carry out continuous processes such as integration and differentiation except by serial approximation, a feature which leads to a conflict between the choice of a large step size (in order to reduce the time necessary for computation) and a smaller step size which may be required for increased accuracy.

## HYBRID COMPUTERS

Digital computers can handle discontinuous and tabulated data, and there is no alternative choice of computer configuration for problems generating data in this form. Apart from this one important category of work, the merits and demerits of analog and digital computers are essentially complementary, the advantages of the analog computer covering many of the limitations of the digital computer and vice versa. If the whole range of biomedical problems involving the handling of continuous input or the simulation of dynamic systems is considered, at one end of the spectrum there are problems where speed and moderate accuracy are required without the need for a computer memory or complex logic, whereas at the other end of the spectrum there are the problems which require a high degree of accuracy, a large memory and complex logic, but in which speed is not essential. In between these two extremes falls a range of work for which neither an analog nor a digital computer can be entirely satisfactory. Under these circumstances the best solution may be obtained by using a computer configuration which contains both analog and digital elements, getting each part of the configuration to carry out those parts of the solution of the problem for which each is best suited. Such mixed computers are increasingly coming into use, and are known as hybrid computers.

### Parallel hybrid computers

The commonest type of hybrid machine is the parallel hybrid computer. The digital computing element is referred to as parallel logic, and is able to carry out both logic and control functions similar to those of the control and arithmetic unit of purely digital computers. The computing units in both the analog and the digital part of the parallel hybrid computer are the same as those in standard analog or digital computers, the only additional specialised units being found at the interface between the analog and the digital components. Three components of the interface unit need to be mentioned.

The main unit interfacing the analog to the digital element is the comparator. In this module the input consists of two analog signals. If the algebraic sum of these two signals is positive, the output is a digital 1 bit, but if the sum is negative the output is a 0 bit.

The main digital to analog computing module is the digital/analog

(D/A) switch, in which the output either opens or closes a circuit in the analog program; input of a 1 bit closes the switch and input of a 0 bit opens it. Digital/analog switches may be used to control the connections between analog computing modules, or to control the mode of one or more analog computing modules. The final specialised computing module in the interface unit is the track/store. This is a modified integrator which can act as a limited analog memory in that it will either follow (track) the input signal, or at any stage can hold (store) the signal until required.

Parallel logic and associated computing modules and the digital portions of the program are patched in a similar manner to the one already described for analog computers. Because of this, the basic methods of programming and running a parallel hybrid computer are the same as those used for a simple analog computer, but the addition of parallel logic produces a much more powerful and flexible machine. The ability to carry out logical functions and decisions means that the hybrid computer can solve complex programs automatically. If necessary, the computer can update its own program and it will continuously re-run with progressive modification of the program if placed in rep-op mode. This technique is known as iteration, and is a powerful technique for tackling problems which involve the solution of partial differential equations or the optimisation of parameters in equations (Chap. 17).

**Full hybrid computer systems**
Parallel hybrid computers still possess some serious limitations, particularly their lack of precision and the absence of a bulk memory store. Where necessary, these limitations can be overcome by interfacing a parallel hybrid computer to a standard digital computer, the combined configuration being referred to as a full hybrid computing system. This represents the most powerful computer configuration at present available for the simulation of dynamic systems and for the solution of multiple complex equations. The critical point in programming for such a configuration is in the preliminary systems analysis and drawing up of flow charts, for this is the stage when decisions have to be taken as to which parts of the solution are to be performed by analog computing techniques and which by digital.

The use of full hybrid systems is at present still subject to two limitations, which must await future computer developments for their solution. In the first place, high level languages must be developed to cover both the analog and digital portions of the solution of a problem. Secondly, automatic programming must be extended from the present servo-setting of potentiometers to systems which will allow automatic patching of the analog and parallel logic modules under the control of a digital computer program. The latter requirement includes the need for a facility to carry out the debug procedure automatically, particularly the debug of the parallel hybrid component; at present, this stage of each static check is laborious.

## THE PRINCIPAL APPLICATIONS OF ANALOG AND HYBRID COMPUTERS

The unique capability of analog and hybrid computers to accept and produce continuous signals means that they are particularly well suited for those biomedical investigations in which there is a desire to study mathematical models of dynamic systems. The applications fall into the three main groups of computing derived functions, data reduction and statistical handling of continuous signals, and the simulation of dynamic systems. These applications are widespread. They are discussed in general terms in the next chapter, and more detailed consideration is given in Chapter 15.

SUGGESTIONS FOR FURTHER READING

BLUM, J. J. (1968). *Introduction to Analog Computation.* New York: Harcourt, Brace & World Inc.

BORSKY, I. V. & MATYAS, J. (1968). *Computation by Electronic Analogue Computers.* London: Butterworth.

CHARLESWORTH, A. S. & FLETCHER, J. R. (1967). *Systematic Analog Computer Programming.* London: Pitman.

HARA, H. H. (1969). Analog and hybrid computers. In *Techniques in Clinical Physiology.* Ed. Bellville, J. W. & Weaver, C. S. pp. 412–485. New York: MacMillan.

MACY, J. (1964). Hybrid computer techniques for physiology. *Annals of the New York Academy of Sciences,* **115,** 568–590.

# CHAPTER THREE

# A General Review of Computer Applications in Medicine

## By L. G. WHITBY

### SUMMARY

THIS chapter serves to link the general introduction to computers given in the preceding chapters with the specific topics selected for consideration in the rest of the book. It also briefly reviews some important areas of computer applications to medicine that have not been included among the specific topics.

## INTRODUCTION

It is not always easy to distinguish what is technically possible, in terms of medical knowledge and of the stage reached in the development of computer technology, from what has been achieved in the practical application of computers to medical practice. The main purpose of later chapters is to select areas of medicine and to describe the part which computers have been shown to be capable of playing in each area, with the emphasis as far as possible on applications that have been made to work. Inevitably, the more detailed treatment adopted in the later chapters could not be comprehensive, and the object of the present chapter is to survey at a more superficial level the spectrum of computer applications in medicine so as to provide a general background against which to set the rest of the book. Several recent publications with titles of this nature are listed at the end of the chapter. None of these accounts claims to be comprehensive, and indeed the range of possible applications for computers in medicine is widening sufficiently fast as to render any review out-of-date by the time it is published.

The capabilities and limitations of electronic computer installations depend on their hardware configurations and on the available software. For some purposes digital computers are more appropriate, whereas for other applications analog or hybrid computer systems are to be preferred. The main characteristics, advantages and shortcomings of the different categories of computer have already been briefly summarised (p. 53), and will be brought out in the discussion of specific applications.

The cost of installing and operating computer systems means that financial authorities usually hesitate before allocating money to computer developments. This certainly applies in Britain, where the funds available to the National Health Service, to the Universities and to the Research Councils for expensive experimental approaches involving the use of computers are distinctly limited, particularly if these approaches are likely to involve any significant element of trial and error. This means in practice that financial authorities want to be assured in advance that a computer system will stand up well to cost-benefit analysis. However, this can be an unreasonable demand, since it overlooks the limitations of present-day methods of cost-benefit analysis, and takes too little account of the contributions to an operation which might only be possible if computer techniques are employed. It can be difficult, for instance, to cost the benefits to be derived from improved patient care or from the better use of data. Nevertheless, it is important to be cost-conscious, and the contributors have indicated the magnitude of computer costs, wherever objective information is available. It is also important, in any experimental situation, to consider how to measure the effectiveness of a new procedure, to show whether it has improved efficiency in operation, but these considerations—which are relevant to cost-benefit analysis—can be difficult to express in measurable form.

Cost-benefit arguments may sometimes be considered to have less immediate importance to the Universities and to the Research Councils. However, the limited funds available to these bodies retard the acquisition of expensive equipment and the employment of the staff required for certain types of research and teaching, and this applies particularly to computing. The expense of computer installations has served to emphasise the need to bring together doctors, computer personnel and organisation and methods (O and M) consultants, and to encourage further cooperation between medical staff in the Universities and in the National Health Service.

## COMPUTERS IN MANAGEMENT: PROBLEMS OF CONFIDENTIALITY

In Britain, most of the Regional Hospital Boards and a few of the larger hospitals have their own digital computer installations. The use of these for accounting procedures and for hospital activity analysis represent examples of batch-processing computer applications which have parallels that are well established outside the medical field, in business administration. These uses are being extended to include hospital information systems, a field of activity in which hospitals in the U.S.A. have adopted computer techniques much more rapidly than in Britain; this is because of the incentive provided by the need for an accurate and rapid means of billing patients on a fee-for-service basis. Hospital information systems can be used to link various events relating to individual patients, and similar principles guide the applications of computers in the maintenance of limited components of the medical record (e.g. age-sex registers, immunisation schedules, 'at risk' registers, etc.). These applications have been shown to be of considerable value in community medical care.

Several aspects of the use of computers in management are considered, mainly in Chapters 4, 5 and 7. The linkage of records presents problems, since it depends for its efficient operation upon reliable (accurate, reproducible and readily available) identification of individual patients. Chapter 5 discusses the importance of capturing such data at source in computer-readable form, and the wider adoption of such procedures would greatly accelerate laboratory requesting procedures, as mentioned in Chapter 8. The linkage of records raises questions of the confidentiality of computer files, a subject in which there is widespread public interest and concern. A good summarising discussion on confidentiality is given in the BMA Planning Unit report (1969), but Chapter 4 points out that computer-held records systems can be made as secure as financial resources permit, besides being almost certainly safer than the present highly insecure manual systems in use in British hospitals. The subject of computers and privacy has been surveyed by Hoffman (1969).

## SIMULATION STUDIES

Hospital activity analysis is attracting attention, and simulation programs for use with digital computers have been written which describe the work of departments of radio-diagnosis (Fraser, 1969) and of pathology (Carruthers, 1970). The purpose of these programs is to assist management in making more informed decisions about the deployment and redeployment of expensive resources, the problems sometimes being aggravated by shortages of suitable staff, or by limitations in availability of equipment or in the reliability of the equipment. These simulations can help to forecast the effect on queue lengths of deploying resources in different ways, and comparable studies have been undertaken to predict the effects of various policies on the use of hospital in-patient resources (Weir et al., 1968).

The characteristic of analog and hybrid computers which is of particular value in research investigations is their ability to simulate rapidly and continuously the behaviour of a dynamic system if it can be described by a series of simultaneous equations. Chapter 17 refers to the wide field of biomedical studies that makes use of mathematical models, for example in studying the kinetics of biochemical or pharmacological actions, or in biophysical investigations into the properties of membranes. Examples of the relationships of pressure and flow in various parts of the body, and the study of biological control systems are discussed in Chapter 15, where the ease and flexibility with which variables can be changed in equations in even a simple analog computer simulation are shown by the example of a teaching simulation. New statistical techniques required for work with analog and hybrid computers, and used in association with a rep-op mode for iteration, have extended simulation studies so that variables may be rapidly optimised either to produce certain pre-defined characteristics in the behaviour of the system, or to obtain the best fit of a proposed model to one or more sets of experimental results.

## THE HOSPITAL MEDICAL RECORD

Computers can store and retrieve data rapidly and reliably, but the extent to which this ability can be applied to the maintenance of medical records is still an open question (Mitchell, 1969). Already the possibility of using computers for holding records has stimulated much useful and critical debate as to how information should be collected, what information should be stored, and for how long it should be held. The growing range of available storage media means that the physical size of patients' records need no longer be a complete bar to their long-term storage. These media now include the possibility of transferring records from a computer's backing store direct on to microfilm, with the capability of subsequently re-entering the microfilmed data into the computer by means of optical character recognition equipment. Any system of computer-dependent clinical records will depend for its success on the accurate identification of patients.

It is proving difficult to decide what information should be stored. The design of documents that render less tedious the collection of information for coding into a form suitable for computer input also requires careful study. It is unlikely that any computer-dependent record system will ever be able economically to hold all the doctor's personal narrative or comments about individual patients, even if the various fields in the medical records format can be made sufficiently variable as to allow for this. Questions about the security of the system would also arise if all the personal details in a patient's medical history were to be held on a computer's file, and doubts of this nature could easily undermine doctor-patient relationships.

The nature of the records and the use to which they are to be put largely determines the computer configuration required and the operating mode necessary to handle these records. In this connection it is useful to distinguish between static and dynamic records systems. In the former, records may be added to or removed from the existing file, but little or no updating or interrogation of individual records is necessary. By contrast, updating and interrogation of individual records is of prime importance in dynamic systems. Most records systems incorporate some facilities for correcting or interrogating individual records so that a purely static system is rare. However, if updating and retrieval are of central importance and if, in addition, accessing of records needs to be done quickly, such an emphasis on dynamic requirements influences the choice of hardware and this is reflected in the cost.

Static records systems are best handled in batch mode, with off-line preparation of input for the most part. However, in those situations where information for storage is gathered from several major sources, remote access immediate response (RAIR) stations (p. 22) may add to the efficiency and convenience of the computer system. With dynamic records systems, frequent access to individual records almost invariably implies requirements for access from many 'users' not stationed in the immediate vicinity of the computer. Because of this the computer configuration must include large, fast random access devices and such systems must also offer extensive on-line console facilities in addition to the usual card or tape readers and line-printers. For on-line interactive requirements a large third generation computer is essential, and all these features contribute to the cost and complexity of such installations.

These various considerations show that there is no simple and uniformly correct way of planning how to harness computers to handle the problems of medical records systems, even though the digital computer can store large quantities of information in rapidly accessible form. Different users have different requirements. Nevertheless, it is true that the form of medical record kept at present by most British doctors is long overdue for improvement, and any system that can obviate the difficulties which arise when written records are temporarily or permanently mislaid would have considerable attractions. Some of the problems relating to the introduction of computer-based systems of medical records are considered in Chapters 4 and 7. More ambitious multi-access real time dynamic records systems are being developed on a research basis, both in respect of hospital practice (at King's College Hospital, London; Anderson, 1971) and in general practice (Abrams et al., 1968), the object of these schemes being to provide and maintain computer-based personal health records. It is too early to say how economically feasible these larger systems will prove, when they move out of the developmental phase into the realm of routine service to patients, but it is worth pointing out that any success that may have been achieved with dynamic records systems has largely been due to the limited and highly structured nature of their records. Preliminary reports have emphasised the difficulties that dynamic schemes may encounter in gaining acceptance (Opit and Woodroffe, 1970a, b).

## COMPUTERS AS CALCULATORS IN MEDICAL PRACTICE AND RESEARCH

It is impossible adequately to summarise the applications of computers related to this heading. A general indication of the value of digital computers in the handling of statistical problems is given in Chapter 6, and the ease with which computers can perform standard forms of statistical calculation has firmly established their role in the routine handling of data, for epidemiological studies as well as in a wide range of administrative and research contexts. It is always necessary, however, for someone knowledgeable about statistics to decide which are the appropriate calculations for the computer to perform—these are not decisions which can be made by the computer program.

In many clinical and experimental biomedical investigations, it is necessary to obtain not only the primary measurements but also derived functions, in which one or more of the primary observations are to some degree independent variables in the equations which define the derived function. A common example is the estimation of the work involved in certain biological activities, and the first extensive use of analog computing techniques for this type of work was in the study of cardiac function by Rushmer and his co-workers (1959). Recent developments in the software available for hybrid computers permit a much more complete analysis of complex functions from the measurable variables. This extends even to the continuous plotting of discrete data, either from primary or from derived measurements, for example in the technique developed for the continuous drawing of ventricular function plots (Strong *et al.*, 1970).

The production of derived functions from primary data, although a significant advance, does not allow more than a qualitative assessment to be made in many instances; certainly it does not permit accurate comparison of experimental results with mathematical models proposed for the system under investigation. One of the principal reasons is that, in many biomedical systems, a steady-state does not exist. Instead, phasic oscillations ranging in cycle length from a few seconds (e.g. sinus arrhythmia) to many hours (e.g. circadian variations) add a noise element to the variable that is being assessed. The cycle lengths with a longer time-scale in their variation are not important in analog data processing, but those with a cycle length of less than one hour may be when it comes to making a comparison between observations at different points in time. If only a few isolated data are selected, it is often impossible to be certain that the differences observed are in fact significant. Instead of isolated observations, measures of a mean value over a finite time period are required, as well as data for the degree of dispersion about the mean occurring during that period.

Data reduction and the statistical comparison of groups of discrete data can be carried out using digital computers. Similar mathematical methods exist for dealing with continuous data, much of the data being amenable to analysis by the theory of random noise (Davenport and Root, 1958). Just as the equations for statistical analysis of discrete data can be solved by digital computing methods, so can the corresponding equations for the analysis of continuous data be solved using an analog computer. Thus, data reduction to give the mean and variance, or to provide a power spectrum, and statistical comparisons such as Student's 't' test, auto-correlation and the fitting of regression curves, can be carried out using analog or hybrid computers.

Specific examples of the role of computers as calculators are mentioned in several chapters, for instance in the clinical laboratory (Chapter 8) and in monitoring situations where data acquisition and data reduction can present major problems (Chapters 10 to 13). For the routine care of patients, computers have established their role as calculators in the planning of radiation treatments (Clifton, 1970; Hope, 1970; Newell, 1970; Orr *et al.*, 1970). This use of computers as calculators has been extensively applied in the treatment of a wide range of malignant tumours by means of high energy radiations (e.g. X-rays, $\gamma$- or $\beta$-radiations, neutrons). Programs have been developed for fixed field and for rotational treatment plans, and isodose charts (resembling contour maps) can be prepared for the different treatment machines, these being varied in practice to take account of the shape and position of individual patients when receiving treatment. These processes together involve large numbers of calculations, and cannot be satisfactorily carried out without the aid of a computer in view of their complexity. With manual calculations, any decision to vary the plan for an individual patient's treatment can mean repetition of the whole range of complex calculations; the computer program, however, can readily accept various specifications of parameters and a range of plans can then be provided from which the radiotherapist can select the treatment schedule most suitable for the patient.

## COMPUTERS AND THE PATHOLOGY LABORATORY

Apart from their roles in hospital administration, and as handlers of numerical data, perhaps the best proved applications of computers in medical practice can be found in the hospital laboratory (*see* Whitehead, 1969). Work has been in progress for several years, not only in clinical chemistry but also in morbid anatomy, bacteriology and haematology. The problems facing these various branches of laboratory medicine differ, but as a whole their work represents some of the most readily quantifiable aspects of medicine. This explains why pathologists have been quick to seek the assistance of computers in handling the many organisational, analytical and data-processing problems which exist in hospital laboratories. These problems increase in magnitude year by year as the calls for pathological investigations continue to rise.

Morbid anatomists have the task of identifying the cause of disease in histological specimens, and recording these diagnoses. Within these data is contained much information relating to the frequency of disease conditions, possible interrelationships between pathological lesions, and the changing incidence of disease. One of the biggest problems facing morbid anatomists is how to reach agreement on the criteria for diagnosing various diseases, so that the information obtained in different laboratories can be uniformly coded. In addition, there is still room for agreement on the system to be used for classification of description—examples in present use include the International Classification of Disease and the Standard Nomenclature of Diseases and Operations.

Few bacteriology departments have so far attempted to apply computers routinely to their diagnostic work. However, Stirland *et al.* (1969) used a survey analysis program designed to provide statistical and epidemiological information from laboratory reports. More recently, Whitby and Blair (1970) described a system which links punched-card request forms, deriving from the central documentation of patients, with the preparation of worksheets and reports within the routine laboratory. The data contained in these reports are subsequently analysed both for laboratory and general hospital purposes, to provide information about the changes in incidence of infection, early indications of the development of antibiotic resistance, and a method of monitoring the quality of the culture media. The weakness of the system developed by Whitby and Blair (1970) is the amount of key-punching of data that it involves, pin-pointing an area where hardware developments are overdue—namely, the interface between the laboratory bench and the computer.

Clinical chemistry and haematology departments share problems relating to process control of automatic instruments, and the need to perform large numbers of repetitive calculations. Much of the output from these departments is in numerical form, and modern data-processing techniques offer the possibility of improving the format and content of reports on individual patients. Statistical techniques can also provide information of value for quality control purposes. Chapter 8 discusses many of these applications, concentrating particularly on the real time process-control and calculation functions of dedicated computers in clinical chemistry laboratories.

## PATTERN RECOGNITION AND PATIENT MONITORING

The human eye is extremely efficient at recognising and evaluating wave forms such as ECG or EEG patterns, or a chart record from an automatic chemical analyser. The eye can also examine chromosome preparations and cytological specimens and rapidly distinguish abnormal from normal appearances at the same time as discarding artefacts. These are all complex processes, and the criteria for differentiating the abnormal from the normal can be difficult to state in quantitative terms. Nevertheless, many attempts have been made to use computers as aids or substitutes for the human eye, since visual inspection of long lengths of ECG tracing, or of large numbers of chromosome preparations, for instance, causes fatigue and human efficiency then deteriorates rapidly.

The statistical applications of analog and hybrid computers also include their use for pattern recognition. In many instances, this depends upon computing a statistical comparison of the magnitude of the variation of the observed pattern from the reference pattern. There are two main classes of pattern recognition which can be carried out by analog or hybrid computers. The first of these is in the recognition of a pattern represented by a finite length of a single continuous wave form, one example of this (involving relatively advanced hybrid software) being the technique for recognising and collecting information on extra-systoles occurring in the ECG; this program includes a facility for continuously updating the normal complex which is used for reference purposes (Vallani and Neilson, 1971). The second category of pattern recognition by analog or hybrid computer is provided by the recognition of a pattern represented by the simultaneous observation of several channels of continuous analog information, of which a simple but nevertheless potentially important example is provided by the use of computers to improve the automatic alarm systems used in patient monitoring. By carrying out calculations aimed at detecting a pattern of change in several different physiological observations, considered collectively, these monitoring systems can be used to detect and to help define at an early stage significant changes in a patient's condition.

Many of these points are discussed in Chapters 10 to 13, where attention is drawn to the fact that special purpose analog computers, or purpose-made small black boxes, are being increasingly used to accept signals from the appropriate transducers and to undertake the prolonged monitoring of pulse rates, blood pressure readings, ECG waveforms, etc. These systems can be programmed to operate alarms, and are extremely valuable in relieving staff of much of the monotony involved in monitoring patients requiring intensive care. Digital computers have also been used for these purposes, after A to D conversion of continuously varying analog inputs, though less often in a real time situation. Examples of these digital computing applications include the use of dedicated machines for the acquisition and processing of the relatively simple signals generated by automatic chemical analysers (Chapter 8), while Chapter 10 discusses the conversion of the more complex analog ECG and EEG signals into a form suitable for analysis by digital computers. In both these examples, when operating on-line, the digital computer is required to accept multiple inputs and the ADC unit contains a high-speed switching device or multiplexor, acting under computer control.

A recent symposium on patient monitoring (Stewart, 1970) surveyed the wide range of potential computer usage in this field, and Chapter 12 discusses one of these applications in detail. Considerations of expense may mean that the more general adoption of these techniques cannot be contemplated until developments in hardware bring down the costs. At the developmental stage it has sometimes proved necessary to employ expensive digital or hybrid configurations but, once a more general system has been satisfactorily developed, it has then been possible to identify components of these general systems for which economically attractive hardware can be designed. This cheaper equipment makes use of special purpose analog computers and purpose-made black boxes, which may include the so-called mini-computers. Some reference to these important developments is made in Chapter 13 but no special definition of a mini-computer can be given. Essentially these are programmable devices capable of storing several hundred instructions costing as a rule between £2000 and £10,000. They may have a core store as small as 1K (12-bit words), but the definition does not extend to include desk-top calculators.

The automatic analysis of chromosomes (Rutovitz, 1968; Rutovitz *et al.*, 1970), and the automatic screening of cytological and other preparations suitable for microscopy (Ward & McMaster, 1970), both use flying spot digital scanners to build up a digital representation of what the eye sees. The object of this work is to develop computer programs which can separate out the normal from the abnormal and so increase the productivity of laboratory workers. These complex but important experiments are still in too early a phase of development to be discussed further in this book.

## THE DIAGNOSTIC PROCESS

In some respects the diagnostic process also involves pattern recognition, but the steps followed in making a diagnosis differ markedly from one doctor to another, and most doctors vary their approach from patient to patient, depending on their assessment of the presenting complaints and on the range of their own expert knowledge. A system of computer-assisted diagnosis which might help a medical student or a newly qualified doctor could prove extremely tiresome to a consultant physician or surgeon, and these considerations in respect of computer-assisted diagnosis overlap into the related topic of teaching about clinical diagnosis. Chapters 9 and 16 consider many of these problems and discuss the difficulties in attempting to use computers to assist with their solution. Although the part that computers may come to play in diagnosis and in teaching could be considerable and important, there will probably need to be several different methods of computer usage available from which the doctor or the medical student can select the one most appropriate to his needs.

A formal, logical and mathematical approach has been adopted by Lusted (1968) and by Card (1970). The classical example of its practical application was to the differentiation of the various acute leukaemias (Hayhoe *et al.*, 1964), but Card (1970) draws attention to its limitations. On present knowledge, the logical approach would only seem usefully applicable to 'simple' diagnostic problems represented by circumscribed situations such as the differentiation of various forms of thyroid disease (Boyle and Anderson, 1968); or the examination of ECG recordings (Wartak, 1970); or the analysis of results of a range of liver function tests (Baron and Fraser, 1968); and one of the most recent examples of this approach has been a multi-dimensional computer-assisted analysis for differentiating patients with hypertension, excess aldosterone and low plasma-renin concentrations into tumour and non-tumour groups (Ferriss *et al.*, 1970). Another circumscribed example, where computers may be able to assist doctors, is in the analysis of stereotyped questionnaires completed by patients themselves on computer-readable documents. This type of simplified self-check history has been incorporated into the health-screening programme operated by the Kaiser-Permanente organisation (Collen, 1968).

Attempts to employ computers for assisting in the diagnostic process, and as aids to learning, have served the useful function of promoting a critical appraisal of how these functions are at present carried out. It is unlikely that computers will ever become as quick and versatile as the eye of the experienced clinician in 'spot diagnosis'. It is also doubtful whether computer programs that logically prohibit short-cuts (e.g. 10 questions should always be asked in order to define fully a complaint of pain, according to some clinical teachers) will prove acceptable. Diagnostic search trees are important but they have limitations (Card, 1970) since few doctors regularly proceed step by step in an undeflected and un-deflectable way through a diagnostic algorithm. Their clinical experience leads them to switch as the situation requires from an algorithmic to a heuristic (trial and error) or to a pay-off approach, and back again. The relative places of these various approaches to diagnosis have been dis-cussed by Dudley (1968) and are considered in Chapters 9 and 16; the versatility of the doctor cannot yet be foreseen as being able to be incorporated into computer-dependent or computer-assisted diagnosis.

## COMPUTERS AND MEDICAL EDUCATION

Computers have several roles to play in this field, and some of these topics are discussed in Chapters 9 and 14 to 19 inclusive. The selection of medical students, the monitoring of their performance throughout the long preclinical and clinical medical course, the correlation of their performance as students with their subsequent career development, the conduct of the examination process itself, the organisation and im-plementation of training programmes, and the better use of medical literature are examples of the type of subject discussed in these chapters.

It is important to consider in general terms how medical students and qualified doctors should be made aware of the use and uses of computers. Computer technology is an essentially practical subject, and only a partial understanding can be gained by attending lectures, or by reading books or articles describing the results or anticipated results of work involving computers. Nevertheless awareness may generate interest, and interest lead on to a desire to learn about the practical details of applying computers to medical problems. The first objective of an educational programme relating to computer technology should, therefore, be to ensure awareness of the broad principles and to back this up with opportunities to learn more about computer programming and to use computing equipment under supervision. The Report (1967) of the President of the United States' Science Advisory Committee on Computers in Higher Education came to this conclusion and has already been referred to in the Preface.

All medical students should attend a few lectures on computer appreciation early in their course (first or second preclinical year). This introduction to computers could usefully be combined with a short series of lectures on statistics, the purpose being to ensure that all students have a uniform basic level of instruction in statistical terms and methods, and in computer appreciation. Later in the medical course, perhaps in the second clinical year, further lectures on specific medical applications of computers can nowadays be usefully included as there are sufficient working applications to make such a course no longer largely theoretical. Again, the aims should not be to give comprehensive coverage but to ensure awareness and to generate interest.

Several universities now offer courses in Computer Science which can be taken by those medical students who show particular interest in computers, and most medical courses include elective periods where the occasional student, in our experience, has chosen to work in the computer field. This type of interest should be encouraged.

As far as doctors who have already qualified are concerned, the increasing emphasis on the continuing nature of medical education, and the greater opportunities to attend 'refresher courses', mean that most doctors in Britain now have the opportunity to hear lectures on computers and their applications to medicine. The growing number of computer installations in hospitals and elsewhere in the health services will also increase the general level of awareness, and provide opportunities to make practical use of these facilities.

REFERENCES

ABRAMS, M. E., BOWDEN, K. F., CHAMBERLAIN, J. & MACCALLUM, I. R. (1968). A computer-based general practice and health centre information system. *Journal of the Royal College of General Practitioners*, **16**, 415–427.

ANDERSON, J. (1971). In *Progress in Real-time Medical Computing*. Ed. Payne, L. C. In preparation.

BARON, D. N. & FRASER, P. M. (1968). Medical applications of taxonomic methods. *British Medical Bulletin*, **24**, 236–240.

BOYLE, J. A. & ANDERSON, J. A. (1968). Computer diagnosis: Clinical aspects. *British Medical Bulletin*, **24**, 224–229.

BRITISH MEDICAL ASSOCIATION (1969). *Computers in Medicine.* Planning Unit Report No. 3, pp. 31–35. London: British Medical Association.

CARD, W. I. (1970). The diagnostic process. In *Medical Computing.* Ed. Abrams, M.E. pp. 29–34. London: Chatto & Windus.

CARRUTHERS, M. E. (1970). Computer analysis of routine pathology work schedules using a simulation programme. *Journal of Clinical Pathology*, **23**, 269–272.

CLIFTON, J. S. (1970). Developing a computer service for radiotherapy. In *Medical Computing.* Ed. Abrams, M. E. pp. 121–132. London: Chatto & Windus.

COLLEN, M. F. (1968). Automated multiphasic screening. In *Presymptomatic Detection and Early Diagnosis.* Ed. Sharp, C. L. E. H. & Keen, H. pp. 25–66. London: Pitman.

DAVENPORT, W. B. & ROOT, W. L. (1958). *An Introduction to the Theory of Random Signals and Noise.* New York: McGraw-Hill.

DUDLEY, H. A. F. (1968). Pay-off, heuristics and pattern recognition in the diagnostic process. *Lancet*, **2**, 723–726.

FERRISS, J. B. and eight co-authors (1970). Hypertension with aldosterone excess and low plasma-renin: preoperative distinction between patients with and without adrenocortical tumour. *Lancet*, **2**, 995–1000.

FRASER, B. J. (1969). *The Organisation of a Radiology Department in a District General Hospital.* Ph.D. thesis, University of Reading.

HAYHOE, F. G. J., QUAGLINO, D. & DOLL, R. (1964). The cytology and cyto-chemistry of acute leukaemias. *M.R.C. Special Report Series*, No. 304. London: Her Majesty's Stationery Office.

HOFFMAN, L. J. (1969). Computers and privacy: A survey. *Computing Surveys*, **1**, 85–103.

HOPE, C. S. (1970). Computer optimization of treatment planning. In *Medical Computing.* Ed. Abrams, M. E. pp. 133–145. London: Chatto & Windus.

LUSTED, L. B. (1968). *Introduction to Medical Decision Making.* Springfield, Illinois: Thomas.

MITCHELL, J. H. (1969). Relevance of the electronic computer to hospital medical records. *British Medical Journal*, **4**, 157–159.

NEWELL, J. A. (1970). Radiotherapy rotational treatment planning on a small slow computer. In *Medical Computing.* Ed. Abrams, M. E. pp. 146–149. London: Chatto & Windus.

OPIT, L. J. & WOODROFFE, F. J. (1970a). Computer-held clinical record system. I, Description of system. *British Medical Journal*, **4**, 76–79.

OPIT, L. J. & WOODROFFE, F. J. (1970b). Computer-held clinical record system. II, Assessment. *British Medical Journal*, **4**, 80–82.

ORR, J. S., CAIN, O., ETCHELLS, A. H., HALNAN, K. E. & HOPE, C. S. (1970). Computing in radiotherapy. *Scottish Medical Journal*, **15**, 370–377.

REPORT OF THE PRESIDENT'S SCIENCE ADVISORY COMMITTEE (1967). *Computers in Higher Education.* Washington: U.S. Government Printing Office.

RUSHMER, R. F., SMITH, O. & FRANKLIN, D. (1959). Mechanisms of cardiac control in exercise. *Circulation Research*, **7**, 602–627.

RUTOVITZ, D. (1968). Automatic chromosome analysis. *British Medical Bulletin*, **24**, 260–267.

RUTOVITZ, D., FARROW, A. S. J., GREEN, D. K., HILDITCH, C. J., PATON, K. A. & STEIN, B. (1970). A system of automatic chromosome analysis. In *Medical Computing*. Ed. Abrams, M. E. pp. 35–65. London: Chatto & Windus.

STEWART, J. S. S. (1970). Editor of a Symposium on patient monitoring, published in *Postgraduate Medical Journal*, **46**, 337–405.

STIRLAND, R. M., HILLIER, V. F. & STEYGER, M. G. (1969). Analysis of hospital bacteriological data. *Journal of Clinical Pathology*, **22**, supplement (College of Pathologists), **3**, 82–86.

STRONG, A. J., TAYLOR, D. E. M. & WHAMOND, J. S. (1970). Continuous automatic plotting of ventricular function using a parallel hybrid computer. *Journal of Physiology*, **210**, 69–70P.

VALLANI, C. W. & NEILSON, J. M. M. (1971). Computer analysis of ventricular ectopic rhythm in acute myocardial infarction. In preparation.

WARD, A. & McMASTER, G. W. (1970). Automatic screening for cervical cancer. In *Medical Computing*. Ed. Abrams, M. E. pp. 76–83. London: Chatto & Windus.

WARTAK, J. (1970). A practical approach to automated diagnosis. *I.E.E.E. Transactions on Bio-Medical Engineering*, **17**, 37–43.

WEIR, R. D., FOWLER, G. B. & DINGWALL-FORDYCE, I. (1968). The prediction and simulation of surgical admissions. In *Computers in the Service of Medicine*. Ed. McLachlan, G. & Shegog, R. A. Volume II, pp. 141–154. London: Oxford University Press.

WHITBY, J. L. & BLAIR, J. N. (1970). A computer-linked data processing system for routine hospital bacteriology. In *Automation, Mechanization and Data Handling in Microbiology*. Ed. Baillie, A. & Gilbert, R. J. pp. 23–32. London: Academic Press.

WHITEHEAD, T. P. (1969). Editor of a Symposium on automation and data processing in pathology, published in *Journal of Clinical Pathology*, **22**, supplement (College of Pathologists), **3**, 130 pages.

RECENT REVIEWS ON COMPUTERS IN MEDICINE

*Computers in the Service of Medicine*, (1968). Ed. McLachlan, G. & Shegog, R. A. 2 volumes. London: Oxford University Press.

Computing in medicine, (1968). *British Medical Bulletin*, **24**, 187–271.

Medicine and the computer, (1968). A series of eight short (one-page) articles published in the *British Medical Journal* by special correspondents.

*Computers in Medicine*, (1969). Ed. Rose, J. Proceedings of a Symposium held in February 1968. London: J. & A. Churchill.

*Computers in Medicine*, (1969). British Medical Association Planning Unit Report No. 3, 55 pages.

The computer in medicine, (1969). *The Practitioner*, **203**, 267–319.

*Medical Computing*, (1970). Ed. Abrams, M. E. Proceedings of a Conference held in January 1969. London: Chatto & Windus.

The use of computers in medicine, (1970). Symposium issues of the *Scottish Medical Journal*, **15**, 353–420.

GENERAL READING

LEDLEY, R. S. (1965). *Use of Computers in Biology and in Medicine.* New York: McGraw-Hill.

LINDBERG, D. A. B. (1968). *The Computer and Medical Care.* Springfield, Illinois: Thomas.

# Specific Applications of Digital Computers Affecting Groups and Populations

# The Use of Computers in a Central Organisation, and Record Linkage

By M. A. HEASMAN

## SUMMARY

THIS chapter classifies the uses of data held on files administered by a central organisation into categories of administrative, statistical and data bank applications, and descriptions of several forms of record are given.

The special problems of preparing data for input to centrally operated data-processing systems are discussed, and the various types of output that can be provided are reviewed. Record linkage and its uses are considered as part of the development of a more comprehensive system, and not as an isolated development. The problems of confidentiality are mentioned, particularly as they affect centrally held computer files of data.

## INTRODUCTION

The costs of health services are such that, even where their organisation by government is restricted, most individuals have to pay for their medical care by means of private insurance. In one sense or another, therefore, all countries have a collective interest in the organisation and delivery of health care. A desire for communication between like-minded organisations and individuals, and the trend towards attaining some degree of standardisation of various aspects of health care, together with the moulding effect of medical education, tend to favour the creation of central co-ordinating organisations even if they have no controlling function. These moves, preceding and taking place alongside the development of medical computing, have led almost inevitably to the co-ordinating or controlling bodies having an interest in the relevant aspects of computing.

This chapter discusses these aspects in so far as they are concerned with the processing of individual summaries of medical history. Although written in the context of the British National Health Service, it must be emphasised that the central organisation need not necessarily be governmental. In the U.S.A. for instance, the medical computing applications discussed here are covered by bodies such as the Commission on Professional and Hospital Activities, a non-profit-making independent organisation. In the British context the applications could be implemented centrally, regionally or perhaps (under an integrated health service of the future) at area health board level. This chapter does not consider the formulation and implementation of a policy for health service or medical computing, except where the topics discussed lead inevitably to the formulation of certain aspects of policy.

## USES OF DATA COLLECTED CENTRALLY

The uses of summaries of medical histories processed centrally are for administrative purposes, for statistical assessments, and as a data bank.

### Administrative uses of centrally collected data

Centrally placed records held on computer files and relating to individual patients, have been and are being used for a number of administrative purposes. The most important pioneering application (also discussed on p. 141) was developed in West Sussex by Galloway (1966). He placed on a computer-held file all notifications of births, and used these as a basis from which to arrange for parents to be notified of the desirability of bringing their children for routine immunisation and vaccination.

The system is arranged so that the computer prints a letter to the parents informing them of the date and time on which to take their child to the clinic or family doctor. The doctor is sent a schedule of appointments, arranged according to his personal wishes (e.g. for an immunisation clinic, or for one or more appointments per consulting session). On completion of the particular procedure, the doctor makes an entry on his schedule and returns it to the computer. Programs then up-date the child's personal record, and arrange for payment of the doctor. If a child fails to attend, a further appointment is made automatically and reminder letters are sent. Repeated failure to attend leads to a print-out for the health visitor, who calls on the parent to see if help is required or to try to persuade the parent to bring the child in future. Statistics about attendances are produced as required from the data held on the computer file. This system has now been introduced by several other local health authorities and has in general been welcomed by general practitioners. It relieves them of much tedious administrative work, has resulted in the saving of clerical and administrative time in the local authority offices, and has ensured a high immunisation rate, the rates in West Sussex for 1968 exceeding those of England and Wales as a whole by about 16 per cent (for diphtheria) and 47 per cent (for smallpox). The comparable unit cost for the computer-dependent system is 36.4 per cent less than the average value for England and Wales where arrangements for immunisation still depend largely on manually operated filing systems (Saunders, 1970).

Further developments in West Sussex now enable women in relevant age-groups to be called for cervical cytology examinations; similar arrangements have been introduced in other countries. Comparable procedures can be used to arrange for the call-up of blood donors, and the computer file can be used for checks to be made on stocks of blood;

requests for donors to attend can be phased in accordance with the need for blood of particular types. A recent development in Scotland has involved the use of similar methods to recall patients who have been treated for thyroid disease (Hedley *et al.*, 1970), and it can be seen how easily this can be extended to the call-up of patients with almost any disease particularly as the computer programs can be adjusted to take account of the characteristics of the disease and the interests and desires of each doctor.

The long-term development of the central administrative use of computer-held files of medical records would appear to lie in the field of population surveillance, provided that the difficult problems of recording changes of address can be solved. In Britain, as long as general practitioners continue to be paid according to the number of patients on their 'list', there exists a ready-made file of the population held by local executive councils. This could, in theory, be rewritten for a computer and used for 'call-up' of patients at appropriate dates for such screening or follow-up examinations as are considered beneficial. The introduction of such a file is perfectly feasible, and it could be commenced at birth. Thereafter it could be amended or added to on suitable occasions throughout life and terminated at death, thus forming the ideal basis for a record linkage scheme (p. 89). The files could be used to produce lists of value in medical administration (e.g. indexes of registered deaths) and could form the basis of accounting and other administrative procedures.

### Statistical uses of centrally collected data

The most widely used and easily understood applications of centrally held medical data probably lie in the area of statistics, where the data have several uses, summarised as follows:

1. To provide national statistics from which trends in mortality and morbidity can be observed.

2. To assist administrators in their organisation and planning of health services—most statistics of morbidity at present relate to the utilisation of the available services, and not necessarily to the needs of the community for these services.

3. To provide a basis for epidemiological investigations.

4. To assist in management, by providing doctors with statistics in standard form that can be used as the starting point for evaluative studies of patient-care.

The statistics obtained from computer-held data have till now been almost exclusively used to provide summaries of records of single events, such as a spell of hospital admission, an attendance at a general practitioner's surgery, or a single immunisation procedure. The computer, however, enables suitable records to be held and processed together.

Thus records of successive periods of admission to hospital can be linked to produce person-based rather than event-based statistics. Development of statistical measures of longitudinal events is as yet in its infancy, and the longitudinal equivalents of (for example) discharge and admission rates are as yet either undeveloped or not widely accepted.

## Data banks

One of the great advantages of computer-held data is the comparative ease with which they can be sorted and analysed, and most computer systems use general purpose programs to facilitate such analysis. It is, however, necessary to maintain some restriction and, on the whole, central organisations only place their data at the disposal of *bona fide* workers who require special statistical tabulations not covered in the routine runs. This *ad hoc* use of data banks is of growing importance, with the increasing use of statistics in administration, management and research, and the facility should be further developed since administrators are usually unable to wait for special research studies to be set up to answer questions that are of immediate concern. Often the manipulation of data already held on file can provide a sufficiently good answer, but for these generalisations to hold the data must not only be readily accessible, but must cover as wide an area of health service functions as possible.

As an example of the application of these sorting and listing principles, it is worth considering the problem which faces a research worker who wishes to obtain access to records (or to patients) known to have a rare disease. It would be time-consuming to write to every hospital asking for appropriate patient records, and many hospitals would be unable to access their records to provide the requisite information. However, if summaries about patients' illnesses were to be kept centrally on a computer, it would involve only a few minutes' work (or at most a few hours' work) to list all the appropriate patients. Access to the individual records would then be considerably simplified, since the research worker would be able to approach the relevant hospitals directly with the case reference numbers of the patients concerned; the permission of doctors in charge of the patients would still be needed, since confidentiality principles usually prohibit the release of the patients' names direct even to *bona fide* research workers.

Information held in a large data bank is inevitably limited, because questions of space and of file access become very real when a large amount of data is held, and because the collection of detailed material in standard form can be difficult. In addition, retrospective research presents many difficulties because data banks and records often do not contain the information required. In general, therefore, the information held in a data bank concerning patients should be restricted to the minimum consistent with usefulness. Identification information, age, sex and marital status of the patient, a few important administrative details (e.g. dates of admission and discharge), and data about diagnoses and operations probably form the minimum. To go much beyond this would soon introduce the law of diminishing returns. Coding of the information should wherever possible be by means of internationally agreed classifications. Despite their undoubted drawbacks, the W.H.O. Classification of Diseases, Injuries and Causes of Death and the General Register Office Code of Surgical Operations remain the most acceptable classifications for use in Britain.

## TYPES OF DATA TO BE HELD ON CENTRAL FILES
### Vital registration data
Probably the first medical events to be recorded on a 'computer', albeit a primitive card-sorting machine, were related to mortality data. Registration of births, marriages and deaths has been a legal requirement in Scotland since 1855. As a by-product of this legal requirement, it has been the practice to collect and analyse the statistics of causes of death. To do this a classification of causes of death has had to be developed, together with rules for the selection of one cause of death from any list giving multiple causes in a single person, and a standardised form on which the original data are recorded. The data are summarised in the form of statistical tabulations of degrees of complexity varying from simple tables of the numbers of deaths from all causes, through tabulations by age, sex, cause and geographical area of residence, to listings of the relevant details of individual deaths.

Over the years, the classifications, rules and forms have changed. The statistical tables have become more refined and processing more sophisticated but the principles remain unaltered, and are as sound today as in 1855. In particular, the collection of statistical data as a by-product of administrative or other needs, and not as an end in themselves, is a principle that continues to need stressing.

### Summaries of periods of admission to hospital (hospital in-patient summaries)
Most of the 'developed' countries have organisations which collect and process data summarising details about periods of treatment as patients in hospital. Usually these data are collected 'anonymously' (i.e. the identification of the patient does not appear on the summary); this is of no value for record linkage purposes; and in some cases identification data are now being recorded. The form used in Scotland for the collection of data is shown in Figure 20. It is prepared in duplicate, with the intention that the second copy be retained in the patient's notes as a summary of an episode of treatment. The Scottish form is atypical in two respects: (1) it allows for identification both of the patient and of the

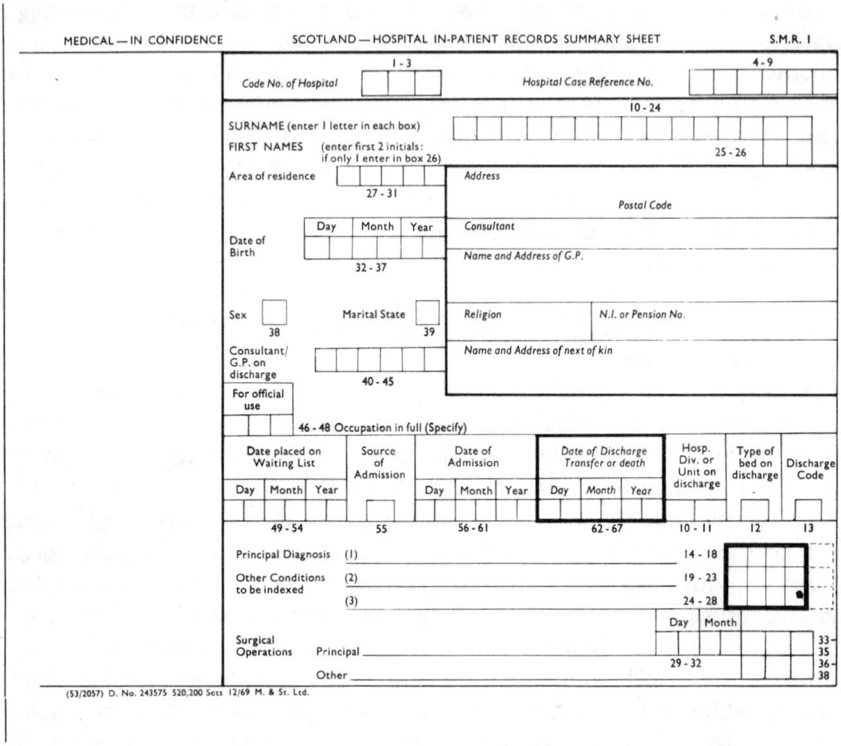

MEDICAL—IN CONFIDENCE SCOTLAND—HOSPITAL IN-PATIENT RECORDS SUMMARY SHEET S.M.R. I

Code No. of Hospital 1-3 Hospital Case Reference No. 4-9

SURNAME (enter 1 letter in each box) 10-24

FIRST NAMES (enter first 2 initials: if only 1 enter in box 26) 25-26

Area of residence 27-31 Address

Postal Code

Date of Birth Day Month Year 32-37 Consultant

Name and Address of G.P.

Sex 38 Marital State 39 Religion N.I. or Pension No.

Consultant/G.P. on discharge 40-45 Name and Address of next of kin

For official use 46-48 Occupation in full (Specify)

| Date placed on Waiting List (Day, Month, Year) | Source of Admission | Date of Admission (Day, Month, Year) | Date of Discharge Transfer or death (Day, Month, Year) | Hosp. Div. or Unit on discharge | Type of bed on discharge | Discharge Code |
|---|---|---|---|---|---|---|
| 49-54 | 55 | 56-61 | 62-67 | 10-11 | 12 | 13 |

Principal Diagnosis (1) 14-18

Other Conditions to be indexed (2) 19-23

(3) 24-28

Surgical Operations Principal Day Month 29-32 33-35

Other 36-38

(53/2057) D. No. 243575 520,200 Sets 12/69 M. & St. Ltd.

FIG. 20. The form used in Scotland for recording data relating to each period of admission to hospital. *Reproduced with permission of the Scottish Home and Health Department and of the Controller of H.M. Stationery Office, Edinburgh.*

doctor in charge, and (2) it is relatively restricted in the amount of information collected. Forms in use in other countries often allow for the recording of more diagnoses and operations and, particularly in the U.S.A., can accommodate more details about the diagnostic tests performed and about the treatment given. The forms are usually completed by medical records clerks; this means that the diagnosis and other details relevant to the summary must be clearly noted on the clinical record. The uses of these forms for administrative purposes are discussed in the next chapter (p. 95). Further elaboration of the basic record would be highly desirable, but it is questionable whether this should be effected at national or at local level. Such elaboration, if designed to be of interest to a particular specialty, can provide useful comparative data for consultants working in different hospitals.

The form (Fig. 20) provides a minimum of basic data suitable for most specialties, but there are at least three areas in which a different approach is required. These are obstetrics, neonatal paediatrics and psychiatry. In obstetrics, the question of 'diagnosis' for statistical purposes raises

Medical In Confidence     SCOTLAND—Maternity Discharge Record     **S.M.R. M.** (Part I)

**Card 1**    ☐ 1 | 1

Hospital _____ 2-4

Case Reference Number _____ 5-10

Current Surname _____ 11-22

Maiden Surname _____ 23-34

*First Names _____ Initials ☐ 35-36

*Home Address _____

_____

Postal Code _____ *Telephone No. _____

Area of Residence _____ 37-41

*Age _____ Date of Birth _____ 42-47

Family Doctor _____ 48-53

_____

*Telephone _____

*Next of Kin _____

*Telephone _____

Marital State (1=Single: 2=Married: 3=Widowed/Divorced: ☐ 54
     9 = Other/Not known)

Husband's Occupation (Specify)    For S.H.H.D. Use
_____ 55-57

Usual Occupation of Woman (Specify)
_____ 58-60

Date of Marriage (Day, month and year) _____ 61-66

Religion (1=None: 2=Protestant (all other Christian ☐ 67
Denominations): 3 = Roman Catholic: 9 = Other/Not known)

**PREVIOUS PREGNANCIES** (Enter appropriate number.
Exclude present pregnancy).

Total Number ☐ 68

Abortions ☐ 69

Still Births ☐ 70

Deaths in First Month ☐ 71

Deaths from 1 Month to 1 Year ☐ 72

Surviving Children ☐ 73

**PAST OBSTETRIC HISTORY** (1=No: 2=Yes: 9=Other/Not known)

Caesarean Section ☐ 74

Rhesus Iso-Immunisation ☐ 75

Eclampsia/Severe Pre-Eclampsia/Hypertension ☐ 76

Antepartum Haemorrhage ☐ 77

Multiple Births ☐ 78

Post-Partum Haemorrhage/Retained Placenta ☐ 79

Other Significant Obstetric History ☐ 80

---

**Card 2**    ☐ 2 | 1

**CURRENT PREGNANCY** ___ DUPLICATE 2-10

Obstetrician _____ Unit ☐ 11

Last Menstrual Period (Day and Month) _____ 12-15

   (1=Date certain: 2=Date uncertain: 9=Date not known) ☐ 16

Estimated Date of Delivery (Day and Month) _____ 17-20

Date of First Ante-Natal Examination anywhere _____ 21-24
             (Day and Month)

Date of Booking for Hospital (Day and Month) _____ 25-28

Original Booking _____ ☐ 29

Blood Group _____ Rh _____ ☐ 30

Rhesus Antibodies (1=No: 2=Yes: 9=Not known) ☐ 31

Antenatal Haemoglobin (Lowest recorded) gms. _____ 32-33

W.R. and Kahn Tests (1=+ve: 2=—ve: 9=Not tested/Not ☐ 34
                   known)

Height ___ ft ___ ins.*    cms. _____ 35-37

Date of Admission (Day and Month) _____ 38-41

Type of Admission _____ ☐ 42

Number of Previous Admissions anywhere this Pregnancy ☐ 43

Date of Delivery (Day, Month and Year) _____ 44-49

Date of Discharge (Day and Month) _____ 50-53

Discharged to _____ ☐ 54

Unit on Discharge _____ ☐ 55

Type of Bed on Discharge (1=N.H.S.: 2=Amenity: 3=Full pay) ☐ 56

Blood Transfusion this Pregnancy (1=No: 2=Yes) ☐ 57

X-Ray this Pregnancy (1=None: 2=Abdominal: 3=Chest: ☐ 58
      4 = Pelvic: 9 = Multiple)

**RECORD OF LABOUR**

Method of Induction (1=None: 2=A.R.M.: 3=Oxytocics: ☐ 59

     4=A.R.M. and Oxytocics: 9=Other)

Presentation at Delivery (1=Occiput: 2=Brow: 3=Face: Baby 1 ☐ 60

     4=Breech: 5=Shoulder: 9=Other) Baby 2 ☐ 61

Total Duration of Labour (Hrs.) _____ 62-63

Mode of Delivery _____ Baby 1 ☐ 64

_____ Baby 2 ☐ 65

Other Obstetric Procedure (1=None: 2=Manual removal of ☐ 66
           placenta: 3=Episiotomy: 9=Other)

Operation not connected with Delivery _____ ☐ 67

Number of Births this Admission ☐ 68

Outcome of Pregnancy _____ Baby 1 ☐ 69

_____ Baby 2 ☐ 70

Sex (1=Male: 2=Female) Baby 1 ☐ 71

                 Baby 2 ☐ 72

Birth Weight Baby 1 ___ lbs. ___ ozs* gms _____ 73-76

        Baby 2 ___ lbs. ___ ozs* gms _____ 77-80

---

**Card 3**    ☐ 3 | 1

**Complications of Pregnancy, Childbirth and Puerperium**   DUPLICATE 2-10

1. _____ 11-15

2. _____ 16-20

3. _____ 21-25

4. _____ 26-30

*Entries at these items are for hospital use only

Case of special interest (1=No: 2=Yes: 3=Transferred to
another hospital for delivery; readmitted within 48 hours) 27

FIG. 21. An example of a specially designed form, used for recording data
relating to patients discharged from maternity hospitals following delivery.
*Reproduced with permission of the Scottish Home and Health Department and
of the Controller of H.M. Stationery Office, Edinburgh.*

problems which demand different treatment, and other special aspects of the case history are important. For instance, it is necessary to record whether a patient was admitted in labour, the mode of delivery, any complications that might have occurred and the time of their appearance. The data collected for 'general' cases do not allow for this, and special arrangements such as those shown in Figure 21 are required. This form contains the minimum data shown in Figure 20 and several important additional facts about the patient's past and current obstetric history; these are all amenable to analysis by statistical means. In addition, the data provided on this form (Fig. 21) provide a concise type of clinical record, which can in itself have the effect of improving standards of medical care. Neonatal paediatrics gives rise to somewhat analogous problems, and work is now in progress on the design of a form suitable for data collection.

Psychiatry, by contrast, is a specialty in which patients are often treated in hospital for long periods of time. Data collected in the usual way, solely on discharge, could mean that records for many patients might not come up for analysis until some years after admission. For this reason, a statistical abstract for this type of case is completed both at the time of admission and on discharge. Occasional censuses of patients resident in hospital are also held.

### Data concerning out-patients

Several *ad. hoc* surveys of out-patient data have been published (for references, *see* Carstairs and Skrimshire, 1968), but the routine collection of statistical abstracts about consultations and treatment involving out-patients is very rarely performed. The reasons for this, at least in Britain, include the large number of patients involved, the short time that they spend at the hospital, and the need for many to attend repeatedly for consultation with doctors. Information that would be of value in statistical analysis includes the reason for consultation, the number of consultations, the interval between applying for a consultation and the actual date of consultation, the special tests performed, and the outcome (e.g. admitted to hospital, referred back to the general practitioner, etc.).

It seems unlikely that any large scale on-going study of data relating to out-patients will be made until the data can be collected and prepared in computer-acceptable form as a part of the normal processes of hospital administration. A possible alternative exists in the collection of data relating to a sample of out-patients, but there are severe sampling problems for a continuing study and such an approach would restrict the uses of the data to statistical analysis. It should be stressed, however, that a wide-scale study of data concerning out-patients is urgently needed, as the tendency of hospital care nowadays is to treat patients as out-patients as far as possible, rather than admit them to hospital.

Some specialties (e.g. dermatology) do most of their work on an out-patient basis.

### Records of patients in general practice

The holding of on-going records for patients in general practice upon computer-based central files, and the analysis of such records, is not a feasible proposition at the moment. The subject is discussed elsewhere (p. 148) and it is sufficient here merely to remark that the maintenance of practice lists centrally on computer files offers possibilities for medical administrative usage similar to those outlined on page 76. As long as the present method of paying general practitioners (on a *per capita* basis) is continued, it would seem to offer an eminently practicable way of calculating the payment due. Production of age-sex registers and population statistics should also be relatively easy.

### Birth notifications

The notification of births to medical officers of health can be used instead of, or as an adjunct to, data on the registration of birth as a computer-based file for population surveillance.

### Social security data

A sample (5 per cent) of data collected as a by-product of the payment of sickness benefits under the National Insurance Acts is used for statistical analysis. Information is produced in relation to age, sex, cause, and duration of incapacity. The analyses are incomplete, however, since they only relate to a part (albeit the majority) of the male and to a restricted and selected part of the female working population. Despite these limitations, the tables produced by the Department of Health and Social Security are of considerable value as indications of morbidity.

Experiments are now in progress which are examining the feasibility of assessing and paying of sickness benefit by computer. If this is introduced on a wide scale, the routine linkage of sickness benefit to other medical data becomes a distinct possibility.

## DATA PREPARATION AND INPUT FOR CENTRALLY OPERATED SYSTEMS

When data are collected from many different sources for input to a centrally operated scheme, it has to be collected in a standardised form. Until recently this required the design of special documents (e.g. Fig. 20) in which the relevant data are inserted in the appropriate spaces on the form. Certain sections (e.g. surnames and initials) can be accepted in alphabetic characters and others (e.g. dates) in numeric form, but a large part has to be pre-coded according to pre-arranged and mutually exclusive classifications. With suitably trained personnel the inter-mediate key-punching which is necessary before this type of form can be converted to computer input may be obviated by the use of either mark-sensing or optical character recognition (O.C.R.) devices. However, when data are being collected from large numbers of hospitals, for example, it is unlikely that sustained interest will be available for completing mark-sensing documents, since the task can become very tedious when data are required that go beyond the contents of circumscribed questionnaires. Even dates of birth can prove difficult to record reliably on mark-sensing documents. Unfortunately, the O.C.R. scanning equipment at present requires characters to be prepared by special equipment, or in standard form, and this again creates difficulties when input data are to be prepared at numerous points. For these reasons it seems likely that the technically more advanced types of data preparation equipment will not be available for this type of computer application for some years to come.

Optical scanning of ordinary manuscript or typescript characters will probably be necessary before key-punching can be entirely obviated, but developments are possible in another direction. With the increase in numbers of locally based hospital computer systems, for example, data required for the central installation should be obtainable as a by-product from the local computer. Most computers can now accept magnetic tape from other installations, but for the data on these tapes to be of any value generally it is essential that the file structure be first standardised at all computer installations when the locally collected data are likely to be required at more than one installation. With such standardisation of file structure the transmission of data between one installation and another should prove simple, but without standardisation interchange will either be very difficult or impossible.

When data are collected from numerous sources for processing centrally, inevitably some variation occurs both in the quality of abstraction of the data from the records and, if this is done locally, in the accuracy of the coding. Although co-operation from hospital staff may be very good, abstraction of data from clinical records is not always easy. Our experience has shown that a lot depends on the design of the written record, or of any summary that is prepared. In addition, the more detail that is required, the more difficult the tasks of abstraction and coding become.

It is important so far as possible to ensure that a check is kept on the accuracy of input data. Improvement in quality is achieved by the provision of feed-back that is of interest and value to the doctors providing the data in the first place. Feed-back of information gives some return for the effort expended in completing the appropriate abstract, and offers tangible evidence that the work done, if performed accurately, has worthwhile results. We have found that the standard of accuracy of the abstracts submitted is remarkably high, provided that the coding of the data does not demand much effort. The only part of the form where accuracy has proved to be seriously at fault has been in the coding of the area of residence; in this operation, a code (of civil parishes) is used that bears little relation to the postal address. Another source of inaccuracy has been in the identification of the consultant responsible for the patient, since the appropriate name cannot always be found on the clinical record.

The importance of validity and feasibility checks, to remove and correct errors of abstraction and coding, cannot be overstressed. Such errors are bound to occur and, if allowed to persist, bring disrepute on the system as a whole. Validity checks are used to ensure that the data have been entered in the correct form (e.g. a surname must not contain numeric characters, and a coding for a disease must be a code that exists, etc.). Feasibility checks, on the other hand, are intended to spot medical 'impossibilities' and provide an opportunity for the entry to be corrected. Such impossibilities would include a man having had a hysterectomy, and checks on unlikely events might include a cross-check in respect of a diagnosis of a case of leprosy in Scotland, or of a man of 25 having had a coronary thrombosis. Impossibilities must be corrected, but the extent of checking for unlikely events that can nevertheless take place is a matter of judgement to decide, within the resources available, what measures allow the minimum number of incorrect records to enter the computer file.

Opinions differ as to the desirability of coding being undertaken centrally or locally, and the decision must depend to a large extent on the resources available. In the future, however, it is likely that the coding necessary for large scale systems will take place in the computer, possibly using developments of the system proposed by Howell and Loy (1968), a system analogous to the gambler's 'fruit machine'. In this, single words are brought together with the 'pay-off' being provided in the form of a unique code number. For example, the word 'myocardial' appears in numerous rubrics of the disease classification, as does the word 'infarction', but when the two are brought together only one code is found to be common to both and this is the code entered into the computer's file.

## THE COST OF A CENTRALLY OPERATED SYSTEM

Large scale studies of the type described in this chapter are not cheap; it is therefore important to ensure that maximum use is made of the data and that duplication of effort is avoided wherever possible. By far the largest part of the cost is incurred in the collection of data, unless this can be achieved as a by-product of other necessary tasks. It is estimated that the completion of each form, as shown in Figure 20, costs between £0·125 and £0·250. If the forms are all completed independently of other tasks, the data collection costs for 600,000 forms (the number collected annually in Scotland) can be as much as £150,000. Central processing costs are between £15,000 and £30,000, so that processing of abstracts for hospital in-patients in a population of five million might be expected to cost annually between £100,000 and £200,000. This may seem a large sum, but it must be seen in the context of the total cost of the hospital service in Scotland; this is in the region of £85,000,000 per annum. The hospital in-patient statistics form the primary data for providing knowledge about the functioning of the hospital part of the National Health Service.

## OUTPUT FROM A CENTRALLY OPERATED SYSTEM
### Administrative uses of data
The administrative uses referred to (p. 76) require the output from the computer to be oriented towards the particular function that the output has to serve. Printed output can be in the form of standard letters addressed and dated appropriately, or appointments schedules filled in on pre-printed stationery, or lists requiring action can be headed appropriately, using either pre-printed stationery or specially programmed output. A problem with most forms of computer output is that the printing type-face is normally restricted to upper case. Until printed output can be produced cheaply in both upper and lower case type, the preferred method of computer output for these purposes will be on pre-printed stationery.

### Statistical output
The virtue of computer-produced statistical output, as opposed to the printed output from punched-card machines, lies in the performance of calculations which previously had to be done separately. In addition, the high-speed of modern line-printers removes restrictions on the amount of output available (indeed one of the great problems of modern computers is the amount of output which is often too much for intelligent interpretation). Suitably programmed, a computer can produce large numbers of tabulations of a common pattern; these would previously have required too much clerical effort to prepare. Standard forms of statistical tabulation do not require description, but the example given in Figure 22 shows the kind of data that can be provided to a single consultant (for further detail *see* Heasman 1968 and 1970). It gives an indication of the amount of his in-patient work during the previous year, generally in derived form (i.e. percentages, means, etc.) which he can then compare with similar national tables. It also gives information about the numbers of cases treated, and the number of deaths. Similar tables are prepared annually for each Scottish consultant, the diagnosis shown varying according to the specialty, and each consultant receives details of his own cases together with a national table for comparison. Thus the computer provides consultants with a few basic facts in a relatively

CONSULTANT –   CODE NO –   SPECIALTY – GENERAL SURGERY   YEAR – 1969

| | NO OF CASES | AGE DISTRIBUTION OF CASES | | | | SOURCE OF ADMISSION | | | | TIME ON WAIT LIST | | | | DURATION OF STAY | | | | SEPARATION | | | | NO OF DEATHS |
|---|---|---|---|---|---|---|---|---|---|---|---|---|---|---|---|---|---|---|---|---|---|---|
| | | 0-14 | 15-44 | 45-64 | 65+ | EMER-GENCY | WAIT LIST | TRANS IM | | QUARTILES 1ST | 2ND | 3RD | | QUARTILES 1ST | 2ND | 3RD | MEAN STAY | HOME | TRAN OUT | DEATH | |
| | | % | % | % | % | % | % | % | WKS | WKS | WKS | DAYS | DAYS | DAYS | DAYS | DAYS | % | % | % | | |
| | | | | | | | | | | | | | | | | | | | | | |
| ICD 174   CA. BREAST | | | | | | | | | | | | | | | | | | | | | |
| MALE | 30 | – | 20 | 37 | 43 | 23 | 30 | – | – | 1 | 1 | 1 | 12 | 14 | 18 | 15 | – | – | – | – |
| FEMALE | | | | | | | | | | | | | | | | | 83 | 3 | 13 | 4 |
| ICD 454   VARICOSE VEINS OF LEG | | | | | | | | | | | | | | | | | | | | | |
| MALE | 11 | – | 55 | 45 | 18 | – | 73 | 9 | 2 | 3 | 8 | 9 | 9 | 9 | 10 | 12 | 100 | – | – | – |
| FEMALE | 40 | – | 43 | | 13 | 13 | 78 | – | 1 | 3 | 9 | 9 | 9 | 9 | 10 | 13 | 98 | 3 | – | – |
| ICD 455   HAEMORRHOIDS | | | | | | | | | | | | | | | | | | | | | |
| MALE | 12 | – | 25 | 75 | – | 25 | 75 | – | 1 | 2 | 4 | 9 | 11 | 13 | 12 | 100 | – | – | – | |
| FEMALE | 2 | – | 50 | 50 | – | – | 100 | – | 1 | 1 | 1 | – | – | – | 11 | 100 | – | – | – | |
| ICD 540-543   APPENDICITIS | | | | | | | | | | | | | | | | | | | | | |
| MALE | 55 | 45 | 42 | 13 | – | 95 | 5 | – | 0 | 3 | 3 | 8 | 8 | 12 | 10 | 96 | 4 | – | – | |
| FEMALE | 53 | 30 | 62 | 2 | 6 | 83 | 15 | – | 1 | 1 | 3 | 8 | 10 | 13 | 12 | 96 | 4 | – | – | |
| ICD 550-553   ABDOMINAL HERNIAE | | | | | | | | | | | | | | | | | | | | | |
| MALE | 57 | 25 | 21 | 33 | 21 | 11 | 74 | 2 | 1 | 2 | 5 | 9 | 9 | 10 | 10 | 100 | – | – | – | |
| FEMALE | 9 | 11 | 22 | 33 | 33 | 22 | 78 | – | 2 | 9 | 22 | 9 | 10 | 11 | 10 | 100 | – | – | – | |
| ICD 574-576   DISEASES OF GALL BLADDER | | | | | | | | | | | | | | | | | | | | | |
| MALE | 7 | – | 43 | 29 | 29 | 29 | 57 | 14 | 1 | 3 | 4 | 12 | 12 | 15 | 14 | 100 | – | – | – | |
| FEMALE | 38 | – | 21 | 47 | 32 | 29 | 45 | 11 | 2 | 2 | 3 | 13 | 13 | 17 | 16 | 89 | 3 | 8 | 3 | |
| ICD 600-602,786.1   URINARY RETENTION AND PROSTATE DISEASE | | | | | | | | | | | | | | | | | | | | | |
| MALE | 35 | – | 6 | 6 | 89 | 66 | 23 | – | 2 | 3 | 4 | 12 | 15 | 22 | 17 | 97 | 3 | – | – | |
| FEMALE | | | | | | | | | | | | | | | | | | | | | |
| ICD 850-854   CONCUSSION AND HEAD INJURY | | | | | | | | | | | | | | | | | | | | | |
| MALE | 26 | 19 | 54 | 19 | 8 | 100 | – | – | – | – | – | 1 | 2 | 4 | 4 | 100 | – | – | – | |
| FEMALE | 5 | 60 | – | 20 | 20 | 100 | – | – | – | – | – | 2 | 5 | 5 | 5 | 100 | – | – | – | |
| ICD 531-534   PEPTIC ULCER | | | | | | | | | | | | | | | | | | | | | |
| MALE | 66 | – | 45 | 38 | 17 | 26 | 53 | 15 | 2 | 5 | 8 | 12 | 15 | 20 | 17 | 95 | 3 | 2 | 1 | |
| FEMALE | 9 | – | 56 | 44 | – | 22 | 44 | – | 1 | 2 | 3 | 4 | 11 | 15 | 11 | 100 | – | – | – | |
| MALE | – | – | – | – | – | – | – | – | – | – | – | – | – | – | – | – | – | – | – | |
| FEMALE | – | – | – | – | – | – | – | – | – | – | – | – | – | – | – | – | – | – | – | |
| ALL OTHER CONDITIONS | | | | | | | | | | | | | | | | | | | | | |
| MALE | 278 | 18 | 23 | 26 | 33 | 41 | 28 | 6 | 1 | 3 | 5 | 5 | 9 | 16 | 14 | 92 | 4 | 5 | 13 | |
| FEMALE | 203 | 10 | 29 | 30 | 32 | 44 | 27 | 5 | 1 | 2 | 3 | 4 | 10 | 20 | 15 | 88 | 5 | 7 | 14 | |
| ALL DIAGNOSES | | | | | | | | | | | | | | | | | | | | | |
| MALE | 547 | 17 | 28 | 27 | 28 | 44 | 34 | 6 | – | – | – | – | – | – | 13 | 95 | 3 | 3 | 14 | |
| FEMALE | 389 | 10 | 33 | 30 | 26 | 43 | 34 | 4 | – | – | – | – | – | – | 14 | 90 | 4 | 5 | 21 | |

FIG. 22. An example of a statistical tabulation provided to an individual consultant giving details of patients treated by him, in diagnostic groupings, as well as total numbers treated. Several other examples are discussed by Heasman and Carstairs (1971).

simple form. The purpose of these data is to assist the consultant in discharging his managerial responsibilities.

The data in Figure 22 provide one example of the use of output from large scale 'central' computers. It must not be forgotten, however, that the modern doctor has had little training in statistics and virtually none in management, and the reception and understanding of this type of information has varied between the extremes of close interest on the one hand to frank antagonism or lack of interest on the other. Adverse comment has to a certain extent been magnified because of the remoteness of the central computer from individual users some of whom have felt that they have had little direct influence on the tabulations produced. It is worth reiterating that centralisation does enable comparative data to be produced, whereas this is impossible on a local basis. Increasing familiarisation on the part of doctors with the computer's output will increase the value they obtain from these data, but this will not remove the need to search for more useful forms of output, two of which are graphical output and exception printing.

The use of graphical output in large-scale analyses implies quite large programming problems and questions of presentation. For example, to present the data shown in Figure 22, together with the comparable national material, would involve not only a large amount of graphical output but quite formidable random access and computational problems for the computer as well.

Exception printing involves the calculation of large numbers of statistical significance tests upon data held in the computer. Print-out in suitable form is produced only for those data where the results exceed a certain level of statistical significance. The advantage of this technique lies in the reduction in the amount of data provided to the user, and immediately focuses interest on factors which may require attention. On the other hand, it may conceal factors of importance which are not presented either because they fail to reach the appropriate level of significance or, perhaps more important, because a particular way of examining the data was not included in the program. In addition, for Gaussian distributions, 5 per cent of the 'normal' results will be printed out as if they were abnormal. This technique has not yet been widely applied in the field of medical statistics.

## Case listings

Experience with Scottish hospital in-patient data has revealed that one of the most useful outputs has been in the form of listings of medical case abstracts. A print-out of most of the original data collected is easy to arrange in either coded or interpreted form. The order of presentation of the data can be made in the form required by the worker; this relates both to the columns and the rows. For example, a listing can be produced in order of diagnostic classification, within age-bands, or just as easily in order of age with respect to diagnosis.

Using a national data bank, it has proved possible to produce diagnostic indexes for all the hospitals in Scotland, for the cost of a few hundred pounds. Many hospitals were previously unable to carry out such a task, while others employed staff specially to do it for them. The use of a computer to produce these indexes could by itself theoretically effect savings equal to the annual cost of the whole study. In addition, the national or regional organisation can produce national or regional indexes which are often used by research workers to obtain lists of cases or for simple statistical abstraction.

**Ad hoc tabulations**
The routine administrative, statistical and tabulation uses of large-scale medical abstraction schemes such as those described in this chapter should suffice to provide answers to a large number of questions. Nevertheless, there will always remain some users needing *ad hoc* special listings, and some questions that require special tabulations to be produced. For these, it is essential that general purpose programs be available that can be adapted easily for special purposes.

On the other hand, it is worth stressing that data banks of medical information cannot in practice cater for all possible requirements. The larger the amount of basic data held, the greater become the problems of economic computer usage. Also, large data files may store the data in such a manner that retrieval of it, if required in a particular form, can become an extremely lengthy and expensive process. Problems of data storage and speed of retrieval, which may not be important for small-scale uses, can become extremely serious with large amounts of data. For these reasons, rather than use a manufacturer's package, the general purpose programs are probably best designed to fit the particular data. It should be remembered, however, that the forms of output available with general purpose programs often restrict the special presentations possible with specially designed single purpose programs.

**RECORD LINKAGE**
The need to be able to relate to each other medical events separated by time has long been recognised, but it is only with the advent of the computer that record linkage has become possible on a routine basis. Record linkage involves the bringing together of data recorded at different times and places into a series of personal cumulative files.

All the data described in this chapter are, if adequately identified, suitable for introduction into record linkage. It has been emphasised that collection of the original data, and its preparation for computer input, together form the largest part of the cost. Record linkage should therefore be regarded, not as a separate entity, but rather as a natural development easily achieved provided that identification is included in standard form on all relevant data.

The computer techniques involved in linking records, although essentially simple, are beyond the scope of this chapter (for a full description of methods, *see* Acheson, 1967 and 1968). Where a perfect match of two sets of identifying data is achieved there is little problem, but difficulties arise when identifying data are similar but not exact. Methods of 'weighting' the various matching and non-matching components are then introduced.

## Problems of identification

If medical records are to be linked by computer-dependent methods or if the computer file is to be used as an aid to the accessing of individual records, a means of identification has to be derived which enables a particular individual's record to be identified with sufficient certainty for the job in hand. This last phrase is important for, if an individual's treatment is to depend upon the ability to effect a match, it is vitally important that the match be correctly made. On the other hand, if a linkage of records is only to be used as the basis for statistical presentation, correct matching in about 85 per cent of possible cases will probably be sufficient. As far as centrally based linkage schemes are concerned, it is unlikely that they will be used for anything other than statistical and research purposes for several years. Precise identification remains a desirable but not an immediately essential aim. Missed or incorrect matches of records are a function of poor information (which may be associated with social class, education, age, etc.), and this may introduce some bias into completely linked statistics.

Certainty in respect of identification can probably be ensured only by a numbering system which is not only unique to an individual but which also contains sufficient in-built checks to ensure that transposition of digits has not occurred (*see* Smythe, 1968). Unfortunately no such system has yet been devised for general use in this country, since neither the current National Health Service nor the National Insurance numbers contain check digits. Apart from this, the British public is markedly resistant to being numbered, unlike the Scandinavians, and it is unlikely that the use of numbers for identification will achieve wide acceptance in the near future. There are, however, other methods involving unchanging characteristics of an individual that offer a high degree of certainty in identification.

The minimum needed for reasonably certain identification of an individual depends on the size of population to be covered. Items which are usually considered, in approximately descending order of importance, are as follows:

1. Surname (and/or birth surname)
2. Initials (or forenames)
3. Date of birth
4. Sex
5. Place of birth
6. Mother's maiden surname

The first four of these items should, if correctly recorded, be sufficient to ensure uniqueness of identification in over 99 per cent of a population of five million. Acheson (1967) described the techniques of record matching and reviewed all aspects of medical record linkage.

## Uses of record linkage

A record linkage file increases in usefulness with the amount of data that it holds, with the size of the population that it covers, and with the length of time it has been in existence. The types of data that might be held on file include all that have been mentioned in this chapter. An ideal medical record linkage file would start at birth, with details of birth registration or notification, contain summaries of all significant medical events, and end with details of death. Apart from the time taken to create such a file, it is unlikely that complete coverage of this sort can be achieved for some years. The most useful file of limited scope is probably one that contains records of hospital treatment and of death certificates, and an attempt to build such a file on a national scale is in progress in Scotland. Other linked files of medical data in existence in Scotland include the Mental Health Register in North Eastern Scotland (Baldwin et al., 1965), and the paediatric register in Glasgow (Richards and Nicholson, 1970). The remainder of this section will deal with the national linkage file relating to hospital treatment and death.

## The Scottish record linkage file

There are several potential uses for this type of file, including the production of person-based statistics. Instead of statistics based upon individual spells of treatment, it should be possible to produce statistics relating to the number of people who have been in hospital, thus enabling reliable estimates of morbidity to be made for many conditions at the more serious end of the spectrum of disease. At present these estimates are not as clear as they could be, because repeated spells of admission of individuals to hospital introduce confusion when morbidity is calculated on data from event-based statistics.

Another use for this file will be to follow up patients who have been treated in hospital, both to subsequent periods of hospital admission and to death. Existing cancer registers have done this laboriously for patients with neoplastic disease, but the existence of a file linking hospital treatment and death would mean that such follow-up studies would become automatic for all diseases requiring treatment in hospital. Survival rates could therefore be calculated much more easily.

The relationship between two events separated in time may be investigated easily, using this type of record linkage file. For example,

Court Brown and Doll (1965) showed the association between ankylosing spondylitis treated by irradiation and leukaemia, and such studies could be repeated and extended.

A fourth application of this file could be for the study of industrial and other hazards. By entering into the file the names of persons exposed to an industrial hazard, for example, the file could be checked thereafter from time to time for the development of any particular disease, or for the cause of death of exposed people, even though the interval between exposure and disease or death might have been many years.

Occasionally, and provided that access time is short enough, a linked file could prove valuable in yielding information about previous periods of hospital admission where a patient was unable to provide this. It is unlikely, however, that a central file will hold more than brief abstracts of an individual's history, and it therefore appears unlikely that this possible application will be used much except perhaps with unconscious patients presenting problems in diagnosis.

One further application deserves mention, namely the possible use of the file for genetic studies. If the identifying information on, for instance, a birth entry were also to give the details concerning the parents such studies would clearly be possible, and indeed one of the first record linkage projects was of this type (Newcombe and Rhynas, 1962).

As yet, the development of medical record linkage anywhere in the world is still in its infancy, and for many years its further development will remain an act of faith. The potential uses, both in retrospective and prospective studies, are vast but the actual uses are very limited so far. Time must therefore be allowed for its full development, together with support for as wide as possible a study of its uses. In general, the uses of a medical record linkage file at present are mainly for research. These uses may be statistical, epidemiological, clinical follow-up, or genetic in nature but at present the applications in respect of patients as individuals are probably limited. With the computer-dependent hospital information systems of the future, however, linkage of each patient's records will be necessary in the computer's files, and the techniques outlined in this section will probably be needed.

## CONFIDENTIALITY AND THE COMPUTER

Confidentiality is only raised as a problem when personal identification is recorded and held on the computer, and the difficulties are of two kinds. On the one hand there are questions relating to the security of data during transmission to the computer and the security of the computer itself, and on the other hand the questions relating to the protection of data held on computer file from inappropriate use.

The first of these problems, up to the time of input to the computer, is no different in kind from the problems of transmission of any other confidential matter by post, and thereafter the computer itself can be made as secure as financial resources permit. Any data held on a computer, even in uncoded form, is probably far more secure than in a records office in hospital, and further checks can be built into the computer-based system. For example, access to data can only be obtained after using an appropriate code word, known only to the authorised user. This, together with stringent security for magnetic tape files, can ensure that the safety of the data is virtually complete. The technical safeguards provided by computer technology have been reviewed by a B.M.A. Working Party (1969), and by Hoffman (1969).

Inappropriate use of the data is more difficult to guard against, although the controls imposed by the code of medical ethics probably means that there is little real danger of misuse. Nevertheless, Acheson (1967) has suggested that medical record linkage files must, as a matter of policy, be kept separate from all other data held, for example, by the government. The reason for this is to ensure that the medical data on file cannot be used, for example, to check that an applicant for a driving licence is medically fit to drive, the licence application being also handled by a computer-based filing system.

Release of information to research workers should only be permitted under strict rules. As already indicated, in Scotland the names of patients are not released, and instead the research workers are provided with hospital case reference numbers. They must then approach the consultant in charge of each case for permission to examine clinical notes. If a worker wishes to approach an individual patient, the patient must state his agreement to his own doctor before contact with the research worker is permitted. Provided such simple rules are adhered to, the confidentiality of medical information held on a centrally based computer file will be maintained. Patients' interests in this matter are paramount, and they must never be embarrassed by incorrect disclosures.

## CONCLUSIONS

There are quite substantial advantages in the central organisation of the aspects of the computer services described in this chapter. They include the collection in one place of relatively simple data from which statistical analyses and listings can be produced covering all individuals and institutions participating. This is essential in many health services of today and becomes very difficult, if not impossible, with too much decentralisation. The organisation is probably cheaper than with decentralised installations.

Record linkage increases in value with the size of the geographical area covered. On the other hand remoteness of the central organisation from the producer of the original data can act as a considerable disadvantage both psychologically and because of the physical communications problems that are introduced. Turnround of data is also usually slower.

In the long term the solution will probably be found in standardisation of file structure enabling easy transfer of data between computers, with the more central organisation being responsible for record linkage and for such statistics as can only be produced at that level, but with administrative uses and local statistical work being carried out by decentralised computer systems. For a fuller discussion of these problems the review by Ockenden and Bodenham (1970) should be consulted.

REFERENCES

ACHESON, E. D. (1967). *Medical Record Linkage*. London: Oxford University Press.

ACHESON, E. D. (1968). *Record Linkage in Medicine*. Edinburgh: Livingstone.

BALDWIN, J. A., INNES, G., MILLAR, W. M., SHARP, G. A. & DORRICOTT, N. (1965). A psychiatric case register in North East Scotland. *British Journal of Preventive and Social Medicine*, **19**, 38–42.

BRITISH MEDICAL ASSOCIATION (1969). *Planning Unit Report No. 3 : Computers in Medicine*. London: B.M.A.

CARSTAIRS, V. & SKRIMSHIRE, A. (1968). The provision of outpatient care at health centres: a review of data available for planning. *Health Bulletin for Scotland*, **26**, No. 3, 12–22.

COURT BROWN, W. M. & DOLL, R. (1965). Mortality from cancer and other causes after radiotherapy for ankylosing spondylitis. *British Medical Journal*, **2**, 1327–1332.

GALLOWAY, T. M. (1966). Computers: Their use in local health administration. *Journal of the Royal Society of Health*, **86**, 213–216.

HEASMAN, M. A. (1968). Scottish hospital inpatient statistics—sources and uses. *Health Bulletin for Scotland*, **26**, No. 4, 10–18.

HEASMAN, M. A. (1970). Scottish consultant review of inpatient statistics (SCRIPS). *Scottish Medical Journal*, **15**, 386–390.

HEASMAN, M. A. & CARSTAIRS, V. (1971). Inpatient management: Variations in some aspects of practice in Scotland. *British Medical Journal*, **1**, 495–498.

HEDLEY, A. J., SCOTT, A. M., WEIR, R. D. & CROOKS, J. (1970). Computer-assisted follow-up register for the North-East of Scotland. *British Medical Journal*, **1**, 556–558.

HOFFMAN, L. J. (1969). Computers and privacy: A survey. *Computing Surveys*, **1**, 85–103.

HOWELL, R. W. & LOY, R. M. (1968). Disease coding by computer. *British Journal of Preventive and Social Medicine*, **22**, 178–181.

NEWCOMBE, H. B. & RHYNAS, P. O. W. (1962). *Proceedings of the Seminar on the Use of Vital and Health Statistics for Genetics and Radiation Studies*. New York: United Nations.

OCKENDEN, J. M. & BODENHAM, K. E. (1970). *Focus on Medical Computer Development*. London: Oxford University Press.

RICHARDS, I. D. G. & NICHOLSON, M. F. (1970). The Glasgow linked system of child health records. *Developmental Medicine in Child Neurology*, **12**, 357–367.

SAUNDERS, J. (1970). Results and costs of a computer-assisted immunisation scheme. *British Journal of Preventive and Social Medicine*, **24**, 187–191.

SMYTHE, M. (1968). Record numbering. In *Record Linkage in Medicine*. Ed. Acheson, E. D. pp. 179–187. Edinburgh: Livingstone.

# CHAPTER FIVE

# The Use of Computers for Administrative Purposes in the National Health Service

By L. M. WILLIAMS and J. C. GRAY

## SUMMARY

THIS chapter indicates the main areas of use for computers in the administrative field, basing the discussion on a typical Regional Hospital Board computer installation. Three applications (payroll, equipment scheduling for new capital projects, and hospital activity analysis) are considered in detail, and some likely areas of future development are indicated. The need for all levels of management to learn how to make better use of the information provided by computer systems is stressed.

The chapter highlights the different ways in which computers can effectively serve administrative functions, and concludes with a warning about possible restrictions in the widespread introduction of computers. Although computers can help to provide a better service to the patient, it is unlikely that their use will give rise to real financial savings.

## INTRODUCTION

In any government industrial or commercial complex a large volume of data is handled daily, and the hospital service is no exception. Staff records, timesheets and duty rosters have to be maintained as well as payments made to staff and suppliers. In addition, details have to be recorded in respect of goods received and issued, and information about the usage of beds and the numbers of patients treated listed in various statistical categories.

Before the introduction of computers these data were handled by manual or punched card methods. Using a sorter and a tabulator it was possible, after punching the data in coded form on to a punched card, to prepare a printed record of (for example) invoices that had been passed for payment, a summary of creditors' payments, and printed cheques for issue to staff. It was also possible to analyse information about patients and other statistical data under various headings. Originally these punched card machines were incapable of performing multiplication or division, but electronic multipliers became available about 20 years ago and these were quickly followed by other machines which could both multiply and divide. With the introduction of these calculators rapid development took place in the processing of financial and other administrative data.

The financial viability of the use of these punched card machines depended largely upon the number of times the original punched card was used. For example, a card punched both with the commodity code of an item held in a bulk store and with information about the amount issued could be used to update the stores records, to price the total cost of the issue for financial expenditure purposes, and to provide the Supplies Officer with the total issues of that particular item over a given period. Similarly, a card punched with the details of a supplier's invoice could be used for preparing the supplier's remittance advice note, the cheque for his payment, and an analysis of expenditure for accounting purposes.

The introduction of computers, with their greater flexibility and speed of input and output, meant that most Regional Hospital Boards changed their method of working about 10 years ago from punched card machines, and thereafter either rented, purchased, or shared the use of a computer with another Regional Board. Principally because of the interest already shown in the machine methods by the staff concerned with finance, the systems initially developed have been mainly on the accounting side, where actual savings could be demonstrated by using the computer.

Examples of the various administrative records maintained on computers by Regional Hospital Boards are listed in Table IV, and the details of three of these systems (payroll, equipment scheduling for new hospitals, and hospital activity analysis) will be discussed.

TABLE IV

Examples of administrative records held on computer file
by Regional Hospital Boards

| Category of record | Main functions served |
| --- | --- |
| Financial ledger | Analysis of expenditure and income under designated headings, together with summaries of hospital running costs. |
| Creditors' file | Remittance advices, cheques, schedules of payments. |
| Payroll operations | Preparation of employees' payslips, together with associated financial analysis, and statistical and management information. |
| Stores ledger | Records of stores transactions, and details of pricing for analysis of expenditure. |
| Equipment schedule | Lists of equipment, room by room, for new hospital building projects, together with commitment recording throughout the commissioning phase. |
| Medical statistics | Preparation of statements on the use made of beds, numbers of patients treated, etc. |

The applications described in this chapter were designed and programmed for a configuration consisting of an I.C.L. 1902A computer (16K, 24-bit words), with peripherals that consisted of four tape decks and a controller (41·7K characters per second), a line printer (120 print positions, 1350 lines per minute) a card reader (600 cards per minute) and a console typewriter. The main programming language was COBOL, chosen because it is comparatively easy to learn and use, and so far about 110 programs have been designed, written, tested and become operational. These specially designed programs incorporate, wherever possible, the computer manufacturer's own sub-routines (e.g. Income Tax calculations) but these represent only a small proportion of the total programming effort. The term data processing unit is used in this article to describe the installation and its associated staff.

## FINANCIAL APPLICATIONS—PAYROLL

Most Regional Hospital Boards have a common broad financial administrative workload for their computers with the processing of payroll for weekly and monthly paid staff, the payment of creditors, the maintenance of stores, etc., and the incorporation of these into an integrated financial system. Payroll has become increasingly complex due to the regulations governing conditions of service and the need to allow for superannuation, for earnings-related sickness benefit payments, for Save-As-You-Earn deductions, contributions to National Savings, etc., as well as to prepare statutory year-end returns; it is now a very time-consuming part of the work of a finance department. A computer-dependent payroll system must set out to alleviate this workload, and a well-designed system should incorporate features discussed in the next two paragraphs.

### Requirements to be met by a computer-operated payroll system

The first requirement of the system, in operation, is that—having established an individual pay record on magnetic tape—the process of making payments can thereafter be implemented without further action by the pay staff, other than the notification of any permanent or temporary variations to this basic record. The next requirement is that certain permanent changes that may become due in the basic record of an individual or group of individuals (e.g. pay awards, salary increments, increased National Insurance rates) can be actioned automatically at the data processing unit and the basic pay records updated accordingly.

The system should also undertake the automatic preparation of a number of documents or lists. These include salary cheques or other methods of payment; the financial analysis needed for incorporation into financial ledgers; the preparation of schedules (e.g. staff making Save-As-You-Earn or National Savings contributions); the issue of year-end returns (e.g. Income Tax and superannuation statements); and the provision of information essential to management (e.g. the number of hours of overtime worked).

## The basic operations of a computer-dependent payroll system

The basic record of the system is a Personnel Record Card, which is a specially designed form that initiates the base record held on magnetic tape for each employee and which serves as an establishment record; this form is completed by the pay clerk. It gives details of the employee's name, pay number, date of birth, date on which employment commenced indicating whether this is in whole-time or part-time employment, the employee's sex, marital status, method of payment, National Insurance number, and bank identification number and bank account number (where payments are made direct to a bank account), Income Tax code, superannuation number and rate of superannuation, details about the position of appointment on a salary scale with a code to identify the particular scale, and information about any special deductions to be made (e.g. savings contributions) before making the salary payment. When completed, this basic record is sent to the data processing unit where the information is punched, verified and read in by the computer for transfer to the magnetic tape file. The system allows the information to undergo validity checks at the time of input, and for error messages to be printed out if a check fails to be met (e.g. an employee designated as female but associated with a National Insurance rate applicable to a male). A final check on the accuracy of the basic record is performed by examining a print out of the information stored on magnetic tape, the staff in the pay department undertaking this check.

Permanent variations in the basic record (e.g. from part-time to whole-time work) are notified on a form containing the same information as the Personnel Record Card; this information is received at the data processing unit, punched, verified, read to tape, checked for validity and the payroll master files updated. Similarly, temporary variations in the basic record (e.g. hours of overtime worked, absence due to sickness, timing of holidays, etc.) are notified and processed. For a weekly payroll of 10,000 employees, the number of temporary variations is about 9,000 due particularly to the frequent entries in respect of overtime working, and absences due to sickness or holidays. The punching and verifying of these variations occupies approximately 70 hours of operator time (i.e. 10 punch operators, each working seven hours on this aspect of their job). Other Regional Hospital Boards have experimented successfully with the use of mark sense document readers as an alternative to the traditional punch card, the reasons for exploring being the difficulty experienced in recruiting and retaining punch operators rather than any possible inadequacy of card input or a need for economy.

After the temporary variations have been input to the computer the pay week computation can commence. Already stored on magnetic tape are the salary and wage scales for all employees, their National Insurance stamp rates, their bank account details and addresses. This information, along with the temporary variations, is merged with the permanent basic record (held on a master tape) of salary and National Insurance deductions, etc.; the computer then computes overtime payments and any other changes in the basic rate of pay, applies deductions such as the Income Tax payable and superannuation payments, and then prints out in triplicate a pay slip showing the make-up of the gross pay, deductions, and net pay. One copy of the payroll is the pay slip for the employee, the second copy provides a permanent payroll hard copy record, and the third copy (which bears the name, number and pay scale and the standard deductions only) is used as the temporary variation sheet for the following week. Using master tapes to hold the salary and wage scales, together with tables of National Insurance stamp values, etc. within the appropriate programs, enables any change in these scales and rates to be altered at the data processing unit, no action being necessary on the part of the pay clerk.

The time to complete each process cycle of update master file, action temporary variations, calculate and print out for a payroll of 10,000 employees paid on a weekly basis depends upon the power of the computer, but the configuration described here completes these tasks in six hours on a single run; a more powerful computer with additional core store and fast access discs would considerably reduce this time scale.

After completing the payroll operation, certain subsidiary documents are processed (e.g. cheques, bank giro credits, time sheets, National Savings schedules, etc.) and a financial analysis of all payroll transactions is prepared. Management information regarding hours of overtime worked and their cost, the incidence of sickness, and staff statistics by grade of employee within a hospital is also provided. The computer holds on its backing store the total gross pay, the Income Tax and other deductions made up to that date for each individual; these amounts are updated each week, so the necessary year-end returns for Income Tax and other purposes can be automatically produced when required.

## Computer-operated payroll: effects on staff

The payroll system was designed and programmed so as to create management reports from the data generated by standard operating functions, as well as to stop pay clerks spending most of their time on tedious repetitive calculations. The need for comptometer and accounting machine operators has been removed, and the number of pay clerks employed has been reduced despite an increasing size of payroll. The pay staff now spend more time keeping abreast of new salary and wage scales and conditions of service, and in following up reasons for high levels of overtime or sickness. The need still exists for pay staff to examine critically the completed computer payroll, for errors that may arise from incorrect information being provided to the data processing unit, and to use fully the management information now available. There has been, therefore, a need for a different approach by staff to computer payrolls.

The details of this payroll system illustrate that it would be wrong to transfer on to a computer without any alteration a manual system for operating financial or other administrative procedures. A complete review of the existing system should be undertaken, and management should be asked what information it would require as well as be advised of the information that can be made available by using computer methods.

## HOSPITAL BUILDING—EQUIPMENT SCHEDULING

The need to consider methods other than purely manual methods of preparing schedules for the component attributable to movable equipment in capital building schemes has been clear for several years. The reasons have been the growing number, complexity and size of major schemes at the planning stage. A careful appraisal of the manual system revealed several defects. In the first place, the equipment lists for each project had to be created manually, in draft, from existing information (e.g. Hospital Equipment Notes). Secondly, there was a lack of detailed description at this early stage; this made the costing of lists difficult, often resulting in variations in cost having to be made later at the stage of actually equipping the building. Finally, the setting out in detail of the cost per item of equipment, the analysing and summarising of the lists, and the typing and duplicating involved were collectively becoming very demanding in time and were beginning to require additional clerical staff.

### Equipment scheduling—the computer files

To consider possible solutions to the problem, a study group of senior members from planning, supply branch, work study and computer sections was formed in the South-Eastern Region, Scotland. The results of this study and investigation have been incorporated into a computer-operated system. In drawing up this scheme, the objectives were to aid planning officers prepare costed schedules of equipment quickly and accurately; to allow amendments to be made to the draft proposals; to make possible earlier submission of lists to the Regional Hospital Board and to the Scottish Home and Health Department; and, after approval, to exert financial control within the approved cost limit throughout the purchasing and commissioning phase. The system is based on four master files:

1. Department Catalogue     Table V

2. Room Catalogue      Table VI
3. Item Catalogue       Table VII
4. Room Library       Table VIII

It was necessary initially to set up these four master files on magnetic tape, giving a commodity code number to each item of equipment and a price per unit. When new items are introduced, or prices alter, the master

TABLE V

An extract from the master file containing the Department Catalogue, used for purposes of equipment scheduling

DEPARTMENT CATALOGUE 30 09 70                    PAGE 01

| DEPT CODE | DESCRIPTION |
|-----------|-------------|
| 01 | CHILDRENS MEDICAL WARD |
| 02 | CHILDRENS SURGICAL WARD |
| 03 | E.N.T. WARD |
| 04 | GENERAL MEDICAL WARD |
| 05 | GENERAL SURGICAL WARD |
| 06 | GERIATRIC WARD |
| 07 | GYNAECOLOGICAL WARD |
| 08 | OPHTHALMIC WARD |
| 09 | ORTHOPAEDIC WARD |
| 13 | STANDARD WARD FLOOR |

TABLE VI

An extract from the master file containing the Room Catalogue, used for purposes of equipment scheduling

ROOM CATALOGUE AS AT 30 04 71                    PAGE 008

| ROOM TYPE | ROOM DESCRIPTION | DEPARTMENT DESCRIPTION | SEQ. NO. |
|-----------|-----------------|------------------------|----------|
| 0112 | SISTERS OFFICE | ALL WARDS EXCEPT PSYCHIATRIC | 01 |
| 0113 | SISTERS OFFICE | A & E TREATMENT | |
| 0114 | SISTER/CHARGE NURSES OFFICE | PSYCHIATRIC WARD-TYPE 1 & 2 | |
| 0115 | SUPERINTENDENT MIDWIFES OFFICE | MATERNITY-RECEPTION & ADMIN | |
| 0116 | DOCTORS ROOM | ALL WARDS | |
| 0117 | PATHOLOGISTS OFFICE | MORTUARY | |
| 0118 | MEDICAL STAFF ROOM | MATERNITY-LABOUR SUITE | |
| 0119 | DOCTORS ROOM | MATERNITY LABOUR SUITE | |
| 0120 | MEDICAL STAFF OFFICE | MATERNITY - RECEPTION AND ADMIN | |
| 0121 | REGISTRARS ROOM | LABORATORY SERVICES | |
| 0122 | PATHOLOGISTS ROOM | LABORATORY SERVICES | |
| 0123 | DOCTORS DUTY ROOM (40 PATIENTS) | A & E TREATMENT | |

TABLE VII

An extract from the master file containing the Item Catalogue,
used for purposes of equipment scheduling

| | | ITEM CATALOGUE AS AT 30 04 74 | | | PAGE 0006 |
|---|---|---|---|---|---|
| GROUP CODE | ITEM CODE | ITEM DESCRIPTION | | EST/UNIT COST | DATE OF LAST REVISION |
| 4 | 00085 | AUDIOMETER SCREENING | | 150.00 | 31 12 69 |
| 4 | 10004 | AUGER | | 4.00 | 26 02 71 |
| 4 | 00031 | AURISCOPE | | 9.50 | 23 01 70 |
| 3 | 00037 | AUTOANALYSER 6 CHANNEL COMPLETE | | 6500.00 | |
| 3 | 00032 | AUTOANALYSER SINGLE CHANNEL COMPLETE | | 3200.00 | 28 02 69 |
| 3 | 00033 | AUTOCLAVE BENCH ELEC. 10 X 11.25 IN. | | 50.00 | |
| 3 | 00093 | AUTOCLAVE INST PORT (LITTLE SISTER) (CL) | | 109.41 | 26 11 70 |
| 4 | 00045 | AUTOSPENSER | | 90.00 | |

TABLE VIII

An extract from the master file containing the Room Library,
used for purposes of equipment scheduling

| ROOM TYPE 0037 | | RECOVERY ROOM | COST LIMIT | £65 | PAGE NO. 0026 |
|---|---|---|---|---|---|
| GROUP CODE | ITEM CODE | ITEM DESCRIPTION | QUANTITY | ESTIMATED UNIT COST | TOTAL COST |
| 3 | A0221 | CHAIR SEMI-EASY | 1 | 12.00 | 12.00 |
| 3 | B0721 | TABLE SIDE VENEERED 4X2.5FT | 1 | 12.00 | 12.00 |
| 4 | D0239 | BOWL POLYPROPYLENE 10IN | 3 | 0.40 | 1.20 |
| 3 | D0828 | COUCH EXAMINATION TUBULAR FRAME | 1 | 22.00 | 22.00 |
| 4 | G0487 | SPHYGMOMANOMETER TABLE MOUNTING | 1 | 8.00 | 8.00 |
| 4 | M0299 | TRAY INSTRUMENT ALUMINIUM 1X1FT (TSC) | 1 | 2.00 | 2.00 |
| 3 | M0357 | TROLLEY DRESSING 18 X 18 IN | 1 | 25.00 | 25.00 |
| 4 | S0120 | CUP FEEDING | 1 | 0.15 | 0.15 |
| 4 | S0899 | TUMBLER GLASS | 1 | 0.20 | 0.20 |
| 4 | T0657 | PILLOW FOAM | 2 | 1.25 | 2.50 |
| | | | COST LIMIT | | 65.00 |
| | | | TOTAL ESTIMATED COST | | 85.05 |
| | | | VARIATION | | 20.05 |

file has to be updated. The extract from the Department Catalogue
(Table V) shows a list of some of the departments within a hospital; at
present the system caters for about 75 different departments. Table VI
shows an extract of the Room Catalogue and the associated detail; the
system currently caters for 1200 different types of room.

As shown in Table VII, the Item Catalogue is a list of about 6000 items
in current use; it is capable of being expanded to 240,000 items. Each
item is given a group code, an item number, a description and an estimated cost. The date of last revision is an indication to the Supplies
Department of the date when the estimated cost was last revised or
checked by them and found to be still valid. For ease of reference the list
is prepared in both alphabetical and in numerical formats. Finally, Table
VIII outlines the contents of the Room Library file, which provides
information relating to the type of room, the cost limit, the itemised list

of equipment contained in the room (priced at the latest known costs), the total cost of the items as listed, and any variation in this total cost from the standard that has been laid down for that room. During operation, the system allows for the amendment and updating of the Department Catalogue and the Room Catalogue as required. The Item Catalogue file is updated at monthly intervals, to allow for changes in prices and descriptions of articles, and for insertions and deletions. The Room Library file is similarly updated at monthly intervals, to incorporate amendments made in the Item Catalogue. The facility exists to amend at any time the contents of individual rooms, to insert new rooms and to delete rooms no longer required; by these means the data base consisting of the four master files is kept up to date.

### Equipment scheduling—the operation of a project

An individual project is created by the planning officer when he specifies the code for a department, the types of room required in the order stated in a sketch plan (using the Room Catalogue to obtain the room code) and the number of each room type in each area specified. These basic data are punched and sorted into the order for the room codes; the Room Library file (Table VIII) is then searched and the project file created. The project file details the rooms specified, sorted to department code order; departmental headings are then inserted and the unique project file sorted to the order required and listed.

The project so prepared is checked and amendments made by the project planning team. The updated project file is listed, further amendments made for each specific hospital project and the file is matched against the Item Catalogue (Table VII) to have the current unit costs inserted. The project is thus costed item by item, aggregated by room and department to provide a total cost. A subsequent list is prepared on duplimat form (i.e. similar to a stencil) and distribution lists are produced by an offset printing machine showing items in item code order and location. A summary file is also produced together with a total category summary.

At this stage the equipment lists are submitted to the appropriate committee of the Regional Hospital Board for approval, and thereafter to the Scottish Home and Health Department. When final financial approval has been received from the Department, the project enters the last cycle of the system. By matching the summary file produced earlier with orders placed, it is possible to compare estimated with actual costs to show under- or over-spending by item, category and project (Table IX). At the same time the total of items still to be ordered is shown category by category. During the ordering phase, the commitment control information is prepared at weekly intervals for the planning division, where management control is exercised.

TABLE IX

An extract from a summary statement showing the state of spending
(under- or over-spending) in an individual project

| PROJECT 07 | PHASE | WESTERN GENERAL HOSPITAL O.P.D. | | | COST VARIATION STATEMENT AS AT 30 04 71 PAGE 7 | | | |
|---|---|---|---|---|---|---|---|---|
| ITEM CODE ID | | ITEM DESCRIPTION | QUAN | ESTIMATED TOTAL COST | ACTUAL TOTAL COST | UNDERSPENT | OVERSPENT | SUPP/ SUBST |
| 00007 01 | ALBUMINOMETER | | 1 | 1.50 | 0.30 | 1.20 | | |
| 00012 01 | ANAESTHETIC APPARATUS PORTABLE | | 3 | 540.00 | 540.00 | | | |
| 00018 01 | APPLICATOR TUBE GAUZE AVERAGE SIZE | | 6 | 4.50 | 0.00 | 4.50 | | |
| 00031 01 | AURISCOPE | | 1 | 8.50 | 8.50 | | | |
| 00050 01 | AMSLER CHART | | 1 | 2.00 | 2.25 | | 0.25 | |
| 00064 01 | APPLICATOR TUBE GAUZE 6&1 | | 1 | 0.75 | 0.00 | 0.75 | | |
| 00065 01 | ANAESTHETIC APP MINI BOYLE | | 5 | 1150.00 | 1250.00 | | 100.00 | |
| 00066 01 | ANAESTHETIC HEAD WALL MOUNTED | | 2 | 300.00 | 338.00 | | 38.00 | |

## Experience with computer-dependent equipment scheduling

This computer-dependent system has now been in operation for four
years, and has excited a wide interest in Britain and abroad. Several
benefits have been derived, and these will be briefly listed.

In the first place draft equipment lists can now be obtained in hours
rather than weeks. Secondly, all listings, calculations, extensions, and
summaries are produced very rapidly and accurately. Thirdly, all information forming the data base can be continuously updated and readily
retrieved. Finally, management control of this part of the commissioning
process is strengthened.

The system is capable of development and it has been kept under
constant review in the light of the requirements of its users; it has been
amended accordingly. It is also capable of extension for inventory control
purposes and, if the average length of life of each item of equipment could
be ascertained, a statement could be made available of the cost of re-
newal of the equipment in future years—an important component of
forward planning.

## HOSPITAL ACTIVITY ANALYSIS

The annual report of any hospital usually includes statements detailing
the number of beds available and the number of beds occupied during the
year under review, together with totals for the number of in-patients and
out-patients treated. Prior to the introduction of the National Health
Service in 1948 these statements were useful in presenting to the general
public, particularly for a voluntary hospital, statements of the work
undertaken by the hospital. Since 1948, it has become important for
Regional Hospital Boards to know, for planning purposes and also to
ensure the best use of their limited resources, details about the bed usage
in each region sub-divided by the speciality, the number of patients
treated, the total numbers on waiting lists and other relevant information.

Since 1948, a half-yearly return has been completed by each hospital

TABLE X

Details of patients treated in hospital and as out-patients

(Figures are for General Surgery: data shown for six hospitals as well as regional totals for the period January 1st to March 31st, 1970)

| Hospital | Details relating to treatment in hospital | | | | | | | | Details relating to out-patients | | | |
| --- | --- | --- | --- | --- | --- | --- | --- | --- | --- | --- | --- | --- |
| | Average number of beds available | Average number of beds occupied | Occupancy of beds (%) | Patients discharged | Average stay (days) | Turnover interval (days) | Number of patients Max | Min | New patients | Total patients | Waiting list | Change in waiting list |
| A | 75·7 | 53·1 | 70·2 | 337 | 14·2 | 6·1 | 69 | 38 | 559 | 1902 | 165 | 41 |
| B | 64·0 | 49·7 | 77·7 | 432 | 10·3 | 3·0 | 61 | 40 | 554 | 1601 | 398 | 38 |
| C | 78·0 | 64·0 | 82·1 | 429 | 13·4 | 2·9 | 74 | 52 | 557 | 2211 | 1040 | 35 |
| D | 96·0 | 72·7 | 75·7 | 541 | 12·1 | 3·9 | 86 | 49 | 668 | 1938 | 127 | 20 |
| E | 62·0 | 50·8 | 81·9 | 307 | 14·9 | 3·3 | 63 | 39 | 183 | 571 | 234 | 38 |
| F | 52·0 | 40·3 | 77·5 | 333 | 10·9 | 3·2 | 51 | 28 | 286 | 791 | 86 | 1 |
| etc. | | | | | | | | | | | | |
| etc. | | | | | | | | | | | | |
| etc. | | | | | | | | | | | | |
| Regional totals | 864·6 | 684·6 | 79·2 | 5221 | 11·7 | 3·2 | — | — | 5931 | 19025 | 3623 | 225 |

TABLE XI

Examples of special tabulations provided by the computer

A. Regional tabulation: admission of patients to beds for general surgery

| Category of information | Sex of patients | Age range of patients | | | | | | | Total admissions |
|---|---|---|---|---|---|---|---|---|---|
| | | Under 1 | 1–4 | 5–14 | 15–44 | 45–64 | 65–74 | Over 75 | |
| Numbers of patients admitted | Male | 11 | 51 | 669 | 4310 | 4203 | 1826 | 1055 | 12125 |
| | Female | 7 | 23 | 404 | 3866 | 3123 | 1508 | 1040 | 9971 |
| Mean length of stay in hospital (days) | Male | 12 | 8 | 8 | 9 | 12 | 16 | 19 | Average stay 12 |
| | Female | 10 | 8 | 8 | 9 | 14 | 17 | 18 | 12 |

B. Hospital tabulation: source of admissions, on a monthly basis

| Source of admission | Sex of patients | Numbers of patients admitted each month | | | | | | | | | | | | Total admissions |
|---|---|---|---|---|---|---|---|---|---|---|---|---|---|---|
| | | Jan | Feb | Mar | April | May | June | July | Aug | Sept | Oct | Nov | Dec | |
| Transfer from other hospital | Male | 34 | 49 | 52 | 41 | 41 | 47 | 55 | 48 | 36 | 52 | 51 | 37 | 543 |
| | Female | 23 | 29 | 33 | 31 | 42 | 32 | 37 | 37 | 28 | 35 | 38 | 17 | 382 |
| Emergency Road Accident | Male | 23 | 26 | 26 | 18 | 22 | 22 | 23 | 32 | 27 | 23 | 18 | 27 | 287 |
| | Female | 9 | 8 | 4 | 5 | 9 | 11 | 7 | 23 | 12 | 20 | 5 | 12 | 125 |
| Emergency—not injury/poisoning | Male | 420 | 352 | 404 | 368 | 374 | 405 | 374 | 356 | 334 | 389 | 365 | 338 | 4479 |
| | Female | 360 | 333 | 282 | 330 | 305 | 303 | 335 | 318 | 289 | 345 | 294 | 310 | 3804 |
| Admission from Waiting List | Male | 398 | 425 | 418 | 363 | 383 | 395 | 386 | 352 | 389 | 429 | 436 | 334 | 4708 |
| | Female | 377 | 349 | 353 | 307 | 364 | 371 | 358 | 333 | 377 | 357 | 370 | 300 | 4216 |
| etc. | | | | | | | | | | | | | | |

collecting together data about the number of beds available, the usage and the number of patients treated by each specialty. Forms containing this information are prepared at each hospital by the medical records staff who manually summarise the relevant statistics for the half year. The completed form is sent to the Regional Hospital Board where the information required by the Board is extracted before sending on the forms for all the hospitals in their region to the Central Health Department, which is responsible for producing national statistics from these data; this gives rise to a considerable delay in the publishing of national statistics. To obtain more up-to-date information, the South-Eastern Regional Hospital Board, Scotland, requests a monthly return from hospitals giving details of beds, numbers of patients treated, length of stay and waiting list numbers for each specialty. The returns were formerly summarised by manual methods and a quarterly return prepared for issue to the appropriate hospital medical committee and used for management purposes. Now, with the computer, the information from the monthly returns is punched in coded form on to cards and a quarterly statement for each specialty is produced (Table X), this information being produced quickly and accurately; any additional cost due to the use of the computer is fully offset by the savings in the time of clerical staff. Monthly, half-yearly and annual statements are also readily produced by the computer for comparative purposes.

These monthly and half yearly statistical statements are valuable in documenting the use of beds, and detailing the total number of patients treated, but they do not provide important information such as the ages of patients, sex, diagnosis and treatment. These statistical statements do not give details about catchment areas nor can they provide individual consultants with medical and other information about their patients. Against this background the Central Health Departments of government supported the introduction of a system of statistics about patients which is now termed 'Hospital Activity Analysis'.

Hospital Activity Analysis was developed in 1967. Before this, in 1961, a form called the Hospital In-patient Enquiry was introduced. In England and Wales this form was completed for one in every 10 in-patients discharged from hospital (other than maternity and mental illness cases), while in Scotland this form has been completed for every in-patient discharged (again excluding maternity and mental illness cases). Since 1967, the Hospital In-patient Enquiry forms have been completed for all in-patients discharged from hospitals in Britain and their use has recently been extended to cover maternity cases.

The introduction of Hospital Activity Analysis has entailed the completion at hospital level of a summary of the main events in a patient's progress in hospital, including the source of admission and clinical particulars such as age and diagnosis; this information is usually recorded and coded by medical records staff and Figure 20 is an example of the form used in Scotland. Thereafter these patient summaries are analysed at a data processing unit, to provide information at Regional Hospital Board and hospital level for management and planning purposes. Provision can be made on special forms to include additional items of interest to a particular region, for instance, or to an individual hospital or consultant, by including details from each patient's record (e.g. Fig. 21) that can be expressed on the output in quantitative terms (e.g. Table XI).

The discharge sheets are processed as computer-readable documents by the Regional Hospital Boards in England and Wales, and a number of statistical tables are produced at monthly or other intervals of time. In Scotland, the coded information is processed currently by the Scottish Office Computer and standard yearly statements are produced although Regional Hospital Boards can request additional information. Examples of the statements which are produced from these records include (1) the numbers of patients by age on admission and sex, subdivided by hospital, hospital ward, or by consultant; (2) the source of admission and the numbers admitted each month, according to specialty or ward; (3) the number of cases treated per specialty, detailing the diagnosis, the regional and the national average length of stay; (4) the number of discharges according to area of residence for each hospital subdivided by sex and age, by specialty, by diagnosis, or by consultant; (5) the number of days after admission before the first operation on a patient took place, tabulated by hospital, and by consultant; (6) the diagnostic index, subdivided by hospital and by consultant, including summaries of the numbers treated, mean stay, etc.; (7) the time spent on a waiting list (e.g. according to specialty or diagnosis, or by consultant); and (8) the average duration of stay, by specialty or diagnosis, for each hospital (by the sex of the patients, and by age on admission). In addition, information can be given personally to a consultant of details of the number of patients who have been under his care for a particular condition, together with their average length of stay and comparative figures for the regional and the national average length of stay (e.g. Table XII).

As pointed out in the previous chapter, the usefulness of these returns depends very much upon the co-operation of the medical staff in ensuring the prompt completion of the clinical summaries within the medical record, and upon the accuracy in coding by the medical records staff. The computer can validate part of the coding but, in the long run, the accuracy depends upon the care exercised in the manual coding. It is estimated that a clerk can complete around 10,000 records each year, so a 600-bed hospital for acute admissions would require two coding clerks. On this basis, smaller hospitals could either have a part-time clerk for coding duties, or share the services of a full-time clerk who undertook the work for two or more such hospitals.

TABLE XII.

Details of patients treated, listed in diagnostic categories

(Figures are for General Medicine: data relate to hospitals administered by the Regional Hospital Board (RHB) in comparison with the corresponding national figures for Scotland)

| Disease category | Sex of patients | Alive at time of discharge | | | Died in hospital | | | Total discharges | | |
|---|---|---|---|---|---|---|---|---|---|---|
| | | Number | Mean stay in hospital | | Number | Mean stay in hospital | | Number | Mean stay in hospital | |
| | | | RHB | National | | RHB | National | | RHB | National |
| Diseases of trachea, bronchus and lung | Male | 113 | 17 | 23 | 82 | 22 | 26 | 195 | 18 | 24 |
| | Female | 17 | 19 | 23 | 24 | 30 | 29 | 41 | 22 | 25 |
| Acute myocardial infarction | Male | 1352 | 18 | 22 | 258 | 34 | 25 | 1610 | 21 | 23 |
| | Female | 595 | 19 | 25 | 205 | 30 | 45 | 800 | 21 | 30 |
| etc. | | | | | | | | | | |

Hospital Activity Analysis, by utilising computer methods, provides a speedier feedback of information to managers, both medical and lay administrators, and a greater flexibility in the range of statements produced. The cost of preparing and processing these statements is not inconsiderable (p. 85).

## THE COST OF COMPUTERS USED FOR ADMINISTRATIVE WORK IN THE NATIONAL HEALTH SERVICE

It is possible to calculate the economic viability of a computer system, installed to perform financial data processing, within about one year of its introduction into routine operation. In the present context, the average cost of processing a payroll by computer is about £0·05 per employee. In a system dealing with 20,000 employees, divided evenly between staff paid on a weekly and a monthly basis, the annual processing costs by the computer total £32,000; each pay clerk can prepare the input and all the necessary pay records for over 220 employees paid on a weekly basis. By contrast, using manual methods, pay clerks could only process on average 125 records for weekly paid staff; thus about 40 more pay clerks would be required to operate the system manually. As the average annual salary of a pay clerk is about £1,000, even if no account is taken of the need to provide space for such extra staff, the computer-dependent method can already be seen to be cheaper. The computer, however, produces in addition information that is of value for management (e.g. the cost of overtime, the turnover of staff, etc.), and this extra information could lead to further economies in the working of the Health Service.

Similar cost-effectiveness studies can be applied to other administrative data processing applications, including the equipment scheduling project. It is, however, more difficult to show direct financial savings on a system such as Hospital Activity Analysis. In this case, the extra information supplied by the computer should enable management to take action to improve the use of available resources, but if management does not do so then Hospital Activity Analysis merely represents an added cost to the hospital service.

## FUTURE DEVELOPMENTS IN THE USE OF COMPUTERS FOR ADMINISTRATIVE PURPOSES IN THE HOSPITAL SERVICE

In the financial accounting field there are unlikely to be any dramatic developments. These will probably consist merely of refinements to existing systems, such as the exchange of magnetic tapes with banks and with large commercial suppliers, to reduce the amount of printout presently required for bank giro credits, and for the ordering and invoicing of goods respectively. If Area Health Boards do come into being, a further degree of centralisation of accounting records will become feasible and should, therefore, bring nearer a standard computer system for payroll and other accounting procedures for use throughout Britain. This example might be taken to represent a test case for the prospects of achieving standardisation—if it is not possible to standardise payroll procedures, there would seem little hope of standardising medical applications throughout the country.

Another general development in the financial field could be in respect of commitment accounting. Most hospital authorities that now use computer methods to produce their monthly budgetary statements have to make manual adjustments, for goods and services ordered but not yet paid for, before preparing their final management statements. These manual adjustments could be eliminated if the estimated cost of the goods or services ordered were to be entered on magnetic tape at the time of preparing the order and, when the invoice is finally paid, any necessary final adjustment could be made. The additional punching and processing costs involved would need to be assessed against the better control of expenditure achieved.

A Working Party is at present studying the possibility of introducing a standard commodity code for each item used in the hospital service. If such a library file can be prepared and maintained (e.g. on magnetic tape), information will become available about the total usage of various items purchased in the hospital service. This should provide industry with a better idea of the total amount of supplies needed, and should enable the National Health Service itself to achieve better purchasing terms from manufacturers for larger production runs.

The capturing of data at source for data processing purposes should be one of the main developments in the computer field in the hospital service. This procedure would dramatically reduce the number of records that have to be maintained at present and would ensure that the data become available promptly and regularly. Two examples will be briefly mentioned. Data for payroll purposes are now provided for each employee (weekly or monthly) and, providing the information on the basic pay record is comprehensive, all relevant staff statistics can be obtained from these records. If the Health Service staff responsible for management require to know, for instance, the number of part-time staff, the rate of turnover, the average period of sickness, or the reasons for staff leaving the service, all this information can be supplied from the pay record. Similarly, statistics about patients could be obtained by arranging that, when the letter for an out-patient appointment or for in-patient admission is sent to the patient, a record of the necessary information is simultaneously prepared for computer input (on punched card or tape), by using a typewriter fitted with a punch accessory (automated typing system). These by-product cards or tapes could be used to set up a file about the patient, and this file could thereafter be updated for the various episodes of the patient's stay in hospital (e.g. operation, laboratory tests, diagnosis, etc.). The preparation of such a record would replace the present method of collecting information and coding retrospectively for the Hospital Activity Analysis, and the information could be used in a forward-planning manner to prepare schedules for out-patient clinics as well as daily in-patient statistics (e.g. for the catering and other departments). This type of system could be introduced as an off-line operation, but it could develop into an on-line system with greater capability of achieving the optimisation of a patient's progress through the hospital, taking into account all the different services the patient may require.

The difficulties of going on-line in a hospital environment are considerable (Opit and Woodroffe, 1970a, b). Under these circumstances, it is perhaps unwise to quote costs for a computer configuration to be used in a hospital, particularly in view of the present developments in the computer market. Nevertheless it might be helpful to give an indication of present day operating costs for a 64K computer fitted with fast access backing store (e.g. magnetic discs), a line printer and approximately 10 terminals, installed on a rental basis to serve a 600-bed hospital. The annual cost of this system would be of the order of £100,000, made up as follows:

| | |
|---|---:|
| Rental and maintenance costs of the computer configuration and its peripherals (excluding terminals) | £50,000 |
| Rental of terminals | £5,000 |
| Staff salaries for computer operators and systems analysts/ programmers | £20,000 |
| Stationery, magnetic tapes and discs | £15,000 |
| Operating costs (electricity, air conditioning, etc.) | £10,000 |
| | £100,000 |

Alternatively, the hardware could be purchased, for about £250,000. If the configuration were to be retained for longer than five years, it would probably be cheaper to purchase the equipment. Working on a single shift basis (i.e. eight hours per day) the cost per hour of computer operation is over £50. Apart from being costly, single-shift operation would not be suitable for many hospital requirements and at least a two-shift system would be necessary; this would reduce the hourly cost of operating the computer to about £30. Expressed in terms of cost per patient week, this size of computer configuration would represent a cost of approximately £3 per in-patient week, which is about 5 per cent of the present running costs of a hospital dealing with acute medical and surgical admissions.

There are many other functions which a hospital-based computer system could serve, and some of these applications are already operational in the USA, or in Canada, or in some European countries. Examples include catering management, drug control and the preparation of nurses' duty rosters. These potential applications will be briefly outlined.

Computer methods are now being used by large commercial caterers and these could equally well be applied to hospital catering departments. It is possible, by holding on a computer file details of the ingredients of a recipe, and the quantities and costs of each component, to establish a system which allows for variations in the numbers of patients and staff and which can provide more information about the size of each helping of food, the costing of the menu, and at the same time considerably reduce waste. It should also be possible for catering managers to cost different menus to obtain the most economic bulk purchase for any season of the year (for references, see St Jeor et al., 1970).

The administration of drugs to patients in hospital is increasingly demanding the attention of both medical and nursing staff. Problems of prescribing and of administration arise because of the wide range of drugs now available, the variations in dosage, the duration of treatment and the cost (Wade, 1968). There is little doubt that errors such as the administering of an incorrect dose or the failure to give the prescribed drug at the correct time are occurring and, just as important, failure to realise the incompatibility of certain combinations of drugs. Interest is being shown in the use of computer methods to assist with the prescribing, dispensing and control of drugs. Such a system, apart from improved stock control, could provide information rapidly if, at some future date, there were to be undesirable side-effects from the use of the drugs. The system could be developed to monitor the actual administering of the drug to the patient, to check if the prescription contained an obvious error, to check that the dose prescribed fell within the limits allowed in the program for a patient of a given age and weight, and to search its files to ascertain whether the patient was allergic to the drug being prescribed. Such an extensive drug-control system would require on-line facilities, but these are unlikely to be available to many hospitals in the foreseeable future because of their cost. However, considerable progress could be made initially with an off-line system.

The preparation of nurses' duty rosters is another task which entails a considerable amount of clerical work in a large hospital, and these schedules demand frequent adjustments (for sickness, holidays, etc.). It is possible to devise a computer system which could take into account training requirements, as well as the different types of workload on various wards. Since nearly 30 per cent of many hospitals' budgets is accounted for by nurses' pay, the primary aim of such a system would be to improve the use made of the nursing staff available.

Inevitably there has been some overlap in the discussion of these hospital-based computer applications with the examples of applications considered in Chapter 4 under the headings of central (government) uses.

These two chapters, considered together, indicate different ways in which computers can be used to serve basically similar administrative functions, and the main point to stress is that these purposes can be achieved with computers installed at different levels of administration. In concluding this review of possible developments in the use of computers for administrative purposes in hospitals, it would only be prudent to sound the warning that financial restrictions will probably delay the widespread introduction of computers into the hospital service. Another big difficulty will be the training and the reorientation of staff. It is also important to comment on the amount of information which can flow from computers, and the problems that this high rate of output can raise (Dodd, 1969).

Computers can print columns of figures and other data at very high speed, but staff involved in management decisions, both medical and lay personnel, do not have unlimited time to read reams of printout. There is a real danger, therefore, that they will be unable to make proper use of all this information. Fortunately, it is possible to program the computer to print out information only when there is a variation from a predetermined norm or other factor. For example, management staff are not particularly interested when the number of staff on the payroll equates with the approved establishment of the hospital, but they want to know if there are several vacant posts in a particular grade or if there has on the other hand been over-filling of establishment. Suppression of unwanted information can be obtained by 'exception reporting'. If this and other sampling techniques were to be more widely used in the application of computers to the hospital service, it should allow all levels of management to make much better use of the information available to them.

The speed of computer developments in the administrative field will largely depend upon the interest and drive of individual administrators, as well as upon the availability of computers. In the long term, it will be essential to measure the cost-effectiveness of each system and to be prepared to amend or discontinue systems which fail to produce any real savings in resources or improvements in operating efficiency.

REFERENCES

DODD, G. G. (1969). Elements of data management systems. *Computing Surveys,* **1,** 117–133.

OPIT, L. J. & WOODROFFE, F. J. (1970a). Computer-held clinical record system. I, Description of system. *British Medical Journal,* **4,** 76–79.

OPIT, L. J. & WOODROFFE, F. J. (1970b). Computer-held clinical record system. II, Assessment. *British Medical Journal,* **4,** 80–82.

ST. JEOR, S. T. DE., MILLAR, R. & TYLER, F. H. (1970). The digital computer in research dietetics. *Journal of the American Dietetic Association,* **56,** 404–408.

WADE, O. L. (1968). The computer and drug prescribing. In *Computers in the Service of Medicine.* Ed. McLachlan, G. & Shegog, R. A. Vol. I, pp. 151–161. London: Oxford University Press.

# CHAPTER SIX

# The Use of Computers for Statistical Analysis

## By W. LUTZ and R. J. PRESCOTT

### SUMMARY

THIS chapter describes the use of readily available statistical packages of digital computer programs, in relation to a system of medical records. It then gives examples of more advanced statistical procedures that can be applied to medical data. The need for reliable and well defined data as a prerequisite for computer storage and analysis is emphasised, as is the continuing need for human ability to judge the validity of statistical analyses that have been performed by the computer.

### INTRODUCTION

Statistics as a subject is concerned with the collection, analysis and interpretation of quantitative data. Many counting, ranking and measuring processes lead to data that are analysable by statistical procedures, the analysis itself being largely mathematical. However, since the methods of collecting, storing and measuring largely determine the type of analysis that can be performed, a full statistical investigation concerns itself from the very start with the definition of terms, with agreement on units, with techniques of measurement as well as with the methods of recording.

The digital computer is an extremely powerful device for storing data and is an extremely rapid calculating machine. Statistical techniques do not necessarily involve complex mathematical procedures or difficult problems of numerical analysis, but they are frequently time-consuming and repetitive. Research investigations often generate data of the 'multivariate' kind, especially in the field of surveys and clinical trials, with some data-collection sheets (or proformas) covering over 100 items. When there are more than about 12 variables or measurements per patient, the number of cross-tabulations that can be, and are, requested becomes very large. Any single one of these tables may involve more than one hour's work on a desk calculator in order to estimate the means, variances, correlations, etc., and to repeat this work for several hundred tables would be unendurable. For all these reasons, statisticians were amongst the earliest users of digital computers.

An increasing number of statistical packages is becoming available, each package being a collection of programs for carrying out a certain set of statistical procedures. These packages cover most of the common statistical techniques and they vary in size, complexity and thoroughness; some are so comprehensive that only the largest computers can hold them in core, and the instruction books are formidable in size.

To enable the more experienced combined statistician and computer user to add special purpose routines, statistical packages are often written in a high level language such as FORTRAN but, to increase operating efficiency, parts of the program may be written in the machine language of the computer on which it was developed. This makes such programs machine-dependent, and some of these statistical packages can then only be transferred to a limited range of similar machines, or to machines with suitable compilers.

## SURVEY PROGRAMS AND PRELIMINARY ANALYSIS

Findings from surveys and research are likely to have their results reported in different ways, and a computer program that demands input in a restrictive manner will therefore have only limited application. These variable needs can be met by special survey programs that extract, retrieve, and tabulate data from very general records in such a way that the extracted data is in a form suitable for input to a statistical program. Some survey programs in addition offer a range of statistical procedures as part of their general facilities.

### An example of a survey program: flow chart

The main stages of the statistical analysis and tabulation of a file of data that is run under a batch processing system are outlined in Figure 23, and more detail about the software stages is given in Figure 24. The example to be considered relates to the processing of case records from patients.

Stage B, as shown in Figure 23, usually includes checking procedures carried out by the computer before the data are stored on file; these procedures augment the manual checking carried out as part of the preparation of data for input. Any records that fail to meet these checks are not read to the magnetic file, and instead diagnostics that outline the nature of the errors are provided for each rejected record. These faulty records are corrected and can then be read in again as the sequence in which data such as completed case records are input is not usually important. Checking by the computer is designed not only to detect errors in data preparation, such as punching figures that fall outside pre-set limits, but is more specifically meant to detect some errors that can arise during the initial recording or interview. In particular, logical errors in which different items on the record are compared for their mutual consistency (e.g. to ensure that the systolic blood pressure exceeds the diastolic) can very easily be looked for and detected by the computer. Unfortunately, with many surveys carried out on records systems, several months may elapse between the time of the interview and the receipt of the proformas at the computer installation, and it may then be very difficult to trace the person directly responsible for any errors in the data submitted.

FIG. 23. The four principal stages in a general system of computer-based
and computer-analysed records.

When all the data have been stored, statistical analysis and tabulation
can commence (stage C in Fig. 23). Separate programs are usually available for this part of the work, these being written as 'general programs',
which means that the detailed values required to handle a particular set
of records have to be inserted into the program prior to the actual analysis.
In particular, the characteristics that identify the items to be analysed,
and the class intervals required in the tabulation need to be given. These
details about the specification constitute a minor initiating program
which has to be prepared for each new request for statistical analysis by
the program package. Tabulation and analysis of all the case records may
sometimes be necessary, but more often an analysis of a special group of
records is wanted. For instance, the distribution by age and sex of all
patients admitted with some specified complaint, rather than the age and
sex distribution for all admissions, may be all that the user requires.

### The software stages in the survey program

The main software stages are outlined in Figure 24, in which the several
stages that together make up the whole procedure called stage C in
Figure 23 are shown individually. During the first stage, C1, the program

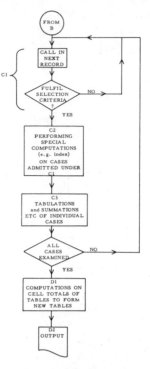

FIG. 24. Flow-chart of the analysis of a record system held on computer file. The lettering of the stages in this figure correspond to the lettering adopted in Fig. 23, but in Fig. 24 stages C and D have been subdivided to indicate subsidiary processing steps. For detailed explanation, see text.

examines the record held in core to see whether it belongs to the required sub-group. If not, the next record is called in from store and this process continues record by record until one belonging to the required sub-group is encountered. The program then passes on to stage C2 (Fig. 24). At this point the computer can if necessary sometimes derive the value of the variable to be recorded from other data in the record. For example, the date of birth is often recorded rather than the age of a patient and, for a distribution giving the 'ages of patients at admission', the computer can derive the age from the recorded dates of birth and of admission before proceeding to tabulate the data about age (stage C3,

LEGEND FOR TABLE XIII

Distribution of systolic blood pressure values among male patients aged 50 to 59 admitted with acute myocardial infarction to a Coronary Care Unit and who were alive at the time of discharge from hospital. For detailed explanation see text. The authors wish to thank the staff of the Coronary Care Unit, Royal Infirmary of Edinburgh, for allowing access to their records, as held on computer file, and to thank Dr P. M. Fulton for her assistance in coding these records.

TABLE XIII

FREQUENCY  TABLE    1

QUALITATIVE CONDITIONS

FIELD ROW NUMBERS

| | | INITIAL | LAST | | |
|---|---|---|---|---|---|
| QUAL | COLUMN | ROW | ROW | MIN | MAX |
| 1 | 105 | 0 | 0 | 1 | 1 |
| 2 | 2 | 0 | 0 | 1 | 1 |
| 3 | 81 | 0 | 0 | 1 | 1 |

QUANTITATIVE CONDITIONS

| QUANT | COLUMN1 | COLUMN2 | MIN | MAX |
|---|---|---|---|---|
| 1 | 3 | 4 | 50 | 59 |

COLUMNS   45 TO   47

| UPPER BOUNDARY | FREQUENCY | PERCENT FREQUENCY | PERCENT CUMULATIVE |
|---|---|---|---|
| 25.000 | 0 | 0.000 | 0.000 |
| 50.000 | 0 | 0.000 | 0.000 |
| 60.000 | 0 | 0.000 | 0.000 |
| 70.000 | 0 | 0.000 | 0.000 |
| 80.000 | 0 | 0.000 | 0.000 |
| 90.000 | 3 | 3.125 | 3.125 |
| 100.000 | 4 | 4.167 | 7.292 |
| 110.000 | 8 | 8.333 | 15.625 |
| 120.000 | 8 | 8.333 | 23.958 |
| 130.000 | 17 | 17.708 | 41.667 |
| 140.000 | 12 | 12.500 | 54.167 |
| 150.000 | 17 | 17.708 | 71.875 |
| 160.000 | 8 | 8.333 | 80.208 |
| 170.000 | 5 | 5.208 | 85.417 |
| 180.000 | 6 | 6.250 | 91.667 |
| 190.000 | 4 | 4.167 | 95.833 |
| 200.000 | 3 | 3.125 | 98.958 |
| INFINITY | 1 | 1.042 | 100.000 |

GRAND TOTAL =        96

NUMBER OF CASES NOT RECORDED =        5

PERCENT NOT RECORDED =    4.950

| MEAN | VARIANCE | STD.DEV. |
|---|---|---|
| 1.3404178 +2 | 7.2204035 +2 | 2.6087081 +1 |

* * * * * * * * * * * * * * * * * * *

Fig. 24). However, if the item of data that is required has already been recorded, no computations are performed at stage C2 and the program passes directly to stage C3. At each stage, if criteria have to be met, the relevant computations are performed before going on to the next stage.

At stage C3 (Fig. 24) the statistical sums, sums of squares, index values, etc. are derived and the tabulation of the results commences. This process is completed later, at stages D1 and D2, when the final output is printed. There are many ways in which the output can be presented and the method adopted in one of our survey programs can best be discussed by considering a specific example. The computer output shown in Table XIII was derived from records for patients admitted to a Coronary Care Unit. It illustrates how hospital case notes, recorded systematically on precoded forms (e.g. Fig. 3), can be used to yield statistical information quickly and easily. Table XIII shows the distribution of systolic blood pressures in male patients, aged between 50 and 59, who had definitely suffered a myocardial infarction and who were alive at the time of discharge from hospital. The conditions set are printed above every table so as to identify the sub-group to which the table refers. The full explanation of these coded details cannot be given here, but the following points should help with the understanding of Table XIII.

1. The heading 'Qualitative Conditions' refers to the conditions imposed upon non-numerical items in the patients' records (e.g. sex, alive or dead at the time of discharge, etc.).

2. The heading 'Quantitative Conditions' refers to restrictions imposed upon numerical items in the record.

3. The above conditions, in the order set by the programmer, were:

(a) Final diagnosis: coded on card 2, column 25; row 0 punched if a proven acute myocardial infarction.

(b) Sex: coded on card 1, column 2; row 0 punched if male.

(c) State at discharge: coded on card 2, column 1; row 0 punched if alive at the time of discharge.

(d) Age: coded on card 1, columns 3 to 4; value punched to be between 50 and 59 inclusive.

4. The heading 'columns 45 to 47' indicates that the readings tabulated in the table (systolic blood pressure) were coded on card 1, columns 45 to 47.

## Running the survey program

Prior to actually running the program it is necessary to set various parameters. These include setting the conditions that define the sub-group of patients required during stage C1 (as shown in Table XIII). It is also necessary to set the values of various program symbols required later at stage C3 (e.g. those of the class intervals, summation and counting symbols). The class intervals for blood pressure shown in Table XIII were set at $C(1) = 25$, $C(2) = 50$, $C(3) = 60$, ..., $C(17) = 200$, in which the first interval includes the values 0 to 24 inclusive but not the value 25 as the upper values are not included in the intervals. The counting variables $F(0)$, $F(1)$, ..., $F(18)$ are all set to zero initially. It should be noted that there are two more counting variables than class interval limits, since $F(0)$ is used to enumerate those patients for whom no systolic blood pressure was recorded, and $F(18)$ counts the number of patients whose systolic pressure exceeded 199 mm Hg. The summation symbols, M and V, are both set to zero initially; these are used to compute the sum and the sum of the squares of the recorded blood pressures.

In this example the data for systolic blood pressure coded in columns 45 to 47 (Fig. 3) have been recorded in the form required so that no additional computations or derivations are needed. Because of this, stage C2 (Fig. 24) is by-passed and the computer program passes directly from stage C1 to stage C3 during the compilation of Table XIII. In order to illustrate how the processing of data by the computer actually proceeds, the data contained in Table XIV, which refers to the first seven cases read into the computer from magnetic disc, will be discussed.

TABLE XIV

Data relating to the first seven hospital records analysed by the survey program outlined in Figure 24

| Case number | Sex | Age | Acute myocardial infarction | Systolic blood pressure mm Hg | Alive at time of discharge |
|---|---|---|---|---|---|
| 1 | M | 56 | Yes | 152 | No |
| 2 | F | 67 | Yes | 97 | Yes |
| 3 | M | 58 | Yes | 145 | Yes |
| 4 | M | 42 | No | 104 | Yes |
| 5 | M | 57 | Yes | 129 | No |
| 6 | M | 59 | Yes | 149 | Yes |
| 7 | M | 56 | Yes | 83 | Yes |
| etc. | | | | | |

The principle on which the program proceeds as it calls in each case is to test first whether the set conditions are met. If these conditions are not met then none of the counting variables are changed (i.e. all the values for F, M and V remain unaltered) and the next patient record is read into core from the disc storage. On the other hand, if the conditions are satisfied, then the program increments by one the value for the particular frequency (F) corresponding to the systolic blood pressure recorded in the case-notes. It adds the systolic pressure value to M, and adds the square of this value to V, before reading in the next record (Fig. 24). Considering the data summarised for each case in Table XIV one by one:

*Case* 1: this case is ignored (i.e. none of the variables change their value) because the stated conditions are not met (dead at discharge); call in next case.

*Case* 2: this case is also ignored, because the conditions relating to sex and age are not satisfied; call in next case.

*Case* 3: in this case, the conditions are met, so the various constants are incremented, as follows: $F(12) = 0$ changes to $F(12) = 1$, since the systolic blood pressure lies within the twelfth interval (i.e. 140 to 149 mm Hg inclusive, Table XIII). All the other values for F remain at zero.

$M = 0$ changes to $M = 145$

$V = 0$ changes to $V = 21025$ ($= 145^2$)

The next case is then called in.

*Case* 4: this case is ignored, as neither the conditions relating to age nor to diagnosis are satisfied; call in next case.

*Case* 5: this case is ignored (did not leave hospital alive); read in next case.

*Case* 6: this is the second case for whom the conditions are satisfied, so the various constants are incremented as follows:

$F(12) = 1$ changes to $F(12) = 2$ (all the other F values still remain at zero)

$M = 145$ changes to $M = 294$ (i.e. $145 + 149$)

$V = 21025$ changes to $V = 43226$ ($145^2 + 149^2$)

The next case is then called in.

*Case* 7: the conditions are again satisfied, and the various constants incremented. In this case $F(6)$ becomes 1 while $F(12)$ remains at 2 with all the other F values still remaining at zero. The value for M becomes 377, and for V becomes 50115. The next case is then called in, and so on.

When all the cases on the file have been examined, the frequency counts (the F values) stored in the computer's memory equal the class interval frequencies as shown in Table XIII. The value for $F(1) = 0, \ldots ,$ $F(6) = 3, \ldots , F(12) = 17, \ldots , F(18) = 1$ and the number of 'not recorded' cases, $F(0) = 5$. The program now passes from stage C3 to stage D1 (Fig. 24). At this stage, it computes the total number of cases, and the total number of systolic blood pressures recorded in the group. The values are respectively 101 and 96, since there were five patients for whom no blood pressure value was recorded. At stage D1, the percentage frequency and the mean, variance and standard deviation are also computed, using the values for M, V and N ($N = 96$). The program now passes to its final stage, D2, and the printout in Table XIII shows the values for the mean, variance and standard deviation given in exponential form (e.g. $1{\cdot}340417 \ @ + 2 = 1{\cdot}340417 \times 10^2$).

This description of the survey program used in the Department of Social Medicine, Edinburgh University, has been deliberately simplified. The actual procedure is more elaborate and in particular the program can extract several tables in a single run, the number of tables that can be requested in a single computer run depending on the size of the computer's internal memory and the size of the tables themselves. Table XIII contains 20 cells (including the 'not known' and the grand total) but two-dimensional tables can easily contain over 200 cells each. Since the computer must store a separate frequency count for each cell in each of the tables requested, the number of tables per run is dependent on the size of the computer core and the number of cells contained in each table requested.

Even the best kept records may reveal unsuspected and improbable errors, and the results in Table XIII illustrate how computer records can draw attention to inadequacies in the recording of data and thereby improve the general level of data collection. It was thought unlikely, for instance, that systolic blood pressures would have gone unrecorded on patients who survived, and yet the computer's tabulation revealed five such cases in 101 records. At a later stage, the survey program was used to 'list' the hospital record numbers for these five cases. A search for these records failed to trace two sets of the case notes; in the other three, values for systolic blood pressure had been recorded, but in one case the value had been recorded in the wrong place (and had not been found) while in the other two cases the data had been recorded but had not been transcribed to the right hand side of the proforma (Fig. 3).

## FURTHER STATISTICAL ANALYSIS ON DATA

The stored data and the survey program together provide the basic tabulations, estimates and derived values (e.g. means, variances, covariances, etc.) on which a more searching statistical analysis can be founded, or on which to construct models useful in research and medical care. It is not feasible, however, to present a comprehensive picture of statistical calculations in medicine capable of being performed by computers. Instead a few examples may portray some of the benefits to be derived from using computers. In selecting these examples, the use of computers for the everyday calculation of $t$-tests, chi-square tests and other elementary but important procedures is undoubtedly of considerable value, but a description of their application to such problems would not be particularly interesting. More convincing examples of the computer's use come from problems involving a number of variables, where the methods to be used require a series of calculations that can only be handled conveniently with matrix algebra.

## The application of a symptom-disease matrix

The example to be considered here is taken from Warner *et al.* (1961). It makes use of a symptom-disease matrix and of statistical rules of probability in order to achieve a differential diagnosis of congenital heart disease. The presence or absence of 50 symptoms and signs (Table XV) is recorded, and these data are used to determine the relative probabilities of 33 different conditions made up of 32 diseases as well as the normal healthy state (Table XVI).

TABLE XV

List of symptoms to be evaluated by the doctor
(from Warner *et al.,* 1961)

$x_1$ = age 1 month to 1 year
$x_2$ = age 1 to 20 years
$x_3$ = over 20 years
$x_4$ = cyanosis, mild
$x_5$ = cyanosis, severe (with clubbing)
$x_6$ = cyanosis, intermittent
$x_7$ = cyanosis, differential
$x_8$ = squatting
$x_9$ = dyspnoea

$x_{10}$ = easy fatigue
$x_{11}$ = orthopnoea
$x_{12}$ = chest pain
$x_{13}$ = repeated respiratory infections
$x_{14}$ = syncope
$x_{15}$ = systolic murmur loudest at
 the apex
$x_{16}$ = diastolic murmur loudest at
 the apex
 etc. up to $x_{50}$

**Note**: symptoms such as the group $x_1$ to $x_3$, and the group $x_4$ to $x_7$, are examples of mutually exclusive symptoms which must be handled as special cases.

The analysis proceeds in two stages, the first consisting of providing the basic data for the subsequent statistical analysis. This stage involves giving a value to the probability of each of the diseases (alternatively called the relative frequency of occurrence or incidence), and to the probability of the various symptoms being present in each of the diseases. These probabilities are stored in a rectangular array, the symptom-disease matrix; this consists of 33 rows and 51 columns, part of which is shown in Table XVII. The 33 rows correspond to the 32 diseases and to the state of normal health. The 51 columns relate to the probability of occurrence of the disease and the probability of occurrence of any one of the 50 symptoms possible with the disease. Thus the entry of 0·100 in the row corresponding to the 'disease' $y_1$ (normal health) and the column headed incidence shows that the probability of any patient being normal is 0·1. Similarly, the entry of 0·02 in the row corresponding to the disease $y_2$ and to the column headed $x_4$ shows that, for individuals with atrial septal defect but without either pulmonary stenosis or pulmonary hypertension, there is a probability of 0·02 that they will exhibit mild cyanosis. In essence, the symptom-disease matrix (Table XVII) provides the computer with a medical memory that describes the relative frequency

TABLE XVI

List of diseases included in the differential diagnosis of congenital
heart disease (from Warner *et al.,* 1961)

$y_1$ = normal health
$y_2$ = atrial septal defect without pulmonary stenosis or pulmonary hypertension
(defined as pulmonary arterial pressure exceeding or being equal to
systemic arterial pressure)
$y_3$ = atrial septal defect without pulmonary stenosis
$y_4$ = atrial septal defect with pulmonary hypertension
$y_5$ = complete endocardial cushion defect (A-V commune)
$y_6$ = partial anomalous pulmonary venous connections (without atrial septal
defect)
$y_7$ = total anomalous pulmonary venous connections (supradiaphragmatic)
$y_8$ = tricuspid atresia without transposition
$y_9$ = Ebstein's anomaly of the tricuspid valve
$y_{10}$ = ventricular septal defect with valvular pulmonary stenosis
$y_{11}$ = ventricular septal defect with infundibular stenosis
$y_{12}$ = pulmonary stenosis, valvular (with or without probe-patent foramen ovale)
$y_{13}$ = pulmonary stenosis, infundibular (with or without probe-patent foramen
ovale)
$y_{14}$ = pulmonary atresia
etc., up to $y_{33}$

of the different diseases and the relative frequency of the symptoms
within each disease category. In preparing this type of table, the authors
would hope that the frequency of the various symptoms would remain the
same from hospital to hospital for any given disease.

Warner *et al.* (1961) utilised the results from 1035 of their own patients
in conjunction with data from the literature to estimate the probability
of the various symptoms within each disease; a part of this estimate is
displayed in matrix form in Table XVII. The probability of witnessing
any of the 32 disease states and the 33rd condition, normal health,
however, varies considerably from place to place, depending on factors
such as the method of referral of patients to the cardiologist. Consequently, anyone wishing to use this type of approach needs to estimate
the 'relative incidence' of the 33 states in his own area. The general
mathematical statement of Bayes' theorem proceeds as follows:

If the relative incidence of disease $y_k$ is denoted by $P(y_k)$, and the
probability of symptom $x_i$ in disease $y_k$ by $P(x_i|y_k)$ then, assuming
the mutual independence of symptoms, the probability that any
disease (e.g. $y_1$) represents the diagnosis in the presence of symptoms
$x_1, x_2, \ldots, x_j$, is given by the expression:

$$P(y_1 \mid x_1, \ldots, x_j) = \frac{P(y_1)\, P(x_1 \mid y_1) \ldots P(x_j \mid y_1)}{\text{Sum for all k } [P(y_k)\, P(x_1 \mid y_k) \ldots P(x_j \mid y_k)]}$$

(Equation 6.1)

TABLE XVII

Part of a symptom-disease matrix prepared by Warner et al. (1961) in connection with the differential diagnosis of congenital heart disease. For further explanation, see text (pp. 124–128).

| Diseases | Incidence | Symptoms: | | | | | | | | | | |
|---|---|---|---|---|---|---|---|---|---|---|---|---|
| | | $x_1$ | $x_2$ | $x_3$ | $x_4$ | $x_5$ | $x_6$ | $x_7$ | $x_8$ | $x_9$ | $x_{10}$ | etc. |
| $y_1$ | 0·100 | ·01 | ·49 | ·50 | ·01 | ·00 | ·01 | ·00 | ·01 | ·01 | ·10 | |
| $y_2$ | 0·081 | ·10 | ·40 | ·50 | ·02 | ·01 | ·02 | ·00 | ·01 | ·35 | ·50 | |
| $y_3$ | 0·005 | ·30 | ·60 | ·10 | ·20 | ·10 | ·20 | ·00 | ·01 | ·60 | ·70 | |
| $y_4$ | 0·001 | ·10 | ·20 | ·70 | ·30 | ·10 | ·25 | ·00 | ·01 | ·80 | ·90 | |
| $y_5$ | 0·027 | ·20 | ·50 | ·30 | ·15 | ·05 | ·10 | ·00 | ·01 | ·40 | ·50 | |
| $y_6$ | 0·005 | ·10 | ·40 | ·50 | ·01 | ·01 | ·01 | ·00 | ·01 | ·15 | ·20 | |
| $y_7$ | 0·001 | ·20 | ·70 | ·10 | ·65 | ·10 | ·05 | ·00 | ·01 | ·70 | ·80 | |
| $y_8$ | 0·018 | ·50 | ·48 | ·02 | ·30 | ·65 | ·01 | ·00 | ·10 | ·80 | ·90 | |
| $y_9$ | 0·001 | ·10 | ·45 | ·45 | ·22 | ·44 | ·01 | ·00 | ·22 | ·80 | ·80 | |
| $y_{10}$ | 0·054 | ·40 | ·55 | ·05 | ·25 | ·25 | ·10 | ·00 | ·30 | ·75 | ·90 | |
| etc. | | | | | | | | | | | | |

The terms on the right-hand side of this expression are precisely those probabilities required in the symptom-disease matrix (e.g. Table XVII). Hence, in this example, given a set of symptoms, probabilities for each of the 33 states (32 diseases and normal health) could be evaluated using this formula. However, as Warner *et al.* (1961) pointed out, the absence of a symptom (e.g. easy fatigue) may also be of importance, but this contingency is not directly covered in Equation 6.1. This eventuality is dealt with by the simple probability relationship:

$$P(\text{symptom absent}) = 1 - P(\text{symptom present}) \qquad \text{(Equation 6.2)}$$

In using this rule, care must be taken to ensure that the absence of a symptom has not been implicitly covered elsewhere. For example, in Table XV age gives rise to three 'symptoms' ($x_1$ to $x_3$) and, in this case, the absence of the 'symptom' $x_2$ would not be significant in itself but would be covered by the inclusion of either 'symptom' $x_1$ or $x_3$. Other examples arise where the absence of a set of symptoms can be important, rather than the absence of one symptom in particular; with cyanosis, only the absence of any of the symptoms represented by $x_4$ to $x_7$ inclusive (Table XV) indicates 'no cyanosis'. Full rules on the appropriate terms to substitute in Equation 6.1 are given by Warner *et al.* (1961). Using these rules, the probability of any of the 33 different states being present can be determined for any set of symptoms; these computations are very tedious if performed manually.

Using a computer, the symptom-disease matrix of probabilities is kept in backing store and is called into core when needed by the operating system. The doctor, while examining a patient, can mark off from a standard list or indicate in some other way the nature of the presenting symptoms. These data are then transferred to a punched card or to some other input medium, and entered into the program. A list of the most likely diagnoses, together with their probabilities, is returned as output. For example, using the data partially shown in Tables XV to XVII, a patient who is over 20 years of age and who complains of easy fatigue, in whom the pulmonary second sound is diminished, whose electrocardiogram exhibits an axis greater than 110° with an R wave greater than 1·2 m.v. in lead $V_1$, and who has a midsystolic murmur unaccompanied by a thrill but which is shown by phonocardiography to be of equal intensity in the pulmonary and the precordial area, can have the probability of various diagnoses automatically reported by the computer. There is a probability of 0·73 that the patient has valvular pulmonary stenosis, a probability of 0·24 of the diagnosis being infundibular pulmonary stenosis, and a probability of 0·02 that the diagnosis is ventricular septal defect with valvular pulmonary stenosis.

As Warner *et al.* (1961) make clear, the value of this type of approach depends upon the accuracy of the estimated probabilities contained in the symptom-disease matrix and upon the independence of the symptoms. If two symptoms are frequently associated, and yet both are included as if they were independent symptoms, there will be an unwarranted tendency to increase the probability of diagnosing those diseases where these symptoms are common. The adequacy of their approach was demonstrated by its application to 36 cases in whom Warner *et al.* (1961) reported that the most probable diagnosis, obtained by the computer, proved to be as accurate as the most probable diagnosis given by three experienced cardiologists. Other workers have also reported some success in applications of this type. Vishnevsky *et al.* (1964), for instance, employed a more highly developed version of the method of Warner *et al.* (1961), using 200 symptoms to obtain a differential diagnosis among 50 different classes of congenital heart disease; they reported an accuracy of diagnosis of between 85 and 95 per cent when applied to more than 200 cases.

## Linear discriminant analysis

This technique is available in a number of statistical packages and, given access to such packages, the programming requirements are limited to a few simple instructions. Linear discriminant analysis is applied on occasions where several variables are measured on each member of two or more distinct groups of patients. In medical applications, these groups are often disease states, the aim of the study being to assign patients, in whom the diagnosis is uncertain, to one or other of the disease groups on the basis of these measurements. The variables used in the analysis are frequently the results of quantitative investigations (e.g. chemical examinations) and measurable characteristics of the patients, such as age, weight, height and the presence or absence of certain symptoms.

The mathematics involved in linear discriminant analysis involve relatively simple operations with matrices, but many potential users may not know the relevant mathematics. However, the advantage of a statistical package is that such knowledge is not essential, provided that the user appreciates the assumptions on which the analysis is based. On this assumption, the computer can be treated as a 'black box' which will accept data from the different groups and produce the appropriate formulae to allow optimal discrimination. For discrimination between two groups or disease states, the linear discriminant function formula is of the form:

$$y = k_1(\text{variable}_1) + k_2(\text{variable}_2) + \ldots + k_n(\text{variable}_n) \quad \text{(Equation 6.3)}$$

Numerical values for $k_1, k_2, \ldots, k_n$ are estimated from the data originally derived from two groups of patients. The formula then enables a single discriminant score (y), based on the observed values of the different variables, to be calculated for any individual. In most applications this score is used to allocate an individual to one or other of the given groups, this being achieved by using the average discriminant score of y in each group, and the relative frequency of occurrence of numbers in the groups, to determine a critical value. Having established this baseline, any subsequent patient can be assigned to the group with the higher mean score if his own individual discriminant score (y) exceeds the critical value; if it does not exceed this value, the patient is assigned to the other group. There is no difficulty in generalising this procedure to more than two groups.

The following example of a linear discriminant function is taken from a very comprehensive investigation by Truett *et al.* (1967). The part of their analysis that we shall be considering is based upon the incidence of coronary heart disease in the succeeding 12 years for 2187 men between the ages 30 and 62 and who were found to be free of coronary disease at first examination. In the 12 year period under review, 258 developed coronary disease which was defined so as to include all definite cases of myocardial infarction, and in addition patients with coronary insufficiency or with angina pectoris or who died and who were found at autopsy to have coronary disease. In this example, therefore, two groups of men can be defined, those who developed coronary arterial disease and those who did not develop it, and for present purposes seven risk factors were investigated (Table XVIII).

TABLE XVIII

Risk factors in an investigation of coronary arterial disease
(after Truett *et al.,* 1967)

| Designation | Description of factor |
| --- | --- |
| $x_1$ | Age (years) |
| $x_2$ | Serum cholesterol (mg/100 ml) |
| $x_3$ | Systolic blood pressure (mm Hg) |
| $x_4$ | Relative weight (100 × weight for the individual divided by the median weight for individuals of the same sex and height) |
| $x_5$ | Haemoglobin (g/100 ml) |
| $x_6$ | Cigarettes per day, coded as:<br>0 = never smoked<br>1 = less than 20 a day<br>2 = 20 a day<br>3 = more than 20 a day |
| $x_7$ | ECG coded as:<br>0 = normal<br>1 = for definite or possible left ventricular hypertrophy, for definite non-specific abnormality and for intra-ventricular block. |

A preliminary step is for the computer to calculate the mean value for every factor in each group, together with the pooled variance-covariance matrix. This information is all that is required to estimate the coefficients $k_1, k_2, \ldots, k_n$ appearing in Equation 6.3, from which the following equation is then derived:

$$y = 0 \cdot 0708x_1 + 0 \cdot 0105x_2 + 0 \cdot 0166x_3 + 0 \cdot 0138x_4$$
$$- 0 \cdot 0837x_5 + 0 \cdot 361x_6 + 1 \cdot 0459x_7 \qquad \text{(Equation 6.4)}$$

It should be noted that the signs of the coefficients are such that higher scores indicate a greater possibility of coronary heart disease.

To illustrate the application of Equation 6.4, a man aged 35 in whom the serum cholesterol level was found to be 195 mg/100 ml, systolic blood pressure 135 mm Hg, whose relative weight was 100, who had a haemo-globin concentration of $14 \cdot 5$ g/100 ml, who did not smoke and who had a normal ECG would score $6 \cdot 93$. On the other hand, a 55-year-old man with a serum cholesterol level of 240 mg/100 ml, a systolic blood pressure of 150 mm Hg, a relative weight of 110, a haemoglobin concentration of $13 \cdot 0$ g/100 ml, who smoked more than 20 cigarettes a day, and who had an abnormal ECG would score $11 \cdot 46$. If discriminant analysis is applied to this kind of result, the mean score for each group can be defined and used to obtain the critical value that yields optimal discrimination. This critical value is $10 \cdot 90$, and hence the first individual considered in this paragraph would be assigned to the No Coronary Heart Disease group, while the second individual would be expected to develop coronary heart disease within the next 12 years.

In this context, the standard approach of linear discriminant analysis, which yields a clear-cut prediction of whether or not coronary heart disease will occur in an individual, is not perhaps the most helpful; such a prediction, based on only seven factors, would understandably give rise to a number of false diagnoses. Truett et al. (1967) adopted an alternative approach by estimating and grading the risk that an individual will develop coronary heart disease within a given period.

They divided individuals into 10 approximately equal groups, or deciles (approximately 215 to 220 patients per group) according to the decreasing rank of their discriminant scores, and then assessed the occurrence of coronary arterial disease within each of these deciles. The numbers observed with coronary heart disease in each decile were 82, 44, 31, 33, 22, 20, 13, 10, 3 and 0. Using the data in this way, the linear discriminant function can be seen to identify a high risk and a low risk group, and the identification of patients at high risk may be of particular value in prospective studies of coronary heart disease, where it may be desirable to restrict the study to a manageable number of high risk patients.

## Regression analysis

In regression analysis interest is focused on the relationship of one dependent variable (y) upon one or more than one variable ($x_1$, $x_2$ etc.). This provides an equation which will predict the value of y from the observed values of the x variables. The simplest and most widely used application of regression analysis is in those cases where there is a linear relationship (linear regression) between y and a single independent variable x. This is written in the form:

$$y = a + bx \qquad \text{(Equation 6.5)}$$

In this equation a and b are constants that are determined from the observed data using pairs of measurements of y and x. For an example see Snedecor and Cochran (1967) who estimated the relationship of blood pressure (y) to age (x).

The more general form of regression analysis is multiple linear regression, in which a linear combination of several variables ($x_1$, $x_2$, etc.) is used to predict the value of y. In a typical example, Mather (1967) estimated the breaking strength of a human femur from observations on the age of the subject, the elasticity, the length of the femur, the maximum anteroposterior and transverse diameters of the shaft as well as the relative cortical thickness of the bone.

Although linear regression is adequate for many needs, some variables are not connected by such a simple relationship and in biological problems logarithmic or exponential terms appear frequently. The assessment of liver function by the elimination of bromsulphthalein (BSP) from the plasma following a single intravenous injection of BSP provides one example. The concentration of BSP in plasma (y) is assumed to conform to the sum of two exponential terms at any time (x) following the injection (Richards *et al.*, 1959), given by the equation:

$$y = Ae^{-k_1 x} + Be^{-k_2 x} \qquad \text{(Equation 6.6)}$$

In this equation, e is the Eulerian constant (e = 2·718 . . .) and A, B, $k_1$, and $k_2$ are constants, the values of which have to be determined from the concentrations of BSP observed at given times. It might be hoped that values for A, B, $k_1$ and $k_2$ would be given by a formula, albeit complicated, which could be evaluated on a computer with little difficulty, but unfortunately this is not so. Nevertheless, methods of solving such non-linear regression problems by iteration have been developed. In these, from an initial approximation to the solution (by giving values A′, B′, $k_1'$ and $k_2'$) mathematical techniques are applied to obtain an improved approximation to the correct values (A′ + $\delta$A, B′ + $\delta$B, $k_1'$ + $\delta k_1$ and $k_2'$ + $\delta k_2$). The process is then repeated with the improved values until successive estimates differ by less than a specified amount. The best known of these iterative procedures is the Gauss-Newton or linearisation method (e.g. *see* Hartley, 1961) but it is outside the scope of this book to describe the method in any detail. It is, however, worth stressing that this iterative procedure is particularly suitable for use on a computer. The initial approximation which the method requires may either be input to the program as data obtained from previous experience of the problem or from manual fitting methods (e.g. Richards *et al.*, 1959), or obtained from preliminary numerical computation which may be included in the program (Foss, 1969).

## A CAUTIONARY NOTE ON THE USE OF COMPUTERS FOR STATISTICAL ANALYSIS

Statisticians may be enthusiastic users of computers themselves, but they are often very reluctant to release statistical packages to other users. This is because, in the application of statistical procedures, judgment and experience play an important role. Having decided upon the suitability of certain statistical procedures or tests, the results of the analysis itself still need to be assessed critically and this interpretation is not yet within the capacity of the computer. There is, nevertheless, a widely held belief that computers can greatly assist in the analysis of any set of records, and the existence of statistical packages seems to strengthen this belief although it is in fact a gross fallacy. No matter how carefully their data are recorded, much of the records of hospital and general practice is not statistically analysable in its present form, and the mere existence of a set of records is not in itself a guarantee that the records are either analysable or worth the effort and expense needed to conduct the analysis. It also deserves stating, if only to avoid misunderstanding, that the mere existence of records is in itself no justification for storing these records on a computer file such as magnetic tape or disc—the justification must lie in the quality of the data and in the usefulness of any derived information.

REFERENCES

Foss, S. D. (1969). A method for obtaining initial estimates of the parameters in exponential curve fitting. *Biometrics*, **25,** 580–584.

Hartley, H. O. (1961). The modified Gauss–Newton method for the fitting of non-linear regression functions by least squares. *Technometrics*, **3,** 269–280.

Mather, B. S. (1967). Comparison of two formulae for in vivo prediction of strength of the femur. *Aerospace Medicine*, **38,** 1270–1272.

Richards, T. G., Tindall, V. R. & Young, A. (1959). A modification of the bromsulphthalein liver function test to predict the dye content of the liver and bile. *Clinical Science*, **18,** 499–511.

Snedecor, G. W. & Cochran, W. G. (1967). *Statistical Methods*. 6th ed. pp. 135–139. Ames, Iowa: Iowa State University Press.

Truett, J., Cornfield, J. & Kannel, W. (1967). A multivariate analysis of the risk of coronary heart disease in Framingham. *Journal of Chronic Diseases*, **20,** 511–524.

Vishnevsky, A. A., Artobolevsky, I. I. & Bykhovsky, M. L. (1964). Cybernetic methods in medicine. *Scientific World*, **3,** 13–17 and 28.

Warner, H. R., Toronto, A. F., Veasey, L. G. & Stephenson, R. (1961). A mathematical approach to medical diagnosis. *Journal of the American Medical Association*, **177,** 75–81.

SUGGESTIONS FOR FURTHER READING

Dodd, G. G. (1969). Elements of data management systems. *Computing Surveys*, **1,** 117–133.

Healy, M. J. R. (1968). Mathematics, computers and the doctor. *British Medical Journal*, **1,** 243–245.

Kennedy, F. (1970). SWITCH—Hospital case history on computer. *Scottish Medical Journal*, **15,** 391–394.

Mitchell, J. H. (1969). Relevance of the electronic computer to hospital medical records. *British Medical Journal*, **4,** 157–159.

# Specific Applications of Computers Affecting the Patient as an Individual

# CHAPTER SEVEN

# Computers in General Practice

## By H. P. DINWOODIE and J. D. GRENE

### SUMMARY

COMPUTERS in general practice have a potential, in the service situation, as data-processors rather than as calculators. The volumes of data create difficulties in selection, processing and storage. Various fields in which experiments have been made with computers are described—for example in practice registers, immunisation schedules, chronic disease recall systems, morbidity recording, and personal files. Directions of possible future developments are surveyed, and it is concluded that computers will ultimately have a profound effect on the nature and efficiency of general practice.

### INTRODUCTION

General practice should mean continuous, comprehensive medical care for patients of all ages, in all their illnesses. The constant aim is to secure early diagnosis, leading to correct treatment and management, and this nowadays includes prevention of long-term chronic disease. Much of the diagnostic skill of the family doctor lies in his marshalling of the many facts, learned after long contact with the family, in relation to his academic knowledge. The general practitioner needs more power to sort the data on which he makes his decisions. It is in this sorting situation that the computer excels.

Computers are thus likely to be useful in general practice as data-processors and as instruments of communication, rather than as calculating machines. If the data that are worth sorting can be stated, then it is possible to collate and correlate on two levels: (1) on the individual level, where all the facts relating to one patient can be handled, leading to a better level of diagnostic skill; and (2) on the practice level, where facts can be marshalled which are general to certain groups in the practice population.

In general practice, sorting, filing, checking and signposting of actions to be taken at foreseeable intervals are all tasks that computers can perform, even if only as an electronic medical records index rather than as a completely computer-dependent records system. The routing to patients' files of information received from hospitals, from laboratories, and even from partners in practice, is not always efficiently done. Use of computers may help to rectify some of the inadequacies of the present methods of keeping records in general practice, and management of the patient as a whole should be better if access to the information concerning each patient is easy and quick. The main problem for the individual general practitioner, if he is to benefit from computer technology, is to learn to record his observations in a form acceptable to the computer, so that access to these observations can be automatic (Grene, 1970).

Indications of applications of computers to large groups and populations have been given in earlier chapters. Examples of applications on a more personal level, affecting patients in general practice, will be considered here, adopting initially the broad classification given by Marinker (1969) when discussing computers and the patient record in general practice. He identified several different levels at which the computer might be used to carry patient records, as follows:

1. A practice register.
2. Demographic data.
3. Immunisation and health surveillance data (recall procedures).
4. Operational coding (workload monitoring).
5. Morbidity recording.
6. The personal file.

## PRACTICE REGISTER

One of the most obvious uses of the computer in general practice is to help to maintain a register of patients. A practice register in its simplest form can be kept in a loose-leaf book. The next stage is to use the 'ASR' (Age-Sex-Register) index cards designed by the Royal College of General Practitioners' Records and Statistics Unit, which enable other data to be coded in addition to the identification data. There are, however, distinct advantages in having a practice register which can be handled mechanically.

Equipment for producing 80-column Hollerith punched cards is now available in the offices of most of the Regional Hospital Boards and is also available in a number of hospitals. Acheson and Forbes (1968) used a hand key-punch (purchase price £80), and have shown that these punched cards could be used for the automatic sorting and printing out of information about groups of patients in the practice concerned.

We have used 80-column punched cards as the basis of an Age-Sex-Address Register. Inclusion of the address in the punched data greatly increases the actual and potential usefulness of the register, although it doubles the initial labour and cost of setting up the file. The punched cards can be used for simple sorting and listing by mechanical methods, but they can also be used as input to a computer for speedier and more extensive sorting, tabulation, cross-reference and linkage. The layout of the card can be made to fit in with existing recording procedures at local hospitals, and Table XIX details the card layout used by Price and his colleagues in the M.R.C. Clinical and Population Cytogenetics Unit, Edinburgh, in a co-operative study with McNair in his practice; this card has subsequently been used with other practices in Edinburgh (personal

TABLE XIX

Layout of 80-column punched card used in a population study in
general practice

| Column numbers | Information coded in the columns |
| --- | --- |
| 1 | Leave blank (for 'type of card') |
| 2 to 6 | Practice patient number (5 digits) |
| 7 | Leave blank (for 'check digit') |
| 8 to 67 | Variable field portion of card, for: |
| | Surname (must start in column 8) followed by comma |
| | Forename, and initials followed by * |
| | Address followed by terminator |
| | Blanks to column 67 thereafter |
| 68 | Column for year of entry (coded) |
| 69 | Code for reason for leaving practice (as Exec. Council) |
| 70 | Leave blank |
| 71 to 72 | Practice number |
| 73 | Marital state |
| 74 | Sex |
| 75 to 80 | Date of birth (6 digits) |

Further details less often required can be coded on a second card, linked by the
practice patient number (e.g. maiden name, N.H.S. number, etc.).

communication). As a by-product of this M.R.C. study, practice registers
of between 5,000 and 10,000 patients have been obtained at a cost of less
than £100 per practice.

Three sets of information are maintained by the practice's secretary,
for punching at regular intervals so as to keep the register up-to-date,
namely an IN-book, an OUT-book, and amendments to the register. The
first two list patients joining or leaving the practice, and the third lists
those patients whose registration details alter; it is most conveniently
obtained by keeping a copy of the Local Executive Council form used for
the same purpose. The secretary verifies and corrects details from the
latest printout when the patient next attends.

Another of the projects in which we have been involved has been
carried out on an IBM 1440 computer. Data preparation costs in respect
of staff for a five-man group practice have been about £800 annually,
and stationery costs between £100 and £200 each year for cards and
other stationery. Registers printed out by the computer come in alphabetical order and contain the details for all the patients recorded. The lists
are used by the reception staff as a quick reference point to check registration or spelling of a name, and there is room on the printout to annotate
removals or deaths. The computer generates a serial number for each

patient, for use by the general practice, as part of the output which produces the practice register. Other forms of listing can also be obtained. For instance, the register can be rearranged so as to show household groups, or it can be sorted into age-groups thereby enabling the age structure of the practice to be examined either year by year or by other group intervals. The register has also been split into the following groups:

1. 1 to 5 years: This list was given to the health visitor to help check the state of immunisation.

2. Over 65 years: This list was given to the health visitor to serve as the basis of a geriatric register.

3. Females aged 35 to 64: This list was used to assist with the registration of patients for cervical cytology examinations.

A practice register showing sex and age distribution is a basic tool of general practice management and research. The method used to originate it, and to keep it up-to-date, depends on the resources available locally, but the computer is the ideal tool for this kind of data processing. It would seem preferable, if a new age-sex register is to be set up in any practice, that the labour be spent in recording the data in a computer-acceptable form. It must be emphasised that it is useless to set up a practice register without budgeting for, and organising the procedures to cope with, the equally large problem of keeping the register up-to-date. Acheson and Forbes (1968) have estimated the initial costs of setting up a register at £250 for a practice of 6,725 patients, and the cost of maintaining the register at £150 each year.

The register can, in summary, be automatically sorted by the computer and printed out in lists or groups by:

1. year of birth (the 'traditional' register);

2. year and month, or by year, month and day of birth;

3. alphabetical order of surname, forename, and initial ('personal' order);

4. alphabetical order of surname, and alphabetical and numerical order of address ('household' order);

5. sex;

6. marital status;

7. selected address groups (areas of the practice);

8. combinations of the above.

Once the register has been obtained on computer file, it can be used for other purposes. These include:

1. Counting and tabulating totals in the groups listed above.

2. Printing names and addresses in other formats (e.g. on adhesive labels) either for appointment cards, or for attaching to laboratory request forms, etc.

3. Introducing a practice patient number; this can then be used in place of the full name and address, both as a labour-saving abbreviation

and as a means of preserving the confidentiality of a patient's identity in any other computer files of clinical data.

4. Linkage with hospital data.

5. A step towards more fully computer-dependent patient records.

## DEMOGRAPHIC DATA

A striking example of what can be achieved with the assistance of computer methods is afforded by the Exeter Community Health Research Project (Ashford and Pearson, 1968). One of its main objectives has been to correlate morbidity experience with personal information among as large a section as possible of the population of Exeter, during a limited period of one year (1967). This involved 70,000 patients, registered on the N.H.S. general practice lists of 35 doctors in Exeter; these figures represent three-quarters of the population of patients, and of doctors.

Information was collected from four different sources, and subsequently linked by computer using a special 6-digit identification number, unique to each patient but common to each section of the project. These sections comprised:

1. General practice registration information;
2. General practice morbidity information;
3. Local hospital morbidity information;
4. Census interview information.

Although using mark-sense cards as the basic computer input medium, much preliminary manual recording had to be carried out. Developments with methods of data input may accelerate this process.

## IMMUNISATION AND HEALTH SURVEILLANCE DATA

There are certain groups of patients who are unaware of, or unable to recognise, their need for primary medical care. Many of these groups can now be identified with some degree of certainty, and general practice rather than hospital or Local Authority services often bears the responsibility for providing such primary care. Where the responsibility rests with general practice, it should logically be responsible also for the system of identifying these patients. The principles can best be discussed in relation to immunisation schedules.

The organisation of immunisation appointments and records by computer was pioneered by Galloway (1966). When the West Sussex County Council installed an IBM 1401 computer in 1962 for payroll purposes, a program was written for immunisation. The manually kept records of immunisation held by the general practitioners were, over the first three years, gradually transferred to a magnetic tape file. Searching and updating the family doctors' records was done prior to transfer by Local Authority staff, and needed from one to one and a half days' clerical assistance per practice.

Following the setting up of the computer file, notifications of births have been made by the midwives, on 80-column punched cards. These lead to the production of record cards and consent forms for use by the health visitors; on these forms the parents indicate whether they would like immunisations arranged at the surgery of the family doctor, or at the Local Authority clinic. These data are entered on the magnetic tape file, and the file is read monthly to select children who have reached an age when the next immunisation is due. Two sets of documents are then produced by the computer: (1) a card is sent to the parent giving day, time, place, and nature of the appointment; and (2) an appointment list for the family doctor (or the Local Authority clinic) identifying the patients and the immunisation procedures to be carried out. The clerical work is minimised—all that is required is an indication whether the patient attended or not, and the signed appointment sheet becomes an attendance record which acts as a claim form for fees due; it is accepted by the Local Executive Council (and the central department) without the need for audit. Records of additional unscheduled attendances, detailing the immunisation procedure given, can be added by hand.

Parents who do not bring their children for immunisation are sent consecutive monthly appointments automatically on three occasions. Further follow-up thereafter is done by the health visitor attached to the general practice; she has only to deal with non-attenders. Refusal of immunisation is only 0·3 per cent and protection indices are now well above the national average for England and Wales. These indices have increased from 33 per cent to 85 per cent for smallpox vaccination, and the other indices (for diphtheria, whooping cough, and poliomyelitis) are all about 95 per cent. At the end of 1969 there were 76,000 records on the file, held on four magnetic tapes which now comprise a small data bank.

The complete cycle of each set of operations (appointment making, immunising, recording, etc.) takes four weeks. The flexibility of the method used has enabled the system to cope with changes in the recommended immunisation schedule, variations in the rate of allocating appointments, changes in the amount of personal data recorded, and with movements to and from practices and to different Local Authority areas. The unit cost is about 40 per cent below the national average unit cost (Saunders, 1970) and the saving in terms of clerical labour and space required for storing records, as well as the increase in efficiency, are manifest. Adaptations of the original program have been introduced in other Local Authority areas, and Saunders and Snaith (1967) have published an account of a similar computer-based technique for the administration of cancer control programs.

Automated recall procedures have been extended from immunisation to other groups of disease. For instance, in Aberdeen (Hedley, 1970; Hedley et al., 1970) and Birmingham (Barker and Bishop, 1969), schemes have been devised to detect iatrogenic thyroid disease. The Aberdeen scheme is a joint venture between family doctor and hospital, the computer program deciding the date for despatch of a questionnaire and blood collection outfit for serum protein-bound iodine (PBI) determinations, and later collating the results. In Birmingham the patient completes a questionnaire and then attends hospital for the estimation of the PBI at an interval which depends on the results of the questionnaire. In both schemes the results are collated and recorded on a magnetic tape file. One of the authors has tried a modification of this scheme to follow up groups of 'at-risk' patients in general practice (e.g. patients with pernicious anaemia, or with a previous gastrectomy, or hypertension, or diabetes, as well as with thyroid diseases); the copious flow of information which resulted was illuminating, and further work is required to define optimum intervals and criteria for recall.

## MORBIDITY RECORDING

Complete recording of the details of all professional contacts between doctors and patients in general practice provides a formidable volume of information. The number of such contacts may total 1,000 per month for one doctor. Multiplied by the number of items of information accruing at each time of contact, the total number of recordings becomes very impressive. Faced with this range and volume of information, it seems imperative to speed up or by-pass some of the obsolescent multi-stage manual data-preparation processes. Visual display units and optical character recognition equipment have obvious attractions, and these methods are being evaluated. They are, however, very costly at present and considerable progress can be made at much less expense if doctors first of all structure the types of information they record and then record the information on a document that the computer can readily handle.

We have experimented with continuous morbidity recording of every contact between doctor and patient, both as individual doctors, and also involving partners as a group. Each doctor codes his own diagnoses, and these are punched up on paper tape and forwarded in batches for computer analysis.

In one project (Dinwoodie, 1969), for each contact the doctor recorded two numbers on a piece of paper which already bore the date of recording; the numbers represented the patient and the coded diagnosis. Latterly, the form shown in Figure 25 was used, and the whole coding procedure for each patient then took 5 to 10 seconds; the patient number (previously allocated to each patient in the practice) was read from the envelope holding the patient's record, and the diagnosis code was read off a list. Subsequently, this sequence of numbers was punched on to paper tape. For the first three years of operation, these data have been processed in batch mode on an Elliott 803 computer, provided with magnetic film

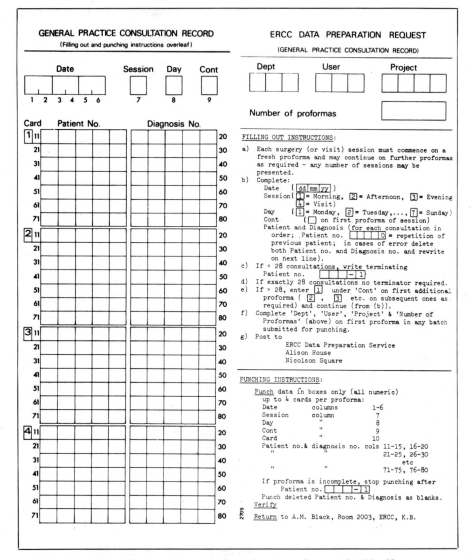

FIG. 25. Proforma used in a general practice surgery for recording identification numbers of patients and diagnosis codes. These forms are processed in batches at the Edinburgh Regional Computing Centre (ERCC).

backing store. The data are now being transferred to a third generation computer in order to explore the benefits of on-line file interrogation, and to utilise more efficient sorting and searching procedures. Data preparation, initially carried out locally on a secondhand tape punch, is now being done by punch operators at the Edinburgh Regional Computing Centre. The data are recorded initially by the doctor on the form shown in Figure

25; data preparation for computer input (i.e. forms and punching costs) has been costed at £90 per annum.

This experiment has shown that the general practice records were serving basically as linkages of only three items: a date, a patient, and an 'event'. The event could be one of many things—for instance the birth of a child, the making of a diagnosis, the result of an investigation, the prescription of treatment, etc. By extending the codings for events to include items of information other than diagnoses (e.g. births and deaths, patients joining or leaving the practice list, the giving of prophylactic injections) the range of data stored has been increased and by manipulating these 'Date-Patient-Event' entries, in various combinations, more extensive and meaningful analyses have become possible. So far, the data have been processed in single annual 'batch-processing' runs, sorting in two main directions—into diagnostic order, and into patient order. The data have then been used to provide the kind of information shown in Table XX. In addition to annual morbidity statistics, the 'Date-Patient-Event' file can be sorted to provide:

1. a month by month analysis of the incidence of individual diseases, such as respiratory tract infections;

2. an identification of patients who make frequent visits to the doctor —6·5 per cent of patients accounted for 21 per cent of consultations;

3. identifying patients with particular diagnoses (e.g. chronic bronchitics with a view to offering them influenza vaccination);

4. a list of patients whose immunisation schedule has fallen behindhand.

In another project, one author (Grene) adapted these methods to record the work of a five-man group practice. The identification number was extended by adding the year of birth, and the work of each of the five doctors was individually identified so that separate analyses could be made. A weekly analysis of data is performed to show the total workload for the week, and a comparison with the weekly mean for the previous year. Twenty groups of procedures or diagnoses are listed separately, so that it can be seen which sector of disease has been responsible for any change in total workload (Fig. 26). Other analyses of the data can be made over longer periods, for instance subdividing the patients into different age-groups to investigate the varying calls made upon the doctor, and the distribution of work between the five doctors in the practice can also be reviewed.

For some years, anticipating the advent of computers, the Royal College of General Practitioners' General Practice Research Unit has advocated the use of records intended from the outset to be 'computer-compatible'. The main types of these record files, with their order of arrangement, are the 'E'-Book (diagnosis order), 'S'-Cards (patient order), 'F'-Book (household order), and the 'L'-Ledger (consultation order).

TABLE XX

Continuous morbidity recording

Numbers of contacts between patients and one doctor for the principal groups of diseases and conditions diagnosed.
Contacts include visits and consultations.

| I.C.D. No. | Disease or condition groups | 1967–68 Total contacts | | 1968–69 Total contacts | | 1969–70 Total contacts | |
|---|---|---|---|---|---|---|---|
| | | Number | Per cent | Number | Per cent | Number | Per cent |
| 001–138 | Infective and parasitic diseases | 560 | 5·2 | 477 | 4·9 | 495 | 5·3 |
| 140–239 | Neoplasms | 255 | 2·4 | 210 | 2·2 | 175 | 1·9 |
| 240–289 | Allergic, endocrine system, metabolic and nutritional diseases | 493 | 4·6 | 436 | 4·5 | 479 | 5·2 |
| 290–299 | Diseases of blood and blood-forming organs | 177 | 1·7 | 207 | 2·1 | 183 | 2·0 |
| 300–326 | Mental, psychoneurotic and personality disorders | 843 | 7·9 | 759 | 7·9 | 645 | 7·0 |
| 330–398 | Diseases of nervous system and sense organs | 926 | 8·7 | 840 | 8·7 | 838 | 9·1 |
| 400–468 | Diseases of circulatory system | 910 | 8·5 | 815 | 8·5 | 750 | 8·1 |
| 470–527 | Diseases of respiratory system | 1318 | 12·3 | 1029 | 10·7 | 1288 | 13·9 |
| 530–587 | Diseases of digestive system | 417 | 3·9 | 427 | 4·4 | 314 | 3·4 |
| 590–637 | Diseases of genito-urinary system | 559 | 5·2 | 453 | 4·7 | 518 | 5·6 |
| 640–689 | Deliveries and obstetric complications | 44 | 0·4 | 68 | 0·7 | 46 | 0·5 |
| 690–716 | Diseases of skin and cellular tissue | 815 | 7·6 | 771 | 8·0 | 793 | 8·6 |
| 720–749 | Diseases of bone and organs of movement | 531 | 5·0 | 459 | 4·8 | 400 | 4·3 |
| 750–759 | Congenital malformations | 11 | 0·1 | 36 | 0·4 | 22 | 0·2 |
| 760–776 (except 763, 764) | Certain diseases of early infancy | 10 | 0·1 | 8 | 0·1 | 4 | 0·0 |
| 780–795 | Symptoms, senility and ill-defined conditions | 1375 | 12·8 | 1377 | 14·3 | 1140 | 12·3 |
| N800–N999 | Accidents, poisoning and violence | 444 | 4·1 | 393 | 4·1 | 365 | 3·9 |
| — | Non-sickness (includes ante- and post-natal examinations, inoculations etc. | 724 | 6·8 | 838 | 8·7 | 786 | 8·5 |
| — | Diagnosis not recorded | 287 | 2·7 | 32 | 0·3 | 15 | 0·2 |
| | All diseases and conditions | 10699 | 100·0 | 9635 | 100·0 | 9256 | 100·0 |

**Note:** The circumstances were closely similar but not identical in each of the three years. Figures do not take account of changes in the number of patients attending the practice, nor of variations in the number of doctors in the partnership present at any one time to attend to patients.

```
GROUP PRACTICE DRS PGHPH WARWICK ENGLAND
         WEEK ENDING 12  9 70
```

R.C.G.P. MORBIDITY CLASSIFICATION

| | | CONSULTS-VISITS | | | | | |
|---|---|---|---|---|---|---|---|
| | | NEW | OLD | NEW | OLD | TOT | PCENT |
| 0 | NO DIAGNOSIS RECORDED | 0 | 0 | 25 | 0 | 25 | 4 |
| 1 | COMMUNICABLE DISEASE | 4 | 6 | 0 | 2 | 12 | 2 |
| 2 | NEOPLASMS | 1 | 0 | 0 | 4 | 5 | 0 |
| 3 | ALLERGY,ENDOCRINE,METABOLIC | 7 | 17 | 1 | 2 | 27 | 5 |
| 4 | DISORDER OF BLOOD | 1 | 6 | 0 | 0 | 7 | 1 |
| 5 | MENTAL AND PSYCHIATRIC | 14 | 41 | 0 | 1 | 56 | 10 |
| 6 | DISORDER NERVOUS SYSTEM | 19 | 13 | 1 | 0 | 33 | 6 |
| 7 | DISORDER CIRCULATORY SYSTEM | 8 | 22 | 1 | 14 | 45 | 8 |
| 8 | DISORDER RESPIRATORY SYSTEM | 22 | 14 | 10 | 6 | 52 | 9 |
| 9 | DISORDER DIGESTIVE SYSTEM | 18 | 13 | 6 | 3 | 40 | 7 |
| 10 | DISORDER GENITO-URINARY SYSTEM | 14 | 15 | 1 | 2 | 32 | 6 |
| 11 | DELIVERIES-COMPL.PREGNANCIES | 6 | 28 | 1 | 19 | 54 | 10 |
| 12 | DISORDERS OF SKIN | 19 | 10 | 0 | 1 | 30 | 5 |
| 13 | DISORDER BONES AND JOINTS | 18 | 22 | 2 | 3 | 45 | 8 |
| 14 | CONGENITAL MALFORMATIONS | 0 | 0 | 0 | 0 | 0 | 0 |
| 15 | DISORDER OF EARLY INFANCY | 0 | 0 | 0 | 0 | 0 | 0 |
| 16 | SYMPTOMS AND UNDEFINED CONDITIONS | 1 | 0 | 1 | 2 | 4 | 0 |
| 17 | ACCIDENT,POISONING AND VIOLENCE | 13 | 5 | 2 | 0 | 20 | 3 |
| 18 | PROPHYLACTIC PROCEDURES | 24 | 7 | 0 | 0 | 31 | 5 |
| 19 | ADMINISTRATIVE PROCEDURES | 13 | 9 | 0 | 1 | 23 | 4 |

```
     TOTAL  DIAGNOSES = 541
     TOTAL ATTENDANCE = 533
                        = 87  PERCENT LAST YEARS MEAN


TOTAL VISITS=111=20.83PERCENT TOTAL SERVICES
STOP
```

FIG. 26. Computer printout of the morbidity classification for one week's
work by a doctor in general practice.

These have been fully described elsewhere (Eimerl and Laidlaw, 1969),
and have so far been used mainly for research projects rather than for
the routine care of patients.

## OPERATIONAL CODING

When morbidity recording is undertaken on a complete and continuous
basis, one by-product is that monitoring of workload can be undertaken
by the addition of simple operational codings. This has been demonstrated by Durno (personal communication) who has used a record form
similar in design to the 'L'-Ledger. He has been able to obtain automatically, for his own practice, periodic analyses of the practice workload
(Tables XXI and XXII), in addition to an annual batch-processing sort
into diagnosis order. Apart from this individual study, a large-scale co-
operative workload study (based on previous similar ones in South West
England and in South Wales) was organised during 1969 to 1970 by the

TABLE XXI

A General Practice Workload Study
(Durno, personal communication)

Analysis of attendances or contacts with patients: December, 1968

| Patients seen by doctor | Prescription issued Yes | No | Not recorded | Total | Patients not seen by doctor | Total |
|---|---|---|---|---|---|---|
| *Type of contact:* | | | | | | |
| *Attendances at surgery:* | | | | | | |
| 1st attendance | 201 | 139 | 17 | 357 | Seen by secretary | 76 |
| Return attendance | 198 | 220 | 3 | 421 | Contact by letter | 28 |
| Total attendances | 299 | 359 | 20 | 778 | Contact by telephone | 146 |
| | | | | | Attendance for prescription | 46 |
| *Visits to patients in their homes:* | | | | | Visit for prescriptions | 11 |
| 1st visit | 115 | 50 | 0 | 165 | Other contact, for | |
| Return visit | 83 | 100 | 1 | 184 | prescription | 7 |
| Total visits | 198 | 150 | 1 | 349 | | |
| *Other types of contact:* | | | | | | |
| Late attendance at surgery | | | | 3 | | |
| Late visit to home | | | | 21 | | |
| Grand totals | | | | 1151 | | 314 |

Department of General Practice, University of Aberdeen, and by the North-East Scotland Faculty of the Royal College of General Practitioners; this co-operative study involved 163 doctors and has recently been successfully concluded (Richardson, Durno and Gill, report in preparation).

## THE PERSONAL FILE
The various methods already described for recording contacts between doctors and patients all have the same ultimate aim, to build up a personal file giving the record of significant medical events in the life of each

TABLE XXII

A General Practice Workload Study (Durno, personal communication)

Analysis of attendances by sex and age: January – June, 1968

| AGE: | Under 5 | | 5–16 | | 16–64 | | 64 and over | | Not known | |
|---|---|---|---|---|---|---|---|---|---|---|
| | Male | Female | Male | Female | Male | Female | Male | Female | Male | Female |
| *New attendances:* | | | | | | | | | | |
| Surgery | 112 | 69 | 79 | 83 | 886 | 418 | 25 | 28 | 0 | 2 |
| Home | 107 | 69 | 55 | 80 | 20 | 185 | 45 | 79 | 1 | 3 |
| *Return attendances:* | | | | | | | | | | |
| Surgery | 174 | 166 | 167 | 149 | 521 | 1773 | 170 | 190 | 3 | 1 |
| Home | 92 | 54 | 62 | 47 | 55 | 311 | 279 | 486 | 2 | 2 |
| *Other attendances:* | 42 | 32 | 55 | 54 | 287 | 327 | 111 | 153 | 1 | 2 |
| Grand totals | 527 | 390 | 416 | 423 | 1769 | 3014 | 630 | 936 | 7 | 10 |

individual. Other attempts have used different approaches towards this aim, but they all come up against the important problems of basic syntax and the need for decisions on how to structure the record (Grant, 1969; Weed, 1969); it is useless to think of employing computers for the storage and total recall of unstructured information. There is no blueprint for the perfect computer-compatible record, and the adaptation of present methods can best be undertaken slowly, by a process of trial and error.

Clarke *et al.* (1969), for instance, are using a typewriter that also generates punched tape to record the significant part of each consultation. As a by-product, prescriptions for the treatment of chronic diseases are typed as needed, and a summary of the medical history is produced at intervals and supersedes the summary already in the file.

In Scotland, at Livingston New Town, a typed record is produced from dictation by the doctor (Gruer and Heasman, 1970). Only a portion of the record is coded for computer storage, using a fixed order of format which takes, on average, about 45 seconds of the doctor's time per patient seen. The full typed record is retained in the practice for day to day use, while the computer-stored summary is used subsequently as an index to the written records rather than as a full personal record. Two main files of 'registration' data and of 'episode' data are kept; so far their main uses have been for immunisation scheduling, for routine pre-school examinations, for arranging cervical cytology, and for maintaining a register of patients sensitive to drugs.

The Thamesmead experiment (Abrams *et al.*, 1968) is based on VDU and teletype units situated in the consulting room; information is put directly on to computer file, whence it is available on demand. This is important work which may indicate the pattern of general practice records in the future, if costs can be brought down and problems of confidentiality of the record overcome. A similar approach was recently demonstrated by Preece and his colleagues (1970); this employed a VDU and line-printer in the general practitioner's surgery linked to a computer 200 miles away.

## BASIC RESEARCH

The analysis of clusters or patterns of signs, symptoms and tests, matching these with complementary clusters of signs appropriate to a specific diagnostic group with a high probability of correct assignment, has been explored in relation to general practice by Crombie and Dobell (1969). This attempt at automatic clinical problem-solving seeks on a mathematical basis to increase the probability of reaching a correct solution to the clinical problem without increasing the amount of clinical effort; the appropriate clinical action then ensues. The logical approach to diagnosis cannot always be followed in general practice, where a pay-off approach frequently has much to commend it and where the appropriate clinical action may take place, and quite correctly, without the need for a formal diagnosis being made. Nevertheless, this type of research should help to support such empirical short cuts, and lead to a better understanding of the diagnostic process.

Increasing numbers of doctors are using computers to analyse results of their own specific surveys, with much greater ease, accuracy, speed, and general productivity than the former customary manual or mechanical methods of analysis. Many examples could be given, but only the Royal College of General Practitioners' Oral Contraceptive Study (Kay, 1970) will be mentioned. This extensive study is still in progress but already the data have been subjected to preliminary analysis, and answers obtained to specific unforeseen urgent and important questions; without computer assistance, these questions could not have been readily answered during the actual course of the enquiry.

## COST-EFFECTIVENESS OF COMPUTERS IN GENERAL PRACTICE

Cost-effectiveness in general practice is difficult to measure. Factors such as a wide application, the volume of work and the routine nature of a task can promise a substantial return from investment in computing (Ockenden and Bodenham, 1970). We have little doubt that actual and potential benefits are to be obtained from setting up an automated age-sex-address register for general practice. These benefits relate to the better use of data, which by their very nature mean improvements in patient care as compared with those obtainable with the traditional manually kept registers. These benefits, although not readily quantifiable, are sufficient to justify the demonstrated outlay of between £20 and £40 per 1,000 patients initially for data preparation, with annual running costs subsequently of about £25 per 1,000 patients. Similarly, the increased effectiveness of immunisation schemes (Galloway 1966, 1969, 1970), coupled with the saving of both medical and clerical time afforded by the reduction in manual documentation procedures, should cause little debate.

The volume of data which accumulates in respect of morbidity is of the order of 12,000 records of contacts between a doctor and his patients each year. If a 'Date-Patient-Event' register is maintained, data preparation and computer processing costs build up and an individual doctor might wish for guidance on costs before setting out to improve his own records system. The initial programming costs for the system described by Dinwoodie (1969, 1970) must have been considerable, but these were borne by the Scottish Home and Health Department and details are not available. Thereafter the cost of a single annual sort (into diagnosis order) has been £75 in respect of time used on an Elliott 803 computer; this cost is additional to the annual data-preparation costs of £90 as mentioned earlier. The corresponding costs for data processing on the third generation computer have not yet been assessed, but they could well be more if the greater potential of the new programs is exploited.

These figures indicate the scale of expense involved in manipulating even simple forms of medical record on magnetic media; the alternative is to continue to keep the records on paper, when the data they contain will be used less. Experience at Livingston led Gruer and Heasman (1970) to remark that 'the amount of data that is continually accumulating may provide problems of processing, if only in terms of computer time'. Hodes (1969), referring to screening projects, also comments that 'computer time is still expensive and, unless receiving special support, computer-assisted projects are not yet an economic possibility'.

## SUMMARY OF THE PRESENT POSITION OF COMPUTERS IN RELATION TO GENERAL PRACTICE

The uses of computers in general practice discussed in this chapter fall into three main categories, which together form a natural hierarchy in terms of complexity, cost and the involvement of the general practitioner. The first two categories of use require access to a central computer, and involve off-line preparation of data followed by batch processing runs on the computer. The third area of work requires on-line access to a computer. These different forms of use will be briefly reconsidered.

Computers have been used off-line in general practice to assist with the recall of selected groups of patients, as with immunisation schemes or in the operation of registers for aged patients or for patients with special categories of disease. The cooperation of the general practitioner is required for filling in forms, preferably in an agreed format suitable for direct computer input, and for returning these forms to the authorities administering the scheme. The main benefits are improvements in patient care and in general administration.

In the other main category of off-line use the general practitioner's own patient record, or rather part of it, is coded and stored on magnetic tape for periodic analysis by computer. This requires more systematic coding and stricter keeping of records than is usually the case in general practice at present, but the potential benefits are considerable. Records, if properly coded and recorded, can contribute to improvements in patient care since they can be searched for patients with particular characteristics or at special risk. If these data are extracted frequently or at regular intervals, the general practitioner can set up a special recall register in his own practice for patients of particular interest. Computer-compatible records can also contribute to improved administration of the practice, for instance by facilitating the analysis of workload, and with these records demographic and epidemiological data become much more readily available (e.g. morbidity data). It is recognised that much demographic and epidemiological data is of more general (research) interest rather than of immediate concern to the running of the surgery.

On-line access to a central computer offers the general practitioner the opportunity to keep records concerning patients in both coded and un-coded form on a magnetic disc or drum for immediate recall during a consultation, using a console or VDU within the surgery. If the data are properly coded (as against free text storage), all the benefits outlined above in respect of off-line usage accrue, and in theory these facilities become available in real time on-line. It must not be disguised, however, that the general practitioner's involvement in terms of recording, coding and supervising the regular input and updating of the computer files can be considerable, and there are distinct limitations in respect of computer storage facilities and cost.

## FUTURE DEVELOPMENTS

This chapter has concentrated on describing early and relatively small-scale explorations of possible applications of computers in general practice; the emphasis has been on schemes which have already become operational. In all these computer applications, the general practitioner is required to participate actively by keeping and coding records and by sending in regular returns; some of the benefits mentioned can be obtained with non-computer based records systems. Bearing in mind how few practices keep systematic records, such as even a simple age-sex register, there must be speculation whether many doctors will be prepared to introduce and maintain a computer-based system of records as a permanent feature of general practice. Nevertheless, areas where the use of computers may extend more widely include:

1. the further automation of repetitive clerical procedures;
2. periodic health examinations (screening) by general practitioners;
3. continuous information about morbidity;
4. monitoring of prescriptions and drug reactions;
5. communications between doctors in general practice and in hospitals.

The direction of further developments will depend considerably on the production of low-cost hardware and other computer facilities, such as VDU terminals, optical character recognition equipment, communications networks and time-sharing systems. In all these developments it is important to remember that the computer should aid, not rule, the doctor. The wider introduction of computers into general practice could help to integrate and rationalise the provision of patient care, and should help to bring general practice and hospital medicine closer, thereby improving the standards of medical care for the community as a whole.

REFERENCES

ABRAMS, M. E., BOWDEN, K. F., CHAMBERLAIN, J. & MACCALLUM, I. R. (1968). A computer-based general practice and health centre information system. *Journal of the Royal College of General Practitioners*, **16**, 415–427.

ACHESON, E. D. & FORBES, J. A. (1968). Experiment in the retrieval of information in general practice. *British Journal of Preventive and Social Medicine*, **22**, 105–109.

ASHFORD, J. R. & PEARSON, N. G. (1968). The Exeter community health research project. In *Computers in the Service of Medicine*. Ed. McLachlan, G. & Shegog, R. A. Vol. I, pp. 173–188. London: Oxford University Press.

BARKER, D. J. P. & BISHOP, J. M. (1969). Computer based screening system for patients at risk of hypothyroidism. *Lancet*, **2**, 835–838.

CLARKE, A. H., DIXON, R. A. & RICKARDS, D. F. (1969). 'Practis': (General) practice recording and computer terminal information system. *Journal of the Royal College of General Practitioners*, **17**, 60–63.

CROMBIE, D. L. & DOBELL, K. (1969). N-Tuplets in computer diagnosis. *Journal of the Royal College of General Practitioners*, **18**, 219–225.

DINWOODIE, H. P. (1969). An elementary use of a computer for morbidity recording in general practice. *Health Bulletin for Scotland*, **27**, No. 3, 6–14.

DINWOODIE, H. P. (1970). Simple computer facilities in general practice. *Journal of the Royal College of General Practitioners*, **19**, 269–281.

EIMERL, T. S. & LAIDLAW, A. J. (1969). *A Handbook for Research in General Practice*. 2nd ed. Edinburgh: Livingstone.

GALLOWAY, T. M. (1966). Computers: Their use in local health administration. *Journal of the Royal Society of Health*, **86**, 213–216.

GALLOWAY, T. M. (1969). *The Health of West Sussex 1968*. pp. 26–30. Hove Printing Co.

GALLOWAY, T. M. (1970). *The Health of West Sussex 1969*. pp. 19–22. Hove Printing Co.

GRANT, D. M. (1969). Communications: Some problems in medical computing in 1969. *Journal of the Royal College of General Practitioners*, **18**, 321–329.

GRENE, J. D. (1970). Computer compatible records in general practice. *Journal of the Royal College of General Practitioners*, **19**, 29–33.

GRUER, K. T. & HEASMAN, M. A. (1970). Livingston New Town—Use of computer in general practice medical recording. *British Medical Journal*, **2**, 289–291.

HEDLEY, A. J. (1970). The use of a computer in patient follow-up in Scotland. *Scottish Medical Journal*, **15**, 395–399.

HEDLEY, A. J., SCOTT, A. M., WEIR, R. D. & CROOKS, J. (1970). Computer-assisted follow-up register for the North-East of Scotland. *Scottish Medical Journal*, **15**, 556–558.

HODES, C. (1969). The computer and screening techniques in general practice. *Journal of the Royal College of General Practitioners*, **18**, 330–335.

KAY, C. R. (1970). British experience of the pill. *Journal of the Royal College of General Practitioners*, **19**, 251–257.

MARINKER, M. (1969). The computer in general practice. *The Practitioner*, **203**, 285–293.

OCKENDEN, J. M. & BODENHAM, K. E. (1970). *Focus on Medical Computer Development*, p. 26. London: Oxford University Press.

PREECE, J. F., GILLINGS, D. B., LIPPMAN, E. D. & PEARSON, N. G. (1970). An on-line record maintenance and retrieval system in general practice. *International Journal of Bio-medical Computing*, **1**, 329–337.

SAUNDERS, J. (1970). Results and costs of a computer-assisted immunisation scheme. *British Journal of Preventive and Social Medicine*, **24**, 187–191.

SAUNDERS, J. & SNAITH, A. H. (1967). Cervical cytology: A computer-assisted population screening programme. *Medical Officer*, **117**, 299–303.

WEED, L. L. (1969). *Medical Records, Medical Education, and Patient Care.* Chicago: Year Book Medical Publishers.

# Computers in the Clinical Chemistry Laboratory

## By L. G. WHITBY

### SUMMARY

THE various ways in which digital computers can contribute to the work of a clinical chemistry laboratory are discussed in this chapter. These activities include taking part in the organisation of laboratory work, the monitoring of automatic equipment, the performance of repetitive calculations, and the preparation of laboratory reports which may contain both quality control and statistical assessments.

Computers have been used in clinical chemistry laboratories since 1964, and their range of applications has been progressively extended. Both on-line and off-line computer systems have been developed, the early dedicated on-line configurations being so expensive that off-line batch-processing methods were preferred. Batch processing of results has many disadvantages, however, and the emphasis shifted so that there are now several commercial systems available for monitoring laboratory equipment, especially AutoAnalyzers, using dedicated computers on-line to the apparatus. The description in this chapter is mainly based on experience gained with one of these dedicated systems.

## INTRODUCTION

Chemical investigations are being performed increasingly frequently to assist in the diagnosis and management of illness, and in recent years as part of screening programmes for the presymptomatic detection of disease. Many laboratories not as yet engaged in screening work have reported increases in their workload year by year at rates of 15 to 20 per cent; these cause a doubling in the output of results every four to five years, and the data summarised in Table XXIII are fairly representative of this situation. Where screening programmes have been introduced, even greater percentage increases in the output of work occurred at the time of starting such programmes.

Laboratories have met the growing demand for chemical investigations by employing more staff, by work study and by job simplification, but especially by introducing automatic methods of chemical analysis; in this latter field the AutoAnalyzer (Technicon Instruments Co., Chertsey, Surrey) has proved invaluable (Table XXIII). The point has been reached where the time required for the performance of the actual chemical analysis represents a small fraction of the interval between the initiation of a request for a laboratory investigation and the arrival of the corre-

TABLE XXIII

Data relating to the work of the Department of Clinical Chemistry,
Royal Infirmary of Edinburgh

| Year | Specimens | Deter- minations | Technical staff | Auto- Analyzer channels | Productivity† | Cost per determination (Pounds sterling) |
|------|-----------|------------------|-----------------|-------------------------|---------------|-------------------------------------------|
| 1950 | 10,800 | 22,000 | 11 | 0 | 2,000 | 0·43 |
| 1955 | 36,400 | 57,000 | 14 | 0 | 4,000 | 0·42 |
| 1960 | 72,500 | 106,000 | 18 | 1 | 5,900 | 0·36 |
| 1963 | 95,800 | 195,000 | 23 | 3 | 8,900 | 0·24 |
| 1966 | 105,300 | 407,000 | 30 | 12 | 14.500 | 0·23 |
| 1968 | 148,000 | 516,000 | 33 | 16 | 16,700 | 0·27 |
| 1970 | 210,400 | 646.000 | 35 | 16 | 20,200 | 0·17 |

† Defined as the average number of determinations performed annually by each member of the technical staff, after making allowance for the numbers attending classes of further education (but no allowance for holidays, sickness, etc.).

* Based on total costs for the year (i.e. including capital expenditure incurred during that year as well as running costs). The computer system represented a major item of capital expenditure in 1968. No allowance has been made for changes in value of money.

sponding report in the hands of the doctor who made the request, Computer techniques can help at several stages in the chain of events that begin with the initiation of requests for investigations, continue with the performance of analytical work in the laboratory itself, and lead on to the preparation and distribution of reports.

## COMPUTER CONFIGURATIONS FOR LABORATORIES

Laboratories carry out several different categories of repetitive process, all of which can be materially assisted by computers. The extent of the assistance derived from the computer depends upon the type of configuration available to the laboratory, and the relatively successful application of computers to clinical chemistry, resulting from experimental work carried out in many countries, means that clinical chemists who are thinking of using computers in their laboratories now have several choices open to them. Four main categories of configuration need to be mentioned:

1. A computer dedicated to the laboratory's programme of work;
2. A share in the facilities offered by a central hospital computer;
3. Use of facilities offered by a bureau installation outside the hospital;
4. Combinations of 1 and 2, or of 1 and 3.

These various configurations do not necessarily all carry out the same functions nor, where they appear to do so, do they always carry them out with the same degree of efficiency and reliability. Perhaps more than in any other field of medical computing today, therefore, the potential user in clinical chemistry needs to define his aims before committing himself to a system. Otherwise considerations of expense, not only in terms of hardware investment but of possible software development, will limit the opportunities of changing from one system to another if the first fails to meet the requirements. Derrett (1970) has surveyed some of these problems of computer selection in general terms.

The first decision is whether to obtain a system that is dedicated to the laboratory's own use. The configuration for the dedicated computer may be sufficient in itself to meet all the department's needs, or a smaller dedicated installation can be obtained for carrying out especially the process-control functions involved in acquiring data from laboratory equipment. The smaller laboratory-based computer can meet requirements if backed by a data-processing installation (e.g. a hospital computer) which can undertake the file-handling and bulk output functions involved, respectively, in the storage and retrieval of records and in the generation of reports. Systems have also been developed for clinical chemistry that are based entirely on the use of off-line batch-processing techniques (Flynn, 1965; Flynn *et al.*, 1966), using a centrally sited hospital computer or a bureau installation, but these have major drawbacks (Whitby *et al.*, 1968) and improvements in communications

TABLE XXIV

Hardware configuration for a clinical chemistry laboratory
based on an Elliott 903 computer

| | |
|---|---|
| Central processor | Elliott 903C computer; 8K core store (18-bit word), 6 microsecond cycle time. |
| Input devices | On-line Teletype (model 33); spare unit held. Paper-tape reader (250 characters per second); spare unit held. Data-acquisition unit receiving signals from Auto-Analyzers—total capacity 31 channels, but present linking limited to 12 AutoAnalyzer inputs. |
| Output devices | On-line Teletype (10 characters per second); same unit as input Teletype. On-line IBM output writer (15 characters per second). Paper tape punch (100 characters per second); spare unit held. Off-line Teletype (model 35; 10 characters per second). |
| Backing store | Magnetic tape controller and three Ampex TM7 tape handlers (9,000 characters per second). |

**Note**: Less powerful systems based on the Elliott 903 computer are operating without any backing store in clinical chemistry laboratories.

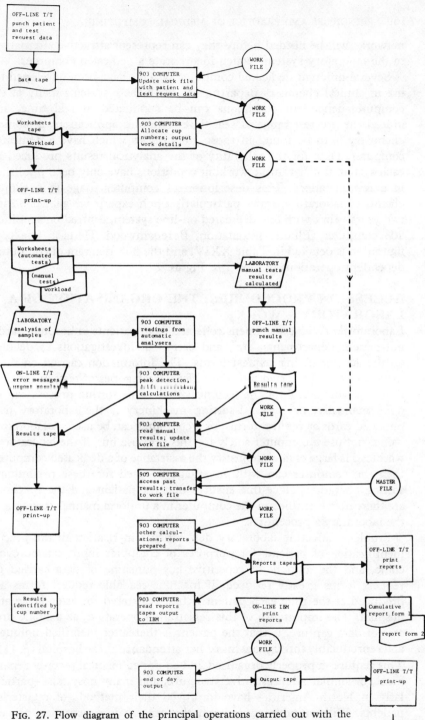

FIG. 27. Flow diagram of the principal operations carried out with the computer configuration in Table XXIV. The computer assists with the preparation of worksheets. It is used for process control, by monitoring analytical equipment for the detection in real time of faults occurring in the operation of the equipment. The computer also calculates the results of analyses and is used for the preparation of various types of report, including quality control and statistical assessments.

networks will be needed before they can represent attractive alternatives to the laboratory systems which incorporate a dedicated computer.

Several different dedicated computer systems have been developed for use in clinical chemistry departments. With these systems many of the computer-dependent operations can be conducted in real time, and indeed the greatest range of real time computer applications in clinical chemistry is to be found in those laboratories which have a dedicated computer. Data for the reliability of the analytical results produced by each system under routine working conditions have only been published in a few instances. This description of computer usage in a clinical chemistry laboratory draws particularly upon experience gained during two years' work with one dedicated on-line system, centred on an Elliott 903 computer (Elliott Automation, Borehamwood, Herts.). The configuration is detailed in Table XXIV, and the flow diagram of computer-dependent operations is shown in Figure 27.

## ACCESSION PROCEDURES: THE ORGANISATION OF A LABORATORY'S WORK

Laboratories receive specimens collected from patients in hospital wards, out-patient departments, etc., and carry out investigations as detailed on the accompanying request forms. The information carried on these forms needs to be sorted into the different categories of test, in order to draw up worksheets for the technical staff. This sorting process can be done manually, or by card-sorting machinery if the laboratory uses punched cards as request forms, or a computer can be used. A laboratory would not use a computer solely for this purpose but, if the laboratory's workload is large enough to justify the assistance of a dedicated computer, then the computer can with advantage be used for these preliminary sorting operations since this ensures that the patient and the specimen are thereafter identified to the computer in a uniform manner throughout the laboratory's procedures.

Problems affecting laboratory departments in relation to the precise identification of patients for purposes of computer input can be overcome, and the amount of repetitive key-punching of data carried on request forms greatly reduced, if machine-readable request forms are produced at the time each patient is first registered for attendance at a hospital. The importance of this registration operation, as a single process of data capture, is that the patient is thereafter identified uniquely and reproducibly throughout his or her attendance at the hospital (p. 111). This requires a properly organised and equipped medical records department, or similar administrative structure, and many hospitals—particularly in North America—have improved their methods of registering patients. With suitable equipment, the central documentation process can be used to generate machine-readable laboratory request forms as one of the documents for routine use within the hospital (e.g. Whitehead *et al.*, 1968); the laboratory request forms can be 80-column punched cards or edge-punched cards.

The analyses to be performed on patients can either be hand-written on to the request cards or checked off on pre-printed cards. This information also has to be coded for input to the computer, but the designation of the analyses to be requested cannot be pre-coded centrally since different patients require different investigations. Nevertheless, the possibility of reducing the amount of repetitive key-punching in the laboratory exists here also, if request forms are designed for use in association with one of the document mark-readers now available; these readers can automatically detect and code marks entered in check-boxes sited on request forms next to the tests that are to be carried out.

It is important to simplify and expedite the coding of information carried on request forms as much as possible if a computer is to be used to provide laboratory staff with worksheets to guide the analytical performance of their work. The initial processes of preparing specimens for analysis (e.g. centrifuging blood samples, separating off plasma or serum, etc.) are usually completed within 20 minutes of the arrival of a specimen in the laboratory, and the specimen may thereafter be required immediately for analysis. The use of machine-readable request forms coded with identification data for patients and designed so that the tests requested can be interpreted by document mark readers can help to ensure that the generation of worksheets keeps pace with the preparation of specimens.

On the basis of information entered into the computer from the request forms received in the laboratory, the computer builds up a file of work to be performed. This workfile can be interrogated periodically for a statement detailing the amount of work for each type of test that has not yet been allocated to worksheets, and these can then be printed up as required, following the appropriate instruction. The computer automatically advances to the first available place on the next worksheet specimens for which analyses are to be performed urgently; its program also determines for the technical staff the order in which the other analyses (standards, quality control samples, specimens from patients) are to be carried out.

## COMPUTERS AND THE ANALYTICAL WORK OF THE LABORATORY

### Analytical considerations

Clinical chemistry departments regularly perform some 50 to 70 different analyses, and many laboratories serving a reference function carry out a much wider range of investigations in response to special requests. Most of these measurements are made on small volumes of blood plasma or serum, and the requirements for accuracy and precision place considerable demands upon laboratory staff when the analytical work is largely or entirely performed by hand. Plasma contains a high concentration of protein (about 7 g/100 ml), whereas many of the constituents of plasma that need to be measured are present in much smaller amount (e.g. urea, 10 to 300 mg/100 ml; uric acid, 2 to 15 mg/100 ml; protein-bound iodine, 1 to 20 $\mu$g/100 ml). The analytical procedures, in general, involve the accurate measurement of a small volume of plasma or serum, usually in the range 20 to 300 $\mu$l, to an accuracy of $\pm 1$ per cent. The sample is then diluted, often the procedure includes a deproteinisation step, and there may then be the addition of reagents in precise volume and in a prescribed order. The resulting mixture may require incubation and one or more of a number of other technical procedures which lead up, in many instances, to the development of a coloured product. The intensity of the colour developed by each specimen as a result of undergoing the analytical procedures is assessed in relation to the intensity of colour developed by a range of standards of known concentration; these standards are carried through the procedure in an exactly similar fashion in order to calibrate the measuring equipment. In addition to colorimetric methods of analysis, many techniques have now been developed which involve a variety of physical or physicochemical procedures, but the basic principles of having to standardise the equipment, and having to relate the behaviour of specimens from patients to the findings with calibrating standards, still hold.

The measuring devices used in clinical chemistry laboratories include colorimeters, flame photometers, reaction rate analysers, and atomic absorption spectrophotometers. They all generate an electrical signal which falls into one of three categories: fixed voltage (square wave); rising analog; or rising and falling (continuously varying) analog signals.

At present there are two widely used automatic systems of analysis in clinical chemistry, the first of which is the single channel AutoAnalyzer. This operates on a continuous flow principle, with specimens entering the equipment one after the other (Skeggs, 1957), and Figure 28 shows the conventional way in which the continuously varying analog output from a Mark I AutoAnalyzer colorimeter is portrayed, after amplification as a tracing on a strip-chart recorder. The other widely used automatic systems are the multi-channel group of analysers (SMA6 and SMA12; Technicon Instruments) which also operate on the continuous flow principle. In these multi-channel systems, each specimen is simultaneously analysed for 6 or 12 different chemical constituents, depending upon the design of the equipment. The technical operation of both the SMA 6 and the SMA 12 equipment has been modified in many ways, as compared with the Mark I AutoAnalyzer, with the result that the final

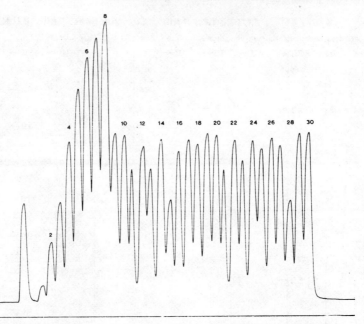

FIG. 28. An example of a chart record obtained with a single-channel AutoAnalyzer. The tracing begins with a peak (unnumbered) to set the computer's peak detection program in operation, followed by a series of calibrating standards (1–8), drift correction standards (10, 20 and 30), quality control serum pool (19 and 29) and patients' specimens (the rest of the peaks). Some of the peaks are sharp-topped, due to deliberately inadequate sampling, and these peaks (11, 13, 21 and 23) were all rejected by the computer; they should all have been the same height as peaks 12, 14, 22 and 24. Analyses were performed at 60 specimens per hour (i.e. one peak every 60 seconds) and the urea content of samples was being measured. The sample in position 9 is not used for calculation purposes; it has the same composition as the one in position 10.

tracing on the chart has the appearance shown in Figure 29; the concentration values for each of the analyses on one specimen appear as a series of approximately horizontal lines crossing the relevant scale on the record paper (Smythe *et al.*, 1968).

## Data acquisition and data processing of the output from Auto-Analyzers by manual methods

Several stages have to be gone through before the raw analog output of AutoAnalyzers (Fig. 28) is ready to be reported in units of concentration. The standard procedure first involves a visual assessment of each peak, to decide whether its overall shape is acceptable. At the start of an analytical run this assessment also takes account of the collective appearance of the peaks recorded for the calibrating standards; thereafter the peak shape and height of each drift-correction standard is specially noted.

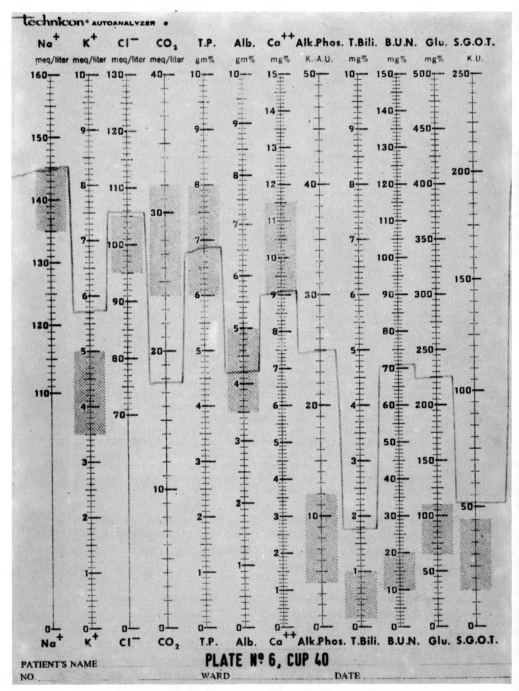

FIG. 29. An example of a chart record obtained with a 12-channel multi-channel continuous flow analyser. The figure shows the results for 12 different analyses carried out simultaneously on a single sample of serum, but phased so that the results for the different channels appear one after the other on the chart record; the detector system switches automatically from one channel to the next, recording the plateau corresponding to each analysis for the same length of time. This record was made with an early model in the SMA (simultaneous multiple analysis) series, operating at 30 specimens per hour, and each plateau lasted for 10 seconds. With the SMA 12/60 and SMA 6/60 models, the duration of each plateau is 5 seconds.

Following this appraisal of standards, the heights of individual peaks are read off the chart records, their raw values corrected for any drift which may have occurred (by linear interpolation between the relevant pair of drift standards), and the corrected values interpolated between the appropriate pair of standards on the calibration curve. The concentration of the constituent in each sample can then be calculated. It is good technique, when these operations are carried out by hand and eye, for another technician to repeat all these chart-reading and calculation steps, to reduce the likelihood that misreading of peaks or miscalculations have occurred.

Many clinical chemistry laboratories now operate 10 or more channels of single-channel AutoAnalyzer equipment, at rates of analysis up to 60 specimens per hour. These figures mean that staff in a busy laboratory may have several thousand repetitive chart-reading and calculation operations to perform each day, when processing the chart records into a form suitable for reporting. It might seem that the chart records for the multi-channel analysers (Fig. 29) would give rise to less work as the appearance of the records suggests that they are direct reading instruments. Unfortunately, the multi-channel analysers are also subject to drift, either electrical or chemical in nature, and processing their chart records can give rise to chart-reading and data processing problems of considerable magnitude. In particular, the application of drift-correction means that repetitive calculations have to be performed in a manner similar to the one outlined above for single-channel AutoAnalyzers, but on a much bigger scale as a SMA 12/60 produces 12 sets of results on 60 specimens during each hour of its operation.

Laboratories that handle large workloads have turned, therefore, to computers for assistance, either when monitoring and acquiring data from automatic equipment or when processing data in the preparation of reports and in statistical assessments. Systems have been developed which use computers off-line for batch-processing of analytical data (Flynn, 1965), and others have been produced which use dedicated computers on-line to the analytical equipment (for a review, see Whitby, 1970). The computer systems have so far been mainly concerned, from the analytical standpoint, with processing the output from single-channel or multi-channel AutoAnalyzers, but it should be noted that those forms of equipment that generate a fixed voltage output, and equipment which generates a rising analog signal, also require to have their performance monitored. Both these other categories of equipment are subject to drift, and checks need to be applied to ensure their continued reliability of performance. If used extensively, therefore, equipment generating fixed voltage output or a rising analog signal can give rise to problems of data acquisition and data processing of magnitudes comparable to the continuous flow analytical systems, as exemplified by the AutoAnalyzer.

### Data acquisition from AutoAnalyzers for batch-processing by an off-line computer

It is necessary first to convert the peak heights on the chart-records into a digital form suitable for input to the computer. This can be performed by a shaft-encoder which detects and records the position of the recorder pen after it has reached a peak, as it changes its direction of movement in falling away from the peak. The voltage reading corresponding to the pen's position is coded in binary form on to punched tape or cards (Flynn *et al.*, 1966; Rappoport *et al.*, 1967). These electromechanical systems only record the fact that a peak has occurred, but can tell nothing about the shape of the peak. In addition, special arrangements have to be made for maintaining the ordered sequence in which data are recorded, to cater for the possibility that peaks corresponding to one or more specimens fail to appear on the chart (e.g. on account of a temporary blockage in the analytical system). Having received the coded peak heights as input, the computer program can undertake various procedures such as testing the acceptability of standard curves or applying corrections for instrumental drift.

As an alternative to using electro-mechanical systems for peak detection, peak heights can be read off the chart records by eye using a Y-plotter or an X-Y plotter. A stylus is placed on the chart at the point corresponding to a peak, and the application of pressure closes an electrical circuit. The position of the stylus is recorded in terms of the relevant coordinates, the value being coded automatically on to punched tape. This equipment is cheaper and more versatile than the electromechanical systems, and has the advantage that an assessment of the shape of each peak is made, even though this assessment requires the attention of a technician.

It is important to note, with all these systems, that data are processed in batch form by the computer at the end of each run of analyses. The time-scale of the batch-processing of the results means that the computer may, and does, sometimes reject results for a whole batch of analyses, often for a seemingly trivial reason. If this occurs, the message indicating rejection by the computer usually is received some time after the laboratory staff thought that the analytical work had been completed, which can be very inconvenient (Whitby *et al.*, 1968). Partly for this reason, interest shifted from the use of off-line to on-line computer methods for clinical chemistry laboratories. However, the importance of the off-line systems as a stage in the development of computer applications for these laboratories should not be underestimated, since the pioneering work of Flynn and his colleagues with an Elliott 803 computer (Flynn, 1965; Flynn *et al.*, 1966) greatly facilitated the introduction of the dedicated systems, based on an Elliott 903 computer, which are now in operation in several laboratories in Britain.

## Data acquisition from AutoAnalyzers using a dedicated computer

Several different dedicated computer systems are now commercially available for use in clinical chemistry laboratories. All of these offer program packages that make possible the monitoring of AutoAnalyzers on-line to the computer. The programs include a series of instructions and criteria on the basis of which the computer can recognise and examine the output of AutoAnalyzers, and builds up in core a representation of each peak as it appears, equivalent to the chart record shown in Figure 28. With most of these on-line monitoring systems, the signals for the computer are generated by a retransmitting slide-wire fitted to the AutoAnalyzer recorder, but the Elliott 903 system (Table XXIV) takes its signals direct from the detector modules (e.g. colorimeter, flame photometer or fluorimeter) and amplifies these for transmission to the computer. These analog voltages have to be digitised by an analog digital converter, and the hardware includes a multiplexor which allows the computer to recognise and accept signals from several different analytical channels on-line at the same time. The frequency with which the computer program examines these inputs varies from once every 40 milliseconds to once every two seconds, depending on the computer system being used.

When a series of readings for a channel has been obtained, the program enters a peak detection routine and, for each acceptable peak, the computer temporarily stores the digital value corresponding to the raw voltage reading obtained at the top of each peak, as seen in Figure 28. For multi-channel analysers, the programs for detecting the digital values corresponding to the voltages at each plateau (Fig. 29) are generally simpler than the foregoing outline description, but the computer again temporarily stores one value per analysis.

At the start of each analytical run, besides applying criteria of acceptability to individual peaks, the computer searches for and validates the calibration curves on the basis of the criteria stipulated in the program. The computer stores the value corresponding to each calibrating standard. In most of the systems, the computer thereafter uses these values for calculation purposes by interpolating the peak value for a specimen of unknown concentration (after any necessary drift-correction) between the peak readings obtained for the appropriate pair of calibrating standards, and then applies a simple linear concentration relationship. Other methods of programming (e.g. Bennet et al., 1970) employ curve-fitting procedures which measure the goodness of fit for values observed with calibration standards by means of a third order polynomial, in which the assay value (A) is expressed as a function of the peak reading (P):

$$A = a + bP + cP^2 + dP^3 \qquad \text{(Equation 8.1)}$$

If a fault is detected in the overall pattern of the calibration curve, as distinct from a fault in an individual peak, a message appears on the control teletype. With the Elliott 903 system, fault messages are provided within 10 to 30 seconds of the appearance on the chart record of the peak corresponding to the last standard (peak 8 of Fig. 28). Calibration curves may contain faults that are so gross that the computer rejects the curve outright, in which case the analytical channel must be stopped, the reason for the fault located, and the analysis restarted. With more minor faults, a message that requires an answer is output, and the technician is given up to 11 minutes in which to inspect the chart record after receiving the fault message. This is sufficient time for the technician to decide whether to stop the analysis and restart the whole analytical process, or whether it is permissible to instruct the computer to ignore the fault. The latter decision could be taken, for instance, if standard 6 (Fig. 28) had inadvertently been replaced by a second sample of standard 5. There would then have been two satisfactorily shaped peaks on the chart record, corresponding to the positions for standards 5 and 6, but both peaks would have had the height of peak 5. If instructed to use a faulty calibration curve of this nature, the computer would have ignored the faulty standard 6, and would have applied a linear interpolation between standards 5 and 7, with a possible loss of reliability of results falling within this region of the curve.

Having accepted the calibration curve, the computer continues its search for peaks and stores the raw values for each until it comes to a drift-correction standard; these occur in regular specified positions (positions 20, 30, etc.; Fig. 28). The peak reading for each drift-correction standard is examined in relation to the value of the drift standard in position 10. If the drift is within acceptable limits, the computer then corrects the values for samples analysed in the interval between the most recent and the preceding drift-correction standard, by applying correction for drift on the basis of an assumed linear change between adjacent drift standards. Having corrected each peak value for drift, the computer interpolates the corrected values in relation to the appropriate pair of calibrating standards (positions 1 to 8; Fig. 28) to obtain the corresponding concentrations. These concentration values are then stored in association with the records for the appropriate patients held on the workfile, and a fail-safe output is generated on paper tape for printing up off-line. The details of the on-line monitoring programs vary from this outline description depending upon the particular computer system used.

It will be apparent from the foregoing paragraphs that, even with trouble-free operation of AutoAnalyzers, computers can relieve laboratory staff from a number of repetitive operations. Dedicated computers, moreover, can serve important process-control functions in real time, by detecting and reporting faults in the operation of the analytical equipment. Included among the messages generated by the computer are warnings to the effect that peaks cannot be detected (suggesting a blockage in the system) or that a peak is misshapen (e.g. due to inadequate amounts of specimen, as with peak 11 in Fig. 28), or that a peak is off-scale, or that unsatisfactory results have been obtained for a quality control specimen of known composition placed in a prescribed position (e.g. positions 19, 29; Fig. 28). A number of other faults, in calibrating and drift-correction standards, may also be reported. It is true that some of these faults can be detected more quickly by a technician whose only duty it is to watch the analytical equipment. A technician solely occupied with these tasks may sometimes recognise a faulty peak within five seconds of its appearance on the chart record. On the other hand, with the Elliott 903 system, the computer does not enter its peak-detection routine until about 15 seconds after the apex of the peak has appeared on the chart-record. Thereafter, depending on the number of other tasks it is currently performing, the computer may take a further 10 to 30 seconds to output an error message. This comparison may reflect unfavourably on the computer, but monitoring of AutoAnalyzer chart records by eye for process-control purposes is an extremely boring task, and attention to the job soon falters.

The hardware detailed in Table XXIV, and the on-line monitoring programs outlined here, have had their performance validated on chemical grounds for 19 of the analyses most often performed in clinical chemistry laboratories (Whitby and Simpson, 1969). For over two years, the computer has been operating regularly on-line to as many as 11 Auto-Analyzer channels at one time, and is now being used for seven days each week. It has become an integral part of the operation of the analytical laboratory, relieving staff of many tedious process-control operations and repetitive chart-reading and calculation steps.

## PREPARATION OF LABORATORY REPORTS

### The various types of report that can be provided

Computers can contribute in many ways to the data-processing steps involved in the preparation of laboratory reports. Apart from cutting down the amount of manual transcription, the generation by the computer of typed reports having a consistent format is helpful in their interpretation. Output programs can be extended to include a variety of statistical routines, which provide additional data needed for the more informed interpretation of results (Flynn, 1969). Despite the computer's potential for ensuring that better use can be made of laboratory data, however, the reporting aspects of laboratory computer systems constitute perhaps the most problematical region when it comes to deciding upon the hardware configuration to install in a clinical chemistry laboratory.

The cost of the system has to be balanced against the type of reports which it can provide; the advantages and disadvantages of different reporting procedures have been reviewed by Flynn *et al.* (1968).

Four different categories of output can be provided by the computer configuration listed in Table XXIV, these being indicated in Figure 27. These four categories should not be regarded as exhaustive—they do not include, for instance, one of the commonest methods of issuing computer-prepared reports, in the form of narrow strips of figures entered on to pre-printed paper, similar to payment-slips used by banks.

The first form of output (Fig. 27) applies to the results of tests which have been requested urgently. These are printed out on the on-line teletype as soon as the work is completed, and are then available for immediate reporting (e.g. by telephone). The second method of output, which applies to all results, is in the form of punched tape generated in segments whenever a batch of calculated results is about to be written away to the magnetic tape files. The paper tape carries the computed results, identified by their position on a worksheet (i.e. without patient identification data), for printing up off-line. When issued in this form, results need to be rounded off to the nearest significant figure, and copied on to standard report forms preferably designed so as to minimise manual transcription (Whitby *et al.*, 1968). These forms at present constitute this laboratory's routine method of issuing reports, but the particular long-term importance of this output is that it provides a fail-safe system for reporting in the event of failure on the magnetic tape units.

The third category of output constitutes a summary of work done, printed up at the end of each day. It consists of a statement of the contents of the computer's workfile, detailing completed work and indicating those tests for which results are still awaited. It provides a document which can be consulted when answering enquiries received about reports which have been issued but which have not yet reached the patients' notes. The slowness of transport and delivery systems in most hospitals, and the delays imposed by sending letters containing reports to doctors outside hospitals, point to the need for extensive rapid data transmission net-works. Major factors determining whether such systems can be intro-duced into medical practice include the costs involved and the difficulty of selecting the most suitable output terminals for hospital wards and consulting rooms.

The last type of report provided by the Elliott 903 system (Table XXIV and Fig. 27) involves the maintenance on computer file of records of work previously carried out on individual patients, the searching of files for these previous records, and the issue of cumulative reports which interrelate past and present findings on individual patients. The system has been shown to be capable of producing these reports (Fig. 30), but

| Date of Birth | SURNAME | | | | INITIALS | Sex | **THE ROYAL INFIRMARY OF EDINBURGH** |
|---|---|---|---|---|---|---|---|
| 17  05  43 | | | | | PD | M | DEPARTMENT OF CLINICAL CHEMISTRY |

Index of Character Codes:
* – Computer (program) suggests special consideration needed.
CS – Contaminated specimen    POST – Post-dialysis
HM – Haemolysed                          TL – Too late for
IS – Insufficient                                      satisfactory analysis
NR – New request needed,         US – Unsuitable specimen
    analysis unsatisfactory.    XX – Test not performed
PRED – Pre-dialysis
Normal ranges are quoted under the test headings for most analyses but if not quoted consult Section D of the Departmental Handbook.

| Ward | Hospital | CONSULTANT/PRACTITIONER |
|---|---|---|
| 26 | RIE | PROF. K. W. DONALD |

BLOOD / PLASMA / SERUM

| Date | Time | Urea (15-40) mg./100ml | Sodium (136-149) meq./l. | Potassium (3.8-5.2) meq./l. | Chloride (100-107) meq./l. | Bicarbonate (24-30) meq./l. | Ion Difference (14-20) meq./l. | Protein-bound Iodine (PBI) (3.9-7.5) µg./100ml. | Cholesterol (140-260) mg./100ml. |
|---|---|---|---|---|---|---|---|---|---|
| 03 02 70 | 0900 | 42 | 138 | 4.3 | 100 | 32 | 10* | | |
| 06 02 70 | 0930 | 43 | 135 | 3.1* | 93 | 34 | 11* | | |
| 09 02 70 | 0900 | 43 | 137 | 4.1* | 101 | 27* | 13 | 4.9 | 220 |
| 24 02 70 | 0830 | 46 | 139 | 4.1 | 105 | 27 | 11* | | |

| Date | Time | Alkaline Phosphatase (3-13) K.A. units/ 100ml. | Thymol Turbidity (0-4) units | Bilirubin ( < 1.0) mg./100ml | Alanine Amino-Transferase (CPT) (10-35) units/ml. | Aspartate Amino-Transferase (GOT) (10-40) units/ml. | Hydroxy-Butyrate Dehydrogenase (HBD) units/ml. | Lactate Dehydrogenase (LDH) (110-400) units/ml. | Creatine Kinase (5-40) I.U./l. |
|---|---|---|---|---|---|---|---|---|---|
| 03 02 70 | 0900 | 12 | | 0.9 | 56* | | | | |

FIG. 30. Part of a cumulative laboratory report prepared with the Elliott 903 computer system (Table XXIV) showing results for investigations performed on four different days. The asterisks are automatically attached by the computer to values which either fall significantly outside the limits of normality for an investigation (e.g. the second result for plasma potassium) or which show significant alterations (more than two analytical standard deviations) from the previous result (e.g. the third values for plasma potassium and bicarbonate, as compared with the second sets of results for these analyses).

limitations imposed by the slow speed of the present output printing equipment means that cumulative reports cannot be issued routinely on the scale required (i.e. about 600 reports each day). Experience has shown that the cumulative type of reporting requires fast output printing equipment (e.g. a line printer), and a later version of the Elliott 903 system incorporating a line printer and the cumulative reporting of results is in an advanced stage of development (Flynn, F. V., personal communication). The rapid preparation of cumulative reports would also be facilitated by keeping records for work in progress in the laboratory on a fast access store (e.g. a magnetic disc or drum); this feature is included in the Clindata System (Digital Equipment Co., Reading, Berks.) and will be available with systems based on the Elliott 905 computer.

## Some special features of cumulative reporting systems
Figure 30 indicates the fact that the computer has been programmed to add an asterisk automatically to the appropriate figure on the report

whenever a single result is abnormal, or when the most recent in a series of results differs significantly from the previous finding. The maximum time-interval for these comparisons is set by the capacity of the computer's file of laboratory records; for this department, this has been calculated as being three months' records. Comparisons of results obtained at different times on individual patients, as presented in cumulative reports, constitute an important aspect of process control of laboratory work which cannot be provided economically by any other method of quality control at present available (Whitby et al., 1967) since these reports allow each patient, to some extent, to serve as his own control or reference point.

Laboratories that aim to issue cumulative reports by computer can either install a relatively expensive dedicated system, or can make use of a hospital or bureau installation to meet the requirements for file-handling and high output capacity associated with cumulative methods of reporting. It is difficult to place a monetary value on the improvements in patient care which should derive from the presentation of laboratory reports in cumulative form, prepared automatically by the computer with attention being drawn to important abnormalities. This difficulty in assessing the cost-benefit attributable to cumulative reports is the main reason for the present lack of agreement about the most appropriate computer system to obtain for a clinical chemistry department.

The preparation of cumulative reports on individual patients by a computer draws attention to the importance of correct and unique identification of patients. In this connection, input and output operations cannot be considered entirely separately. Using manual filing systems, it is possible to compare each request form with records of previous work already on file in a laboratory, and to make some allowance for imperfect matching of identification for patients who are probably one and the same individual—if necessary after consultation with the doctor who completed the request form. With computer-operated records systems, however, the ability to carry out this type of matching and correcting procedure is limited to record linkage techniques (Acheson, 1967), and the advantages of generating computer-acceptable documents for use as laboratory request forms at the time of first registering a patient in a hospital records department (p. 111, 160) can now be better appreciated.

Cumulative reporting systems sometimes draw attention to the possibility that specimens or results may have been interchanged, and become associated with the wrong patient, inasmuch as these reports allow comparisons to be made between consecutive sets of results obtained on individual patients. It would be better, however, to reduce the possibility of interchange of results occurring, and progress is being made with the development of equipment that positively associates specimens obtained from patients in relation to the corresponding request forms. Immediately after collection, a pre-punched stub-card coded with a unique number is attached to the specimen tube; this same number has also been punched into an 80-column punched card which is detached from the specimen's stub-card and is completed as the laboratory request form. The stub-card remains attached to the specimen tube and passes through a card reader at the time the specimen is sampled for analysis, the number on the stub being held in hardware and related in a machine-readable, computer-acceptable way with the peak that appears later on the chart record. This special punched-card equipment has been developed for use with AutoAnalyzer and other automatic apparatus, and sets out to render automatic the identification of specimens, but it is still being evaluated and is currently very expensive.

### The automatic addition of diagnostic comments on reports

Computers have begun to be used for carrying out diagnostic assessments based on the results of laboratory investigations, and diagnostic comments are then sometimes printed automatically on reports. One example is provided by the interpretation of electrophoretic separations of serum protein fractions and of the isoenzyme patterns of lactate dehydrogenase (Pribor *et al.*, 1968). Another example is in the evaluation of acid-base disorders (p. 228), and a third is in the application of numerical taxonomy (or classification processes) to the study of liver disease where the data include the results of a range of chemical investigations (Baron and Fraser, 1968).

The use of a computer to assist in the interpretation of chemical findings must not be allowed to divert attention from the fundamental requirement for reliable data on which to base these diagnostic assessments. This cautionary note needs to be sounded because there would seem to be a tendency, for instance, to attribute a greater degree of quantitative significance to the results of electrophoretic separation than is justified by the semi-quantitative nature of the analytical technique. The 'diagnostic assessments' provided by the computer (Pribor *et al.*, 1968) give an appearance of confidence that the data do not in fact justify.

## STATISTICAL AND QUALITY CONTROL DATA

The different computer systems developed for use in clinical chemistry laboratories all offer opportunities for applying statistical quality control procedures, and the programs written for the configuration listed in Table XXIV include the provision of quality control data in real time. Results for pooled specimens of serum of known composition placed in stipulated positions (19, 29, 39, etc., as in Fig. 28) are examined, and fault messages are generated if the values observed fall outside limits set by the precision of the analytical method. In addition, fault messages drawing attention to excessive drift are printed out if the drift-correction standards (in positions 20, 30, etc., as in Fig. 28) give unacceptable results.

These statistical checks, together with the other on-line monitoring programs, constitute important process-control features that are provided by computers dedicated to the work of clinical chemistry laboratories. Off-line batch-processing systems cannot provide this information in time to influence the operation of the analytical equipment. It would be wrong, however, to claim that this process control is anything other than rudimentary when compared with the completely automated computer-controlled chemical plants operated, for instance, by the petroleum industry. Clinical chemistry laboratories still have a long way to go before any of their work can properly be described as fully automated.

In addition to the real time statistical quality control data mentioned above, several assessments based on the results obtained in each batch of analyses can be carried out at the end of the batch. For instance, the mean value and standard deviation for the results obtained on specimens from patients, in some cases after excluding very abnormal findings, may be calculated. These values for 'patient means' have been shown to be remarkably stable from batch to batch, and to be suitable for plotting cumulative sum charts (Whitehead, 1965). The computer provides these data sufficiently quickly for them to be taken into consideration when the results of each batch of analyses are being assessed prior to issue from the laboratory as reports. These statistical assessments based on batch calculations can be derived from either off-line or on-line computing techniques.

## RELIABILITY OF DEDICATED COMPUTER SYSTEMS IN CLINICAL CHEMISTRY LABORATORIES

Departments which provide a diagnostic service on a routine basis require reliable equipment for their successful operation, and computers are no exception to this requirement. Few data have been published so far, but information is available for the equipment described in Table XXIV. Initially this equipment was operated on an entirely developmental basis, but since the middle of 1969 it has been used daily for a large number of routine operations.

All the peripheral components have developed faults at various times, but spare units are held for some of these, and faults on others do not render the equipment completely unworkable. For instance, a failure on the magnetic tape controller does not prevent the computer being used for its important on-line process-control and calculation functions, even though records cannot be updated on the magnetic tape file. Many of the faults recorded in routine operation have been essentially minor, being detected at the start of a day's work by the laboratory staff and not requiring the services of an engineer. Clearly the system cannot survive failure of its central processor, but the percentage down time due to the computer itself has been 0.4 per cent; this would appear to be an acceptable figure.

## COST CONSIDERATIONS
### Experience with the Elliott 903 system

The equipment listed in Table XXIV cost £33,000 in 1968, and the additions needed to overcome existing limitations (i.e. an extra 8K core, a line-printer, additional channels for monitoring a wider range of equipment, and an edge-punched card system for requesting procedures) will raise the total cost of hardware to about £60,000. The costs of systems analysis and programming expenses are additional, as are the salaries of laboratory staff in so far as their time has been devoted to the developmental aspects of the work. Software costs have been estimated at approximately £25,000, and the chargeable component of laboratory staff salaries is at least £10,000. Operating costs (including staff salaries) attributable solely to the computer system are approximately £8,000 p.a.

To give an idea of time-scale for this relatively circumscribed and definable computer application, problem definition and systems analysis began early in 1966, and the hardware was delivered in mid-1968. There followed an intensive period of program testing, debugging and program rewriting before the system began in 1969 to contribute to the routine operation of the laboratory.

The capital cost of this laboratory's computer system should be seen in relation to the overall running costs of the department; these were approximately £110,000 in 1970. Table XXIII shows the changes which have occurred in the cost per determination, the figures in the table being based on expenditure which includes staff salaries, consumable materials (glassware, chemicals, etc.), building overheads, and the cost (attributed to the year of purchase) of capital equipment. It is worth noting that the average cost of an investigation has been falling during the 20-year period for which figures are available, despite changes in the value of money. These costing figures relate to investigations performed in response to specific requests, since the department has not yet embarked upon a regular programme of screening investigations.

### The influence on costs of different types of configuration for use in laboratories

Comparable figures for the cost of other laboratory-based computer systems are only partly available, the information being restricted usually to the cost of hardware. For dedicated computer systems, the wide variation in capital cost (£10,000 to £60,000) is attributable to differences in the range of analytical equipment that can be monitored on-line, and in the degree of sophistication of the monitoring programs. A large part of the variation in hardware cost is, however, due to the type of backing store (some systems have no backing store), and to the type of output printing equipment.

For a laboratory that aims to provide cumulative records of its work, backing store and high speed output printing equipment (e.g. a line printer) are practically essential, and the backing store should preferably be in the form of a fast access disc or drum. Magnetic discs and line printers are, however, expensive items of hardware to provide as part of a dedicated computer system since their use (especially the use of the line printer) may only be for short periods each day. On the other hand, these items are almost standard features of a central hospital computer installation and of a computer bureau. On a cost-effectiveness basis, therefore, there are strong arguments for favouring one of the combined systems referred to on p. 157. Unfortunately, present indications suggest that there will be few opportunities for considering such combined installations for several years, in view of the overall shortage of money for computer developments in the health services (e.g. Ockenden and Bodenham, 1970). For this reason, many clinical chemistry laboratories have installed computer configurations which aim to meet their total requirements, justifying this decision on the grounds that these departments provide one of the areas where computing in medicine has been shown to work.

The choice of backing store for a dedicated computer largely determines the potential and the limitations of the system. The Elliott 903 configuration (Table XXIV), for instance, can only be provided with a magnetic tape system, which means that the computer cannot be rapidly interrogated about enquiries for results on individual patients (e.g. an urgent telephone call) and respond in real time. This type of reporting requires a fast random access storage device, such as a magnetic disc or drum, and a response time comparable to the modern airline booking systems.

The installation of fast access storage devices for handling enquiries about individual patients in real time depends, for its success, upon accurate unique patient identification. If this basic requirement can be met, and the cost of data transmission networks and terminals becomes more acceptable, the technology already exists for doctors to be able to interrogate laboratory records about the results on their patients. The response time would be slower for results of tests performed several months ago, by then probably on a demounted magnetic tape, than for results obtained within the last few days or hours.

## CONCLUSION
Peacock et al. (1965) described the first major attempt to organise the

work of a clinical chemistry department and its data-processing problems on the basis of a punched-card oriented system, and their description was soon followed by the first account of a process control computer's use in clinical chemistry, on-line to AutoAnalyzers (Blaivas, 1966). These papers heralded a major concentration of interest by clinical chemists on the applications of computers to assist with the wide variety of organisational and analytical problems which together make up much of the daily concern of the staff in these departments.

It is by now widely accepted that computers have much to offer to the clinical chemistry laboratory, and a considerable amount of the experience gained in these experimental studies could be transferred to other hospital laboratory disciplines, especially to haematology. The enthusiasm with which clinical chemists have incorporated computers as powerful extensions to their facilities has had some drawbacks, however, as critical appraisal of the cost-benefits achieved in the laboratory, and evidence for significant effects upon the patterns of medical care, are still lacking. Attempts are now being made to obtain such information, as described in HM(70)50 (1970), but the difficulties of deciding how to determine the effects properly attributable to the introduction of a computer into a constantly developing environment such as a hospital laboratory should not be underestimated. The decision to introduce a computer may in itself require changes in organisation and analytical procedures, and will certainly demand a complete reappraisal of the laboratory's method of working. These effects fall into the category of so-called computer catalysis, and it may be difficult or impossible to disentangle any improvements they may achieve in themselves from the changes in performance properly attributable to the introduction of the computer.

REFERENCES

ACHESON, E. D. (1967). *Medical Record Linkage*. London: Oxford University Press.
BARON, D. N. & FRASER, P. M. (1968). Medical applications of taxonomic methods. *British Medical Bulletin*, **24,** 236–240.
BENNET, A., GARTELMANN, D., MASON, J. I. & OWEN, J. A. (1970). Calibration, calibration drift and specimen interaction in AutoAnalyser systems. *Clinica Chimica Acta*, **29,** 161–180.
BLAIVAS, M. A. (1966). Application of a process control computer in the automated clinical chemistry laboratory. In *Automation in Analytical Chemistry*. Ed. Skeggs, L. T. pp. 452–454. New York: Mediad.
DERRETT, C. J. (1970). The selection of a small real-time computer for bio-medical application. *Bio-medical Engineering*, **5,** 482–492.
FLYNN, F. V. (1965). Computer-assisted processing of biochemical test data. In *Progress in Medical Computing*, pp. 46–51. London: Elliott Medical Automation.

FLYNN, F. V. (1969). Problems and benefits of using a computer for laboratory data processing. *Journal of Clinical Pathology*, **22**, supplement (College of Pathologists), **3**, 62–73.

FLYNN, F. V. and eleven co-authors (1968). Data processing in clinical pathology. *Journal of Clinical Pathology*, **21**, 231–301.

FLYNN, F. V., PIPER, K. A. & ROBERTS, P. K. (1966). Equipment for linking the AutoAnalyzer to an off-line computer. *Journal of Clinical Pathology*, **19**, 633–639.

HM (70)50. (1970). *Hospital Laboratory Services*. London: Department of Health and Social Security.

OCKENDEN, J. M. & BODENHAM, K. E. (1970). *Focus on Medical Computer Development*. London: Oxford University Press.

PEACOCK, A. C., BUNTING, S. L., BREWER, D., COTLOVE, E. & WILLIAMS, G. Z. (1965). Data processing in clinical chemistry. *Clinical Chemistry*, **11**, 595–611.

PRIBOR, H. C., KIRKHAM, W. R. & FELLOWS, G. E. (1968). Programmed processing and interpretation of protein and lactic dehydrogenase isozyme electrophoretic patterns for computer or for manual use. *American Journal of Clinical Pathology*, **50**, 67–74.

RAPPOPORT, A. E., GENNARO, W. D. & CONSTANDSE, W. J. (1967). Cybernetics enters the hospital laboratory. *The Modern Hospital*, **108**, 107–111.

SKEGGS, L. T. (1957). An automatic method for colorimetric analysis. *American Journal of Clinical Pathology*, **28**, 311–322.

SMYTHE, W. J., SHAMOS, M. H., MORGENSTERN, S. & SKEGGS, L. T. (1968). SMA 12/60: A new sequential multiple analysis instrument. In *Automation in Analytical Chemistry*. Vol. I, pp. 105–113. New York: Mediad.

WHITBY, L. G. (1970). Computer processing of data from AutoAnalyzers in clinical chemistry. *Laboratory Practice*, **19**, 170–176.

WHITBY, L. G., MITCHELL, F. L. & MOSS, D. W. (1967). Quality control in routine clinical chemistry. *Advances in Clinical Chemistry*, **10**, 65–156.

WHITBY, L. G., PROFFITT, J. & McMASTER, R. S. (1968). Experience with off-line processing by computer of chemical laboratory data. *Scottish Medical Journal*, **13**, 181–191.

WHITBY, L. G. & SIMPSON, D. (1969). Experience with on-line computing in clinical chemistry. *Journal of Clinical Pathology*, **22**, supplement (College of Pathologists), **3**, 107–124.

WHITEHEAD, T. P. (1965). Computer-assisted statistical uses of laboratory data. In *Progress in Medical Computing*, pp. 52–56. London: Elliott Medical Automation.

WHITEHEAD, T. P., BECKER, J. F. & PETERS, M. (1968). Data processing in a clinical biochemistry laboratory. In *Computers in the Service of Medicine*. Ed. McLachlan, G. & Shegog, R. A. Vol. I, pp. 113–133. London: Oxford University Press.

SUGGESTION FOR FURTHER READING

Automation and data processing in pathology (1969). Symposium organised by the College of Pathologists, London (Edited by Whitehead, T. P.). *Journal of Clinical Pathology*, **22**, supplement (College of Pathologists), **3**, 130 pages.

# CHAPTER NINE

# Computer-assisted Diagnosis

## By F. T. de DOMBAL

## SUMMARY

THIS chapter reviews the concept of clinical diagnosis and draws attention to differences between the way in which the 'diagnostic process' is taught to medical students and the way in which the process is practised. These considerations are fundamental to an understanding of the possible roles of computers, in computer-aided diagnosis, and various ways of applying computer techniques to reduce the uncertainty of the diagnostic process are discussed.

## INTRODUCTION

THE technical problems of introducing computers into the sphere of clinical decision-making may be serious, but they are completely over-shadowed by conceptual problems that stem mainly from the shortage of information about the diagnostic process itself. Thus, Card (1970) stated that 'until we have formulated a theoretical structure, a logic or a calculus of medicine . . . it is not possible to transfer the activities of clinical medicine as we know them . . . to a computer', and Eden (1964) wrote: 'Until the clinician is willing to investigate his own terminology, his own methodology, all the computer engineer, the physical scientist, or the mathematician can do is stand in the wings and help out in very minor ways.' Many other pertinent quotations could be cited, but Scadding's (1967) comment on disease is particularly relevant: 'The word "disease" is in general use without formal definition—most of those using it allowing themselves the comfortable delusion that everyone knows what it means.'

There is general agreement on the nature and size of the problem of what is meant by 'diagnosis', but much less agreement about possible solutions. Discussion has mainly centred around questions such as whether it is better to tackle the conceptual problem or to attempt pragmatic solutions, or again whether to investigate the decision-making process or the clinician in his role as decision-maker.

Ledley and Lusted (1959) pioneered the attempts to develop a formal structure for clinical medicine, and have been supported in this approach by Card and his co-workers (Card 1967; Card 1970; Card and Good 1971). Others (e.g. Edwards, 1962; 1966a, b) accept the need eventually to formulate 'diagnosis' in general terms but argue that, in selected areas of clinical practice, much can already be accomplished using available knowledge and techniques. In practice, short-term studies can help with the long-term development of a formal structure which will describe clinical medicine in mathematical terms.

Significant effort in recent years has been directed towards the problem of whether to investigate the system of decision-making or the man who uses it. A high proportion of the work until recently concentrated on the development of techniques and systems, often computer-based, for improving the process of decision-making. However, as recently pointed out by several authors (Dudley, 1968; Linn, 1969; de Dombal, 1970), these experiments needed to be complemented by studies concerned with the clinician himself, including assessments of his role as a decision-maker, and the methods, strategies and tactics which he employs in making clinical decisions. Again, these two avenues of research are not mutually exclusive, but undue attention has perhaps been directed towards the production of devices and techniques for 'improving' the diagnostic process, and insufficient to the study of doctors, the central figures in clinical decision-making.

Computers have an important part to play in processing medical data in an attempt to discover hitherto unsuspected relationships among clinical attributes, in performing the tedious calculations inherent in such mathematical analysis, in simulating and analysing the performance of doctors and so on. Nevertheless, the central pivot is not the computer. As Lusted (1966) cogently remarks, talk of 'computer diagnosis' or of 'computers doing diagnosis' is not helpful at this time—the central theme must be the diagnostic process itself together with the clinician whose function it is to make medical decisions.

## THE DIAGNOSTIC PROCESS

The term 'diagnosis' is used in many different senses (Engle and Davis, 1963). For some it is synonymous with the diagnostic process, for others with the end-point of the diagnostic process, and for others with the disease that is responsible for the patient's illness. In this chapter, the term 'diagnostic process' is preferred—it can be generally stated as the process whereby a doctor collects information from a patient, evaluates the information, and makes a clinical decision on the basis of this information and evaluation.

### Modelling the diagnostic process

Simulation of the entire diagnostic process cannot be attempted at present because of lack of information (p. 320), but this does not mean that modelling the diagnostic process is impossible. There is an essential difference between modelling and simulation—whereas modelling attempts to represent reality, simulation tries to imitate it. Modelling is, in general, a necessary first step prior to simulation, which then involves the manipulation of a previously constructed model. One of the main tasks in any investigation of the diagnostic process is the construction of a model which will enable the experimenter to predict and explain the phenomena that do in fact occur with a high degree of accuracy.

There is a considerable difference between the diagnostic process as it is currently taught (Fig. 31) and as it is currently practised (Fig. 32). The latter model derives from the early results of our own survey into the methods, strategies and tactics of human and computer-aided diagnosis (de Dombal *et al.*, 1969a, b). It is an example of a basically sequential model, and is by no means finalised—indeed, there are compelling reasons why the model should not be considered as finalised since there is a real danger, in any modelling exercise, that the model itself will acquire a sanctity during its development that makes it difficult to evaluate subsequently in any objective fashion (Ackoff and Sasieni, 1967).

It is somewhat chastening to note the difference between the way in which clinical diagnosis is taught and the way in which it is in fact practised, assuming for the present that the two models both approximate to reality. Comparison of Figures 31 and 32 clearly shows that the two processes bear only a superficial relationship to one another, and this may well have important implications as far as future teaching is concerned. It is the author's view that doctors are not teaching the diagnostic process as such at present, but that techniques of interrogating patients are being taught instead, and it is his belief that it would help clinical medical students if this were to be made clear.

Figure 32 does help to identify areas within the overall framework of diagnosis where computers may be able to assist the clinician, whether it be in obtaining or in evaluating his data. These potential modes of computer assistance will be discussed shortly, but before doing so it is necessary to consider another fundamental question, namely the basic purpose of the diagnostic process. This calls for a consideration of the relative merits of accuracy and certainty.

**Accuracy and certainty in the diagnostic process**
Accuracy of diagnosis is clearly the desired objective, but in clinical decision-making accuracy is perhaps less important than certainty, as decisions have to be made and acted upon. This concept of the diagnostic process is partly illustrated in Figure 32.

The diagnostic process can be thought of as involving three 'phases' if it is to be effective. First, the doctor must consider 'the correct diagnosis' as one of a list of practical possibilities. Secondly, he must consider 'the correct diagnosis' to be the most likely possibility, and finally he must reach a degree of certainty about the diagnosis that allows him to take a decision in respect of treatment. Most doctors can manage

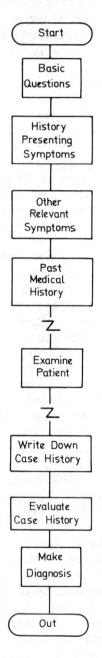

FIG. 31. Schematic model of the diagnostic process as commonly taught at present.

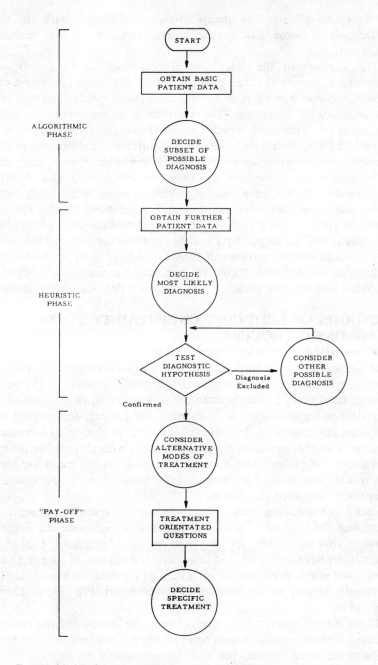

START

OBTAIN BASIC
PATIENT DATA

ALGORITHMIC
PHASE

DECIDE
SUBSET OF
POSSIBLE
DIAGNOSIS

OBTAIN FURTHER
PATIENT DATA

DECIDE
MOST LIKELY
DIAGNOSIS

HEURISTIC
PHASE

TEST
DIAGNOSTIC
HYPOTHESIS

Diagnosis
Excluded

CONSIDER
OTHER
POSSIBLE
DIAGNOSIS

Confirmed

CONSIDER
ALTERNATIVE
MODES OF
TREATMENT

"PAY-OFF"
PHASE

TREATMENT
ORIENTATED
QUESTIONS

DECIDE
SPECIFIC
TREATMENT

FIG. 32. Model of the diagnostic process as currently practised (de Dombal
and Gill, 1970).

the first two phases, but many encounter difficulty with the third, particularly if some risk to the patient attaches to the method of treatment.

This concept of the diagnostic process leads on to an important proposition, namely that the prime function of a system designed to aid clinical decision-making is to reduce uncertainty rather than to increase the accuracy of diagnosis. The distinction is important. Instead of 'diagnosis by computer', which Lusted (1966) rightly described as unhelpful, the aim should be to secure 'computer-aided diagnosis' in which doctors can use computers just as they use other special methods of investigation, to strengthen the basis on which they take decisions. Doctors do not require a computer-based system which will, for any given case, scan all known diseases and select from its files the 'most likely' diagnosis, even if such a system were possible. On the other hand, they might well be helped by a number of more limited systems, each of which would operate for a small subset of related diseases, within these constraints helping the doctor by reducing his uncertainty about the diagnosis and thereby assisting him to take a decision about treatment.

## METHODS OF REDUCING UNCERTAINTY IN THE DIAGNOSTIC PROCESS
### The provision of further information
The doctor who passes through the type of process modelled in Figure 32 but who still has no clear idea as to the 'correct' diagnosis, or the optimal form of treatment, generally attempts to acquire more information. He may ask further questions, or re-examine the patient, or request a series of special investigations. It would be possible, in theory, to increase the clinician's level of certainty by providing him with all possible information about the patient, and a computer-based system could be devised that would even obtain such detailed information from the patient before the patient contacted the doctor.

This is a misleading view, since there is no guarantee in practice that increasing the amount of available information increases the degree of certainty that the doctor can achieve in respect of diagnosis. Indeed, our own studies have indicated that increasing the volume of data can have a deleterious effect, even though each item of information may in itself be potentially helpful to the solution of the problem (Fig. 33; de Dombal et al., 1970).

There is thus a major difference between the human and the computer in terms of diagnostic accuracy, since additional information may benefit a computer-based system, but will not necessarily do so for a human. This can be exemplified by comparing two information situations, in which a computer achieves accuracy and certainty levels of $x'$ and $y'$ on the basis of, say, 25 items of information and corresponding levels of x

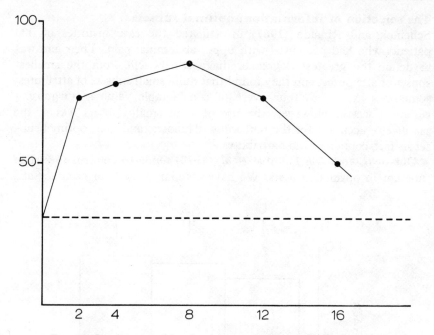

Fig. 33. Pattern recognition by doctors; this figure shows the average percentage of patterns correctly identified by a group of doctors when provided with increasing numbers of elements of intrinsically helpful information and asked to ascribe the patterns to one of three categories (de Dombal *et al.*, 1970). There were 100 patterns in each series, and the interrupted horizontal line shows the number of patterns that would have been correctly identified by chance alone. In this example, 'diagnostic accuracy' becomes impaired as the amount of information exceeds eight items. *Ordinate*: the number of patterns correctly identified; *Abscissa*: the number of elements in the pattern matrix.

and y on the basis of 10 items. For the computer, the levels x′ and y′ would almost certainly be higher than x and y, provided that the additional 15 items of information were themselves helpful. As far as a human is concerned, however, there would be no guarantee that this would be the case—indeed, for the human, levels of x′ and y′ might even be lower than their counterparts x and y. In practical terms, therefore, there is reason to question the relevance or validity of any computer-based system for which the prime function is to provide more information to the doctor.

There is an interesting corollary to this. If doctors are conservative processors of information, becoming less efficient as the input of information increases, the question arises whether a system should set out to provide him with less information rather than more, provided the same amount of certainty can be extracted from the smaller volume of data. This introduces the concept of optimal subsets.

## The selection of information: optimal subsets

Scheinok and Rinaldo (1967) investigated the case histories of 300 patients who had presented with upper abdominal pain. Their aim was to define the greatest degree of diagnostic benefit from the smallest subset of attributes, and they found that quite small subsets of attributes, sometimes as few as four, were of considerable value in diagnosing certain diseases. However, the use of such small subsets was at the sacrifice of accuracy for the remaining diagnoses, and their optimal subset in fact contained nine attributes.

Our own work (de Dombal *et al.*, 1970) tends to confirm the value inherent in optimal subsets. We have compared levels of accuracy and

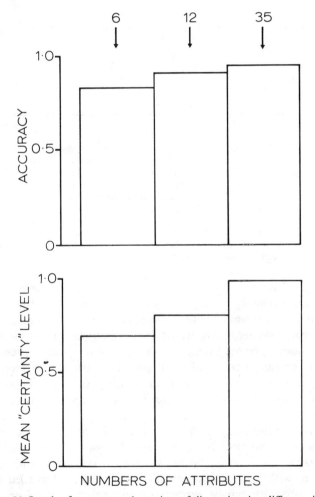

FIG. 34. Levels of accuracy and certainty of diagnosis using different sizes of subsets of attributes (for explanation, see text).

certainty using a subset of six attributes, a subset of 12 attributes, and a 'full' analysis involving as many as 35 attributes (Fig. 34). In our relatively small series, we found a higher level of diagnostic accuracy than did Scheinok and Rinaldo (1967), who obtained an overall ratio of 0.58 for accuracy of diagnosis. Figure 34 is of interest, however, in comparing the levels of accuracy and certainty obtained using the subsets. It would appear that six attributes were sufficient to obtain a fair degree of overall accuracy, and that 12 attributes were almost as effective as 35 in terms of accuracy, but that the additional attributes improved the certainty of diagnosis.

## The selection of information: sequential analysis

Several authors have suggested an alternative method of obtaining maximal levels of certainty from minimal amounts of information (e.g. Gorry, 1970; Taylor, 1970). They replace the simple model (Fig. 31) by a sequential model (Fig. 35) in which the doctor first assesses the diagnostic problem and decides upon the attribute most likely to be of value in that particular situation. He then receives the relevant item of information, reassesses the problem, and repeats the process until his degree of certainty reaches the desired level. A major problem with this scheme is how to select the next best test and both Gorry (1970) and Taylor (1970) suggested that a computer-based system, using variants of Bayes' theorem, might be of value in suggesting this test to the doctor. With the aid of such a system, Taylor (1970) demonstrated a diagnostic accuracy of 93 per cent in a series of 56 cases of thyroid disease, usually arriving at a final probability level of over 0.99 using less than 12 tests.

In principle, this is an extremely useful way of solving the problem of having too much information available. The doctor can be assisted in his processing of information, and can be 'guided' (Taylor, 1970) towards a diagnosis using a minimal amount of information. In practice, however, there are problems since we would question the assertion by Taylor (1970) that this sequential approach is already carried out in clinical practice. Indeed, our own preliminary results indicate that in many cases exactly the opposite occurs, clinicians tending to think in subsets of questions rather than in terms of individual attributes (de Dombal *et al.*, 1970).

Another, and far more important, objection to the sequential analysis of data is the fact that none of the systems so far introduced has contained any concept of cost, as the authors themselves have pointed out. It may be easy to select the next best test (Fig. 35) on the basis of the usefulness of the information it will contain, but it can be far more difficult to balance its value against the cost (not necessarily monetary) of obtaining the information. For instance, when presented with a patient suffering

from an 'acute abdomen' the most informative test is immediate lapar-
otomy, but the cost of such a step to the patient is such that this is
rarely the initial test. Again, in the investigation of thyroid disorders, the
'optimal' sequence suggested by Taylor (1970) involves the elicitation of

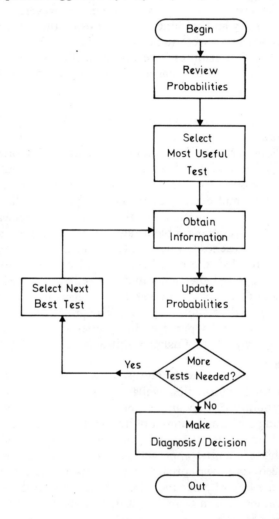

FIG. 35. Sequential model of the diagnostic process, after Gorry (1970) and
Taylor (1970).

one physical sign, followed by a series of lengthy biochemical tests,
followed by the elicitation of a further physical sign; this sequence
ignores any cost to the patient in terms of the time involved. Unfortunately, as Card (1970) points out, we have no means as yet of estimating in
quantitative terms the cost of each investigation.

**Sequential analysis and decision trees**

Attempts have been made (e.g. Lusted, 1966; Edwards, 1970) to formalise the sequential approach to diagnosis into a flow chart or 'decision tree' (Fig. 36), and to provide this for doctors to use. This is another useful idea, in principle, but in practice it suffers from several disadvantages. Unless restricted to a circumscribed situation, the 'tree' can become very

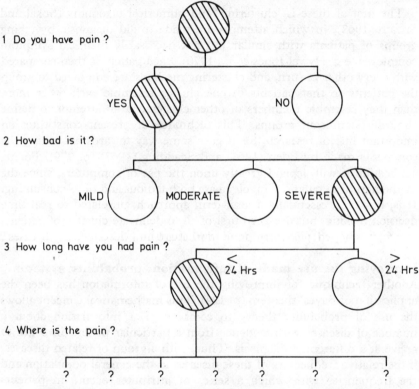

1 Do you have pain ?

2 How bad is it ?

3 How long have you had pain ?

4 Where is the pain ?

FIG. 36. The use of a 'decision-tree' in an approach to the diagnosis of abdominal pain showing the limitations of this approach. The 'severity' of pain is an arbitrary and subjective assessment, and the 'site of pain' shows considerable variation.

unwieldy (Edwards, 1970), but the use of 'trees' in very limited situations reduces their value considerably. Another major disadvantage of a 'logical decision tree' is that it loses that degree of flexibility which is perhaps the doctor's greatest asset at present, by restricting each successive course of action, and by assuming a small number of alternatives in the patient's responses.

**Improving the use made of information: clustering techniques**

We have already suggested that the provision of additional information may confuse rather than help the doctor. Conversely, reduction in the amount of information may diminish the accuracy and certainty of diagnosis. There is, however, a possible answer to this dilemma, namely to provide a system which enables the doctor to extract a greater degree of certainty from the information which he routinely collects from the patient. Several techniques have been suggested for accomplishing this aim.

The first of these is 'clustering' and numerical taxonomy (Sokal and Sneath, 1963), in which attempts are made to aid diagnosis by taking groups of patients with similar but not necessarily identical symptom complexes (e.g. Hywel Jones et al., 1970). Each patient is then compared with every other in turn, and clustering methods are employed to group the patients so that patients in one cluster resemble each other more than they resemble members of other clusters, in an attempt to define clinically significant groups. This technique at present constitutes an important line of research, for it goes some way towards answering the comments made by Eden (1964) and Scadding (1967) (p. 179). For its application it will depend greatly upon the use of computers, since the mathematical calculations involved are both tedious and time-consuming. It is, however, essentially a long-term approach, unrelated to real time decision making, but designed first of all to delineate clusters of patients which, it is hoped, will correspond to what are now described as 'diseases'.

**Improving the use made of information: probability systems**

Another technique for improving the use of information has been the application of Bayes' theorem (p. 124). This mathematical concept allows the use of probability theory to combine prior information about a number of diseases with evidence from a particular patient in order to arrive at a differential diagnosis. Thus, with a group of related diseases, if the relative frequencies of these diseases in the general population and the frequencies with which a series of attributes occurs in patients suffering from each disease are known, the probability can be calculated that a new patient with a particular symptom complex (S) suffers from a certain disease (D) (Table XXV).

Variants of this concept, employing the calculating ability of computer-based systems, have been applied to the computer-assisted diagnosis of thyroid disease (Winkler et al., 1967; Taylor, 1970), Cushing's syndrome (Nugent et al., 1964), bone tumours (Lodwick, 1963), congenital heart disease (Warner et al., 1964) and abdominal pain of acute onset (de Dombal et al., 1970). Of particular interest are those studies which have attempted to compare the performance of doctors, aided by some form of 'Probability Information Processing' (PIP) system, with the performance of unaided doctors (e.g. Edwards, 1966a, b; Kaplan and Newman, 1966). It would appear that human estimation of probabilities

TABLE XXV

Data-base of probability values for groups of patients with various diseases, all of which gave rise to acute abdominal pain (100 patients in each group)

| Disease | PS/D Sex | | PS/D Age (years) | | | | | | PS/D Duration of pain (hours) | | |
|---|---|---|---|---|---|---|---|---|---|---|---|
| | M | F | 0–9 | 10–19 | 20–29 | 30–39 | 40–49 | Over 50 | 0–12 | 12–24 | Over 24 |
| Appendicitis | 60 | 40 | 22 | 33 | 22 | 8 | 5 | 10 | 13 | 47 | 40 |
| Diverticulitis | 39 | 61 | 0 | 0 | 2 | 2 | 10 | 86 | 9 | 10 | 81 |
| Perforated duodenal ulcer | 85 | 15 | 0 | 4 | 7 | 9 | 26 | 54 | 65 | 12 | 23 |
| Non-specific pain | 42 | 58 | 14 | 41 | 19 | 7 | 5 | 14 | 25 | 12 | 63 |
| Cholecystitis | 32 | 62 | 0 | 1 | 8 | 4 | 9 | 78 | 28 | 12 | 60 |
| Small bowel obstruction | 60 | 40 | 2 | 6 | 24 | 6 | 14 | 48 | 14 | 24 | 62 |

PS/D represents the probability (P) that a symptom complex (S) would be observed with a particular disease (D) of alternative diseases may be inferior to that obtained with Bayes' theorem by using a PIP system, and our experience (de Dombal *et al.*, 1970) also suggests that PIP systems would merit further study.

There are several drawbacks, however, to the use of Bayes' theorem in clinical medicine, and these need to be briefly mentioned. In the first place, attributes need to be mutually exclusive. For example, the use of nausea, vomiting, and dehydration as unrelated attributes would raise problems, since these attributes are interdependent in a way which we do not as yet fully understand. Secondly, Bayesian PIP systems do not cater well for very rare diseases, and thirdly these systems depend upon an accurate 'data-base' of clinical information; unless such a base (e.g. Table XXV) can be constructed, final probabilities are open to considerable inaccuracy.

### Improving the use of information: matching to stereotypes and the use of weighting

A relatively simple method of increasing certainty in the diagnostic process is to match individual cases to stereotypes for various diseases previously constructed from data such as those shown in Table XXV. In this example, the stereotypes of appendicitis, perforated duodenal ulcer and small bowel obstruction would be male, and those of the other diseases would be female. In addition, appendicitis occurs mainly below the age of 30, diverticulitis in patients over 50 and so on. By extending this approach, it may be simple to match additional cases to the stereotypes for each disease, and to make the assumption that the most likely disease in each new case is that with the largest number of matching factors.

The chief merit of this system is its simplicity, but a major drawback of this type of pattern-matching is that it does not extract all the information inherent in the data. For instance, using Table XXV, a 'match' for appendicitis as regards sex (where the distribution is 60 to 40) would be treated in the same way as a 'match' for perforated duodenal ulcer (where the distribution is 85 to 15). In an attempt to remedy this, various authors (e.g. Lipkin, 1964; Ledley, 1969) have used 'weights' or some form of discriminant function analysis, replacing a simple positive or negative 'match' (which carries a score of plus or minus one respectively) by a positive or negative 'weight' the numerical value of which is a function of the significance of that attribute in the diagnosis of that disease. The numerical values of these weights may be calculated using discriminant function analysis or likelihood ratios (Lusted, 1966; Ledley, 1969).

It is a useful simplification to regard the 'weighted stereotype' form of analysis as a process intermediate between the complex and precise probability systems, and simple stereotype matching systems which pay little heed to probability. The successful application of any system of weighting clearly depends upon the use of computers and their calculating facility, at least in the early stages. However, once a discriminant function analysis has been satisfactorily performed, simple weighting systems for specific groups of differential diagnoses should be able to be drawn up for general availability to doctors.

## THE ROLE OF THE DOCTOR

This brings us back to the central figure, the clinician himself. In the last few years, interest in his role has increased enormously, and several important observations and studies have been published (e.g. Scadding, 1967; Dudley, 1968; Linn, 1969; Young, 1970). There has been much debate on how best to 'investigate' the clinician, for instance by observing him or by constructing an analogous situation and then, using models and simulation techniques, to measure his performance. It is possible to combine these methods, and to compare results obtained in real life with those obtained in artificial situations. There are many problems in making these observations, since the intrusion of an observer into a real-life situation is in itself bound to alter that situation, and there is no guarantee that a clinician's performance in an artificial environment will reflect what he does in real life.

An interesting approach has been the production of 'cognitive' structures from observed behaviour. In this, doctors are asked to 'think aloud' during diagnostic problem-solving sessions, and there is some evidence (e.g. Reitman, 1964; Taylor, 1966) that subsequent analysis of these data may enable computer programs to be written which in certain respects parallel the observed behaviour. Arising out of such studies has been the development of several interesting hypotheses concerning doctors' approaches to the diagnostic process. Thus, Dudley (1968) has distinguished between such approaches as pattern-recognition, heuristic or goal-seeking behaviour, and 'pay-off' where the chief consideration is the probable outcome to the patient after a number of alternative decisions about treatment. This is a very interesting concept, and Dudley is almost certainly correct in asserting that these three methods feature extensively in the diagnostic process as applied by many clinicians in their own practice.

Our own studies (de Dombal and Gill, 1970) allow us to suggest what is perhaps a logical extension of this argument. In addition to the three possibilities discussed by Dudley (1968), we believe there is a fourth, the logical decision-tree or 'algorithmic' approach and that all four approaches are used by clinicians in a flexible way. To illustrate this, in the model of the diagnostic process (Fig. 32), the first steps can be described as 'algorithmic', since doctors generally begin their questioning of patients in a fairly standard fashion until they have some idea of the specific problem that is being presented to them. They next move to a phase which is certainly not algorithmic, in which they attempt to achieve both accuracy and certainty of diagnosis, and heuristics coupled with pattern-matching may both form important parts of the activities at this stage. Finally, doctors move to yet another phase, in which their prime interest is in the impending decision about treatment, and in this phase the pay-off approach predominates (Fig. 33). The length of each phase is affected by factors such as seniority, experience, urgency of the situation and difficulty of diagnosis (de Dombal and Gill, 1970).

It might be thought that the computer can play a relatively small part in investigating the decision-maker, but this is not in fact the case. Computer programs that parallel human thought-processes have been written (p. 180, 187). In addition, computer-based systems can be used to provide Bayesian analyses for comparison with human estimates of probability (e.g. Edwards, 1966a, b), or to provide artificial patterns for doctors to analyse (de Dombal *et al.*, 1969c, 1970), or to produce on the basis of known probabilities artificial 'patients' (Chapter 16) which can be used for the analysis of performance of both doctors and students.

## PROBLEMS OF INTRODUCING COMPUTERS INTO THE FIELD OF CLINICAL DECISION-MAKING

### The lack of clinical data and the existence of observer error
Any computer-based system for assisting the diagnostic process can only be as good as the clinical data provided to it. For example, our own simple system was initially informed that 99 per cent of patients with appendicitis suffered from rectal bleeding, because of an undetected transposition of data, and this temporarily caused confusion in the computer-based decisions between appendicitis and diverticulitis. The provision of an adequate and accurate 'data-base' drawn from a representative sample of patients is a mandatory first step as far as any system based on probabilities is concerned, or else a system that works well in the computing laboratory will fail dismally when applied to clinical practice.

As a corollary, the problem of observer error has to be considered. Observer error is an inherent part of medicine, both in respect of patients' descriptions and doctors' observations. We must accept this and try to take it into account as part of the process which measures the lack of certainty. This means that, at no point in the program of a computer-based system, should a decision hang upon a subjective assessment such as a distinction between pain that is described as severe or as only moderately severe.

### The selection of attributes or variables
There is little reason to assume that the clinical attributes and variables

which are currently measured and recorded are necessarily the best that can be devised, either in the sense of yielding the maximum statistical information or in any other sense. For instance, pulse rate and temperature have probably reached their pre-eminence in the clinical world not because of any major intrinsic value but because they can be measured easily and with a reasonable degree of accuracy (Maloney, 1968).

## Rare events and diseases

Computers are notoriously inefficient when dealing with rare events or diseases. For example, unless a computer-based system is aware of the possibility that pain in the right iliac fossa may be caused by right lower lobe pneumonia, such a diagnosis cannot by definition be entertained by the system. However, in order to allow a computer-based system to consider this possibility, which may not happen often but which can usually be recognised by doctors, much additional information concerning pneumonia and several other similar but nevertheless rare possibilities must be provided to the system, which then becomes unwieldy.

This impasse is inevitable as long as computers are expected to perform in essentially the same way as doctors making the 'correct' diagnosis from a large number of possibilities, some of which are common and some rare. If, however, the computer's function is seen as complementing the doctor's role by increasing certainty rather than accuracy in diagnosis, then the problem of the significant but rare event becomes much less important.

## Considerations of costs and of effectiveness

Discussions of cost are premature until the role that the computer is to perform has been defined, and studies of cost-effectiveness are therefore ruled out at present. Also, to judge the effectiveness of a computer-based system, it is necessary to decide first what the system is to do, and then to compare it with a doctor when carrying out the diagnostic process with his unaided faculties. The difficulties here again must not be underestimated, since the qualities which contribute to effectiveness in decision-making are difficult to define.

Often a doctor is characterised as 'brilliant' if he makes 'spot diagnoses' of unusual complaints which ultimately turn out to be correct, but is this really the aim of diagnosis? The difficulty in assessing effectiveness in decision-making can be highlighted by asking how one compares such a 'brilliant' clinician with his colleague who never succeeds in recognising diagnostic rarities but who rarely makes a mistake as far as the common diseases are concerned; and again by asking how one compares either of the foregoing with a third doctor, perhaps a very experienced general practitioner, who may care little for the finer aspects of diagnostic accuracy but whose decisions about treatment may almost invariably be correct. When eventually computer-based systems are introduced to help clinicians, on any scale, not the least of the problems will be the measurement of their effectiveness in so helping.

## Clinicians – a heterogeneous group

This leads on to perhaps the greatest problem of all in the introduction of computer-based systems into the procedures involved in making clinical decisions. Not only are we faced with patients and diseases, both of which are variable, but also with a group of clinicians who are in themselves heterogeneous. Each clinician has his own method of making a diagnosis, and any attempt to generalise on the basis of a few observations is fraught with danger. Equally, any attempt to provide a computer-based system for clinicians to use must be preceded by a very careful study of whether the particular group of doctors involved actually want or need such a system.

There are three possible ways of overcoming this problem. First, by studying groups of clinicians, it may be possible to extrapolate enough to produce a system which will be sufficiently flexible in a general way to conform to the clinical practice of most of those who are hoping to use it. As an alternative, because conformity to the clinician's practice may be impossible or undesirable, his diagnostic technique may have to be altered to conform with the system that he will use. The third possibility is to devise a system that is so personalised that it will adapt to the individual clinician. In the Department of Surgery at the University of Leeds, we consider that an adaptive system has many advantages.

The prime purpose of an adaptive system is to assist the individual doctor in whatever fashion seems most appropriate to him at the time. For instance, if the doctor wishes to increase his level of certainty before taking a decision about treatment, then the system should adapt to this wish. If on the other hand the doctor wants to be reminded of some uncommon diagnostic possibilities, the system should be able to meet this requirement. Another use for the adaptive system would be for it to monitor the doctor's methods of collecting data rather than his evaluation of the data, and there are other possible methods of use. We believe that the only computer-based diagnostic systems that are likely to find acceptance in the long term will be those that can accept individual variations and seek to conform to them, but these are very demanding requirements.

Any adaptive system requires a vast amount of data, not only about diseases and patients but about clinicians also. Our own studies on clinicians, with a current accumulation of about 50,000 data points, have probably only scratched the surface. In addition, many ethical questions are raised by the advent of such systems. For example, it is perfectly feasible for a clinician's 'opinion', based on probabilities, to be given without the clinician being aware of the patient's existence. But if this opinion should happen to be wrong, the question arises as to who is to blame. The possibilities include the clinician, whose 'opinion' is being taken for granted, the computer scientists, and the clinician who collected the data. Without making any extravagant claims for the future of adaptive systems, it is perhaps safe to assert that it is high time serious thought was being given to this type of problem.

## CONCLUSION

As a general principle, it cannot be over-emphasised that the introduction of computers into the processes of making clinical decisions should be orientated towards the consumer and not the computer. As Baumeister (1970) has pointed out, enormous harm has already been done by individuals—usually with little or no biomedical experience—whose claims that medicine can be revolutionised overnight by computers seem based more on fantasy than reality. Whatever the merits of on-going research, we must realise that computer-aided diagnosis, as a routine procedure, is not yet in sight. Even more important is the realisation that the desired 'end-point' is not merely the provision of such a system but its widespread acceptance by an extremely diverse group of individuals.

REFERENCES

ACKOFF, R. L. & SASIENI, M. W. (1967). *Fundamentals of Operations Research,* p. 384. New York: Wiley.

BAUMEISTER, C. F. (1970). Practical everyday uses for the computer in medicine. *Medical Times,* **98,** 182–193.

CARD, W. I. (1967). Towards a calculus of medicine. *Medical Annual,* **85,** 9–21.

CARD, W. I. (1970). The diagnostic process. *Journal of the Royal College of Physicians of London,* **4,** 183–187.

CARD, W. I. & GOOD, I. J. (1971). Logical foundations of medicine. *British Medical Journal,* **1,** 718–720.

DE DOMBAL, F. T. (1970). The teaching of clinical diagnosis using a computer-based system. In *Proceedings of the IFIP World Conference on Computer Education.* Ed. Scheepmaker, R. Vol. 3, pp. 77–78. Amsterdam: International Federation of Information Processing.

DE DOMBAL, F. T. & GILL, P. W. (1970). Unpublished data.

DE DOMBAL, F. T., HORROCKS, J. C., STANILAND, J. R. & GUILLOU, D. (1970). Unpublished data.

DE DOMBAL, F. T., HARTLEY, J. R. & SLEEMAN, D. H. (1969a). A computer assisted system for learning clinical diagnosis. *Lancet,* **1,** 145–150.

DE DOMBAL, F. T., HARTLEY, J. R. & SLEEMAN, D. H. (1969b). Teaching surgical diagnosis with the aid of a computer. *British Journal of Surgery,* **56,** 754–757.

DE DOMBAL, F. T., WOODS, P. A. & HARTLEY, J. R. (1969c). Digoxin: a computer-based diagnostic game. *British Journal of Surgery*, **56**, 625–626.

DUDLEY, H. A. F. (1968). Pay-off, heuristics and pattern recognition in the diagnostic process. *Lancet*, **2**, 723–726.

EDEN, M. (1964). The taxonomy of disease. In *The Diagnostic Process*. Ed. Jacquez, J. A. (Proceedings of a conference held at the University of Michigan, May 1963.) pp. 47–51. Ann Arbor, Michigan: Malloy Lithographing Co.

EDWARDS, W. (1962). Dynamic decision theory and probabilistic information processing. *Institute of Electrical and Electronics Engineers (IEEE), Transactions on Human Factors in Electronics*, **4**, 59–73.

EDWARDS, W. (1966a). Introduction to Revision of opinions by men and man-machine systems. *IEEE Transactions on Human Factors in Electronics*. Special issue, pp. 1–6.

EDWARDS, W. (1966b). Non-conservative probabilistic information processing systems. *Report ESD–TR–66–404*. University of Michigan, Ann Arbor: Engineering Psychology Laboratory, Institute of Science and Technology.

EDWARDS, D. A. W. (1970). Flow charts, diagnostic keys and algorithms in the diagnosis of dysphagia. *Scottish Medical Journal*, **15**, 378–385.

ENGLE, R. J. & DAVIS, B. J. (1963). Medical diagnosis; past present and future. *Archives of Internal Medicine*, **112**, 512–519.

GORRY, G. A. (1970). Modelling the diagnostic process. *Journal of Medical Education*, **45**, 293–302.

HYWEL JONES, J. and six co-authors (1970). The application of numerical taxonomy to the separation of colonic inflammatory disease. *Advance Abstracts of 4th World Conference of Gastroenterology*.

KAPLAN, R. J. & NEWMAN, J. R. (1966). Studies in probabilistic information processing. *IEEE, Transactions on Human Factors in Electronics*, **7**, 49–63.

LEDLEY, R. S. (1969). Practical problems in the use of computers in medical diagnosis. *Proceedings of the IEEE*, **57**, 1900–1918.

LEDLEY, R. S. & LUSTED, L. B. (1959). Reasoning foundations of medical diagnosis. *Science*, **130**, 9–21.

LINN, B. S. (1969). Statistics, computers and clinical judgment. *Lancet*, **2**, 48–60.

LIPKIN, M. (1964). The role of data processing in the diagnostic process. In *The Diagnostic Process*. Ed. Jacquez, J. A. pp. 255–281. Ann Arbor, Michigan: Malloy Lithographing Co. (See Eden (1964) for full details.)

LODWICK, G. S. (1963). A probabilistic approach to the diagnosis of bone tumours. *Radiological Clinics of North America*, **3**, 487–497.

LUSTED, L. B. (1966). *Introduction to Medical Decision Making*. Springfield, Illinois: Thomas.

MALONEY, J. V. (1968). The trouble with patient monitoring. *Annals of Surgery*, **168**, 605–614.

NUGENT, C. A., Warner, H. R. & Dunn, J. T. (1964). Probability theory in the diagnosis of Cushing's disease. *Journal of Clinical Endocrinology*, **24**, 621–627.

REITMAN, W. R. (1964). Information processing models in psychology. *Science*, **144**, 1192–1198.

SCADDING, J. G. (1967). Diagnosis: the clinician and the computer. *Lancet*, **2**, 877–882.

SCHEINOK, P. A. & RINALDO, J. A. (1967). Symptom diagnosis: optimal subsets for upper abdominal pain. *Computers and Bio-medical Research*, **1**, 221–236.

SOKAL, R. R. & SNEATH, P. H. A. (1963). *Principles of Numerical Taxonomy*. London: W. H. Freeman.

TAYLOR, D. W. (1966). Cognitive processes in solving algebra word problems. In *Problem Solving*. Ed. Kleinmuntz, B. p. 120. New York: Wiley.

TAYLOR, T. R. (1970). Computer-guided diagnosis. *Journal of the Royal College of Physicians of London*, **4**, 188–195.

WARNER, H. R., TORONTO, A. F. & VEASEY, L. G. (1964). Experience with Bayes theorem for computer diagnosis of congenital heart disease. *Annals of the New York Academy of Sciences*, **115**, 558–567.

WINKLER, C., REICHERTZ, P. & KLOSS, G. (1967). Computer diagnosis of thyroid diseases. *American Journal of Medical Science*, **253**, 27–34.

YOUNG, J. Z. (1970). What can we know about memory? *British Medical Journal*, **1**, 647–652.

CHAPTER TEN

# The Analysis of Electrocardiogram and Electroencephalogram Recordings

## By H. R. A. TOWNSEND

### SUMMARY
THIS chapter briefly considers the principal features revealed by electrocardiogram and electroencephalogram recordings, and discusses methods which have been used for the analysis of normal and abnormal records with particular emphasis on computer-based techniques.

### INTRODUCTION
The essential difference between an electrocardiogram (ECG) and an electroencephalogram (EEG) is apparent at first glance (Fig. 37). This difference determines the very varied methods which are used in an attempt to analyse the signals derived by these closely related techniques.

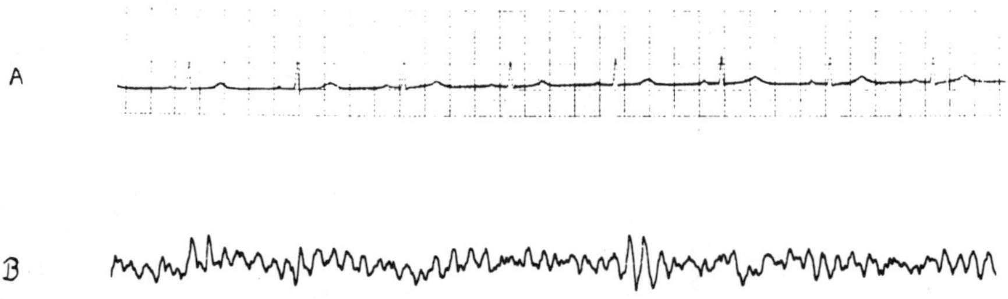

FIG. 37. Upper tracing: An electrocardiogram recording (Lead 1). Lower tracing: A single channel (occipital) of an electroencephalogram recording.

The heart is a single muscle formed from a network of interconnected muscle fibres, each contraction being associated with an electrical change which spreads through this muscle. If the heart is damaged or deformed, the size of the potential and the route by which it travels are altered. In recordings of the electrical potential from the limbs, a complex disturbance occurs with each heart beat. The 'complex' contains a number of component waves which can be identified with the spread of electrical activity over particular parts of the heart muscle, and the object is to infer as much as possible about the mechanism of the heart's contraction from an analysis of these potential changes.

The EEG is essentially a continuous and irregular signal, but it is not completely random. The most obvious feature is its rhythmicity, there being an approximately sinusoidal rhythm occurring at about 10 waves per second (the 'alpha rhythm'). The exact mechanism by which this rhythm is produced is not known, but it is closely related to the activity of the nerve cells of the cortex of the brain which are organised in a very complex manner. The object of the analysis is to characterise the activity statistically in order to permit quantitative comparison and correlation.

## ANALYSIS OF THE ELECTROCARDIOGRAM

### Automated measurement of conventional parameters

Figure 38 illustrates some of the measurements which it is conventional to make on an ECG complex, and automatic ECG analysis attempts to derive these measurements with a minimum of human intervention. The first requirement is to identify the complex, and the reference point which has almost universally been adopted is the instant of maximum rate of change (i.e. the apex of the R wave). It is interesting to note that this is not the way in which the human eye identifies a complex, and that this technique is also inherently liable to be misled by artefacts.

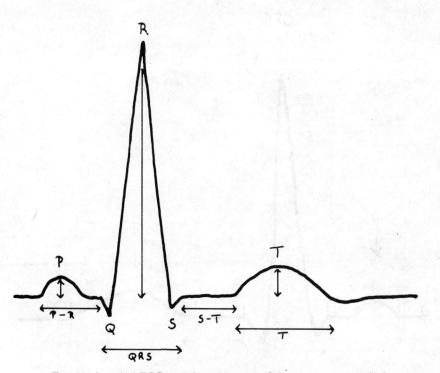

FIG. 38. A typical ECG complex with some of the assessments routinely made illustrated. These include the amplitudes of the P, R and T waves and the duration of the P–R interval, the QRS complex, the S–T interval and of the T wave.

The most successful programs have been those pioneered by Stallman and Pipburger (1961) and developed by Caceres *et al.* (1962). These were designed for a specific purpose, the rapid and economical processing of routine ECG records obtained during large-scale surveys or periodic health check-ups, and they reflect the engineer's approach. Starting from the central reference point the limits of the QRS complex are first determined, the P and T waves on either side are then identified, and finally the starting and finishing points of the P and T waves are fixed and the various measurements recorded.

As an example we may consider the method described by Lawrie and Macfarlane (1968). The moment of maximum spatial velocity or maximum inscription velocity is used as the reference point, and this velocity is determined from three leads simultaneously; it is thus less sensitive to artefacts than the more usual 'maximum negative rate of change'. The QRS complex is defined as 'a continuous region in which the spatial velocity exceeds 3 mv/sec' and the limits of this region approximately define the points at which the complex starts and finishes. Similar

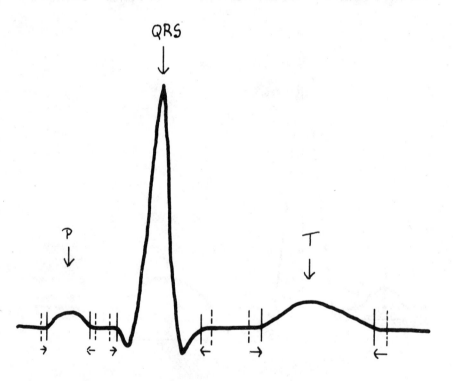

Fig. 39. Diagram of an ECG complex to show the method of searching inwards from the approximate limits of the P wave, QRS complex and of the T wave to determine the exact starting and finishing points of each (after Lawrie and Macfarlane, 1968).

techniques are used to define the approximate limits of the P and T waves. All these points of reference are derived from the three leads considered together, either using orthogonal leads or else conventional leads selected so as to be approximately orthogonal. The actual measurements, however, must be obtained from individual leads considered in isolation, and are derived by determining the times when approximate differentials (measured inwards from the previously identified starting and finishing points) exceed predetermined values (Fig. 39). The strength of this program is the way in which the physics and physiology of the situation have been used in order to make the signal to noise ratio as large as possible. The task of the pattern recognition program is thereby simplified and its accuracy improved.

This approach to the well defined problem of obtaining standard measurements from the ECG exploits available techniques nearly to the limit. Even so, it would clearly be unsuitable as a general purpose program for assessing the ECG recorded from patients with severe cardiac abnormalities, or from infants or animals, at least without a radical redesign. It is, therefore, worth considering whether more general pattern-recognition techniques would have a place in this field. They will probably be more costly in terms of computing time and the computer power required, but may be justified in some situations.

## Pattern matching of electrocardiograms using a computer on-line

A very different approach is exemplified by a device developed for monitoring the ECG and for recognising the occurrence of extrasystoles (Neilson, personal communication). This apparatus makes use of hybrid computing techniques and is therefore relatively inexpensive. It has been specially designed for use in a ward environment, particularly for the long-term monitoring of severely ill patients.

The first section of the device comprises circuits for the detection of cardiac complexes. The incoming signal is differentiated and filtered so as to minimise the ratio of (unwanted) noise to the ECG signal. The latter is then detected by comparison with the residual random noise level, and recognition is confirmed by logical checks. Meanwhile, the original signal is delayed so that, when the occurrence of an R wave is signalled, the complete complex can be compared with a pattern stored in the machine. This stored pattern is set up in the first place by allowing the machine to learn which of the complexes it detects are 'normal', using a doctor or a skilled technician as the teacher. When the machine is first connected to the patient, the 'teacher' observes the ECG and, during a period when the incoming complexes appear normal, depresses a button marked 'learn'. While this button is depressed, a normal ECG pattern for that patient is built up and stored in the computer. Thereafter,

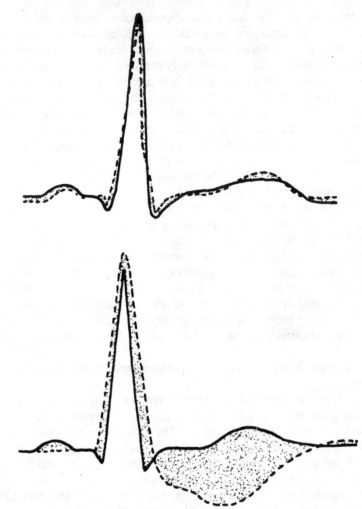

FIG. 40. Diagrams which compare two ECG complexes, the upper tracing representing a good match and the lower tracing a poor match. The size of the area between the interrupted and the continuous lines is inversely proportional to the goodness of the match. The representation of the normal complex is held in the computer's memory.

whenever a complex is encountered which matches the stored pattern sufficiently closely (Fig. 40), a proportionate amount is added to the stored pattern. The stored pattern is therefore a moving average of 'normal' complexes, and the machine can accommodate to gradual changes in the shape of the ECG. Whenever a complex is detected which fails to match the stored pattern, an alarm is activated or an appropriate record is made.

This instrument, therefore, detects phenomena by comparison with an ostensibly defined 'normal' pattern. A minimum number of prior assumptions is made about the shape of the complexes concerned, and the only requirement is that the occurrence of the complex can be unambiguously determined.

## General purpose pattern recognition and its possible application to the electrocardiogram

A much more general class of devices for pattern recognition depends on detecting relationships between features. Such 'machines' can be considered as two linked sections, a feature extractor and a relationship processor. Feature extraction is necessarily performed on an *ad hoc* basis, the difficulty being that 'features' are not in general susceptible to precise definition. They may overlap or be indifferently defined in time, and feature extraction is essentially a device for data reduction. The fact that a feature is present, although superficially a simple 'yes or no' statement, should really be associated with a confidence level.

Perceptrons and allied devices (Arkadev and Braverman, 1967) rely on a very large number of simple features, and assume that the patterns to be recognised are linearly separable in terms of these features. They appear to model closely the mechanism that might be used by living organisms, and have been applied to the recognition of patterns in two dimensional pictures or drawings, but not as yet to ECG recognition.

Syntax-directed analysis has been applied by Ledley (1962) to the recognition of chromosomes but again, apparently, never to the ECG. This may seem surprising because syntax analysis applies naturally to features which are strung together, or concatenated. It was developed for the study of natural language in which words follow each other in sequence, just as do the waves of an ECG. Unfortunately, however, little progress can be made with syntax analysis unless the terminal elements or features can be precisely and clearly separated from one another, like letters in a line of text.

More abstract techniques may compensate for poorly defined features, by searching for multiple correspondences. If, for instance, a feature extractor could recognise 'waves', this could be applied to a section of ECG record to resolve it into a number of roughly designated waves (Fig. 41). By comparing pairs of waves with respect to different properties, the relations between them can be mapped in different ways. Three samples of such mappings are drawn as graphs in Figure 41—for the relationships 'after', 'larger than' and 'wider than'. Each graph consists of a number of nodes (each node represents a wave) connected by lines which represent the relationship between a pair of nodes. The relationships are all directed (e.g. W4 is larger than W3 is represented as 0———◄———0). Given two such graphs, or a set of pairs of such graphs,

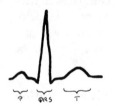

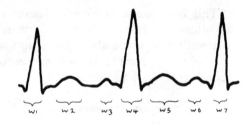

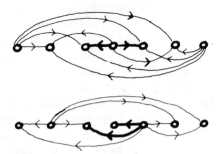

FIG. 41. A series of graphs indicating the relationships between waves comprising a single ECG complex and a series of ECG complexes. In the correspondence plots shown below the ECG complexes, each node represents a 'wave' and the three relationships shown, from above downwards, are: 'immediately follows', 'is larger than' and 'is wider than'.

The relationships are arranged in a straight line in the order in which the waves occur, so as to make them easy to follow. The 'immediately follows' graphs are very simple but the 'is larger than' set are more complex in the continuous tracing. Here the lines and arrows indicate that waves W1, W4 and W7 are significantly 'larger than' (i.e. of greater amplitude than) any of the other waves, by means of arrows going from each of the big waves to each of the smaller waves. The 'is wider than' graphs convey similar information, on the assumption that there is no significant difference in width (i.e. duration) between the various P and T waves.

In the right hand set of graphs, only one set of nodes has relationships corresponding to those of the target complex, thereby identifying waves W3, W4 and W5 collectively, as an ECG complex. These relationships have been drawn in with heavier lines and in such a way that the correspondence is easy to see.

techniques have been developed for use with a computer that will find regions of the graphs in which similar nodes are inter-connected by arcs in the same way—for instance, when searching for matching patterns in chemical compounds (Unger, 1964; Sussenguth, 1965), or when attempting to discover whether a particular electrical network has been previously patented (Cornog and Bryan, 1966). The important point of these techniques is that they may be extended to cope with cases in which correspondences are not exact, enabling recognition to be established even when feature extraction is less than perfect (*see also* Burstall, 1969).

### The recognition of arrhythmias

The normal heart beats regularly and produces similar complexes with each beat, but in certain heart disorders the heart may beat irregularly producing a cardiac arrhythmia. Study of the intervals between beats (e.g. the heart rate) demands in the first place that the occurrence of a complex can be reliably recognised, and to this extent depends on the techniques of recognition already described (Haywood *et al.*, 1970). Detailed measurements (as in the first section) are not required, but the pattern recognition techniques described in the last section may be important, not only for the precise definition of complexes but also because complexes of abnormal shape are often found in particular kinds of arrhythmias.

## ANALYSIS OF THE ELECTROENCEPHALOGRAM

When Berger first observed the EEG, he considered that it was composed of alpha and beta waves, with about three beta waves to each alpha wave. In a diagram of an idealised EEG, the alpha and beta waves were triangular rather than sinusoidal in shape. Dietsch (1932), however, subjected small portions of Berger's tracings to Fourier analysis. He showed that quite a wide spectrum of activity was present, and it would thus seem that 'analysis' proper is out of the question. Furthermore, although early concepts of the EEG were based on the notion of masses of nerve cells forming dipole oscillators, each with its characteristic frequency, it is now accepted that there is necessarily a large random element.

### Visual analysis of the electroencephalogram

The trained human being is probably the most efficient pattern-recognising system at present available and evaluation of the EEG for clinical diagnosis will, for the foreseeable future, be carried out simply by examining sections of the conventional recording (e.g. Fig. 42). The role that a computer can play in this process is mainly that of collecting large numbers of such observations and enabling firmly estimated probabilities to be associated with the occurrence of certain recognisable features in the EEG.

Margerison *et al.* (1970), for instance, tackled the problem of how to localise ruptured intracranial aneurysms by means of the EEG. They made a detailed study of a consecutive series of 133 patients with spontaneous subarachnoid haemorrhage, 70 of whom were known to have had ruptured intracranial aneurysms. A total of 180 distinct

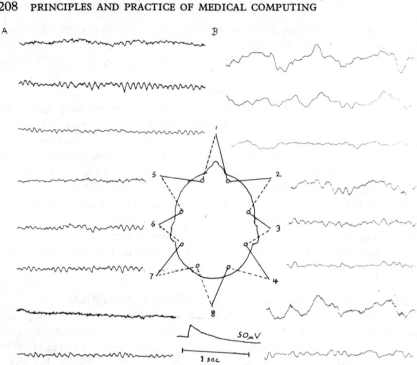

FIG. 42. Two short sections of conventional eight-lead clinical EEG records. The left-hand tracing is an example of a 'normal' record and the right hand is abnormal.

phenomena were tabulated, and these were sought in each tracing. Coefficients of association between each of the sites and each of the features, together with levels of significance based on Fisher's exact probability test, were computed. As a result of this study, 35 signs were selected and the authors claim that, on the basis of these signs, useful predictions can be made among the six major anatomical sites of ruptured aneurysms.

### Evoked potentials

The engineer's approach to the study of the brain is to consider it as a black box, and the standard technique for dealing with black boxes is to input a signal and observe what comes out. The simplest input to the brain is the unit impulse, and physiological approximations to this have been used to investigate many sensory cerebral systems. Stimuli have included brief flashes of light to test the visual system, clicks to test the auditory system, electric shocks applied to peripheral nerves, and tapping (e.g. on a tooth, finger nail, or tendon) to stimulate the fast conducting sensory fibres. The responses to these stimuli each involve rather a small region of the cerebral cortex, and the associated potentials produced on the scalp are therefore very small, typically only a few microvolts. The spontaneous activity in the same part of the field is about one order of magnitude greater, however, and this led to the introduction of the technique of averaging several responses, so as to diminish the effect of uncorrelated spontaneous activity (Dawson, 1954); this was rapidly recognised as being a very powerful tool for investigating sensory systems in the intact human being. Many different devices have been used for performing this averaging process, but systems based on digital computing techniques are undoubtedly the best, even if not the cheapest.

Many very small computers have been developed for the special purpose of averaging responses to impulsive stimuli. For example, the Biomac (Data Laboratories, Wates Way, Mitcham, Surrey) is a special purpose device which uses the techniques of digital computers but which does not have a stored, and therefore a changeable, program. Cost is very much the determining factor in this field, and although the suitability of small digital computers for this sort of work is unquestioned, the apparatus is sufficiently expensive to be outside the category of ordinary laboratory equipment.

The small general purpose computer is even more costly than the special purpose devices mentioned in the previous paragraph, but has the great advantage of being highly flexible in its application. The ability of the small on-line computer to control a complex experiment, at once precisely and flexibly, makes it invaluable and a good example of such an application in the present context is the work on the contingent negative variation.

Any impulsive stimulus, or a stimulus which takes the form of a step (e.g. switching a light on or off) will produce a so-called non-specific evoked response. This is a complex disturbance, containing a prominent surface-negative sharp wave which predominantly involves the frontal regions of the scalp. The response is called non-specific because it is substantially the same whatever the modality of the exciting stimulus. Walter and his colleagues (1964) have demonstrated that, if paired stimuli are used in a conditioning situation (where the first stimulus acts as a warning or anticipatory signal and the second is linked to a motor response), then a build-up of potential can be shown between the two stimuli which seems to reflect the degree of preparedness or 'expectancy' of the brain (Fig. 43). This potential build-up has been termed the contingent negative variation or CNV. Both the evoked potentials and the CNV are quite small, usually only a few microvolts. The spontaneous activity in the frontal regions is also small, but averaging techniques are nevertheless essential in order to show the potential shift clearly. Not only do the responses have to be recorded and averaged (commonly each response lasts several seconds) but the paired stimuli have to be given

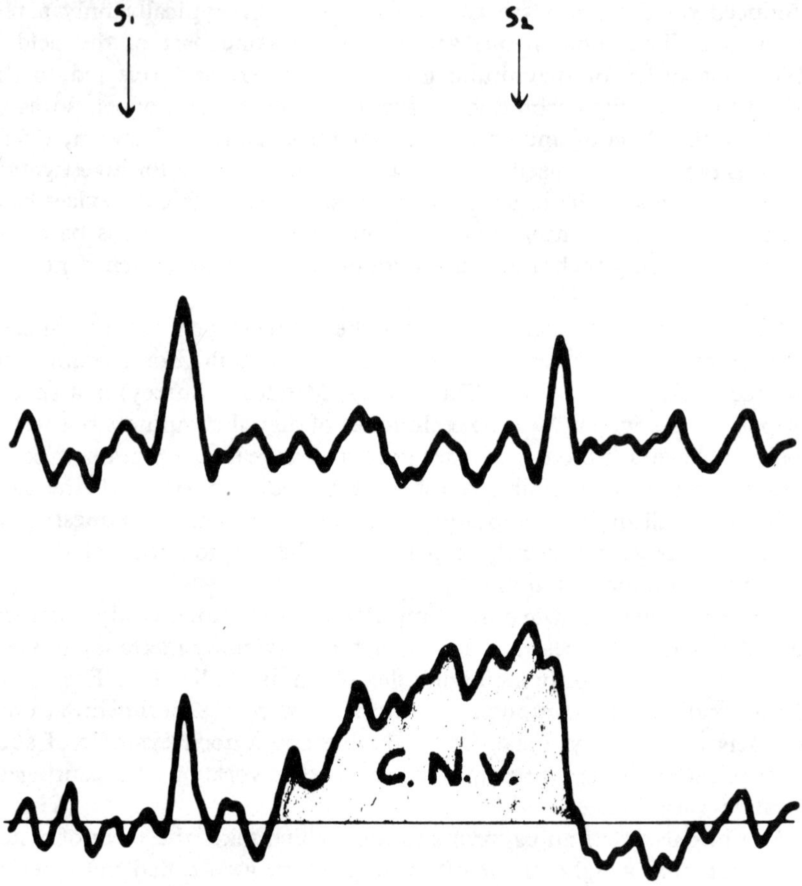

FIG. 43. The upper tracing shows the non-specific evoked responses to two stimuli, $S_1$ and $S_2$. In the lower tracing, a motor response is made to the second stimulus and the two stimuli have become associated; a contingent negative variation (CNV) is shown to be building up in the interval between the two stimuli (after Walter *et al.*, 1964).

at random intervals so that the complete experimental situation is quite complex. With the aid of a small on-line general purpose digital computer, it is possible not only to carry out these experiments much more easily but to extend the technique to allow multiple channel simultaneous recordings to be undertaken in even more complex experimental paradigms. For instance, the effects of dilution or distraction can be tested and the interaction of stimuli in different modalities can be compared (*Attention in Neurophysiology*, 1970).

## Spectral analysis
Spectral analysis starts from the observation that there are rhythmic

components present in the EEG. It attempts to separate out the mixture of activity into discrete frequency bands, estimating the amount of activity in each band. The Fourier analyses of Dietsch (1932) were performed by hand, but the idea was quickly followed up and many varieties of 'analyser' have been used to obtain estimates of the frequency spectrum of EEG activity. The most successful of these analysers was the one developed by Baldock and Walter (1946). This passed an EEG signal into a bank of filters tuned to various frequencies between 1 and 24 cycles per second. The output of each filter was averaged over a fixed period of time (usually 10 seconds), to obtain an approximation to the spectrum of the signal during that interval. Early machines of this sort suffered from instability of the tuned filters and required constant adjustment, but modern apparatus is adequately stable. Recently, several workers have developed digital programs to perform essentially the same function.

There are two approaches to the digital computation of spectrum estimates. The first involves the initial step of obtaining an auto-correlogram. Calculating each element of the autocorrelogram involves multiplying the whole of the sample of EEG with a copy of itself, an operation known to mathematicians as 'convolution'. In spite of the considerable amount of computation involved, the process is relatively simple and can be programmed economically. The EEG is a continuous signal that is sampled and presented as a sequence of amplitude measurements to the computer. A series of measurements like this, representing a time-varying phenomenon and arranged in chronological sequence, is called a 'time series'.

Denoting an element of the time series by $x_t$ and the following elements by $x_{t+1}$, $x_{t+2}$, etc., the first term of the autocorrelogram is obtained by summing the products $x_t \star x_t$ over all the available values, i.e. $\sum x_t x_t$. Successive terms are obtained by delaying the second value in time so that the autocorrelogram is a function of time delay. It is usually represented by the symbol $r_\tau$, the $\tau$ (measured in seconds) being termed the lag, as follows:

$$r_\tau = \sum_{t=0}^{T} x_t x_{t-\tau}; \ \tau = 0, 1, 2 \ldots L \qquad \text{(Equation 10.1)}$$

In this equation T is the number of samples available and L is the maximum lag. If T is small enough, the entire sample of time series can be held in the fast access store. The algorithm used by the author (see Appendix, p. 222) avoids this, however, thereby enabling much larger values of T to be used; this is particularly valuable for small computers.

When an autocorrelogram is available the spectrum can be obtained as its 'Fourier Transform'. Fourier transformation is also a convolution operation, each element of the spectrum being obtained by summing the products of corresponding elements of the correlogram and a cosine function. Unfortunately, when this process is applied to a finite correlogram, the resulting estimates are unbiased but highly variable, giving a very 'noisy' representation of the spectrum. Most workers, therefore, smooth the resulting spectrum estimates, a process referred to as 'Hanning' (Blackman and Tukey, 1958). The author has followed an alternative suggestion (Milner, 1954) which involves multiplying the correlogram by a compensating function; this gives a good approximation to the desired spectrum estimates.

The alternative method, which has become popular since the introduction of the Fast Fourier Transform (Cooley and Tukey, 1965), involves deriving the spectrum estimates directly from the original sample record. It has the disadvantage that it requires the whole of the sample to be held in the fast access store of the computer, to take advantage of the increase in computation speed, and hence is only suitable for larger machines. This technique retains information about the relative phase of components in the original signal. It therefore has the advantage that phase relations between spectral components may be compared not only between simultaneously recorded samples of different signals (Dummermuth and Fluhler, 1967) but also within a single sample of a signal by an extension of the technique.

The advantages of digital computing methods, when used for spectral analysis, are threefold. In the first place, there is no possibility of the filters drifting out of tune, and the results are therefore more consistent from one observation to another. Secondly, the analysis is much more flexible because the epoch length, band-width and frequencies at which estimates are to be made can all simply be given as parameters to the computer. The third advantage is that the computer can be used to process the results.

The main disadvantage of the digital computer method is that it is difficult to arrange for a graph of the spectrum to be available during the actual recording itself (i.e. on-line). Because of this, the observations have to be made blind and may have to be repeated later if minor alterations in technique are suggested as necessary by the results. In some cases it may not be possible to repeat an observation and on-line working then becomes essential.

Spectral analysis has had disappointingly little impact in the clinical use of the EEG, although it is certainly possible to follow alterations in the major rhythms in many conditions which affect the metabolism of the brain, for example during the menstrual cycle (Margerison et al., 1964) or in liver disease (Laidlaw and Read, 1963; Hawkes et al., 1970). Much simpler techniques may be equally useful.

The EEG signal is essentially symmetrical about a zero baseline, because of the characteristics of the amplifiers if nothing else, and one of the simplest ideas proposed has been to rectify and integrate the signal;

this is equivalent to adding the total of the areas above and below the baseline (Fig. 44). This technique has been successfully used (Drohocki, 1948, 1969) for the assay of drugs, and a similar method used in the study of reactivity of the alpha rhythm measures the total rise and fall of the curve in a given time. Alternatively, intervals between the crossings

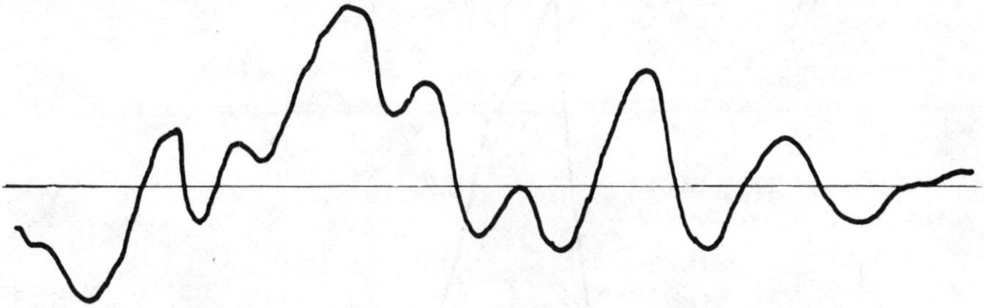

FIG. 44. The 'integral' of the EEG, obtained by rectifying and integrating the signal. This is equivalent to adding the total of the areas above and below the baseline (after Drohocki, 1948; 1969).

of the baseline may be measured in order to give an approximate estimate of the waves at different frequencies present in the trace. A good review of these techniques was given by Burch (1959), and a more general coverage of the subject of automatic analysis in clinical electroencephalography is given by Matousek (1967).

## The study of sleep

The EEG has proved an invaluable tool in the study of sleep, as well as in other disturbances of consciousness. Perhaps the best known result of such investigations has been the discovery of 'paradoxical sleep'. This is a state which occurs frequently throughout the night when the subject appears to be deeply asleep and is difficult to arouse, although the appearance of the EEG would suggest a state of alertness. Many workers have suggested that these states correspond to times when the subject is dreaming.

A major difficulty in studies on sleep, apart from the obvious disincentive to the investigator of having to conduct experiments at night, is the immense volume of data to be examined after each night's recording, rapidly growing to miles of paper record. It is not surprising, therefore, that several attempts have been made to devise procedures for the automatic recording of the different stages of sleep to reduce the tedium of these studies. Some of these systems have relied on frequency analysis, but a pragmatic approach which makes use of measures related to mean amplitude or to the statistics of baseline crossings is probably more practical (see Itil et al., 1969).

## Models of cerebral activity

One of the simplest models proposed to explain the generation of EEG activity is that of 'filtered noise'. This model suggests that the cortex acts as a simple filter, modifying the random afferent impulses from the periphery. These afferent impulses are not random in the sense of being

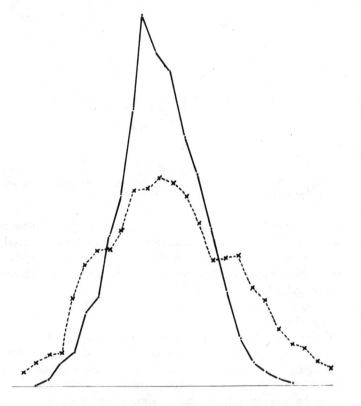

FIG. 45. The full line is the observed distribution of amplitudes from a 20 second tracing of a model EEG; it consists of narrow band filtered noise. The interrupted line shows the observed distribution of amplitudes from a 20 second tracing of a normal EEG recorded from an adult with the eyes closed.

The ordinate shows the number of times that a measurement of the given amplitude is observed in each 20 second sample. Amplitude is plotted on the abscissa.

'meaningless', but random in the sense of being 'unpredictable' from the point of view of the EEG observer. This model has a testable corollary—if it is an adequate description of the EEG, then the amplitude probability density function of the EEG trace should be Gaussian. An approximation to the probability density function can be obtained by plotting a histogram constructed from all the sample amplitudes of the signal (Fig. 45).

Amplitude histograms of samples of EEG have been studied (e.g. Saunders, 1963; Elul, 1969) and there is general agreement that, although under some conditions there is a very close approximation to the Gaussian form, in general the approximation is less good. This probably explains the relative lack of usefulness of spectrum analysis in clinical situations, but has not inhibited the study of suitably selected samples of the EEG from this point of view.

Another way of looking at this model of 'filtered noise' is to consider the EEG record as having been generated by a multi-order Markov process (Hill, 1969; Mitchie, 1970). If we consider a short sample of record (Fig. 46), the model consists of an equation which enables us to

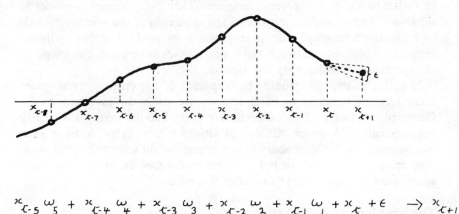

FIG. 46. The 'autoregressive model' of the EEG, showing the method of predicting the value of $x_{t+1}$. The expression used is:
$$x_{t-5}w_5 + x_{t-4}w_4 + x_{t-3}w_3 + x_{t-2}w_2 + x_{t-1}w_1 + x_t \longrightarrow \mu_{t+1}$$
where $\mu_{t+1}$ is the predicted value of $x_{t+1}$.

predict the amplitude value of the record at the next time interval, $x_{t+1}$, from a weighted average of past values, by the equation:

$$x_{t+1} = x_t + x_{t-1} w_1 + x_{t-2} w_2 + \ldots x_{t-n} w_n - \varepsilon \qquad \text{(Equation 10.2)}$$

where $\varepsilon$ is a small error term. The expression given in Figure 46 may be applied repeatedly to give a pseudo-EEG of indefinite length, by setting $x_{t-(n+1)} = x_{t-n}$ throughout, (thus $x_{t-5}$ becomes $x_{t-4}$, . . . and $x_{t-1}$ becomes $x_t$) and finally setting $x_t = \mu_{t+1} + \varepsilon_t$ before applying the equation again to get a new value for $\mu_{t+1}$. This procedure should be compared with the algorithm for computing the autocorrelogram (p. 222). The pseudo-EEG may be compared by eye with the original samples as an empirical test of the relevance of the analysis, while the weights form a compact quantitative description of the record as a whole. It is possible to take this model a step further (Fenwick, 1970), by substituting an impulse function for the series $\varepsilon_t$ and comparing the result with the effect of administering impulsive stimuli to the subject from whom the records are being derived.

Zetterberg (1969) has fitted to observed EEG signals a linear difference equation of the form:

$$x_v + a_1 x_{v-1} + \ldots + a_n x_{v-n} = e_v + b_1 e_{v-1} + \ldots + b_q e_{v-q} + c$$

(Equation 10.3)

The equation of the model (Fig. 46) may be re-written as:

$$x_{t+1} - x_t - w_1 x_{t-1} - \ldots - w_5 x_{t-5} = \varepsilon$$

(Equation 10.4)

in order to show the correspondence. This more complex model is capable of approximating closely to the spectrum of the observed EEG, and has the advantage that it is possible to establish more easily an intuitive connection between the a and b parameters and the shape of the spectrum to which they correspond.

Non-linear models would be capable of describing even more accurately the majority of EEG samples in which the assumption of a Gaussian amplitude histogram (amplitude probability density) is clearly not applicable. However, the complexity of a non-linear model is such that heuristic rather than analytic techniques would seem to be indicated. The main aim of the author and his colleagues is to explore these approaches to a non-linear model of the EEG.

## The problem of stationarity

The techniques so far described all presuppose that the EEG signal is statistically constant, at least over the interval being studied. The actual functioning of the brain, however, is rarely so dull, and a moving average of any of these indices has the advantage of allowing the observation of spontaneous fluctuations in these statistical parameters of the EEG. Such an average, however, always involves a compromise between the smoothing out of local random fluctuations on the one hand, and the blurring of actual changes on the other. Display of the integral plots (Byford, 1963; Burns and Melzack, 1966) affords an ingenious way of avoiding the dilemma (Fig. 47).

The display of integral plots permits a very great reduction in the amount of data, and enables filtering to be performed easily by eye. Where the line formed by the plot is sensibly straight, it is legitimate to use ordinary least squares techniques to fit a straight line to the points and so obtain a best estimate of the value of the index during that period. Fully automatic analysis of the data to produce the same result would either involve the inspired setting of parameters in a curve-fitting program or else would require very complex logic. Cumulative displays have been used to study small evoked potentials (Townsend, 1967) and

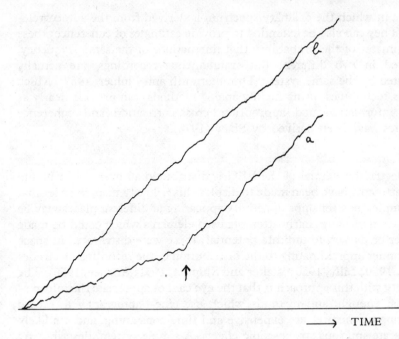

FIG. 47. Displays of the integral plots of the EEG (after Byford, 1963). The phenomenon to be plotted is either observed continuously, in which case the value of the plot at any instant (T) is the integral with respect to time, $\int_0^T x dt$, or the observations are discrete in which case the value of the plot is the equivalent sum, $\sum_0^T x_t$.

In the cumulative sum traces shown, curve (a) is altered by an 'event' at the time indicated by the arrow and increases to a new value thereafter, whereas curve (b) remains at a constant value throughout.

contingent negative variation (Rousseau *et al.*, 1969). The ideal solution, using present day techniques, would be to develop this type of display as part of an interactive system, using a CRT graph plotter and light pen. Interactive use of a computer in this way will probably prove to be one of the major fields in which digital computers can contribute to the analysis of brain activity.

## Multi-channel analysis
Spectrum analysis, and allied techniques which concentrate on the statistical structure of a single fluctuating potential, do not take into account similarities and differences between electrical activity at different places on the head whereas Fourier analysis proper preserves information about the phase of constituent components. In fact, from a full Fourier analysis, an exact copy of the analysed sample can be reconstructed. These techniques can be extended, therefore, to provide cross-spectra which can be derived from a cross-correlogram in a manner similar to

the one in which the ordinary spectrum is derived from the autocorrelogram. They can also be extended to provide estimates of coherence; these are estimates of the probability that fluctuations of the same frequency, observed in two different but simultaneous recordings, are actually generated by the same system (Dummermuth and Fluhler, 1967). Much simpler techniques, using mainly analog methods, can provide nearly as much information and appropriate cross-correlation and coherence estimates have been derived by Shaw (1970).

**Toposcopes**
The electrical potential of the EEG is distributed all over the scalp and many attempts have been made to display this field as a map, in order that the complex relationships of activity appearing at different places may be appreciated visually. Early attempts used elements which could be made brighter or darker, to indicate potential; these were distributed in space in a manner approximating to the distribution of the recording electrodes (Cohn, 1950; Lilly, 1950; Walter and Shipton, 1951; Ananev, 1956). The difficulty with this approach is that the eye cannot appreciate the information fast enough, and methods which use cine-photography to record the changing pictures are expensive and time-consuming, and are likely to generate spurious stroboscopic effects. A simple system, described by Naitoh and Walter (1969), can be used for the manual as well as automatic plotting of topographic data.

A digital computer has been used to construct potential maps by interpolation (Rémond, 1961; Rémond and Lesevre, 1967), but efforts have mostly been concentrated on a single spatial dimension; the other dimension is used to plot time while electrical potential is indicated by contours and shading. Rémond has used the facilities afforded by the digital computer to take the process a stage further, to produce not only maps of electrical potential but of current sources and sinks. This is an interesting concept which depends on the fact that, in order that a potential difference may exist on a conducting surface, a current must be flowing—if a current flows, it must come from somewhere and go to somewhere. From the pattern of potentials, the location of these sources and sinks of current may be calculated and mapped. It seems likely that the pattern of sources and sinks will approximate more closely to underlying physiological mechanisms than the patterns of the currents or potentials derived from them.

The author and his colleagues are developing apparatus for recording from arrays of EEG electrodes directly on to digital magnetic tape which can then be replayed under computer control. One of the many uses anticipated for such a data acquisition system will be in connection with a program for displaying on a CRT a continuously changing contour map representing potential distribution, or sources and sinks, on the scalp. If the play-back is at one-tenth to one-twentieth of the recording speed, this will slow down the changes sufficiently for the eye to be able to appreciate what is happening, and may thus yield useful information about physiological mechanisms.

## CONCLUSION

This chapter has reviewed several areas of application of computer-based techniques to the examination of normal and abnormal ECG and EEG patterns.

In electrocardiography, the digital computer finds its main use in the fast automatic measurement of routine ECG records. On the other hand analog and hybrid methods find their main application in the prolonged monitoring of records obtained on-line from more or less severely ill patients, for the detection of arrhythmias and other irregularities.

The study of the electroencephalogram has attracted much interest. It is obviously complex in nature and has a close relationship to the functioning of the living brain. The main lines of investigation where computer techniques have been found necessary have been in the study of responses to stimuli and in the study of steady states. It is possible, by giving the same stimulus repeatedly, to study the 'average' response to a stimulus. Steady states investigated have usually been closely related to states of consciousness, as in sleep, or else coma and various diseases which cause impairment of alertness.

REFERENCES

ANANEV, V. (1956). Elektroenkefaloscop. *Fisiologicheskii Zhurnal SSR Imeni in Sechenova*, **42**, 981–988.

ARKADEV, A. G. & BRAVERMAN, E. M. (1967). *Teaching Computers to Recognise Patterns*. New York: Academic Press.

*Attention in Neurophysiology* (1970). Edited by Evans, C. R. & Mullholland, T. B. London: Butterworth.

BALDOCK, G. & WALTER, W. G. (1946). A new electronic analyser. *Electronic Engineering*, **18**, 339–344.

BLACKMAN, R. B. & TUKEY, J. W. (1958). *The Measurement of Power Spectra*. New York: Dover Publications.

BURCH, N. R. (1959). Automatic analysis of the encephalogram: A review and classification of systems. *Electroencephalography and Clinical Neurophysiology*, **11**, 827–843.

BURNS, S. K. & MELZACK, R. (1966). A method for analysing variations in evoked responses. *Electroencephalography and Clinical Neurophysiology*, **20**, 407–409.

BURSTALL, R. M. (1969). Graph family matching. *Research Memorandum, MIP–R– 62*. Department of Machine Intelligence and Perception, University of Edinburgh.

BYFORD, G. (1963). A technique for measuring changes in EEG activity. *Journal of Physiology*, **169**, 62–64.

CACERES, C. A. and six co-authors (1962). Computer extraction of electrocardiographic parameters. *Circulation*, **25**, 356–602.

COHN, R. (1950). Cerebral toposcopy in clinical EEG. *Electroencephalography and Clinical Neurophysiology*, **2**, 358.

COOLEY, J. W. & TUKEY, J. W. (1965). An algorithm for the machine calculation of complex Fourier series. *Mathematical Computing*, **19**, 297–301.

CORNOG, J. R. & BRYAN, H. L. (1966). Search methods used with transistor patent applications. *I.E.E. Spectrum*, **3**, (1), 116–121.

DAWSON, G. D. (1954). A summation technique for the detection of small evoked potentials. *Electroencephalography and Clinical Neurophysiology*, **6**, 65–84.

DIETSCH, G. (1932). Fourier-analyse von elektroencephalogrammen des menschen. *Pflugers Archiv fur die Gesamte Physiologie*, **230**, 106–112.

DROHOCKI, Z. (1948). L'integrateur de l'electroproduction cerebrale pour l'electroencephalographie quantitative. *Revue Neurologíque*, **80**, 619.

DROHOCKI, Z. (1969). Electroencephalographie quantitative—Les limites de variabilité individuelle et collective de l'electrogenese cerebrale. E.G.N. chez l'homme normal. *Revue Neurologique*, **121**, 280–288.

DUMMERMUTH, G. & FLUHLER, H. (1967). Some modern aspects in numerical spectrum analysis of multichannel electroencephalographic data. *Medical and Biological Engineering*, **5**, 319–331.

ELUL, R. (1969). Gaussian behaviour of the electroencephalogram: Changes during performance of a mental task. *Science*, **164**, 328–331.

FENWICK, P. (1970). *Computer Analysis of the EEG in Coma*. M.D. Thesis, University of Cambridge.

HAWKES, C. H., MACPHERSON, A. I. S., PRYOR, H. & TOWNSEND, H. R. A. (1970). The value of EEG frequency analysis in hepatic encephalopathy. *Journal of the Royal College of Surgeons of Edinburgh*, **15**, 151–157.

HAYWOOD, L. J., MURTHY, V. K., HARVEY, G. A. & SALTZBERG, S. (1970). On line real time computer algorithm for monitoring the ECG waveform. *Computers and Biomedical Research*, **3**, 15–25.

HILL, G. (1969). Appendix to Electroencephalography (Computer Analysis) by Townsend, H. R. A. In *Computers in Medicine*. Ed. Rose, J. pp. 67–69. London: Churchill.

ITIL, T. M., SHAPIRO, D. M., FINK, M. & KASSENBAUM, D. (1969). Digital computer classifications of EEG sleep stages. *Electroencephalography and Clinical Neurophysiology*, **27**, 76–83.

LAIDLAW, J. & READ, A. E. (1963). The EEG in hepatic encephalopathy. *Clinical Science*, **24**, 109–120.

LAWRIE, T. D. V. & MACFARLANE, P. W. (1968). Towards automated electrocardiogram analysis. In *Computers in the Service of Medicine*. Ed. McLachlan, G. & Shegog, R. A. Vol. I, pp. 103–122. London: Oxford University Press.

LEDLEY, R. S. (1962). High speed automatic analysis of biomedical pictures. *Science*, **146**, 216–223.

LILLY, J. C. (1950). A method of recording the moving electrical potential gradient in the brain. *AIEE–IRE Joint Conference on Electronics in Nucleonics and Medicine. A*, 37–43. New York. American Institute of Electrical Engineering.

MARGERISON, J. H., ANDERSON, W. & DAWSON, J. (1964). Plasma sodium and the EEG during the menstrual cycle. *Electroencephalography and Clinical Neurophysiology*, **17**, 340–344.

MARGERISON, J. H., BINNIE, C. D. & McCAUL, I. R. (1970). Electroencephalographic signs employed in the location of ruptured intracranial aneurysms. *Electroencephalography and Clinical Neurophysiology*, **28**, 296–306.

MATOUSEK, M. (1967). Automatic analysis in clinical electroencephalography. *University of Prague, Research Reports*. Report No. 9.

MILNER, J. A. (1954). A method of frequency analysis. *Technical Note, No. A.R.M. 547*. Royal Aircraft Establishment, Farnborough.

MITCHIE, P. M. (1970). Ph.D. Thesis, University of London. In preparation.

NAITOH, P. & WALTER, D. O. (1969). Simple manual plotting of contours as a method of EEG analysis. *Electroencephalography and Clinical Neurophysiology*, **26**, 424–428.

RÉMOND, A. (1961). The Matide (Méthode d'analyse et de traitement integrée des donnes électrographiques. *Electroencephalography and Clinical Neurophysiology*, **13**, 484–485.

RÉMOND, A. & LESEVRE, N. (1967). Variations in average visual evoked potential as a function of the alpha rhythm phase (Autostimulation). *Electroencephalography and Clinical Neurophysiology*, **26**, (Supplement), 42–52.

ROUSSEAU, J. C., BOSTEM, F. & DONGIER, M. (1969). Intérêt de l'enregistrement de la construction progressive de la courbe integrée, dans l'étude de la variation contingente négative. In *Variations Contingentes Négatives*. Ed. Dargent, J. & Dongier, M. *Congrès et Colloques Université de Liège*, **52**, 38–44.

SAUNDERS, M. G. (1963). Amplitude probability density studies on alpha and alpha-like patterns. *Electroencephalography and Clinical Neurophysiology*, **15**, 761–767.

SHAW, J. C. (1970). A method for continuously recording characteristics of EEG topography. *Electroencephalography and Clinical Neurophysiology*, **29**, 592–601.

STALLMAN, F. W. & PIPBERGER, H. V. (1961). Automatic recognition of electrocardiographic waves by digital computer. *Circulation Research*, **9**, 1138–1143.

SUSSENGUTH, E. H. (1965). A graph-theoretical algorithm for matching chemical structures. *Journal of Chemical Documentation*, **5**, 36–43.

TOWNSEND, H. R. A. (1967). A technique for studying the time course of small evoked potentials. *Electroencephalography and Clinical Neurophysiology*, **23**, 397.

UNGER, S. H. (1964). *GIT*: A heuristic program for testing pairs of directed line-graphs for isomorphism. *Communications of the Association for Computing Machinery*, **7**, 26–34.

WALTER, W. G., COOPER, R., ALDRIDGE, V. J., McCALLUM, W. C. & WINTER, A. L. (1964). Contingent negative variation: An electric sign of sensori-motor association and expectancy in the human brain. *Nature*, **203**, 380–384.

WALTER, W. G. & SHIPTON, H. W. (1951). A new toposcopic display system. *Electroencephalography and Clinical Neurophysiology*, **3**, 281–292.

ZETTERBERG, L. H. (1969). Estimation of parameters for a linear difference equation with application to EEG analysis. *Mathematical Biosciences*, **5**, 227–275.

**Appendix**

Algorithm for computing the Autocorrelogram

```
procedure raw correlogram (R, B, N, T, S);
    value       N, T;  integer N, T;
    array       R, B;
    comment       array R[0: N] will hold the autocorrelogram on exit
                  array B[0: N + 1] is used as a buffer;
    real  S;
    comment real S is used later to correct for the non-zero mean;
begin   integer   JK;  real   B0, X;   S: = 0;
    for K: = N step  − 1 until 0 do
        begin
            B[K]: = INEEG; comment INEEG is a real procedure whose value
                                   is the next element of the time series;
            R[K]: = 0
        end   this loop fills the buffer and clears array R;
    for J: = 1 step 1 until T do
        begin
            B0: = B[0];   S: = S + B0;
            for K: = N step  − 1 until 0 do
                begin
                    X: = B[K];   B[K + 1]: = X;
                    R[K]: = R[K] + B0*X;
                end   this loop performs the multiplications
                      and also shifts up the elements in the buffer;
            B[0]: = INEEG; comment reads elements of the time series;
        end this loop is repeated for each element of the time series;
end of procedure raw correlogram;
```

# CHAPTER ELEVEN

# Computer Applications in Clinical Respiratory Physiology

## By D. C. FLENLEY

### SUMMARY

THE collection and evaluation of quantitative data has been essential in the growing application of physiological knowledge to the practice of clinical respiratory medicine. This chapter begins with a brief consideration of the functions of the respiratory system. Thereafter, since no computer can compensate for errors in input, attention is directed particularly to the problems of the collection of data relevant to respiratory function in the automatic monitoring of patients. Later, some applications of computers to the study of ventilatory mechanics, blood gas exchange, acid-base balance and control of ventilation are discussed. Essentially this chapter constitutes a review of a wide field of both theoretical and experimental studies, and should be read in conjunction with the following chapter which describes a limited number of specific applications in greater detail.

## INTRODUCTION

### The function of the respiratory system

The overall function of the respiratory system is to provide normal concentrations of oxygen $(O_2)$ and carbon dioxide $(CO_2)$ in the blood flowing in the systemic arteries. This is achieved by ventilation of air drawn into the 3 million lung alveoli, through rhythmic contractions of the inspiratory muscles driven by the respiratory centres in the brainstem. The alveoli are richly perfused with venous blood, high in $CO_2$ and deficient in $O_2$ concentration; this blood becomes arterialised by losing $CO_2$ and gaining $O_2$ from alveolar gas. Gaseous diffusion in the alveoli is very efficient, for it is only during exercise under extreme hypoxia that equilibrium fails to be achieved between $O_2$ and $CO_2$ tensions in alveolar gas and blood leaving the alveolus. The resultant partial pressures of $O_2$ and $CO_2$ ($Po_2$ and $Pco_2$ respectively) in both alveolar gas and pulmonary capillary blood depend upon the relative amounts of ventilation and blood flow received by each alveolus. This ratio of alveolar ventilation to perfusion $(\dot{V}_A/\dot{Q})$ is a critical index of the efficiency of gas exchange, since under-ventilation of one area of lung cannot be corrected by over-ventilation of another.

The body monitors the adequacy of ventilation in maintaining normal levels of $Po_2$ and $Pco_2$ in the arterial blood by means of the chemo-receptors. These sensors (the carotid and aortic bodies) 'taste' the arterial blood, and are particularly sensitive to a fall in arterial $Po_2$. Increases in $Pco_2$ and in blood acidity are also very powerful stimuli for ventilation in their own right, activating central mechanisms through changes in the acidity of the cerebrospinal fluid (CSF) bathing the lateral border of the brain stem. In addition to these chemical factors, respiratory activity is influenced both by a wide range of somatic afferent stimuli (which are responsible for the increase in breathing at the start of exercise) and by receptors in the lungs and air passages.

Ventilation is therefore controlled by a negative feed-back mechanism. The sensitivity of this feed-back loop is such that, in normal life, the arterial $Pco_2$ is maintained within the range 38 to 42 mm Hg, even during strenuous exercise when $CO_2$ excretion can increase as much as 20-fold. Although the arterial $Po_2$ falls as people become older, it normally exceeds 70 mm Hg in a subject breathing air at sea level.

### Monitoring of blood gas tensions in disease

In many forms of lung disease, arterial hypoxia is combined with low or normal $Pco_2$ levels. This situation is called Type I respiratory failure, the major functional disturbance in these conditions lying in maldistribution of $V_A/\dot{Q}$ ratios amongst the alveoli. However, in bronchitis and emphysema, hypoxia is often combined with an elevation of $Pco_2$, and this life-threatening complication can supervene in a number of other conditions. There is then overall hypoventilation due to a disturbance in ventilatory control mechanisms, and this combination is called Type II respiratory failure or ventilatory failure.

Physiological monitoring of arterial blood gas tensions is a valuable aid to the care of patients with severe respiratory disease, and reliable direct measurements of $Po_2$, $Pco_2$ and pH in blood samples withdrawn from patients have been in clinical use for about 14 years. However, automated systems, able to monitor these variables continuously *in vivo* and thereby utilise the full potential of these measurements, have not yet been developed for routine use. Continuous measurements of $Po_2$, $Pco_2$ and pH by conventional external electrodes in a cuvette system have been used in animals (Sugioka, 1968), and arterial $Po_2$ and $Pco_2$ levels have been successfully monitored by a mass spectrometer in animal studies. Band and Semple (1967) described a rapidly responding indwelling arterial pH electrode for use in man or animals, and mixed venous pH has been continuously monitored during surgery and anaesthesia by a catheter tip glass electrode (Staehelin *et al.*, 1968), but none of these methods has passed the developmental stage.

## MEASUREMENTS IN RESPIRATORY PHYSIOLOGY

### Monitoring of respiratory frequency and tidal volume

Calculation of the minute volume of ventilation ($\dot{V}_E$) depends upon a knowledge of the volume of air drawn in with each breath (the tidal volume, $V_T$) and of the rate of respiration (f). Respiratory rate can be recorded from a heated thermistor sited in the nose, or from a rapidly responding hot wire anemometer, but the positioning and comfort of these devices over the long term leave something to be desired. Measurement of $V_T$ presents greater difficulties.

During treatment by intermittent positive pressure ventilation (IPPB), $V_T$ and f are pre-set on the machine, but actual recordings have shown that the gas volume delivered to the patient may sometimes be considerably less than that pre-set on the machine. A leak-tight connection to the patient's airway by a cuffed endotracheal tube is essential when IPPB is used. A pneumotachograph then records the flow of gas into and out of the patient, and this flow can be integrated against time to give $V_T$. The integral is prone to error due to changes in gas viscosity, if the composition of the inspired gas changes, or due to changes in temperature and humidity. This integrated airflow signal provides both $V_T$ and f, from which $V_E$ is calculated. Measurement of the $O_2$ and $CO_2$ concentrations of the inspired and expired gases, in addition, allows the $O_2$ uptake and $CO_2$ output of the patient to be computed. This approach has been extensively used by Osborn *et al.* (1968), along with measurements of blood gas contents of systemic arterial and mixed venous blood, to obtain measurements of the cardiac output by the direct Fick principle.

In patients who are not being treated by IPPB, leak-tight connections to the respiratory tract are extremely difficult to maintain over a period of time. Thus integrated pneumotachograph measurements are really only practicable in cases where IPPB is being used. Any value to be gained from computers in monitoring respiratory function in ill patients will depend upon the quality of the input data. It is only in patients being ventilated by IPPB that sufficiently accurate data on $V_T$, f, and on values for the concentrations of inspired and expired gas are available at present. Further advances in this field will depend greatly upon reliable automation of blood gas and pH measurements.

## Ventilatory mechanics

During inspiration a pressure gradient from the mouth to the alveoli is developed by the inspiratory muscles. This pressure difference between the mouth and the pleural surface is the transpulmonary pressure ($P_L$). If the change in lung volume (the integrated flow signal) is displayed on an X-Y recorder as a function of $P_L$ during a breath, the resultant loop can be divided into areas representing the elastic and the viscous work of inspiration (Fig. 48). These areas can be summed, after analog computation of their value, so as to give the inspiratory work of inspiration which is done on the lungs. The resistance ($R_L$) and the compliance ($C_L$) of the lungs can also be computed from this plot, by an analog

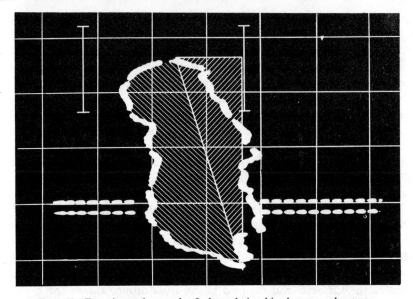

FIG. 48. Experimental record of the relationship between the trans-pulmonary pressure and changes in volume of the lung in a normal subject during quiet breathing. Volume is plotted on the vertical axis (the vertical lines representing 0.34 litres), and pressure horizontally, the distance between the calibration marks being 10 cm water. The trace is interrupted five times each second, the interrupted parallel horizontal lines indicating the duration of the breath. From the lowest point of the loop, at the end of the previous expiration, the trace moves at first to the left on inspiration, reaching maximal volume at the end of inspiration, then returning during expiration on the right. The slope of the diagonal line joining the highest and lowest points of the loop represents the dynamic compliance ($C_L$) of the lungs. The area shaded \\\ denotes the pulmonary viscous work of inspiration, and the area shaded /// the pulmonary elastic work of inspiration. (Reproduced with permission of the authors and the Editor from Flenley, D. C. and Miller, J. S. 1968. *Clinical Science*, **34**, 385–395.)

computer which incorporates sample and hold circuits to retain the values of pressure and volume as the flow signal crosses zero at the beginning and end of expiration; these are the points at the top and bottom of the pressure volume loop. In practice, these analog methods are plagued by noise on both the pressure and the flow signals, particularly as the cardiac artefact on the pressure trace is only four to five times the frequency of the respiratory signal. Sampling with analog to digital conversion and storage of digitised data on magnetic tape, with subsequent digital filtering and analysis by a LINC computer, has been successfully applied to this problem (Stacy and Peters, 1965).

Transpulmonary pressure cannot be measured safely by direct methods in man, but the pressure in a balloon sited in the lower third of the oesophagus adequately measures the mean intrapleural pressure for patients in the upright or seated position (Milic-Emili *et al.*, 1964); in the supine position the oesophageal balloon is partially compressed by the heart. Measurements of $P_L$, volume and airflow were made in seated patients maintained on IPPB following intrathoracic and abdominal surgery (Hilberman *et al.*, 1969), and a digital computer used to determine $C_L$ and $R_L$ from the phase angle between $P_L$ and airflow. These observations showed that, whereas $C_L$ fell as resistance rose following cardiac surgery, this was much less evident after abdominal operations. These authors discuss the future use of such measurements for automating the control of a ventilator providing IPPB (i.e. using a computer as part of a fully automatic or closed loop system).

## Carriage of oxygen and carbon dioxide in blood

The relationships between the $Po_2$ and $Pco_2$ values and the content of these gases in whole blood were established by chemical analysis, as was the oxyhaemoglobin dissociation curve for human blood. Digital computer subroutines to describe these relationships for $O_2$ (Kelman, 1966) and for $CO_2$ (Kelman, 1967) are available, but have no advantage over a specially designed slide-rule (Severinghaus, 1966) when used for this purpose alone. However, these subroutines have led to a description of the interactions between $O_2$ and $CO_2$ carriage, and this description is of great value in computing changes in the $Po_2$ and $Pco_2$ of blood from the mixed venous level, as it undergoes exchange with the alveolar gas (Kelman, 1968)

In an important contribution, West (1969a) utilised these subroutines to examine the theoretical consequences of maldistribution of $\dot{V}_A/\dot{Q}$, by increasing the standard deviation of a log-normal distribution of $\dot{V}_A/\dot{Q}$ in the lung. His analysis applied to differences in the numbers of compartments and in the levels of overall ventilation and of blood flow, etc. The simplified flow diagram of the program is shown in Figure 49 (West, 1969a). This analysis demonstrated, in contradiction to earlier suggestions, that inequality of $\dot{V}_A/\dot{Q}$ values would have little effect on $CO_2$ transport while having a profound effect on $O_2$ transport, and that both gases were in fact similarly affected by maldistribution of ventilation to perfusion. However, $CO_2$ retention is rapidly reversed by increase in ventilation, induced through chemical control mechanisms, whereas this increase in ventilation has little effect in improving oxygenation in a patient with maldistribution of $\dot{V}_A/\dot{Q}$ ratios. In a further study using similar methods, West (1969b) concluded that the difference in slope (but not in shape) of the $O_2$ and $CO_2$ dissociation curves explained the greater vulnerability of $O_2$ uptake to $\dot{V}_A/\dot{Q}$ inequality. These papers indicate the potential usefulness of digital computers in the analysis of some of the more difficult problems of respiratory physiology.

## Acid-base balance

The acidity of the blood and of the body fluids is largely dependent upon

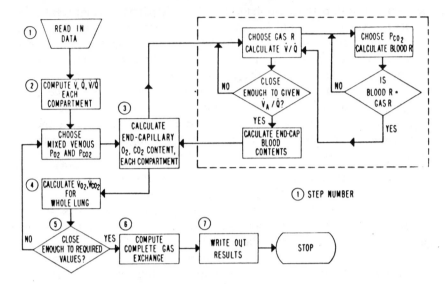

FIG. 49. A simplified flow diagram of the program for analysis of the effects of maldistribution of ventilation to perfusion ratios ($\dot{V}_A/\dot{Q}$) in the lung. The main steps in the program are numbered. The box indicated with broken lines shows the two iterations needed to find the gas exchange corresponding to a given $\dot{V}_A/\dot{Q}$ value. (Reproduced with permission of the author and Editor from West, J. B. 1969. *Respiration Physiology*, **7**, 88–110.)

the bicarbonate buffer system:

$$H_2O + CO_2 \rightleftharpoons H_2CO_3 \rightleftharpoons H^+ + HCO_3^- \qquad \text{(Equation 11.1)}$$

In plasma the three variables, pH, $Pco_2$ and $HCO_3^-$ are related by the Henderson-Hasselbach equation:

$$pH = pK^1 + \log \frac{[HCO_3^-]}{S.Pco_2} \qquad \text{(Equation 11.2)}$$

Graphical solutions of this equation are numerous, and digital computer programs for these inter-relationships are also available (Dell *et al.,* 1967), but cannot compete with the special purpose slide-rule described by Severinghaus (1966) in terms of cost or general utility.

Bleich (1969) recently described a much more sophisticated system, based on a time-sharing computer program which incorporates current concepts in acid-base disorders. This program can be used in a conversational mode to assist the physician in treating his patient. The program is written for a PDP–1D computer (Digital Equipment Corporation, Maynard, Mass., U.S.A.) and permits time-sharing between as many as 64 terminals. Information storage occurs without regard to length or content, with special features for handling non-numerical input that allow effective processing of illegal entries, and which render the program auto-instructional. In addition, insertion, deletion and editing of text instructions by other programs in the same interpretive language are greatly facilitated.

When the program is called from a teletype terminal connected to the telephone system, the computer asks for acid-base data and values for the serum electrolytes (Fig. 50); it then checks this input for internal physiological consistency, including compatibility with life. If the information requested by the computer is unavailable, only an 'enter' key is pressed; mistakes are erased with a 'rub out' key. The program then produces an evaluation note varying in length from four words to two pages, with suggestions in respect of differential diagnoses, calculations of appropriate therapy, and measurements which should be recorded subsequently; the printout concludes with pertinent references to the medical literature (Fig. 51). The program has been translated into BASIC, allowing it to be run on the GE–365 computer from Dartmouth College, New Hampshire, U.S.A. Computer time costs only $0.50 for each evaluation note; there are in addition teletype hire and telephone charges. In practice the program has proved of particular educational value, both in sharpening the clinician's discipline in accepting laboratory data, and in encouraging him to consider the wider implications of pathophysiology. More will be heard of this approach to clinical medicine in other fields besides acid-base disorders.

**Ventilatory control**

The basic concept of feed-back control of ventilation, with a rise in $Pco_2$ stimulating an increase in ventilation, has been known for many years. In 1954, Grodins et al. applied the theory of engineering control systems based on a two compartment model of lungs and tissues to describe the ventilatory system. The second order differential equations involved were solved by an analog computer, and the model gave a satisfactory simulation of the ventilatory response to inhalation of exogenous $CO_2$. Experimental physiologists have since discovered more about the mechanisms controlling ventilation. It has been shown, for instance, that the acidity of the CSF overlying the lateral border of the brainstem is probably a major determinant of the central $CO_2$ drive to breathing. This acidity depends upon the bicarbonate ion concentration of the CSF and the $Pco_2$ of the arterial or jugular venous blood (Brooks et al., 1965).

In 1967, Grodins et al. modified their earlier model in the light of this new knowledge. Their revised model consisted of a controlled system of three compartments (lung, brain and tissue), connected by the circulating blood, the brain compartment being separated from a CSF reservoir by a membrane only permeable to $CO_2$. The controlling system included receptor elements monitoring concentrations in CSF and arterial blood.

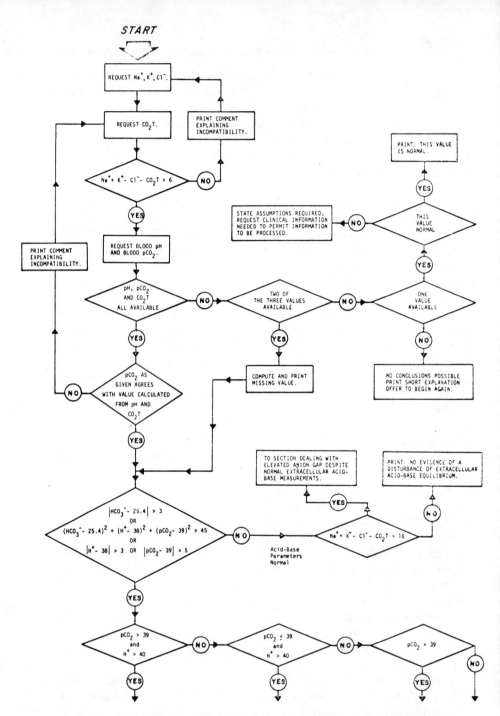

FIG. 50A. Collection of acid-base data when sodium, potassium, and chloride have been provided. Serum electrolytes are expressed as mEq/litre, carbon dioxide tension as mm Hg, and hydrogen ion activity as nEq/litre. Not shown in the figure are additional pathways that check each entry to proper syntax and for compatibility with life. The terminating arrow in the lower left corner leads to the pathways shown in Figure 50B; the remaining terminating arrows lead to sections of the program not shown in the figures.

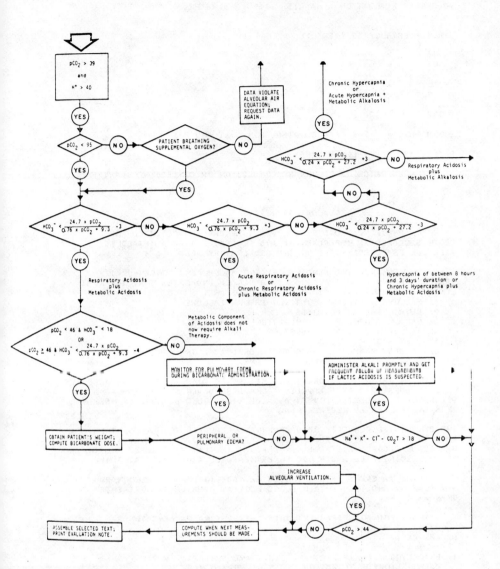

FIG. 50B. Partial diagram of some of the pathways used to characterise an acid-base disturbance. In these pathways the patient's data are compared with whole-body carbon dioxide titration curves in order to determine whether or not the values are compatible with acute or chronic hypercapnia, and whether or not a metabolic acidosis or alkalosis is superimposed. Equations for the titration curves and for the width of the confidence bands have been derived from the literature.

(Figures 50A, 50B and 51 have been reproduced with permission of the author and Editor from Bleich, H. L. 1969. *Journal of Clinical Investigation*, **48**, 1689–1696).

ACID-BASE EVALUATION    MAY 15, 1969    5:46 PM

SERUM ELECTROLYTES (MEQ/L):

    NA    =    140
    K     =    40
    K     =    4.0
    CL    =    110
    CO2T  =    20

BLOOD PH    =    7.19

BLOOD PCO2 =    49.9   (CALCULATED FROM CO2T AND PH)

PATIENT'S WEIGHT (IN POUNDS)    =    150

IS THERE EVIDENCE OF PULMONARY CONGESTION OR CONGESTIVE HEART FAILURE?
NO


                    EVALUATION NOTE

        THE PH OF 7.19 UNITS IS LOWER THAN CAN BE ACCOUNTED FOR
BY THIS DEGREE OF HYPERCAPNIA, AND INDICATES THAT A METABOLIC
ACIDOSIS IS SUPERIMPOSED ON THE RESPIRATORY ACIDOSIS.

        FURTHERMORE, THE FINDING OF A NORMAL PLASMA CONCEN-
TRATION OF UNMEASURED ANIONS (14.0 MEQ/L) INDICATES THAT THE MOST
LIKELY CAUSES OF THE METABOLIC ACIDOSIS ARE:
        1) PYELONEPHRITIS WITHOUT GLOMERULAR FAILURE
        2) RENAL TUBULAR ACIDOSIS
        3) CARBONIC ANHYDRASE INHIBITION (DIAMOX)
        4) AMMONIUM CHLORIDE INGESTION
        5) URETEROSIGMOIDOSTOMY
        6) MASSIVE DIARRHEA, PANCREATIC DRAINAGE, OR
           FISTULAE OF THE SMALL INTESTINE.

        IN AN EFFORT TO CORRECT THE METABOLIC COMPONENT OF THE ACIDOSIS
IT IS SUGGESTED THAT SUFFICIENT ALKALI BE GIVEN TO RAISE PLASMA
BICARBONATE CONCENTRATION TO A VALUE THAT WOULD BE MORE IN KEEPING
WITH UNCOMPLICATED HYPERCAPNIA.

THE CALCULATED QUANTITY OF BICARBONATE REQUIRED TO ACHIEVE THIS GOAL
IS APPROXIMATELY 250 MEQ.   IT IS SUGGESTED, HOWEVER, THAT 132 MEQ
OF SODIUM BICARBONATE BE GIVEN DURING THE NEXT FEW HOURS, AND THAT
SERUM ELECTROLYTES AND BLOOD PH BE MEASURED AGAIN AT THAT TIME.

        FINALLY, EVERY EFFORT SHOULD BE MADE TO IMPROVE PULMONARY
VENTILATION AND TO MAINTAIN BLOOD PCO2 AT A VALUE OF NO GREATER
THAN 45 MM HG.

        THANK YOU FOR REFERRING THIS INTERESTING PATIENT TO US.

REFERENCES:

1) BRACKETT, N.C., JR., COHEN, J.J., AND SCHWARTZ, W.B.
   CARBON DIOXIDE TITRATION CURVE OF NORMAL MAN.
   NEW ENG. J. MED., 272, 6, 1965.

2) BEESON, P.B. AND MCDERMOTT, W.
   CECIL-LOEB TEXTBOOK OF MEDICINE
   12TH EDITION (1967), P.763.

<*>

        FIG. 51. Entry of patient's data and computer-generated evaluation.
Underlined information was typed by the physician, everything else by the
computer. Note that the initial potassium entry was rejected as being
unreasonable, and that the computer supplied the pCO$_2$ when the physician
pressed only the enter button. The bicarbonate deficit is calculated on the
basis of two-thirds of total body water, but the suggested dose (usually less
than the deficit) is rounded off to the nearest ampoule when the patient's
weight exceeds 50 kg.

From this model, and drawing extensively on the physiological literature, these authors deduced six sets of equations for $O_2$, $CO_2$ and nitrogen, defining material balance for each compartment, equilibria between alveolar gas and arterial blood, dissociation curves for blood transport, blood brain equilibria, relationships between blood flow and gas tensions, and transit delay times as a function of these flow rates. These relationships defined the open-loop operations of their model, and the controller function had to be chosen so as to close these loops. The equations were solved in a differential difference form, including an allowance for variable time lags in the model, by a program written in FORTRAN and run on an IBM 7044 computer. Iterative procedures yielded solutions to the complex interactions between $O_2$ and $CO_2$ transport in blood. The final controller function, defining dependence of ventilation upon CSF hydrogen ion concentration and upon arterial pH and $Po_2$ at the carotid chemoreceptors, was illustrated as computer-generated plots of these variables against time, following simulation of $CO_2$ inhalation, hypoxia at sea level, altitude hypoxia and metabolic disturbances in acid-base balance. The program required one minute of computer time for every four minutes of experimental simulation. Although this model undoubtedly represented a highly sophisticated description of the behaviour of the ventilatory control system, it still made no allowance for the mechanical factors concerned in the regulation of ventilation.

The perfect ventilatory control model does not yet exist. Most models assume two or three compartments in which $CO_2$ is distributed, but knowledge of the way in which $CO_2$ is stored and transported in the body is essential for accurate simulation of chemical ventilatory control mechanisms. Matthews et al. (1968a) studied the kinetics of radioactive $CO_2$ distribution during rebreathing, and simulated their results using analog models based on five tissue spaces (brain, well and poorly perfused extracellular fluid, and intracellular bicarbonate ion in equilibrium with both these extracellular fluid spaces), in addition to a pulmonary compartment and arterial and venous blood $CO_2$ pools (Matthews et al., 1968b). They suggested that hydration of $CO_2$ in intracellular fluid might be an important rate-limiting factor, and presented a model of ventilatory control during rebreathing, $CO_2$ inhalation, and hyperventilation, with equations based on $CO_2$ buffering relationships of their compartments, again solving the differential equations by digital computer.

## Routine pulmonary function tests

In the clinical practice of respiratory medicine, a wide variety of 'pulmonary function tests' is available. Ventilatory tests, such as the forced expiratory volume in one second ($FEV_{1.0}$) and forced vital capacity (FVC), allow rapid and simple evaluation of airways obstruction. Spirometric measurements of lung volumes, by helium dilution or body plethysmography, enable restrictive and obstructive patterns of functional defect to be separated. Measurements of the single breath transfer factor for carbon monoxide ($T_{CO}$) can aid diagnosis of pulmonary fibrosis of whatever aetiology; this test is also very useful in following therapy.

In all these measurements numerical values for patients' results must be calculated, and comparison made with the 'normal values' predicted from height, weight, age and sex from various surveys carried out in normal subjects. These routine tasks are eminently suitable for performance by a digital computer, and a time-sharing system for this work has been described by Moser (1969). The program prints out values for individual patients in respect of lung volumes and $T_{CO}$, and compares these findings with the 'predicted normal' results; manual methods cost $3.50 per patient, whereas the computer system costs at least $4.50 per patient depending very much on the rate of use. With the computer, greater accuracy and relief of skilled personnel for other tasks are claimed, but it seems that the full value of the computer in this field will only be utilised when diagnostic and therapeutic information are directly obtained, as in Bleich's (1969) work on acid-base analysis.

## CONCLUSION

The potential ability of computers to rationalise decision-making, by comparing a variety of directly acquired and derived data with previously acquired information and with the sequelae of previous decisions, mimics the human processes of judgement based upon experience. In some areas of the management of acutely ill patients, the harnessing of computers so as to fulfil this function is in sight (e.g. Bleich, 1969), and the next chapter describes some important work in this field. In many areas, however, the major problem is how to secure the automatic provision of reliable accurate data for analysis by the computer, and this chapter has had as one of its main aims the need to draw attention to the 'transducer problem'. Much more effort is required in this field, and success will require much more active collaboration between the instrument engineer, the physiologist, and the clinician before turning to the computer to solve the problems. Without this collaboration, there is a real danger that engineers will design instruments that can record clinically irrelevant data while the clinician, upon whom the ultimate responsibility for action devolves, will come to ignore the flood of accurate but irrelevant information with which he is provided.

REFERENCES

BAND, D. M. & SEMPLE, S. J. G. (1967). Continuous measurement of blood pH with an indwelling arterial glass electrode. *Journal of Applied Physiology*, **22**, 854–857.

BLEICH, H. L. (1969). Computer evaluation of acid base disorder. *Journal of Clinical Investigation*, **48**, 1689–1696.

BROOKS, C. M., KAO, F. F. & LLOYD, B. B. (1965). *The Cerebrospinal Fluid and the Regulation of Ventilation.* Oxford: Blackwell.

DELL, R. B., ENGEL, K. & WINTERS, R. W. (1967). A computer program for the blood pH; Log $pCO_2$ nomogram. *Scandinavian Journal of Clinical and Laboratory Investigation,* **19,** 29–37.

GRODINS, F. S., BUELL, J. & BART, A. J. (1967). Mathematical analysis and digital simulation of the respiratory control system. *Scandinavian Journal of Clinical and Laboratory Investigation,* **22,** 260–276.

GRODINS, F. S., GRAY, J. S., SCHNOEDER, K. R., NORINS, A. L. & JONES, R. W. (1954). Respiratory responses to $CO_2$ inhalation. A theoretical study of a non-linear biological regulator. *Journal of Applied Physiology,* **7,** 283–308.

HILBERMAN, M., SCHILL, J. P. & PETERS, R. M. (1969). On line digital analysis of respiratory mechanics and the automation of respiratory control. *Journal of Thoracic and Cardiovascular Surgery,* **58,** 821–828.

KELMAN, G. R. (1966). Digital computer subroutine for the conversion of oxygen tension into saturation. *Journal of Applied Physiology,* **21,** 1375–1376.

KELMAN, G. R. (1967). Digital computer procedure for the conversion of $pCO_2$ into blood $CO_2$ content. *Respiration Physiology,* **3,** 111–115.

KELMAN, G. R. (1968). Computer program for the production of $O_2 - CO_2$ diagram. *Respiration Physiology,* **4,** 260–269.

MATTHEWS, C. M. E., LASZLO, G., CAMPBELL, E. J. M., KIBBY, P. M. & FREEDMAN, S. (1968a). Exchange of $^{11}CO_2$ in arterial blood with body $CO_2$ pools. *Respiration Physiology,* **6,** 29–44.

MATTHEWS, C. M. E., LASZLO, G., CAMPBELL, E. J. M. & READ, D. J. C. (1968b). A model for the distribution and transport of $CO_2$ in the body and the ventilatory response to $CO_2$. *Respiration Physiology,* **6,** 45–87.

MILIC-EMILI, G., MEAD, J., TURNER, J. M. & GLOUSER, E. M. (1964). Improved technique for estimating pleural pressure from oesophageal balloons. *Journal of Applied Physiology,* **19,** 207–211.

MOSER, K. M. (1969). Practical computer program for routine spirometric testing using the time sharing concept. *Diseases of the Chest,* **56,** 92–97.

OSBORN, J. J., BEAUMONT, J. O., RAISON, J. C. A., RUSSELL, J. & GERBODE, F. (1968). Measurement and monitoring of acutely ill patients by digital computer. *Surgery,* **64,** 1057–1070.

SEVERINGHAUS, J. W. (1966). Blood gas calculator. *Journal of Applied Physiology,* **21,** 1108–1116.

STACY, R. W. & PETERS, R. M. (1965). Computations of respiratory mechanical parameters. In *Computers in Biomedical Research.* Ed. Stacy, R. W. & Waxman, B. D. Vol. 2, pp. 269–288. New York: Academic Press.

STAEHELIN, H. B., CARLSEN, E. N., HINSHAW, D. B. & SMITH, L. L. (1968). Continuous blood pH monitoring using an indwelling catheter. *American Journal of Surgery,* **116,** 280–285.

SUGIOKA, K. (1968). A method of measuring continuously in vivo-blood $pCO_2$, $pO_2$ and pH in the intact animal. *Biomedical Sciences Instrumentation,* **4,** 185–189.

WEST, J. B. (1969a). Ventilation—perfusion inequality and overall gas exchange in computer models of the lung. *Respiration Physiology,* **7,** 88–110.

WEST, J. B. (1969b). Effect of slope and shape of dissociation curve on pulmonary gas exchange. *Respiration Physiology,* **8,** 66–85.

# CHAPTER TWELVE

# Real Time Processing of Data by Computer for the Clinical Monitoring of Patients

By J. C. A. RAISON

## SUMMARY

THE real time processing of data deriving from patient monitoring and clinical measurements under conditions requiring intensive care represents an important area of application for on-line computer systems. Computers can serve useful functions at every stage of these systems, beginning with the operation of measuring instruments and proceeding through the steps of data acquisition, calculation, correlation, interpretation, information display and storage; computers can even serve functions in relation to the direction of treatment. The various processes listed are all interrelated, and this suggests that they might usefully be integrated by a computer-dependent system. This chapter refers to a real time system having wide application in an intensive care unit and discusses in detail the sub-system for ventilatory and respiratory measurements so as to illustrate the part played by the computer. The benefits that derive from the system are examined.

## INTRODUCTION

Small computers, used as rapid calculators, can serve important functions when attached on-line to one or a number of measuring instruments, but the greatest potential of real time computing when applied to the direct clinical care of the acutely ill patient is in the realm of complex high speed function. In this situation computers can be used for acquiring data, performing calculations, and undertaking correlations rapidly and on a time-sharing basis from a number of different physiological functions. Important information can be made available rapidly to influence and improve the standards of care for individual patients.

## MONITORING PATIENTS IN A CARDIOPULMONARY INTENSIVE CARE UNIT

A computer-dependent system of this nature was developed for clinical use, to serve a cardiopulmonary intensive care unit, and this became operational at the Pacific Medical Center, San Francisco, in 1966 (Osborn et al., 1968; 1969a). One sub-system, ventilatory and respiratory measurement, has been selected for detailed description in this chapter and its accompanying appendix since this sub-system illustrates many of the different uses of a computer operating in real time under these conditions. By itself, this sub-system would not justify the provision of facilities on the scale described; some of the benefits it confers can be considered in isolation, but others depend on its interaction with the other sub-systems.

Figure 52 illustrates in diagrammatic form the standard procedures involved in monitoring patients, and shows where computer-dependent process control features have been introduced by the system as a whole. The technical details of the computer system, its hardware and software organisation, are outlined in the Appendix (p. 251) together with more information about the operation of the monitoring equipment itself. It should be made clear that the system outlined in Figure 52 has been operated in parallel with the more traditional processes of (1) making a clinical observation in respect of a patient's condition, (2) consideration of possible courses of action and the taking of such action by staff, and (3) the further observation of the patient.

## Calibration of the ventilatory sub-system
This sub-system employs several transducers. A modified Fleisch pneumotachograph is linked to the bedside computer console, which incorporates the other data input channels, switching apparatus and displays. The pneumotachograph is attached as close as possible to the endotracheal or tracheostomy tube, and allows gas sampling to be performed as well as the making of pressure recordings. There are four 'primary gas signals' available for processing:
1. Differential pressure (to provide an estimate of flow rate);
2. Absolute airways pressure;
3. Oxygen concentration;
4. Carbon dioxide concentration.
The analog signals are amplified for transmission to the computer room, where they are each sampled every 4.2 milliseconds. The signals are digitised before being read into the computer, where they are held in a data buffer.

To calibrate the equipment, a known volume of air is pumped through the pneumotachograph by a hand-operated piston, under conditions of airway pressure which give calibration values for tidal volume and minute volume, compliance and work, and the gas sensors are then calibrated at two different known gas concentrations. The computed values for total $O_2$ uptake and total $CO_2$ output are then checked by using a hand-operated double-barrelled syringe, which serves as an artificial lung; this draws a fixed volume of gas of known composition in through the sensing head, through a measured amount of dead space, and then 'expires' an identical volume of a different 'alveolar' gas. Since the volume and concentration of gas flowing in each direction is known,

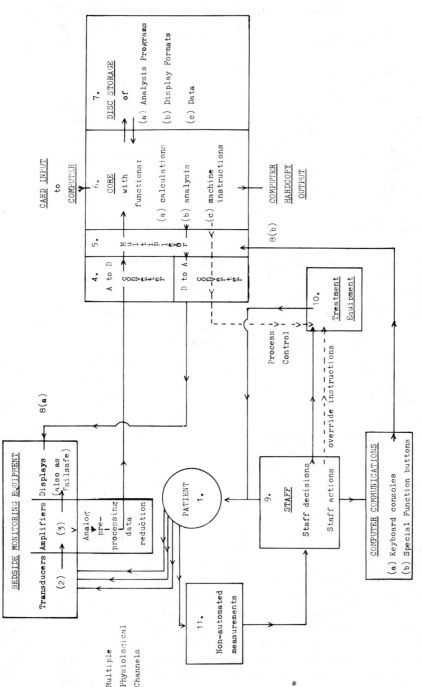

SIMPLIFIED PATIENT SERVO-CONTROL DIAGRAM

FIG. 52. This figure shows the general interrelationships of components making up the on-line real time patient monitoring system described in Chapter 12 and its accompanying Appendix. The stages in the computer-dependent parts of the system are numbered, beginning with the patient (1) and proceeding eventually to 8(a), the computer operated displays and 8(b), the hard copy output. Staff (9) receive this information in addition to the results of their own observations, and the results of non-automated measurements (11), on the basis of which they may treat the patient directly, or adjust the treatment equipment (10), or communicate with the computer. Operations involving process control of equipment (10) are indicated by broken lines, the computer-originated process control data being examined by the staff before the equipment is adjusted or the computer's instructions overridden.

$O_2$ uptake and $CO_2$ production during calibration can be calculated. The keyboard or console entry indicating the start of this procedure modifies the ordinary analytical programs and ensures that the data for instrumental calibration are noted in the computer's history file. A technician observes that the values calculated are acceptable before instructing the computer that the sub-system may be used for accepting measurements from patients and monitoring their condition. Normally, the calibration procedure needs to be performed once daily.

## Operation of the ventilatory sub-system: the 'alarm' mode

To the observer, the system operates in one of two modes, either 'full analysis' or 'alarm'. Full analysis is undertaken for 30 seconds every 10 minutes, and at other times when demanded by a dedicated process interrupt button at the bedside; it is described in the next section. The alarm mode operates in the remaining periods.

The alarm analysis programs reside permanently in the computer's internal memory and are carried out at different frequencies depending upon the physiological data involved; the cardiovascular channels are checked most frequently. For the ventilatory sub-system, the alarm analysis program is required every 30 seconds, to identify the existence of air flow and to measure the peak inspiratory pressure, which should fall within pre-set limits. Any of these alarm signals initiates a highest level interrupt calling in the 'Alarm Alert and Display' program. The limit that has been exceeded is intimated as a flashing signal of words appearing at the bottom of the display oscilloscope, this being accompanied by illumination of a red alarm light and an audible warning signal; this information is also recorded on the hard copy detailing the full data. These alarm signals contain further information capable of indicating more precisely the probable nature of the emergency. For instance, the messages suggest whether the emergency is due to the patient having become apnoeic or having developed an airway obstruction, or draw attention to the possibility of a connection having been broken or of a gas leak having developed. If the alarm analysis program detects nothing abnormal, the data in core for that particular cycle are not stored but are removed from the buffer table when this becomes filled. The buffer table is limited in size and is therefore liable to overflow since data are being continually acquired; at the stage of the recycling procedure where this is liable to occur, the latest set of data replaces the data which were acquired most remotely (i.e. data from the beginning of the table are displaced). A button beside the bed can be operated to suppress the alarm analysis process by staff when they have observed the warning; this eliminates for a pre-set period the inevitable recycling into the alarm mode. In the electrocardiogram sub-system, operation of the alarm program initiates a more detailed analysis of the waveform. All the alarm limits that have to be pre-set for a particular patient, and any other limits which are used in the alarm analysis programs, are entered into the computer through the ward keyboard or bedside terminal. More details of the collection of input and the operation of the system are given in the Appendix (p. 251).

## Operation of the ventilatory sub-system: the 'full analysis' program

The ventilatory respiratory subroutines illustrate a number of ways in which a real time system can operate uniquely so as to be clinically effective in an intensive care ward. The first is in the co-ordination of sample signals. The signals produced by the flow and pressure transducers are virtually instantaneous, but there is a delay of about 0.05 seconds for the corresponding data points in respect of the $O_2$ and $CO_2$ concentrations; this delay represents the sum of time taken for gas to travel along the sampling line and the response time of the gas analysers (p. 252). The delay can be measured by inspection of simultaneous signal recordings on a chart recorder in the bedside console, the point corresponding to the start of inspiration (start of inward gas flow) being marked by a sudden decrease in the $CO_2$ and a sudden increase in the $O_2$ concentrations. The data points for the signals from the flow transducer must be 'delayed', for purposes of calculation, by this amount before being correlated with the corresponding values for $O_2$ and $CO_2$ analyses. The identification and measurement of the delay time can be carried out by the computer, but it was found in practice that the delay was constant for a given set of physical conditions, and the program was later modified so that the observed delay period could be input via the ward keyboard when setting each new patient up on the system.

On the basis of the readings from the flow and pressure transducers, and the $O_2$ and $CO_2$ concentrations, the computer makes three volume calculations for each inspiration and expiration during the period under analysis. These are the tidal volume, by integration of the flow signal, and the corresponding $O_2$ and $CO_2$ volumes by integration of the product of flow and gas concentration. Average values for inspiration and expiration are next calculated for each of these three volumes and for the pressure readings in respect of the period of analysis. Any individual observation deviating by more than 10 per cent from the mean is discarded. The computer then applies a correction for errors that would otherwise arise because of differences in pressure, temperature, humidity and gas concentration occurring at the pneumotachograph between the periods of inspiration and expiration. Full details of this procedure have been described elsewhere (Osborn *et al.*, 1968; 1969a; Raison *et al.*, 1968; Beaumont *et al.*, 1968), and do not require to be repeated in this short account.

Finally, a number of indices of ventilation and respiration are cal-culated (Osborn *et al.*, 1968; 1969a). These indices are:

| | |
|---|---|
| Minute tidal ventilation | Tidal volume |
| Non-elastic airway resistance | Respiratory rate |
| Alveolar oxygen tension | Oxygen uptake |
| Inspired oxygen tension | Carbon dioxide output |
| End-expiratory $CO_2$ partial pressure | Respiratory quotient |

'Total' compliance of ventilatory system (pulmonary plus chest wall)
Work of inspiration during positive pressure breathing.

Some of these calculated values are compared with stated limits, which can be varied by keyboard entries. All these calculations commence during the period of 'full analysis', and are completed within about five seconds of the 30-second period required for the complete series of observations and their related calculations and correlations. The results are stored on magnetic disc in a history file for each patient, together with a computer-averaged transient of the inspiratory pressure-volume loop; this file is serially addressed so that any tendency for data to overflow leads to obliteration of the earliest information. Taking account of the data arising from all the different sub-systems, and the many and various keyboard entries, the intention initially was to provide sufficient storage space for at least 24 hours per patient with simultaneous monitoring of two patients. In practice, it was found that the 500,000 words of storage allowed for this was being under-used, and the system has since been extended in its application so that it can now accept signals from six monitoring systems operating on-line simultaneously with a file capacity for data collected during a minimum period of three days.

**Operation of the ventilatory sub-system: special applications**
Two special on-line applications have been found necessary. The first, operated by a function selection switch at the bedside, starts a breath-by-breath analysis of ventilation and continues this until switched off. Respiratory rate, tidal volume, and peak inspiratory pressure are dis-played for each breath almost instantaneously, together with a graphic plot of the inspiratory part of the pressure-volume loop for each; this information appears on a cathode ray display tube at the bedside. The scale factors of the horizontal (pressure) axis are moved one unit to the right for each successive breath, so that distinction and comparison between them is made easy. This has become the standard method by which each patient is established on mechanical ventilation.

In the second special on-line application, averaged pressure-volume inspiratory loops from previous and current analyses are retrieved and displayed in a similar progressive manner, on request entered via the ward console. These comparisons of changes in ventilatory pattern have been found very useful in observing progress when monitoring for acute trends in improvement or deterioration.

When blood gas analyses (pH, $Pco_2$, $Po_2$) are performed with conventional instruments and manual recording of the scale readings, the data can be entered into the computer through a standard keyboard in the laboratory or through the keyboard on the bedside console. For the standard keyboard, the code entry 'EG' ('Enter Gas Value') causes the production of a row of names of the variables to be entered (e.g. time of analysis, pH values, etc.) below which data may be typed in quickly. More recently, a cathode ray screen has been used; this requires selection of the appropriate display, followed by keying in of the digital analysis values in the order outlined on the screen. The data appear on the screen and can be corrected before storage is ordered by pressing the 'End' message key.

The most recent introduction has been the connection of a semi-automated blood gas analyser on-line to the computer. After a doctor or nurse has attached a syringe containing a 2 ml specimen of blood to the equipment, and pressed the 'Start' button, all procedures and measurements are carried out automatically. The computer scans the single meter output (the various electrodes are multiplexed to it), calculates the corrections and displays the results; corrections are applied for temperature, for pH, and in the case of potassium determinations for the concentration of sodium. With any of these methods of input, the blood gas results are correlated with the appropriate respiratory analyses to produce and display calculations of alveolar-arterial difference, alveolar ventilation, and the ratio of dead space to tidal volume. All these values are of considerable importance in managing patients during prolonged periods of mechanical ventilation.

### Operation of the ventilatory sub-system: display programs

The display methods have been fully described (Osborn et al., 1968, 1969a; Raison, 1970); they are called in by bringing the appropriate display format subroutine from the magnetic disc after the completion of a set of 'full analyses'. Several different 'standard' displays have been constructed, of which four can at any one time be selected by switches on the bedside console; each set of displays can be selected with either a 4-hour or a 24-hour time base.

The most useful displays have proved to be X-Y plots of the most recent values of up to three measurements, together with the digital values for the latest set of analyses and derived calculations (accompanied by their descriptive codings for purposes of identification). In addition to the standard displays, other X-Y plot formats, or numerical tables of data, may be obtained on demand by keying in the appropriate simple coded instruction through the ward keyboard. Similarly, keying in the relevant code selects the time base for the various displays. A manual of the available keyboard entries is kept on the ward but, in addition, entry of 'SOS' initiates an instructional program outlining to the keyboard the command or entry options available. Because of the limited life of storage oscilloscopes, each display is erased after 30 seconds unless a 'hold display' switch is operated by the observer. Displays can also be called between a set of full analyses by using an interrupt button on the bedside console. Alarm messages always appear at the bottom of any existing display, and are distinguished by the fact that they flash on and off.

In addition to the oscilloscope displays which are used for minute-by-minute and hour-by-hour care, a graphic plot of all variables is produced daily at 7 a.m. This is the prime document for clinical 'daily rounds' and serves as a preliminary scan of the data collected in the previous 24 hours, in connection with any research and development in progress on the system. This graphic display helps with the subsequent examination of the mass of digital data on the hard-copy tabular output from the line printer. A first attempt has also been made to produce, via the ward keyboard, a brief cumulative report of 'vital signs' formerly recorded by the attending nurse.

## Correlation of the ventilatory sub-system with other sub-systems

The ventilatory sub-system is also correlated with other computer procedures. When a 'Fick cardiac output' is requested via the bedside console, a measurement of the $O_2$ uptake extending over four minutes is commenced. When these observations were first made, a double wavelength automated oximeter (Eberhart, 1968) was used, directly connected to indwelling catheters for collecting the two specimens of arterial and central venous blood; sampling was controlled by the computer and occurred at the midpoint of the $O_2$ uptake measurements. More recently, to avoid the cost of a separate oximeter having to be connected on-line to each patient, blood has been withdrawn manually during the $O_2$ uptake measurements, following a signal from the bedside console. Having collected the specimens, the syringes are immediately attached to the oximeter and remainder of the procedure is carried out automatically under computer and local control. The results are immediately displayed following completion of the calculations.

## Program writing and 'going live'

Application programs have been written in FORTRAN. Quite major changes (e.g. in the methods of calculation, correlations, frequency and priority of various analyses, etc.) can be effected quickly by alteration to the program cardstacks, and this experience has confirmed the value of careful documentation. In the special situation of 'going live' where critical clinical conditions exist, the ability to introduce changes to the system at short notice, on request, is very important. Equally important has been the ability to revert to the unmodified and hitherto familiar method, if the latest change proves unacceptable when it comes to be tried. The ability to make these changes, and to reverse decisions easily, have been significant factors in obtaining the enthusiastic co-operation of the clinical staff.

## THE CONTRIBUTION OF A COMPUTER-DEPENDENT MONITORING SYSTEM TO THE OPERATION OF AN INTENSIVE CARE UNIT

The ventilatory sub-system described illustrates a number of ways in which a real time computer system can help with the running of an intensive care unit. In the first place, instrumentation may be improved. In the present context, a number of the limitations of a pneumotacho-graph as a means of 'continuous' measurement have been offset, rendering it useful in clinical care. The ability to make use of this particular instrument renders possible measurements which, in these clinical circumstances, could otherwise only be occasionally carried out with conventional methods of spirometry.

Another big advantage has been the high speed of data collection from several sources concurrently—from the pneumotachograph, the pressure transducer, $O_2$ and $CO_2$ analysers as well as from the transducers serving all the other sub-systems. These various forms of input have then been subject to calculation at high speed. It would be impossible to use this technique and this range of instrumentation, regardless of the problems of data acquisition, if calculations had to be performed by 'manual' methods. This speed of calculation makes frequent use of measurements such as cardiac output estimations and alveolar ventilation measurements practicable.

In addition to data acquisition and high speed calculations, the system allows for the rapid performance of correlations between the various data. This may take place during the process of acquisition (e.g. gas flow and gas concentration signals) or take the form of correlations between different sub-systems (e.g. cardiac output estimations), or correlations with previously recorded data (e.g. alveolar ventilation, and the ratio of dead space to tidal volume). On the basis of these various measurements and some of the correlations, the system has also been programmed to assume in part an interpretative function. This is perhaps least well illustrated by the ventilatory-respiratory sub-system (an example is an alarm stating 'respiratory obstruction'), and a better example is provided by the cardiovascular sub-system, in the form of diagnoses made on the basis of ECG recordings. Finally, the system has proved very helpful in the areas of data recording and display.

It should be pointed out that the work described here has employed a digital computer system, and that some of the activities summarised above require digital computing techniques. However, it would be possible, particularly now that the development work has been undertaken, to design special purpose analog computers to undertake many of the high speed data acquisition and calculation operations, and they could contribute to the use of improved instrumentation at the stage of data capture.

## Some specific advantages that have been noted

The assistance provided by an effective system of data collection and display should not be underestimated, and indeed the monitoring system at the Karolinska Hospital, Stockholm, has this function as its prime objective; considerable benefits have been derived (Norlander, 1968; William-Olsson et al., 1969). In San Francisco, a preliminary survey suggested that up to 40 per cent of the time of nurses specially trained for work in the intensive care unit was being taken up by measurements that were able to be performed automatically, and by the subsequent procedure of calculation and recording, including recording on graphical displays. It is not claimed that a corresponding saving of effort has yet been achieved by the computer system. However, some relief has undoubtedly been achieved and more time can now be devoted to the personal nursing of the patient.

Parallel operations carried out during the early stages of implementing the project, and the research activities stemming from these, drew attention to the incidence of errors in manual transcription, particularly in respect of pH and blood gas values. These have been almost entirely eliminated by using automatic computer-dependent systems, as have other quite remarkable and hitherto unappreciated errors related to the interval of time between an event actually occurring during a very busy period of work and the time later ascribed to that event when it came to be recorded; on some occasions the discrepancy was more than one hour, yet the existence of any discrepancy was not appreciated. It has also proved invaluable to have continuing and accurate records which go on being obtained during critical events, a time when they are most needed and yet, with manual methods, a time when they usually have to be abandoned.

The techniques required by the computer for setting patients up on ventilators, and for monitoring changes of airway, have become indispensable to the staff and are readily acknowledged as having improved the care of patients.

The intense metabolic demands of shivering, particularly when it is of a scarcely recognisable degree, have been demonstrated and it has been possible to institute treatment much earlier so as to avoid this (Raison et al., 1970).

A recent study has shown that, out of eight otherwise 'unexplained cardiac arrhythmic crises' which occurred in spite of uninterrupted nursing by highly skilled staff, five had their origin in a respiratory episode which had occurred several hours earlier; this respiratory event would have been able to be detected and recognised by the computer (i.e. computer diagnosis), and the subsequent cardiac crisis might therefore have been capable of being avoided (Osborn *et al.*, 1969b). It is not suggested that automatic diagnosis did take place but the sequence of events, once identified from the computer records, was capable of definition as trends and is amenable to programming. It should be stressed that advances in patient care, deriving from a study of trends detected in correlated data, can call for extensive multivariate analysis of very large amounts of data in order to design new methods and to set limits for variables which will thereafter provide effective 'diagnostic' procedures without an unacceptable number of false alarms. Such progress depends on the development and testing of hypotheses which, for instance, associate undesirable physiological observations or measurements that would not in themselves normally be regarded as potentially serious, at least until a much more marked degree of abnormality had developed, with a mass of earlier data collected from other measuring devices. This demands repeated testing by selection from a large volume of data, probably with several degrees of refinement starting (1) from coarse approximations, and progressing (2) to the application of different values for variables to be applied in the trial of new programs. This is not an argument in favour of collecting all possible data, much of which is subsequently found to be unusable. Instead the thesis is that new programs can be based on on-line measurements and that these programs should then be tested against real data, in real time but as a background or research activity, to allow an early assessment of their relationship to observed clinical phenomena. This objective can be achieved by logging the operation of such programs.

The incidence of abnormal trends relative to the amount of data acquired is small, and background testing needs to be arranged in such a manner that a large number of different values for the variables which can be set are tested, simultaneously, to identify the most effective diagnostic (or detection) programs, in close relation to the clinical course. These developmental assessments are too demanding to be able to be adopted using only human effort, and the present studies indicate that a computer-based system is itself an important tool in the generation of new techniques, by facilitating studies which would not otherwise be practicable. In general, computers have now shown their value in promoting a greater appreciation and use of measurement, as opposed simply to alarm monitoring, in the management of patients under intensive care.

## Impact on clinical staff

The impact of the system as a whole (not just the ventilatory sub-system) on clinical staff has been favourable. Systems of this sort are bound to require considerable activity in research and development, and this may distract from the objective of devising a practical system of caring for patients. It is important to excite and retain the interest of doctors and nurses, since a good system depends on reliable input and those responsible for input (in this case principally nurses and junior doctors) must themselves obtain from the system at an early stage output that improves upon their existing facilities. The importance of obtaining and maintaining the cooperation of ward staff in computer projects directly concerned with patients has recently been emphasised, although in a different context, by Opit and Woodroffe (1970a, b).

The flexibility afforded by a large computer installation has contributed to the provision of useful output. The presence of professionals among the computer systems staff and the programmers, many of whom have become competent physiologists, has been important. It has, however, been equally important that some of the medical staff should be able to 'talk the language' of the professional computer staff.

Following the proving of the system, the established method of computer operation has not required the constant attendance of a computer operator. After a few months, it proved possible to run the system to acceptable standards of clinical performance by enlisting volunteers for an on-call rota, to operate a simple start-up routine should bugs arise outside normal working hours. After nine months of operation, it became possible to leave the computer unattended every night and at weekends, the longest period unattended being 66 hours.

## A cautionary note

The application of computers working in real time to patients requiring intensive clinical care can be confused by the issue of precision. The scientist or mathematician may be unaware of the relatively coarse degree of accuracy required—recognisable clinical changes may be associated with variations of as much as 15 to 20 per cent. Searching for greater precision should be possible as a result of the development of improved methods of measurement applicable to such patients, and this will be invaluable. However, to search for and detect these early changes may render immediate progress towards better standards of care frustrating, and may also discourage doctors from using the less sensitive methods presently available to them to refine existing knowledge. The contrary situation can also arise—for instance, nurses who had been accustomed to rounding off their own recordings of blood pressure became seriously worried by the 'inaccuracy of the computer', which reported pressures of 118/88 rather than 120/90. Astute programming and education of the users can help to avoid such sources of misunderstanding.

## Limitations of the system, and its further development

The system so far developed has intentionally not attempted to 'close the loop', by making the computer initiate treatment. Places where this could become applicable are indicated in Figure 52, and their introduction would make the system resemble full industrial process control function. While there might be hesitation about introducing this mode of operation until greater confidence exists in the precision of equipment, and in the criteria on which clinical decisions are based, attention should be drawn to the system in use in Birmingham, Alabama (Sheppard *et al.*, 1968). This system controls and monitors blood replacement by reference to arterial and venous pressures and blood loss, all of which are measured automatically; the limits for the variables are input by the doctor. It seems probable that the more effective and safer use of vaso-active drugs in shock will be provided by computer-dependent monitoring and control.

The object of this project was to explore the potential of a 'medium range' industrial process control computer, and there was no immediate plan to match the available hardware to the processing requirements of the system. When the system was serving two beds continuously, only 20 per cent of the potential processing time was being used by the intensive care project, but linkage of the computer has been increased to six beds on a full-time basis with a number of other beds connected intermittently. As the slack in the system is taken up, it may become necessary to queue analysis data in core for sequential processing. There is, however, room for considerable reduction in the amount of data, and this has at least two connotations for the present system. Few of the physiological signals used in monitoring have a high frequency component that is sufficiently well understood at present to justify sampling rates that are as great as 200 per second. Trials applied to the measurements in the respiratory sub-system have shown that sufficient information can be obtained for processing with existing programs at a sampling rate of 50 per second. With presently available high speed multiplexors, this reduction in the amount of input data should be of value either in widening the service to more beds or in increasing the number of input channels.

At the other end of processing, data reduction is equally important. The need to present information as statements in words summarising the data on which they are based, rather than the presentation of large tables of digital values, has clearly emerged from these experiments. At present, however, there is only a limited amount of such information presentation since, in the developmental stage, there has been a need to retain in store all the primary data from which any processed information is derived. This may prove to be just an interim state, while confidence in the computer grows and its usefulness is extended, and it is to be hoped that much of the primary data and derived calculations will in course of time be eliminated from store; if retention of data should be required solely for legal reasons, this need could be met by obtaining regular printouts. It should be noted, however, that the task of devising automatic facilities for editing, to achieve data reduction, is a very large task and little progress has been made so far.

Limitations on manpower resources answer another possible major criticism, that the full potential of relatively powerful computing facilities lies in a considerable expansion of the correlative role. This requires the devising of interpretative programs, if simultaneous multi-channel physiological measurements are undertaken. Already three phases of the ventilatory inspiratory pressure-volume loop, of established clinical value, have been shown to be capable of definition and this should lead on to identification by the computer of abnormal developments, rather than continuing to rely on periodical reviews of graphic presentations by the staff in the intensive care unit. A program capable of differentiating changes due to cardiac tamponade, to hypovolaemia, or to primary cardiac failure, based on measurements already obtainable, now seems possible (Osborn et al., 1969b); these conditions are often confusing clinically. It is also forecast that the system will be increasingly used to identify automatically the premonitory ventilatory features of cardiac arrhythmias, as mentioned earlier.

## Cost considerations
The project did not include provisions for assessing its cost-effectiveness. The pre-requisite of pioneering the introduction of the system under circumstances that in no way disrupted the existing high standards of patient care meant that staff could not be asked to experiment with any reduction in numbers, and there is no definite evidence in respect of possible savings in staff time. Similarly, the information needed to obtain the real costs of the system, operated as a service and excluding research applications, cannot yet be provided. Sheppard et al. (1968) have put forward cost estimates suggesting that a similar computer-based full system, for 14 beds, would increase the charges for intensive care by about 50 per cent, taking into account a figure for the amortization of capital investment.

It is nevertheless possible, on the basis of considerations of the experience already gained, to suggest that the hardware costs for the digital system (as detailed in the Appendix), and having sufficient power for multichannel, multiprogram real time measurement and monitoring of six patients, would cost between £60,000 and £120,000. Below an investment of £60,000 it would probably be necessary to accept limitation to very specialised applications, for which it might be possible to devise relatively fixed program purpose-built machines. A certain amount of analog processing, notably for cardiac arrhythmias, is already available for monitoring systems, and the advantages of hybrid processing in such a system require examination. The advantages to be gained from the relatively cheap methods of 'black box' analog pre-processing relate to a system that has actually been devised, often on the basis of work initially carried out with more powerful and more flexible digital computing techniques. A 'black box' unit filtering all but the systolic and diastolic turning points of the arterial pressure waveform can yield information of considerable assistance in monitoring patients, but it cannot meet requirements if the first derivative of the upstroke of the pressure wave is to be used to provide information about ventricular function and peripheral resistance. The place of these 'black box' analog machines, as alternatives to the type of digital installation described in this chapter, requires further evaluation and considerations of cost-effectiveness will be necessary.

Digital systems do give power and flexibility, and these features should receive proper recognition despite the apparent cost. They represent strong arguments in favour of the more expensive multi-functional digital installations being designed to serve many similar purposes simultaneously. This would mean that such installations would be more likely to show a favourable cost-benefit comparison in hospitals with several types of intensive care facilities, as well as a number of specialist investigation units responsible for advanced techniques in the fields of cardiac catheterisation or respiratory function. Comparative cost-benefit analyses of this type have still to be carried out, and the difficulty of performing such studies should not be underestimated since both objective and emotional factors come into consideration.

ACKNOWLEDGEMENTS
The practical work and most of the ideas developed in this chapter resulted from close collaboration with Dr J. J. Osborn, Dr J. O. Beaumont, and Dr F. Gerbode, at the Heart Research Institute, Pacific Medical Center, San Francisco, and the author also wishes to thank the many other medical, nursing and technical members of the team. The project was jointly supported by the Research Institute, I.B.M. Advanced Systems Division, and grant no. 5P01-HE-06311 of the National Heart Institute, National Institutes of Health, Bethesda, Md., U.S.A.

**Appendix**

# COMPUTER SYSTEM FOR PATIENT MONITORING AT THE PACIFIC MEDICAL CENTER

## Configuration and operation of the installation

An IBM 1801 (2D) central processor with 32K (18-bit) word store was operated initially by Time Sharing Executive System (TSX) and later by a Multi-programming Executive Operating System (MPX). The central processor has a 2 microsecond memory cycle time, nine data channels and 32 interrupt levels. Applications software, analytical programs and display formats, reside in one part of an IBM 2310 3-disc unit, the other two discs being used respectively for data storage and unrelated batch-processing work. Other peripherals include a card reader, keyboard, line printer and graph plotter.

Time Sharing Executive (TSX) allowed the time sharing of programs loaded from disc by exchanging between disc and core on demand of an interrupt. Because of the comparatively long period required for disc access, this discouraged the use of time-slicing for different programs each of less than a few seconds' duration. The operating system occupied 11.5 K words, and 2K was reserved as an immediate data buffer. A further 10.5 K words formed the working area for programs and data. The remaining 8K core was available for special analysis programs (e.g. respiratory mechanics, ECG analysis), for program development or for unrelated processing activities; these last groups of programs were only in core one group at a time.

Multi-programming Executive (MPX) offered the facility of segmenting the core and overlapping peripheral transfer activity with central processor activity, control being switched between programs in the different areas automatically. In view of the high proportion of input and output involved in processing, this allowed several independent programs to operate simultaneously with very little reduction in efficiency. The core load was designed for the specific needs of the project, 15.8K words being allocated to the System Director; this included subroutines which were commonly used by many programs held in other parts of the core, and a data logging program. A special program area (768 words) housed programs for handling interrupts generated in response to user terminals. The remaining core was allocated in sections of 6K and 3K words respectively to programs executed relatively slowly (i.e. in less than 4 seconds) and to programs executed relatively quickly; the latter were executed on a higher interrupt level. Approximately 7K words could still be allocated to special or unrelated work. All applications programs were written in FORTRAN.

The main display system operates in the following manner. Character generation and display formats, together with any data held in store for a patient, are called as and when required from the disc into core, merged if necessary with data currently in core, and output to one of three 5-inch Tektronic 564 storage oscilloscopes. The computer is not engaged in character regeneration for the display oscilloscope. For enlargement, and because of the need to carry displays over 1,000 feet from the computer to the bedside, images are then transferred by closed-circuit television to ordinary portable 11-inch television screens. As well as being the output of the analytical routines, displays are used in a 'tree-branching' manner, in combination with a small portable special purpose 16-position keyboard, to call special procedures or to input alphanumeric data; these operations are designed so as to require a minimum of keyboard activity by the operator. These display and keyboard units are situated at the bedside. A full keyboard is also available in the computer room itself for input. Most input to the system is in the form of directly measured physiological variables, and the interfacing equipment consists of transducers (2), amplifiers (3), multiplexors (4), and analog digital convertors (5) (for numbering see Fig. 52). Separate multiple beam analog 14-inch display oscilloscopes are also operated from the primary amplifiers in the intensive care ward, partly to provide the reassurance of familiar signals to staff, and partly as a fail soft provision in the event of the computer 'going down'.

For the ventilatory sub-system, several transducers are employed. A Fleisch pneumotachograph is placed as close as possible to the patient's airway. Initially it is usually attached to the endotracheal tube, or occasionally to a tracheostomy tube, but at a later stage in treatment it can be attached to a tightly fitting facemask, which is, however, only applied for short periods. In this way, the same piece of measuring equipment is applied as a rule to each patient throughout the various successive modes of ventilation.

The pneumotachograph is the only part of the equipment that is situated close to the patient. It is electrically heated to $39°C$, and has been modified by the addition of a fine bore gas sampling tube, fitted to the distal side of the airway baffle. This sampling tube divides after about one inch into two similar plastic tubes and these two gas sampling tubes, together with the two tubes which transmit the proximal and distal pneumotachograph pressures, are carried together to the bedside computer console situated about 5 feet away. The console incorporates all the other data input channels, switching apparatus and display instruments.

In the console, the pressure tubes from the pneumotachograph lead to a Statham PM5 differential transducer which has been carefully balanced volumetrically, the proximal tube also being led to a separate gauge which measures the 'absolute' transient airway pressure. One of the gas sampling lines is further subdivided in the bedside console so that gas may be drawn, during periods when the system is in 'full analysis' mode, at rates of 1.5 litres per minute through two rapid response electrodes, (1) a Beckman LB150 infrared analyser and (2) a modified Westinghouse high speed hot ceramic oxygen electrode (Elliott et al., 1966). In between the periods of 'full analysis' the rate of withdrawal of gas is slightly increased, while at the same time warmed dry air is blown gently down the other division of the sampling line and the pressure lines at a combined rate equivalent to the withdrawal rate. These gas flows are in fact very small and constant, so do not interfere with ventilatory measurements, the net gas loss from the system at the pneumotachograph being constant. The effect of this arrangement is to keep sampling and pressure lines free from condensation during the periods between full analyses. This technique, together with automatic resetting of the differential strain gauge to zero before every analysis, has made it possible to leave the pneumotachograph *in situ,* and to obtain reliable measurements, for periods well in excess of 24 hours; this matches the clinical requirements in respect of the management of patients. The switching of valves needed to perform these operations is controlled automatically, by the computer. The system as a whole has a capacity for six patients and in two of the bedside consoles the use of these transducers is switched by the computer alternately between two beds for successive analyses. There are also two smaller consoles, where the use of the transducers is dedicated to one patient, and the present description relates to this simpler arrangement.

There are four 'primary' gas signals available for processing: (1) differential pressure (to provide flow); (2) 'absolute' airway pressure; (3) $O_2$ concentration; and (4) $CO_2$ concentration. Each signal is transmitted double-ended, by a twisted wire pair, from the bedside console to the computer multiplexor, with primary amplifiers in the intensive care ward and line-terminating differential amplifiers at the multiplexor in the computer room. This system was required as an electrical safety precaution because of a difference of ground potential between the intensive care unit and the computer room (Osborn et al., 1969a).

Each analog signal is sampled every 4.2 milliseconds by a solid state multiplexor, working under stored program control. The signal is then converted to digital form, by an analog digital converter, and read into the computer's core memory. For the data from each signal, the immediate store is a table of 100 addresses, serially ordered in such a manner that, on filling the last address, the next data value replaces that in the first address, and so on down through the table and round the loop. Interrupts to initiate analyses are forced immediately following filling of the 50th and 100th addresses. Thus processing commences on 0.25 second periods of data. The program which periodically establishes the 'full analysis' mode (the Periodic Patient Data Analysis program) is held on magnetic disc until called into the computer's internal memory, the trigger for this particular program being the completion of one of these tables of 50 addresses.

REFERENCES

BEAUMONT, J. O., OSBORN, J. J., RAISON, J. C. A. & RUSSELL, J. A. G. (1968). Respiratory measurement and monitoring based on an on-line computer. *Proceedings of the Conference of the Association for the Advancement of Medical Instrumentation,* Houston, Texas, U.S.A.

EBERHART, R. C. (1968). An automated sampling whole blood photometer. *Biomedical Sciences Instrumentation,* **4,** 197–204.

ELLIOTT, S. E., SEGGER, F. J. & OSBORN, J. J. (1966). A modified oxygen gauge for the rapid measurement of $PO_2$ in respiratory gases. *Journal of Applied Physiology,* **21,** 1672–1674.

NORLANDER, O. (1968). An integrated patient monitoring system with display terminals. *Fourth World Congress of Anesthesiologists.* Amsterdam: Excerpta Medica.

OPIT, L. J. & WOODROFFE, F. J. (1970a). Computer-held clinical record system. I, Description of system. *British Medical Journal,* **4,** 76–79.

OPIT, L. J. & WOODROFFE, F. J. (1970b). Computer-held clinical record system. II, Assessment. *British Medical Journal,* **4,** 80–82.

OSBORN, J. J., BEAUMONT, J. O., RAISON, J. C. A., RUSSELL, J. A. G. & GERBODE, F. (1968). Measurement and monitoring of acutely ill patients by digital computer. *Surgery,* **64,** 1057–1070.

OSBORN, J. J., BEAUMONT, J. O., RAISON, J. C. A. & ABBOTT, R. P. (1969a). Computation for quantitative on-line measurements in an intensive care ward.

In *Computers in Biomedical Research*. Ed. Stacy, R. W. & Waxman, B. D. Vol. 3, pp. 207–237. New York: Academic Press.

OSBORN, J. J. and six co-authors (1969b). Respiratory causes of 'sudden unexplained arrhythmia' in post-thoracotomy patients. Scientific sessions. *22nd Conference of the American Heart Association.*

RAISON, J. C. A., BEAUMONT, J. O., ELLIOTT, S. E. & OSBORN, J. J. (1968). Breath-by-breath analysis of respiratory gases in acutely ill patients. *Proceedings of the 21st Annual Conference on Engineering in Biology and Medicine, Houston.* Institute of Electrical and Electronic Engineers, New York, 2, 6.

RAISON, J. C. A. (1970). Graphic presentation of clinical measurement and monitoring. *Proceedings of the Internal Symposium 'Computer Graphics 70',* *Brunel University.* Middlesex, England.

RAISON, J. C. A., OSBORN, J. J., BEAUMONT, J. O. & GERBODE, F. (1970). Oxygen consumption after open-heart surgery measured by a digital computer system. *Annals of Surgery,* 171, 471–484.

SHEPPARD, L. C., KOUCHOUKOS, N. T., KURTTS, M. A. & KIRKLIN, J. W. (1968). Automated treatment of critically ill patients following operation. *Annals of Surgery,* 168, 596–604.

WILLIAM-OLSSON, G., NORLANDER, O., NORDENT, I. & PETERSON, S. O. (1969). A patient monitoring system with display terminals. *Opuscula Medica,* 2, 39–46.

SUGGESTIONS FOR FURTHER READING

DURFEY, J. Q. & LEEMING, M. N. (1966). An on-line system for measuring respiratory parameters using a hybrid analogue/digital computing system. *Aerospace Medicine,* 37, 474–478.

RAISON, J. C. A. (1970). Patient monitoring: on-line computing. *Postgraduate Medical Journal,* 46, 360–365.

WARNER, H. R., GARDNER, R. M. & TORONTO, A. F. (1968). Computer-based monitoring of cardiovascular functions in postoperative patients. *Circulation,* 37, Supplement 2, 68–74.

# Some Examples of the Use of Computers in Research and Medical Education

# Digital Computers in Physiological Laboratories – On-line Applications

## By A. IGGO

### SUMMARY

DEVELOPMENTS in the use of digital computers in physiological laboratories are reviewed. Two recent major advances, the fixed-program bench computers and programmable general purpose digital computers, are considered in some detail and their respective merits for off-line and on-line applications are discussed.

The use of on-line computer systems to control experiments is an especially important advance. Examples of the ways in which this control has been achieved in neurophysiological laboratories to program the experiments, to acquire and process data, and to use the results to decide the subsequent course of the experiment, are taken from research work currently in progress.

### INTRODUCTION

The alert reader might well ask why a physiologist working in a Faculty of Veterinary Medicine should be contributing to a book on medical computing. The answer lies in the fact that there is much which is common between the physiology of man and animals, and in their response to a wide range of stimuli. In man, however, ethical considerations prevent the performance of many procedures until they have become established on a sound experimental basis as being justifiably applicable to man. Research on animals can therefore be very relevant to the treatment of disease, and the use of computers in veterinary physiology is no exception, particularly in the area of recent developments with computers linked on-line and forming part of closed loop control systems.

### FREQUENCY-MODULATED RECORDING AND OFF-LINE WORKING

The complexity of the mechanisms investigated in physiology, and the sheer quantity of data that can be collected by sophisticated electronic apparatus, has generated considerable interest among laboratory workers in the benefits to be gained by using computers in association with their experiments. To begin with, the main uses were based on off-line facilities, in the fields of data reduction and data analysis, and in these applications the computers functioned as elaborate high-speed calculating machines.

The testing of hypotheses and the making of models are two examples of the extension of statistical testing into more elaborate programmes of work where a variety of possible solutions can be tested quickly, using large general purpose digital computers. Specific examples of this type of application are in the testing and validation of the Hodgkin-Huxley equation for the membrane and action potential. In particular, the relevance of this equation to cardiac action potentials has been studied by Noble and his colleagues (*see* Noble, 1966), and the generation of input-output functions in a model neurone has been investigated (Moore *et al.*, 1966). In these applications, use is made of the large internal memory and the high processing speeds of big general purpose computer installations located in computing centres, situated at a considerable distance from the experimental laboratory. Much of the effort in this kind of computing has been directed towards the generation of the appropriate software, and the physiologist may never even see the computer hardware; the main programs are held at the centre and it is only necessary for a short instruction program to be sent together with the data that are to be processed. The latter are usually supplied to the computing centre in the form of punched cards or paper tape.

A variant of this method of computer usage is in the off-line analysis of data where the data are collected and stored in analog form on magnetic tape. The recent availability of reliable and relatively cheap frequency-modulated (F.M.) instrumentation magnetic tape recorders has led to a rapid growth in this field. The data are collected during the experiment and stored on magnetic tape, and may take several forms. Examples include the voltage outputs from transducers such as thermistors, strain gauges, or blood pressure manometers, and bioelectric potentials such as nerve impulses or electroencephalograph or electrocardiograph recordings. These data are later transformed, using analog-to-digital converters, into digital data in which form they can be used as input to a general purpose digital computer. Because multi-channel recorders can be used, it is possible to compute correlation coefficients between simultaneous events at several loci to yield cross-correlograms or auto-correlations between successive events at a single locus.

An important advantage of the processing by a computer of the data recorded off-line into a F.M. magnetic tape recorder is the elimination of a particularly tedious step in analysis, namely the measurement of the records by hand. In many kinds of physiological investigation an important measurement is the time-interval between events. In experiments performed in the classical manner, this time was usually determined by obtaining in the first place a record of the events (e.g., the arterial blood pressure, a record of respiration, an electromyogram) with the aid of an optical recording device such as a camera (or more recently an ultra-violet recorder, electronic ink-writer, polygraph, etc.), and then laboriously measuring manually the appropriate time-intervals on the record. Physical limitations usually led to only a part of the available data being analysed in this way and the results, after appropriate transformation of the data, were then presented in either tabular or graphical form. This whole sequence was slow and laborious, although it might be said to have afforded the opportunity of concentrating the investigator's interest on the most significant part of his data, an important advantage. By contrast, the whole sequence can now be compressed, using the storage of F.M. data and its off-line reduction prior to analysis, particularly since incremental graph-plotters can be used as output devices to provide hard copy from the general purpose computer. Using this modern equipment, the investigator can collect data during the course of the experiment, store it in analog form on magnetic tape and then, via an analog-to-digital converter, input the data to a general purpose computer. Working with software provided by or at the request of the investigator, the computer can carry out the necessary calculations and present the results in either tabular or graphical form as a direct automatic output. In such a sequence, the task of manual analysis of data is replaced by the need to write the appropriate software; this is a not inconsiderable task, but it is one which is fully justified if an experimental procedure is to be used regularly.

## LABORATORY DIGITAL COMPUTERS

A major advance in computer technology transformed the scene in the last 10 years. This was the development and large-scale manufacture of small digital computers; these machines have an internal memory of 4 to 16K words (12 to 18 bit in size). The development has taken two forms.

### Fixed-program digital bench computers

These computers are small and usually portable. They have a number of fixed programs and the instrument can be switched from one to another of these programs, but it cannot be otherwise changed by the user. The forerunner of these instruments was the Mnemotron Corporation's Computer-of-average-transients (the CAT).

The pre-wired bench computers represented a dramatic advance leading to an expansion in the use of computer technology in the laboratory. In particular, they have enabled on-line computing to become a part of the armoury of the experimental worker, and this has made possible the very rapid extraction of results from the biological data. However, their use is limited to this kind of application, and the low cost and ease of use obtained by pre-wired programming has to be balanced against the inflexibility of such systems; the limited repertoire of programs means that only the collection time, or the number of repetitions or the number of samples can be varied. The further analysis of the data processed, and thereby reduced, by these machines calls for additional hardware.

Instruments of this kind basically combine an analog-to-digital converter with a small central processor and a set of pre-wired programs. They are usually able to perform the following:

1. Compute an average for analog input data, digitised into 400 to 4,000 addresses, and with a substantial improvement in the signal-to-noise ratio.

2. Generate several kinds of histogram, for instance:
    (a) time-interval histograms for repetitive events;
    (b) post-stimulus interval histograms;
    (c) amplitude histograms;
    (d) time dwell histograms (a plot of event number against time-interval between consecutive events).

The contents of the memory stores can be displayed on a cathode ray tube, which is an integral part of the machine, but can also be obtained at output terminals as voltages used to drive supplementary peripheral instruments such as a plotter, or a paper tape punch. The punched tape can then be used as input to a general purpose digital computer for further numerical analysis. New peripherals have recently become available which allow a certain amount of statistical analysis to be carried out locally without recourse to computing centres.

These pre-wired program instruments are often very fast, and are of particular value, therefore, in neurophysiological experiments where the individual impulses may last only 500 $\mu$sec. The Biomac 1000 (Data Laboratories Ltd., 28 Wates Way, Mitcham, Surrey), for example, has a minimal collection time of only 10 $\mu$sec. It is therefore capable of dissecting an action potential into 50 components, and can thus detect small changes in the temporal configuration of nerve or muscle action potentials.

The particular merits of the wired-program computers are their relatively low cost, their ease of operation and their small size. These three factors make them suitable and available for use in the laboratory. This has the important and far-reaching consequence that they can be used on-line to an experiment. They can also be used in a real time mode of operation, since they can either analyse or control external events happening concurrently, or they can in some instances undertake both the analysis and the control operations.

Before giving an example of the use of these systems, there is another important feature of their function that needs to be considered. Physiological experiments in general are designed to analyse the mechanism of interest by initiating a disturbance of basal conditions and recording the subsequent responses. An integral feature of the design of these experiments is the application of one or more stimuli to the experimental preparation, with analysis of the subsequent response. It is sometimes necessary to deliver several stimuli in succession, at definite intervals, in order to test, for instance, the time-course of the response to the original stimulus. Thus a chemical compound or a drug may be administered intravenously, and the effects of the infused material may then be tested by delivering electrical stimuli to a nerve, at pre-determined intervals. Traditionally, this sequence of events is controlled by the investigator, who operates a number of switches in a given sequence and at pre-set times. More recently, however, the developments in digital pulse technology have made available instruments such as the Digitimer (Devices Instruments Ltd., Welwyn Garden City, Herts), designed to deliver up to five electrical pulses at adjustable pre-set times, and to repeat a given cycle of stimuli at pre-set repetition rates. When statistical evaluation of a particular test under standardised conditions is necessary, equipment delivering digitally-controlled stimuli has proved extremely valuable, and is now widely used in many of the biological sciences.

The pre-wired bench computers, when used on-line, require a means of synchronising their averaging or counting activity with the biological events that are being examined. This can be achieved in two ways. In the first method, the counting or averaging cycle in the computer is initiated by an electrical pulse derived, or 'triggered', from the stimulator used to evoke the biological response. At the completion of one passage through the program, the computer is re-set internally and is then ready for the next trigger pulse. Repetition of the stimulus initiates an identical number of cycles in the computer, with accumulation of data according to the program selected. An alternative procedure is to use a Digitimer to synchronise both the stimulator and the computer.

The second method of synchronising events is to use the computer to deliver an electrical pulse that initiates the stimulus to the biological preparation. In the ensuing computer cycle, output pulses (as described above) are used to trigger the stimuli to be delivered to the biological preparation. These output pulses from the computer can be set to occur at stipulated times relative to the time at which the computer started its own cycle. Each computer cycle can be arranged to start automatically (i.e. by repetition of the basic computer cycle), or it can be initiated manually by the use of push-buttons, or it can be started by a pulse generated from some external synchronising instrument, as in the first method. This last possibility indicates a way in which the computer can be made to interact with the experiment, if it were to be triggered, for example, by a stipulated biological event. Since the output pulses from this type of computer are rigidly determined by switch settings, however, such a method of interaction has not proved very flexible.

Several important features of on-line work, and the steps by which skill and confidence in the use of more complex systems can be acquired, are illustrated by these fixed-program digital bench computers. These features include:

1. The presentation of data in a form suitable for analog to digital conversion (e.g. as analog voltages).

2. The control of the experiment by a program, albeit simple, together with the constraints placed on the experiment and on the experimenter (e.g. the inadvisability of changing the parameters to be observed during the course of a sequence of tests).

3. The rapid extraction of significant features from the data, especially during averaging procedures making use of on-line techniques.

4. The need to store data for further analysis by the use of some bulk storage device (e.g. F.M. magnetic tape).

5. The importance of electrical control of stimulating and recording apparatus, and the need for transducers to convert electrical into mechanical or thermal events, and *vice versa*.

The use of computers on-line in this way is only possible if the physiological response that is of interest can be converted into analog voltages or digital pulses for reading into the computer. This presents an important and expensive hardware problem. However, in most physiological laboratories the problem has already been recognised and attacked, even if it has not been solved, by the widespread use of electrical or photographic recording devices, which require the conversion of the variable under investigation into an analog voltage. The analog voltage is then used as input to the recording instrument, which may be an oscillograph and camera, a hot-wire recorder, an ultraviolet recorder or some other device.

### Programmable general purpose digital computers

These machines, of 12, 16 or 18-bit word length and with a memory of 4 to 16K words or more, are the basis of the second major development in the use of small and medium-sized computers in physiological laboratories and have had a very considerable impact. These computers, especially the PDP range of DEC equipment (Digital Equipment Corporation, Maynard, Mass., U.S.A.), and more recently the Modular One (Computer Technology Ltd., Hemel Hempstead, U.K.) are now a familiar part of the laboratory scene in disciplines extending from astrophysics to micro-electrophysiology. A common configuration for a system to be used in a physiology laboratory, and built around such a computer, consists of the type of equipment listed in Table XXVI. This basic configuration can be supplemented in various ways, including the addition of other input devices (e.g. a card reader), extension of the core storage, and the addition of peripheral units such as light pens or graph plotters, the need for which will depend on the use to be made of the system.

The feature which distinguishes these machines from standard general

TABLE XXVI

General purpose digital computer configuration for a
physiology laboratory

| | |
|---|---|
| Central processor | 4K (12, 16 or 18-bit) words of internal memory, or multiples thereof. Cycle time 0·6 to 1·6 $\mu$sec. |
| Input devices | Control typewriter keyboard<br>Analog digital converter in association with a real time clock for accepting analog inputs<br>Paper tape reader |
| Backing store | Magnetic tape or disc |
| Output devices | Teletypewriter<br>Paper tape punch<br>Cathode ray screen for visual display<br>Relay controls, for communication with experimental apparatus |

purpose computers, and the one which is of paramount importance for experimental work, is their in-built capacity to accept analog input and provide a digital pulse output that can be used to control other electronic equipment. The analog input is handled by the analog to digital (A/D) converter, with a sample-and-hold unit that can systematically and rapidly examine as many as 64 input terminals, either sequentially or as instructed by the computer. The digitised data are held by the sample-and-hold unit until they have been accepted by and transferred to the central processor, after which new data can be sampled and collected at the input A/D converter.

A variant of this kind of input system makes use of an independent, oscillator-controlled sampling device that can be switched by the occurrence of pulsatile events or voltage changes at the input; this device can be made in such a way that it stores the time-interval between events at the input. Once an event has occurred the sampling unit stores its count, interrupts the central processor of the computer, transfers the number it holds, and then resets itself ready to start counting again until the next event. Because of the very high speed of operation, the whole sequence following the occurrence of an event requires only a few microseconds before counting is resumed. This means that the time lost is insignificant and, even more important, no events will be missed or lost because they occur during the 'dead time' of the sampler.

The more sophisticated input characteristics of the laboratory-oriented general purpose digital computers extend the range and kind of use that can be made of these instruments far beyond the capabilities of the pre-wired laboratory computers. However, this versatility can only be exploited if the necessary software is provided. Unlike the pre-wired computers, the general purpose systems cannot just be plugged into the mains, switched on, connected to the source of input and immediately used to generate output that can be varied with the turn of a switch. Instead, it is necessary to prepare all the programs appropriate to the particular use to be made of these programmable computers. Some manufacturers provide an extensive software service and, with machines based on the LINC system, a certain amount of sub-programming is incorporated but there is nevertheless still the need to write programs in order to use these machines. Thereafter, exploitation of the capacity of these general purpose computers to sample a variety of inputs and to process the data, in the specific way required for a particular experiment, is limited only by the ingenuity of the user in constructing suitable programs.

The LINC (Laboratory INstrument Computer) grew from research programs at the Massachusetts Institute of Technology and was subsequently sponsored by the U.S. National Institutes of Health. The original LINC machine was a stored-program 12-bit binary parallel digital computer, and was intended to allow research workers to have the maximum degree of control over the computer; it provided direct control from the console, with effectively instantaneous display of the data and the results on an oscilloscope (Clark and Molnar, 1965). Later computers based in part on the LINC include the PDP 12 (D.E.C.) and the micro-LINC (Spear Computers, 335 Bear Hill Road, Waltham, Mass., U.S.A.); these incorporate a variety of improvements and are much faster.

## THE USE OF DIGITAL COMPUTERS TO CONTROL EXPERIMENTS

The great advantage which stems from the introduction of specialised general purpose digital computers into the laboratory is the possibility of using the computer to exert control over the experiment. The first kind of control to be considered is well illustrated by the experiments of Werner and Mountcastle (1965), who took part in the LINC evaluation project. In their investigations, the stimulus-response characteristics of certain cutaneous receptors were examined very rigorously using electro-physiological methods. The basic design of the experiment was to deliver, via an electro-mechanical transducer, an exactly controlled displacement of the skin; the evoked nerve impulse discharges were stored on F.M. magnetic tape, or in digitised form in the computer's memory. After a specified time the stimuli were repeated, using an amplitude chosen at random by the computer from within the available range. Detailed statistical analysis was carried out subsequently, using the data which had been stored on magnetic tape.

In experiments of this type the computer program controls the experiment in a predetermined way, with appropriate instructions being delivered to many electrophysiological instruments in a sequence stated by the program. Variation, for example, of the order or sequence of the control instructions can be made by modifying the program, but to do this it is necessary to stop the computer. One facility common to this kind of laboratory instrument and to earlier and simpler large general purpose computers is the 'sense-switch'. These are instrument switches which are set by hand in the on or off position, and there may be several of these switches. Their condition (i.e. on or off) can be made to determine the subsequent execution of the program by the computer, if an instruction to read them is included in the program. The particular relevance in this context is that the 'sense-switch' can be set during the experiment, and can therefore be used either to stop the program running (e.g. to allow an adjustment of some kind to be made, which is perhaps dependent on the results so far obtained) or to determine which alternative path the program should take. This type of application shows the power of a laboratory computer, used on-line, both to control a physiological experiment according to a pre-determined but variable program and to accept data of various kinds from the animal preparation via transducers and analog digital converters. Considerably more flexibility is available to the investigator, therefore, when he uses a programmable as compared with a fixed program pre-wired laboratory computer.

The second kind of control application introduces another important development. This is the ability of the computer to take a decision on the subsequent course of the experiment according to the information received from the animal preparation. This kind of interaction with the experiment is a striking attribute of the on-line general purpose digital computer, since it introduces a great degree of flexibility and may enable the computer to 'learn' to issue the appropriate commands. The following example again comes from neurophysiology.

In many neurophysiological experiments it is necessary to insert electrodes into the brain or spinal cord, with the intention of recording from a particular nucleus, tract or individual cell. The electrodes are usually fixed to a micro-manipulator, attached to the sub-frame assembly holding the animal; in neurosurgical work this kind of micro-manipulator would be attached to the patient's skull. The position of the electrode relative to the brain is adjusted by some kind of mechanical or pneumatic device. A recent improvement has been to use a pulse-motor, in which the rotation of the shaft of the motor is controlled by voltage pulses; these motors can make between 30 and 800 steps per revolution, to 'drive' the electrodes. Since the electrode movement is controlled by a voltage pulse, the micro-manipulators can in their turn be placed under the command of a computer which delivers control pulses according to the program it is following.

In experiments on the neural connections between the caudate nucleus and the cerebellar cortex, Fox and Williams (1968) recorded the electrical responses at different depths in the cerebellar cortex while the caudate nucleus was being stimulated. The recording electrode, made from a glass micropipette, was driven forward by a pulse-motor in steps of $6 \times 10^{-4}$ mm, under the control of a LINC-8 computer. The program caused the motor to stop every 0·05 mm. It then applied electrically controlled stimuli to the caudate nucleus, started an analog tape recorder which stored the responses, computed the average response to a number (usually 16) of identical stimuli, stopped the analog tape recorder, displayed the results of the computer's oscilloscope and stored the data on the computer's digital tape recorders. The stored results could subsequently be played back for more detailed analysis using appropriate programs. The electrode can, therefore, be advanced or retracted by a specified number of steps, and the program can be used, for example, to evaluate responses obtained along the track taken by the electrode at whatever sampling distances are required. The computer can prepare a chart of the spatial distribution of responses to a given set of stimuli, also selected according to the program. This kind of control can be extended by installing pulse-motors to adjust the horizontal co-ordinates of the micro-manipulator. A three-dimensional map produced under the computer's control then becomes possible, and an instrument of this kind is now being used in the author's laboratory, but a full description of it has not yet been published.

A more sophisticated kind of control system that is under development in this department makes use of the information derived from the recording electrodes to determine the instructions that the computer gives to the pulse-motor driving the micro-electrode. One of our aims is to program the computer so that it can direct the recording micro-electrode to record intracellularly. To do this it is necessary to write a program that will accept the voltage level recorded by the micro-electrode, recognise the sudden and large change of voltage that occurs, from 0 to $-70$ millivolts, when a micro-electrode enters a nerve cell, and which will then modify the output instructions going to the pulse-motor so as to prevent further movement of the electrode. As a refinement of this procedure the program could be extended so that, once a nerve cell had been entered by the micro-electrode, a series of computer-controlled tests could be carried out to determine if the nerve cell were of the required type, and to accept or reject it accordingly. These tests might include the electrical stimulation of nerves prepared beforehand, or the application of natural stimuli such as movement of the skin or a change in skin temperature. Used in these ways a dedicated on-line computer could make a considerable impact on the design and productivity of laboratory experiments, by taking over 'responsibility' for much of the management of the experiment. Of course there are draw-backs, one of which is the relative inflexibility of computer control, since any 'spur-of-the-moment' decision to modify the course of the experiment might be difficult to implement, depending on the program in use at the time and on the sophistication of the computer system itself.

The final example, also selected to illustrate the versatility of digital computers used on-line in laboratory experiments, comes from the field of behavioural physiology, and differs from the previous examples since it relates to the control of activity of unrestrained conscious animals. This is made possible by the use of telemetering instruments which can be fitted to the animal, for instance under the skin. These instruments can receive signals, transmitted as radio waves from a remote transmitter, and can transmit radio waves to be detected by a remote receiver. Two-way communication can thus be established between a control station and the unrestrained animal. Suitable electrodes and amplifiers have to be provided on the mobile station attached to the animal. These electrodes and associated equipment can be used either to record and transmit bio-electrical potentials from the selected part of the animal, for instance the electrocardiogram, or to deliver electrical stimuli to a part of the animal such as the brain. With the computer system, the responses to these signals can be monitored on-line under practically normal conditions.

The control systems briefly described in this section have for the most part already been developed and are in use in the author's department, where a computer-controlled set of laboratories is being established. The general principles relating to computer applications can be extended in various directions. One interesting possibility (Delgado et al., 1970) is to use the computer to control the behavioural activity of freely moving animals by the use of telemetering systems that transmit information two ways between the animal and the computer-linked transmitting and receiving station.

REFERENCES

CLARK, W. A. & MOLNAR, C. E. (1965). A description of the LINC. In *Computers in Biomedical Research*. Ed. Stacy, R. W. & Waxman, B. D. Vol. 2, pp. 35–65. New York: Academic Press.

DELGADO, J. M. R., JOHNSTON, V. S., WALLACE, I. D. & BRADLEY, R. J. (1970). Operant conditioning of amygdala spindling in the free chimpanzee. *Brain Research*, 22, 347–362.

FOX, M. & WILLIAMS, T. D. (1968). Responses evoked in the cerebellar cortex by stimulation of the caudate nucleus in the cat. *Journal of Physiology*, 198, 435–450.

MOORE, G. P., PERKEL, D. H. & SEGUNDO, J. (1966). Statistical analysis and functional interpretation of neuronal spike data. *Annual Review of Physiology*, 28, 493–522.

NOBLE, D. (1966). Application of Hodgkin-Huxley equations to excitable tissues. *Physiology Reviews*, **46**, 1–50.

WERNER, G. & MOUNTCASTLE, V. B. (1965). Neural activity in mechanoreceptive cutaneous afferents: stimulus-response relations, Weber functions, and information transmission. *Journal of Neurophysiology*, **28**, 359–397.

# CHAPTER FOURTEEN

# Computer Applications to the Use and Operation of Libraries

By A. J. HARLEY and ELIZABETH D. WHITTLE

## SUMMARY

ARTICLES of biomedical interest are published in very large numbers and in a wide range of journals. Every individual who is seeking particular information gains access to this literature in two phases, selection and acquisition.

Selection of literature can be achieved through subject guides such as *Index Medicus*. Computers are being used to automate the compilation of these guides, and the retrieval of references by computer is a by-product of this process. MEDLARS (*MEDical Literature Analysis and Retrieval System*), which has been in operation since 1964, is described in detail and compared with other computer-based retrieval systems.

The acquisition of literature involves the provision of efficient library services, and the uses of computers to automate some of the housekeeping functions of libraries are briefly reviewed.

## INTRODUCTION

Progress in science and medicine, both theoretical and practical, rests on communication between individuals—for instance, between colleagues in research and practice, or between teacher and student. Oral communication is flexible and subtle and is a two-way process in 'real time'. Printed records are equally necessary; they can be widely distributed and can be stored in libraries for study when required.

The most fundamental records of science are the articles published in primary journals, where the results of research are first published, and which therefore record the step by step advances of science. Review articles, monographs and textbooks distil the essence from the articles, and abstracts and indexes are guides to their existence and contents. For the whole of science, technology and the social sciences, there are now more than 34,000 different primary journals of which perhaps 4,000 contain some papers of relevance to medicine. Clearly, therefore, no single individual can keep in touch with developments in the entire field. Ten journals regularly scanned may serve to keep the specialist in a well-established field reasonably informed, but at times he will want information that cannot be found in these. There is not only the problem presented by the sheer volume of medical literature published annually, but there is also the scatter of articles, as is expressed by Bradford's Distribution Law (Bradford, 1948; Brookes, 1969). If $x$ papers relevant to a particular topic can be found in $n$ 'core' journals, then it is likely that $2x$ are to be found in $(n^2 + n)$ journals, $3x$ in $(n^3 + n^2 + n)$ journals, and so on. The problem of scatter is currently made worse by the inter-disciplinary approach of much research work in biomedicine.

The scientist or medical practitioner, therefore, is confronted with a twofold problem, the first of these being how to identify the papers that he wants to read, and the second being the problem of obtaining the full texts. A partial solution to the first problem lies in the provision of adequate subject guides to the literature, and the second problem requires for its solution an efficient library organisation at both local and national levels.

A reasonable target for a good library is to be able to supply on demand from its own stock of journals 80 per cent of requests for papers, and the remainder by means of inter-library loans. With the advent of the National Lending Library for Science and Technology, 80 per cent of inter-library requests for loans or photocopies can be met by return of post—if the request is sent by telex, the paper may be available in the requesting library within 24 hours.

During the last decade, computers have been introduced into the library situation. In this chapter, their application to the compilation of indexes, to reference retrieval, and to library automation will be discussed. A description of the computer-based MEDLARS information retrieval service and experience of its operation will be given in most detail.

## AUTOMATION OF INDEXES

Abstracting and indexing journals are well-established aids for obtaining access to the literature, especially to the more recently published articles in the primary journals. A number of these exist for the biomedical field, both those with a broad subject coverage (e.g. *Index Medicus*) and those with a more specialised coverage (e.g. *Leukemia Abstracts*). Their essential feature is a subject index, which is usually an alphabetic list of terms. The scientist looks up a term that he believes to be related to the subject matter of his interest, and from there is led either to the titles of papers (as in *Index Medicus*), or to abstracts of their contents (as in *Excerpta Medica, Biological Abstracts, Chemical Abstracts*). From the information provided, he judges whether the article seems sufficiently interesting for him to want to examine the full text.

With the increasing volume of medical literature published, input to indexing journals with a broad coverage has become considerable, involving a vast amount of repetitive processing in addition to the intellectual effort of specialist indexers. A relatively early application of computers was to use them for the sorting of index entries, and it is undoubtedly economic to automate the compilation of indexes.

The use of computers to analyse the content of articles has so far met with little success (Stevens, 1965). The human process of understanding an article and assigning subject headings to describe its contents is more subtle and complex than anything a computer can do as yet. In any case, at present, before the computer can attempt to 'read' an article, someone has first to keypunch and verify the keypunching of every word. These operations are together much lengthier than having a human indexer read and understand the article. By contrast, computers are currently being used to produce speedily and efficiently new types of index that are either partly or completely independent of the human analysis of documents. The Keyword in Context (KWIC) index is formed by the alphabetic listing of significant words in the title or enriched title (as in the *Biological Abstracts Subjects In Context,* or B.A.S.I.C.) printed in the context of other words in the title (Fischer, 1966). Thus, if there are five keywords in the title, the reference appears in five different places in the index. The usefulness of the KWIC index depends on the extent to which the title is indicative of the article's content; this tends to be better in the basic sciences than in medicine. The citation index (e.g. the *Science Citation Index*) is another type of index which profitably exploits the efficient sorting capability of the computer; it is a directory of cited references listed alphabetically under their first authors, where each is accompanied by a list of the corresponding citing references. Thus, by looking up the reference to a paper known to be of interest, one can find out what papers have cited it more recently. This somewhat indirect approach to subject access to journals is a useful alternative in some bibliographic problems.

The scientist often wants information on a more complex topic than can be expressed by a single subject heading; with a printed subject index, he can only look under one heading at a time. Information retrieval by computer, however, potentially has the advantage of increased selectivity, by employing its power to retrieve references on the basis of combinations of terms; literature searches by computer may therefore be particularly useful for producing bibliographies on the more complex topics. For economic reasons, a computer-based information retrieval system is usually designed to serve both for the production of printed indexes that have a wide general use, and for the retrieval of references by computer for specialised topics on demand. MEDLARS, which stands for *MEDical Literature Analysis and Retrieval System,* is one of the largest of these systems and is one of the first to have been widely used.

## MEDLARS 1

MEDLARS developed primarily out of the need to automate the production of the printed *Index Medicus.* The first version, MEDLARS 1, was developed by the U.S. National Library of Medicine (NLM) between 1960 and 1963 for use with second generation computers; it became fully operational in January, 1964 (U.S. National Library of Medicine, 1963; Austin, 1968).

## Input to MEDLARS 1

The input to the MEDLARS system is determined by its coverage of articles, and by the information content of the record made for each article. The coverage of MEDLARS in the field of biomedicine is comprehensive but not exhaustive; it comprises about 2,300 primary and review journals. Letters to the editor, editorials and biographies that have a substantive content are indexed, but abstracts of papers delivered at meetings are not. Those journals with a wider scientific interest (e.g. *Nature* and *Science*) are selectively indexed only for articles in the field of biomedicine. In the journals covered by MEDLARS, approximately 50 per cent of the articles are written in English.

For each article, a 'unit record' is produced, containing essentially the following items:

1. The author's name or authors' names;
2. The title of the article in English;
3. The title of the article in the original language, if other than English;
4. The journal reference;
5. Up to 30 keywords describing the content of the article.

A characteristic feature of MEDLARS as an information storage and retrieval system is the manner in which the keywords are selected and applied (i.e. the indexing process). Indexing is performed by staff who are highly trained indexers but not subject specialists; they index the content of the whole article as explicitly stated. No attempt is made by the indexer to form a value judgement of the paper to decide its acceptance by or exclusion from the system. All articles within the pre-defined coverage of MEDLARS are indexed for the system but, for articles of relatively slight content, fewer indexing terms are applied. The indexer scans the article, picks out those concepts that he judges to describe its content and, for each concept, assigns an appropriate and most specific term from the fixed vocabulary of MEDLARS Medical Subject Headings. This vocabulary is of such fundamental importance to the operation of the system that it needs some description.

The MEDLARS vocabulary consists essentially of three types of term —main headings, subheadings and check tags. Main heading terms, at present totalling about 7,500, are structured into a hierarchical classification by means of an alphanumeric coding system. The arrangement, which is best illustrated with an example (Fig. 53), facilitates computer manipulation and retrieval of references. Subheadings, of which there are now 60, when used in conjunction with main heading terms, act as

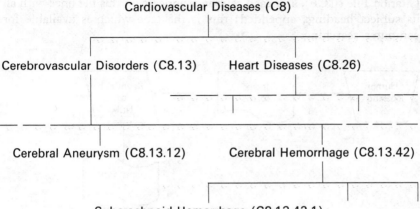

Cardiovascular Diseases (C8)

Cerebrovascular Disorders (C8.13)        Heart Diseases (C8.26)

Cerebral Aneurysm (C8.13.12)        Cerebral Hemorrhage (C8.13.42)

Subarachnoid Hemorrhage (C8.13.42.1)

FIG. 53. Example to illustrate the hierarchical structure of the MEDLARS vocabulary (Medical Subject Headings).

modifiers of them. For example, the subheading SURGERY associated with the main heading term SUBARACHNOID HEMORRHAGE describes more specifically 'surgical management of subarachnoid haemorrhage'. Check tags are a limited number of rather general terms that are considered to be sufficiently important for retrieval purposes as to be routinely looked for in an article by the indexer and recorded. For example, if an article is about the case history of a 3-year-old boy, the check tags CASE REPORT; HUMAN; MALE; and CHILD, PRE-SCHOOL; will be included in its unit record.

Each term ascribed to an article is marked according to whether it is to be 'print' or 'non-print'. Print terms are those main heading terms which reflect the major theme of the article, and are the terms under which the reference appears listed in *Index Medicus*. Non-print terms, which include check tags, are available in addition for computer searching only. On average, 10 terms are assigned to an article, three of which are print terms.

The record of an article prepared in this way by an indexer is punched on to paper tape and read into the computer. In 1969, 233,980 records were processed, bringing the total since January, 1964, to over one million. Two main files on magnetic tape are produced (see Fig. 54) and each record appears on both. One, the 'GRACE tape', includes type-setting instructions added to it during the computer processing, and each reference appears on it arranged under each of the appropriate print headings; it is used to drive the photocomposing machinery for the production of *Index Medicus*. The other main file is the Compressed

Citation File (CCF), and each reference appears on this file once with all its subject headings appended; this is the tape which is available for computer searching.

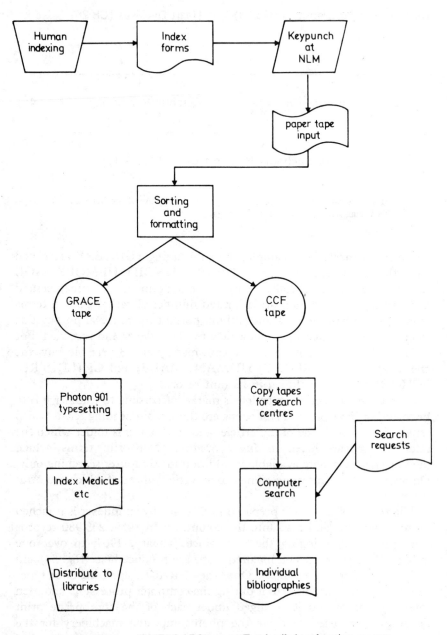

FIG. 54. The overall MEDLARS system. For detailed explanation, see text.

## Information retrieval by computer, using MEDLARS 1

The topic on which references are sought from MEDLARS has first to be clearly defined by the requester. A search formulation for it is then written, using only terms selected from the MEDLARS vocabulary linked appropriately together by the three operators, *or*, *and* and *not*. The basic principles of writing a search are best illustrated by an example. Suppose the topic on which a search is to be carried out were to be described as the 'Effects of radiation on female germ cells in mammals, particularly human'. It can be considered as consisting of three concepts: there is a 'radiation' concept (A); a 'tissue' concept (B); and a 'species' concept (C). For each concept, one or more appropriate terms from the MEDLARS vocabulary are used (Fig. 55). The search statement, *Ra*,

Topic: Effects of radiation on female germ cells in mammals, particularly humans.

*'Radiation' concept (A)*
A1  Radiation Effects
A2  Radiation Injury
A3  Radiation Injury, Experimental
A4  Radiation Genetics

*(Tissue) concept (B)*
B1  Ovum
B2  Graafian Follicle
B3  Ovary

*'Species' concept (C)*
C1  Human
C2  Mammals (all types excluding humans)

*Search statements*
*Ra:* = (B1 *or* B2 *or* B3) *and* (A1 *or* A2 *or* A3 *or* A4) *and* (C1 *or* C2);
*Rb:* = C1;
For simplicity, no distinction has been made between the different types of search terms, i.e. single main headings, subheadings and categories.

FIG. 55. Example to illustrate the principles of search formulation.

instructs the computer to retrieve all references from the citation file that have been indexed with at least one of the B terms (B1 to B3) *and* one of the A terms (A1 to A4) *and* one of the C terms (C1 to C2). The other statement, *Rb*, carries the further instruction that references to articles about humans are to be selected from the *Ra* search and printed out first as a subsearch. The operator *not* is used in those instances where it is required to exclude references which have been indexed with certain terms.

For the retrieval process, the computer acts as a serial matching device, comparing the indexing terms that have been assigned to each of the articles in the citation file against all those combinations of terms in the search formulation. It selects those references for which a match is obtained, and the printout consists of a list of references arranged in specified order (e.g. alphabetically by first author). For each reference, the usual bibliographical details are given plus a list of the indexing terms that were assigned to it, these terms augmenting the information content as given by the title.

As an information retrieval system for medical literature, MEDLARS is used in a somewhat different way from, say, a system designed to retrieve records for patients in hospital. A hospital records system is not functioning satisfactorily unless, in response to a specific request, all the relevant records in its data base can be retrieved, and none besides—in other words, both 100 per cent recall and 100 per cent precision are essential. In MEDLARS, computer retrieval on the basis of combinations of terms is just as efficient, but these combinations are necessarily to some extent an approximate expression of the user's actual requirements. The question is, how far does this method of retrieval, which is in principle quite simple, in fact meet the user's need for a comprehensive bibliography on a given topic?

The effectiveness of a MEDLARS search is limited by two independent factors—the inherent limitations of MEDLARS itself, and the problems of communication between the user and the system which lead to less than maximal exploitation of MEDLARS. If the precision of a search is defined as the percentage of references on the printout that are relevant, and recall is defined as the percentage of all relevant references present in the data base that are in fact retrieved, then a MEDLARS search is inevitably a compromise between precision and recall. Indeed, these factors tend to be inversely proportional to each other. There is, in general, no uniquely correct way of formulating a search, and a certain degree of flexibility in the process allows the search to be weighted primarily for high precision or for high recall, according to the individual needs of the person requesting the search.

If we consider first the inherent limitations of the system, irrelevancy on the printout may be caused by absence of the specific term that is required from the MEDLARS vocabulary. The appropriate more general term may then have to be used, or perhaps the concept cannot be expressed at all. Irrelevancy can also be caused by false association of the concepts of the search topic in the retrieved article. For example, a search formulated on the coexistence of two named diseases in the same patient can also retrieve unwanted references to articles in which both diseases are described but in different patients. Less than 100 per cent recall may result, apart from indexing discrepancies, from the inevitable limitation of a finite depth of indexing.

Sometimes the limitations of MEDLARS may be overcome by indirect approaches. For instance, the topic 'The handling, transfer and storage of antigens by the reticuloendothelial system' looks at first sight unpromising from the point of view of a MEDLARS search, since the concepts 'handling, transfer and storage' cannot be expressed in terms of the MEDLARS vocabulary. To leave these concepts out altogether and retrieve only on 'antigens' and 'reticuloendothelial system' would lead to a large printout with a high degree of irrelevancy, but the difficulty can be overcome by including the practical methods by which the subject may be studied (e.g. autoradiography, immunofluorescence, etc.) as a third concept; in practice, a search formulated along these lines proved quite successful. Again, a search on 'The biochemistry of $\gamma$-hydroxybutyric acid' needs to be handled with care, since there is a term HYDROXY-BUTYRATES in the MEDLARS vocabulary, but no distinction is made between the $\beta$- and the $\gamma$-forms; the former is a ketone body produced under certain conditions of metabolic stress, whereas the latter is a drug that has anaesthetic properties. Since one might expect the biochemistry of $\gamma$-hydroxybutyric acid to be studied in nervous tissue, much potential irrelevancy on the printout can be avoided by combining the term HYDROXYBUTYRATES with a 'nervous tissue' term as well as a 'biochemical action' term.

Superimposed on the inherent limitations of MEDLARS 1 are problems of communication between the user and the system. The MEDLARS service has been made widely available, to all medical and scientific workers in several different countries, and only a fraction of its users have sufficient familiarity with the operation of computers to realise the need for precision in formulating their questions. With MEDLARS 1, it has been found necessary to have a search editor who acts in an interpretative role between the user and the system. To write a search formulation that will produce the best results, the search editor has to understand exactly, and in some detail, the nature of the topic on which the requester requires references.

Despite the limitations of MEDLARS 1 for information retrieval by computer, it has been found to be a valuable bibliographic aid in appropriate situations (Harley, 1967). During its six years of operation, various studies have been carried out (e.g. Lancaster, 1968; King, 1969) to assess the needs of users and the present effectiveness of MEDLARS, and to suggest ways in which the effectiveness may be improved.

**Organisation and developments in MEDLARS 1: decentralisation**
A computer in just one geographical location, at the National Library of Medicine (NLM, at the National Institutes of Health, Bethesda, Md., U.S.A.), is sufficient for compiling the monthly and annual cumulated versions of *Index Medicus* for publication and world-wide distribution. However, international exploitation of the data base for information retrieval by computer demands at least national search centres in the

larger countries, each with its own copy of the updated Compressed Citation File. Early in the MEDLARS project, NLM began a policy of decentralisation. There are now 11 other centres within the U.S.A., and MEDLARS centres have been operating in the United Kingdom since 1966 (Harley and Barraclough, 1966), Sweden (since 1967), France (since 1969), and Germany and Australia (since 1970), while more are planned. Each overseas centre receives monthly from NLM, for addition to its citation file, a tape containing the index records equivalent to that month's *Index Medicus*.

Indexing for MEDLARS is also becoming increasingly decentralised. In exchange for the monthly tape, each foreign centre now produces index entries for articles from journals published in its own country. The British quota is 15,000 articles each year, and is performed by a team of four science graduates whose tasks also include the formulation of searches. Constant effort is required to maintain a high standard of consistency in indexing between one centre and another, and between individual indexers at the same centre. Indexers are given a careful and prolonged period of training, after which their work is still checked by sampling, and 'workshops' are held periodically in the U.S.A. and in Europe.

### Organisation and development in MEDLARS 1: computer programs

The original MEDLARS programs at NLM were written for the Honeywell 800 computer in its machine language (Argus). There was an unsuccessful attempt to rewrite the programs in COBOL for general use, and four of the overseas MEDLARS centres wrote their own set of programs. In Britain the computer chosen was an ICL KDF9 at Newcastle University, with 16K of core store (48-bit words), four tape drives, and the usual range of input and output devices; the programs were written in KDF9 Usercode (an assembly language) and represented altogether about two man-years of work. Essentially there are two kinds of programs, housekeeping and search. The housekeeping programs, for example, take the new tapes produced monthly in the U.S.A. (7 channel, half-inch tapes at 556 bits/inch) and convert them for the KDF9 (16-channel, $\frac{3}{4}$ inch, 400 bits/inch), re-formatting the records in the process.

Figure 56 is an overall flowchart of the search programs. At the input stage, a batch of up to 50 searches (punched on paper tape) is read in and tested against a dictionary file. Each entry on the dictionary consists of a subject heading from the MEDLARS vocabulary, the equivalent 17-bit binary code which is used to represent it on the citation file tape, and a tally, which is the number of times that the indexers have used the term. If the searcher has used a term that is not in the MEDLARS vocabulary, or has merely mis-spelled a term in the vocabulary, that particular search

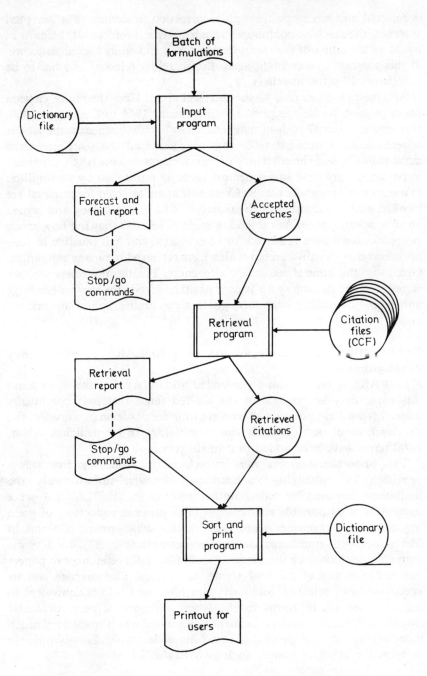

FIG. 56. The MEDLARS 1 overall search process. For detailed explanation, see text.

is rejected and has to go through a correction procedure. For accepted searches, the machine computes a rough statistical forecast of the output, based on the tallies of the terms in the search and on its logical structure. If this forecast is very high, again the search is rejected and has to be re-examined by the searchers.

Accepted searches pass to the retrieval stage. Here the entire citation file is processed; for the period from January 1964 to December 1969, this amounted to 37 reels of magnetic tape. Each reference on the tape is tested against a decision table that represents all the searches in the current batch, and the efficiency of this decision process is of paramount importance; any time saved per reference is multiplied by one million in a search of the whole file. References that are selected for retrieval are labelled with the number of the search to which they belong and copied on to a working tape. At the end, a table is printed showing how many references have been retrieved for each search, and it is possible to suppress searches or sub-searches which have retrieved too many references. Generally, the limit is set at 500 references. Finally, the references are sorted, and the dictionary file is used again to decode the subject headings into their English language forms before the bibliographies are printed out.

## Organisation and developments in MEDLARS 1: vocabulary developments

MEDLARS operates with a controlled vocabulary. On the other hand this vocabulary is dynamic in the limited sense that it is continually under review, and periodic alterations to it are made so as to reflect the development of new concepts and terminology in biomedicine. About 1,000 terms have been added to it in six years.

Two important features were introduced in 1966. The first was a provision for qualifying subheadings, although unfortunately the limitations imposed by the computer records in MEDLARS 1 set a maximum of 63 possible subheadings. The other introduction, of great importance for computer searching, was the arrangement of terms in hierarchies with numbered codes. For example (Fig. 53), by a single matching operation for the category code C8.13.42, references to papers indexed with any of the four terms for cerebral haemorrhage and its specifics can be selected. Similarly, matching for C8.13 is equivalent to matching for all 17 terms in the whole category of cerebrovascular disorders. A broad search is frequently requested and is made very much more efficient by this process of matching codes, which is only possible in a fixed vocabulary system such as MEDLARS.

## Cost-effectiveness of MEDLARS 1

There is a debt that cannot be measured owing to NLM for originating and developing the MEDLARS system and for making its expertise available. Apart from this, during the experimental period, the total cost of providing the service in the United Kingdom has been met by the Department of Education and Science, through the Office for Scientific and Technical Information and the National Lending Library.

At a turnover of 3,000 searches per year, the total cost per search is about equally divided between overheads, such as computer house-keeping and the indexing operation, and the operating cost. For any search, about 90 per cent of the operating cost is the cost of computer time. With the British system, on the KDF9, the time (T) in minutes attributable to one computer search processed along with others, in a batch of optimum size (30 to 40 searches), is given by the equation:

$$T = 3.2 + 0.14rk + 0.016n, \qquad \text{(Equation 14.1).}$$

In this equation, 'r' is the number of reels of tape, 'n' is the number of references retrieved, and 'k' is the number of terms up to the first *and* operator in the search statement. For instance, for the *Ra* statement in Figure 55, k would be 3. Thus, for a typical search of the last 2.5 years of file (r = 15), with 3 terms in the first concept (k = 3) and retrieving 125 references, we arrive at a requirement for computer time of T = 11.5 minutes which would cost approximately £10.

The alternative to a machine search is for the user to go to a library and search by conventional methods. For simple problems such as 'Find some good recent papers on kidney transplantation', the conventional search is undoubtedly cheaper than using MEDLARS and is just as effective. However, the greater the extent to which a complex and exhaustive search is needed, the more economic a computer search becomes.

Because *Index Medicus* contains essentially the same records as the MEDLARS computer tapes, there is a unique opportunity to compare outputs for computer searches with the equivalent manual searches performed in *Index Medicus*. The measure used (Harley, 1968) was to compare the number of titles to be scanned in reading the computer printout with the number to be scanned in searching *Index Medicus*. Typically, the hand search involved more scanning by a factor of 10 for every *and* operator in the computer search. Thus, in the example given in Figure 55, the manual search might be expected to involve the scanning of 100 times as many titles as would appear on the computer printout. Although computer time is costly, a MEDLARS search tends to be economically justified for this kind of search, on a reasonably complex topic, where the computer's high selecting power is used.

Other types of search for which the computer is particularly suitable are:

1. Searches involving very rare combined occurrences of certain index

headings (e.g. a search for all papers indexed with both PANCREA-TITIS and INFLUENZA).

2. Searches where one or more of the concepts sought is likely to be a minor one, covered by the indexer as a non-print heading and generally not mentioned in the titles of articles (e.g. the use of a certain technique).

3. A search on a broad topic, for which a comprehensive hand search could be too time-consuming and too tedious to contemplate.

## MEDLARS 2

The main impetus to develop a new version of MEDLARS arose from the development of third generation computers having large random access stores. These offer an escape from the increasingly time-consuming searches of records arranged serially on magnetic tapes. It is expected that MEDLARS 2, phase 1, will be operational at NLM by November, 1971, and in Britain by the spring of 1972.

In MEDLARS 1 the system operates with two files, the dictionary and the citation files, whereas in MEDLARS 2 there will be three. The new one is to be an inverted or directory file, held on magnetic disc and interposed between the others. In it, each subject heading appears once, followed by a list of the citation numbers of all the references on the Compressed Citation File to which it has been applied. A search on a simple combination of two terms (e.g. TELEMETRY and ELECTRO-ENCEPHALOGRAPHY) will involve the following steps:

1. Accessing the dictionary to validate the terms and to find their directory addresses.

2. Retrieving from the directory the two lists of citation numbers to which these terms have been applied.

3. Matching the two lists to find citation numbers common to both.

4. Retrieving only the references that have these citation numbers from the citation file.

Searching by this method can of course be extended to combinations of any number of terms.

Apart from this new and potentially more efficient search technique, MEDLARS 2 offers the possibility of a much expanded vocabulary. The main subject headings used to organise the lists of titles in *Index Medicus* will remain approximately the same, at about 7,500 headings. However, a large number (20,000 to 100,000) of more specific terms will be added and will be available for searching by computer. For example, a paper on 'Telemetered EEG from a football player in action' is indexed with (among other things) SPORTS in MEDLARS 1, but in MEDLARS 2 it will probably be indexed with FOOTBALL. However, by means of a mapping instruction from the minor heading FOOTBALL to the major heading SPORTS, it will appear in *Index Medicus* automatically under SPORTS, as at present. Thus, in a computer search it will be possible to retrieve papers on very specific topics (such as football), while retaining the present convenient grouping of references in *Index Medicus*.

In association with these developments comes the possibility of on-line search formulation and retrieval. Small-scale experiments have been in progress since 1969 on an IBM 360/67 computer at Newcastle University, as well as in the U.S.A. It is planned to include regular use of on-line searching in the second phase of MEDLARS 2, which is expected to be in operation in the U.S.A. about 1972.

## OTHER COMPUTER-BASED RETRIEVAL SYSTEMS

There are two types of information-retrieval system which depend on the words acceptable for matching purposes by the computer. The first type is based on a relatively small vocabulary of strictly controlled subject headings, as exemplified by MEDLARS. The second type admits the use for matching purposes of any word, and is known as a natural language system.

The *Biological Abstracts* (BA) organisation issues the BA-Previews tapes as products of a natural language system. The titles used by the authors of papers, edited into American English, and with the addition of some phrases and classification codes from the abstracts prepared for *Biological Abstracts*, are read into a computer. Output consists on the one hand of a KWIC index (B.A.S.I.C., p. 271) and, on the other, of a retrieval tape on which these enriched titles take the place of the subject headings of the MEDLARS system.

Writing a search formulation with a natural language system involves choosing, in the main, words which the authors of relevant papers might have used in their titles. Thus, if the concept required is 'cat', we might include CAT, CATS, and FELINE. There is also a word truncation facility, so that BACTERI* will retrieve BACTERIA, BACTERIAL, BACTERICIDE, etc., but this facility must be used with caution since the use of CAT* will retrieve not only CAT and CATS but also CATALYST, CATHODE, CATASTROPHE, etc. The words or parts of words chosen may be linked, as in MEDLARS, by using the operators *and, or* and *not*.

Other examples of natural language systems are those used by the CA (*Chemical Abstracts*) service (Veal, 1968), which produces the Chemical Titles, Chemical-Biological Activities and CA Condensates retrieval tapes. The ASCA (Automatic Subject Citation Alert) tapes are produced as a by-product of the *Science Citation Index* (Cawkell, 1968); in addition to titles and authors, these ASCA tapes contain cited references that are also available for retrieval purposes.

The advantages of a natural language system include the cheapness of the input and the speed of its production, especially for a system based only on titles and cited references. Another advantage of the natural language systems is their flexibility, because new words become available in the system as soon as authors start to use them in their titles. By contrast, the chief advantages of fixed vocabulary systems such as MEDLARS are their uniformity of indexing, and the ease with which the indexing words can be represented as codes on the retrieval tapes. This makes retrieval faster, and therefore less expensive, than for natural language systems by at least one order of magnitude. Effective retrieval by natural language systems depends much more upon whether informative words have been used in the titles given by authors than is the case with fixed vocabulary systems.

The relatively slow process of searching by a computer for words represented alphabetically rather than as codes has meant that the natural language systems have been used mainly for 'current awareness' services rather than, like MEDLARS, for retrospective searching. In current awareness services, each new tape containing the most recently added references, produced weekly or monthly, is matched against a set of word combinations that represent the users' interests, and the users are provided regularly with a printout. Systems of the MEDLARS type can, of course, be used for this kind of service also.

A further important example of a fixed vocabulary system is the one operated by the Excerpta Medica Foundation (about 1969). This has a vocabulary of 40,000 preferred terms and allows for 500,000 synonyms to be automatically mapped to them, so has some of the advantages of a natural language system. The Excerpta Medica system began in 1969 and has a data base similar in coverage to the MEDLARS data base.

The handling of chemical structural formulae presents special difficulties for computer retrieval. The solution adopted by *Chemical Abstracts* is to represent a formula by a connection table, showing how and to what other atoms each atom is bonded (Morgan, 1965). The main alternative is the Wiswesser Line notation (Smith, 1968) in which, for instance, the formula for acetylsalicylic acid is represented uniquely as QVR BOV1. The Excerpta Medica system uses Wiswesser Line notations, whereas MEDLARS 2 will be linked to the *Chemical Abstracts* system.

## LIBRARY HOUSEKEEPING

There are several activities within libraries that involve the manipulation of large files of uniform records which need to be sorted in various ways to produce different outputs.

A classical application of computers is for book purchase. The library receives requests to purchase books. These are checked; funds are earmarked, if available, orders are placed, reports are received from booksellers, or they may have to be prompted with reminders after some time has lapsed. If the book is unavailable, these reports from the booksellers give information such as 'publishers are out of stock' or 'not yet published, due on . . . (date)'. Later the books are received and finally the bills are paid. Each of these steps is amenable to batch processing of standard records with a computer, and numbers of large libraries in Britain have already successfully experimented with such systems, notably at Newcastle University (Grose and Jones, 1967).

Oddly enough, although in science and medicine the sheer bulk of journals is much greater than the number of books, the handling of journals by computer-dependent systems has proved more difficult and less economic to automate. This is because of the wide variety of ways in which the individual parts are identified, whether by month or by issue number, etc. (Bishop *et al.*, 1965). There is also the problem of irregularity. Many journals (e.g. *The Lancet*) arrive in the library like clockwork, but others appear when the editor has collected enough material, and between these extremes lie other irregularities. For instance, some French journals publish 11 monthly issues, omitting August. Setting up a computer algorithm to handle all these variations is formidable, whereas a library assistant can learn to do it in a few weeks.

The automated processing of catalogue entries for books is to some extent similar to the processing of order records, involving the updating, sorting and listing of these records in various ways. In many systems, the machine-readable order record is the starting point to which cataloguing data are added. The NLM handles its catalogue records by computer (Weiss and Wiggins, 1967). In the full MEDLARS 2 system at NLM, ordering of both books and periodicals, cataloguing of books and indexing of articles in periodicals, will be controlled by a comprehensive computer system containing 16 distinct files.

In the U.S.A., the majority of libraries use the same classification system as does the Library of Congress, which has the most comprehensive collection. It is therefore sensible for the Library of Congress to catalogue each book once and for all, and to distribute copies of its catalogue on magnetic tape to other libraries. Individual libraries can then select the records which they require and use these for purchase ordering, control, and for the printing of catalogue cards. This is the MARC project (Avram, 1969); MARC stands for MAchine Readable Catalog of the Library of Congress. In Britain, however, scarcely any two scientific libraries use exactly the same system of classification, and it is therefore harder to avoid duplicating the work of cataloguing, but a project has now been launched by the British National Bibliography (BNB) in association with the MARC project (Coward, 1968).

Circulation control is a library activity that requires separate handling (Wilson, 1970). A typical example is afforded by the library at Southampton University, where each user is provided with a card, and another is kept inside each book. When a user borrows a book, his card and the book card are read by a machine at the library exit and the transaction is recorded. The master file of items on loan is updated by daily runs on a computer, and from these runs recall notices for overdue books, etc. can be generated.

## FUTURE DEVELOPMENTS IN COMPUTER APPLICATIONS TO LIBRARIES AND LIBRARY USAGE

Discovering relevant or stimulating scientific papers is either a matter of browsing through journals and serendipity, or of painstaking logical searching, or more usually a combination of both. Computers are essentially machines with the capacity to relieve intellectual drudgery, and it would seem that there is a considerable future for them in the carrying out of logical searches of the literature.

So far, computer-based information retrieval systems such as MEDLARS 1 have been relatively crude, since the user must first specify his needs to an intermediary who formulates the search in the computer's terms, and the user must then wait days or weeks for the result. The most significant advance that is immediately foreseeable will be the introduction of on-line searching carried out by the user, thereby allowing him to interact directly with the system. With MEDLARS 2, phase 2, it is expected that the user will be able to explore the vocabulary, to assemble trial searches, and to ask for sample output to test his strategy. Eventually it may be possible to make the system so responsive that the user will need little specialised training to exploit it fully. On-line searching is likely to be considerably more expensive, however, than the presently available off-line methods. Future developments and tests must be awaited, therefore, before it can be decided whether the extra cost of on-line searching is justified, and if so how such searches should be made available.

There will undoubtedly be expansion in the use of computers for library housekeeping, in those places where the scale of operations is sufficiently large for it to be profitable. The importance of continuing the education of doctors in practice is recognised, and the need in consequence for greatly improved and more widely available medical library facilities, especially outside the main teaching hospitals. It has been suggested that some form of regional medical library network would be the most effective way of fulfilling this need (e.g. Oxford Working Party, 1968; Tabor, 1970). It is in the medical library, at the centre of network operations, that a very useful place for the computer can be envisaged.

REFERENCES

AUSTIN, C. J. (1968). *MEDLARS 1963–1967*. Washington: U.S. Government Printing Office. USPHS Publication No. 1823.

AVRAM, H. D. (1969). MARC program research and development: a progress report. *Journal of Library Automation,* **2,** 242–265.

BISHOP, D., MILNER, A. L. & ROPER, F. W. (1965). Publication patterns of scientific serials. *American Documentation,* **16,** 113–121.

BRADFORD, S. C. (1948). *Documentation,* pp. 106–121. London: Lockwood.

BROOKES, B. C. (1969). Bradford's law and the bibliography of science. *Nature,* **224,** 953–956.

CAWKELL, A. E. (1968). Search strategies using the Science Citation Index. In *Computer Based Information Retrieval Systems.* Ed. Houghton, B. pp. 25–44. London: Bingley.

COWARD, R. E. (1968). BNB and Computers. *The Library Association Record,* **70,** 198–202.

EXCERPTA MEDICA FOUNDATION (about 1969). *Excerpta Medica Automated Storage and Retrieval Program of Biomedical Information.* Amsterdam: Excerpta Medica Foundation.

FISCHER, M. (1966). The KWIC index concept: A retrospective view. *American Documentation,* **17,** 57–70.

GROSE, M. W. & JONES, B. (1967). The Newcastle University library order system. In *Organization and Handling of Bibliographic Records by Computer.* Ed. Cox, N. S. M. & Grose, M. W. pp. 158–167. Newcastle-upon-Tyne: Oriel Press.

HARLEY, A. J. (1967). MEDLARS in context. *Journal of Royal College of Physicians, London,* **1,** 261–270.

HARLEY, A. J. (1968). MEDLARS: A comparison with hand searching in Index Medicus. *Information Scientist,* **2,** 59–70.

HARLEY, A. J. & BARRACLOUGH, E. D. (1966). MEDLARS information retrieval in Britain. *Postgraduate Medical Journal,* **42,** 69–73.

KING, M. (1969). Report on the operation of the MEDLARS service in the Newcastle Region from 1966 to 1968. University of Newcastle-upon-Tyne.

LANCASTER, F. W. (1968). *Evaluation of MEDLARS Demand Search Service.* Washington: U.S. Government Printing Office.

MORGAN, H. L. (1965). The generation of a unique machine description for chemical structures—a technique developed at Chemical Abstracts service. *Journal of Chemical Documentation,* **5,** 107–113.

OXFORD WORKING PARTY (1968). *An Integrated Medical Library Service for the Oxford Region.* Oxford: Oxonian Press.

SMITH, E. G. (1968). *The Wiswesser Line-formula Chemical Notation.* New York: McGraw-Hill.

STEVENS, M. G. (1965). Automatic indexing: A state-of-the-art report. *National Bureau of Standards Monograph No. 91,* 164–172.

TABOR, R. B. (1970). Medical library and information services. *Postgraduate Medical Journal,* **46,** 149–153.

U.S. NATIONAL LIBRARY OF MEDICINE (1963). *The MEDLARS Story at the National Library of Medicine.* Washington: U.S. Government Printing Office.

VEAL, D. C. (1968). An experiment in the selective dissemination of chemical information. In *Computer Based Information Retrieval Systems.* Ed. Houghton, B. pp. 65–92. London: Bingley.

WEISS, I. J. & WIGGINS, E. V. (1967). Computer aided centralized cataloguing at the National Library of Medicine. *Library Resources and Technical Services*, **11,** 83–96.

WILSON, C. W. J. (1970). A bibliography on U.K. computer-based circulation systems. *Program,* **4,** 55–60.

# CHAPTER FIFTEEN

# Simulation Studies Using Analog and Hybrid Computers

## By D. E. M. TAYLOR

## SUMMARY

BIOMEDICAL computer simulations use a series of mathematical equations to reproduce the behaviour of a biological system. Simulations can be produced on any of the three basic computer configurations, the optimum choice varying according to the system being simulated. Simulations can be useful both for teaching and for research. For teaching, the simulations should be relatively simple and designed in such a way as to allow a high degree of 'hands-on' control by the student. For research purposes, the equations used must be able to be justified, on a theoretical basis, and the simulation should be able to be used for predictive purposes. In this chapter, examples of both a teaching and a research simulation are considered in some detail, to bring out the differences in their requirements.

## INTRODUCTION

The concept of simulation is discussed in general elsewhere (p. 305, 319). In the present context of mathematical models, particularly models for a biomedical system, some assumptions and approximations may have to be made and the resulting model may not fully reproduce the behaviour of the system it is designed to represent. To take a simple example, if the object in some part of a simulation were to be to reproduce the interrelationship between pressure and flow in an artery, the Poiseuille equation is probably the most familiar equation for expressing the relationship:

$$(P_1 - P_2) = L\eta \left(\frac{8Q}{\pi r^4}\right) \text{ or } \frac{8L\eta}{\pi r^4} \cdot Q \qquad \text{(Equation 15.1)}$$

In this equation, $(P_1 - P_2)$ represents the pressure gradient, L is the length of the tube, $\eta$ is the viscosity, Q is the volume flow and r is the radius of the tube. The Poiseuille equation is, however, a considerable over-simplification of the true relationship, and applies only to flow in rigid tubes.

The general equation for flow in a tube in response to phasic changes in pressure is more complex, being represented by:

$$(P_1 - P_2) = L\eta \left(\frac{1}{v} \cdot \frac{\partial V}{\partial t} - \frac{\partial^2 V}{\partial r^2} \cdot \frac{\partial V}{\partial r}\right) \qquad \text{(Equation 15.2)}.$$

The symbols are the same as for Equation 15.1, with the addition of $v$

as the kinematic viscosity (viscosity/specific gravity) and V as the velocity of flow. This is a second order partial differential equation and requires for its complete solution a not inconsiderable complement of analog and parallel hybrid computing modules. Even then the solution of Equation 15.2 can only be an approximation, as it relates to a straight uniform bore system and does not fully take into account the visco-elastic properties of the arterial wall. The equation can be simplified for a site such as the ascending aorta, by making assumptions and approximations on the basis of the properties of flow in a tube immediately distal to its inlet (Fry et al., 1957). Equation 15.2 then reduces to:

$$(P_1 - P_2) = L\eta \left( \frac{1}{\nu} \cdot \frac{dV}{dT} + \frac{a}{L\rho} \cdot V \right) \qquad \text{(Equation 15.3)}.$$

Equation 15.3 is a first order differential equation in which the symbols are as before, but with the addition of a constant (a) and the symbol $\rho$ representing specific gravity. It can be simulated with analog modules alone, and with relatively few of these. A final approximation can be made if it is assumed that the properties to be studied are all determined by the mean pressure gradient. The equation then reduces to the Poiseuille formula (Equation 15.1). Since the term $\frac{8L\eta}{\pi r^4}$ is constant, the relationship between pressure and flow can be simulated by a single potentiometer.

The three mathematical models represented by Equations 15.1 to 15.3 are all valid in the appropriate circumstances. The problem of computer simulation is to devise a series of mathematical equations and logical statements which reproduce the behaviour of a biomedical system within the limits of the study. Equally, the limits of the model will govern the extent to which predictive or extrapolative results obtained from the model can be justified. Different criteria are required, depending on whether the simulation is to be used for teaching about already established observations, or for research into the physical properties of a system of which not all the properties have yet been determined by observations.

With simulations used for teaching purposes, the principal requirement is to be able to reproduce those characteristics that it is desired to illustrate. Subsidiary requirements include the need for the simulation to occur at a rate that can be followed by the student, either in respect of slowing down complex simulations or in speeding up other simulations so as to demonstrate broad principles when the amount of time available for teaching is limited. Also the variables which simulate known biological variables should be easily and, as far as possible, uniquely changed. Finally, the output should be in a readily interpreted form such as an oscilloscope trace or an X-Y plot. Analog and hybrid computers are particularly fitted to meet all these requirements.

For research purposes, the mathematical models require to be much more exact. In this context, simulation is often useful for its predictive value by indicating critical experiments to be performed later, and many of these simulations require the solution of simultaneous partial differential equations. They may require the determination of boundary values, or the optimisation of constants to give the best fit of a model to the experimental observations.

The complexity of the equations and of the computer configurations used for the simulation should be determined on a basis of cost-effectiveness, the relative compute time being one of the important factors to be taken into account. With the present generation of computers, the cost and time required for the solution of a problem by digital as compared with parallel hybrid computing techniques are nearly equivalent when approximately 20 simultaneous differential equations are involved for any problem (Figs 8 and 19). Hybrid computer techniques may provide the best configuration because of their ability to carry out simultaneously all stages in the solution of a problem; they may also be the best when using iterative techniques for optimisation. For the optimisation, however, it is often necessary to use a full hybrid computer system, since a parallel hybrid computer has insufficient digital arithmetic and memory capacity. An example of the use of an extensive full hybrid simulation, fully justified in terms of the saving of human life, occurred in the extensive simulation studies carried out in preparation for the Apollo manned moonflights.

In this chapter, two examples of simulations, one used for teaching purposes and the other for research, will be described in some detail in order to illustrate these general points.

## A SIMULATION USED FOR TEACHING PURPOSES: BODY TEMPERATURE REGULATION

In this example, the object is to teach medical students the physical and physiological principles governing body temperature regulation; no previous knowledge of the subject is assumed. The programs used are progressive, and only the control of heat loss will be simulated.

### First stage in the simulation of body temperature regulation

The first stage is to simulate Newton's law of cooling in a two compartment model, and to show the effect of adding a constant heat source to the hotter compartment. This law states that the rate of cooling (i.e. the negative heat flow) is proportional to the temperature gradient. Mathematically, the rate of cooling (in joules per second) may be expressed as:

$$\frac{dT}{dt} = -k\,(T_a - T_b) \qquad \text{(Equation 15.4)}.$$

In Equation 15.4, k is the constant of heat transfer and $T_a$ and $T_b$ are

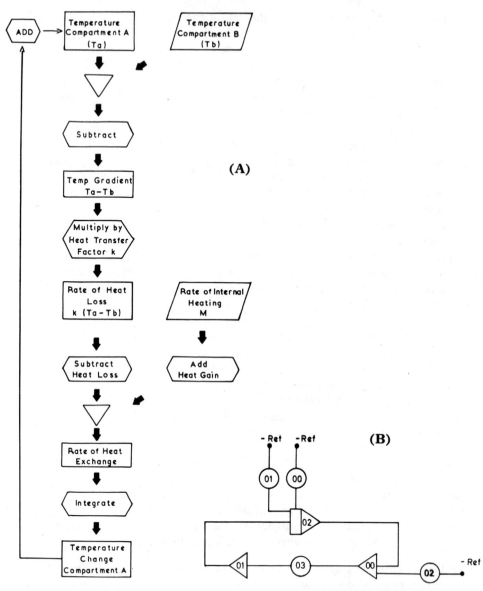

FIG. 57. (A) Flow chart and (B) program diagram for an analog simulation of a two-compartment model used to demonstrate the laws of heat exchange. In the computer program, integrator A:02 represents the compartment with which heat exchange is occurring (e.g. body core), potentiometers P:01 represent the rate of internal heating (e.g. metabolic heat production), P:02 the temperature of a second compartment of infinite thermal capacity (e.g. the environmental temperature and, in consequence, the skin) and P:03 the heat exchange factor between these two compartments. For further explanation, see text.

the temperatures in compartments A and B respectively. If a heat source is now added so as to heat compartment A at a rate of M joules per second, equilibrium will be reached when

$$\frac{dT}{dt} + M = 0 \qquad \text{(Equation 15.5)}.$$

If compartment B is very large (i.e. has infinite heat capacity) T becomes constant and Equations 15.4 and 15.5 can then be combined to give a closed loop solution suitable for simulation by an analog computer (Fig. 57). The biological analog of this would be the transfer of heat between the body core (compartment A) and the skin (compartment B) when the skin is kept at a constant temperature. The constant (k) in Equation 15.4 can be varied so as to represent blood flow from the core to the skin, and M becomes the heat of metabolism. To demonstrate this stage, M is initially set at zero and the effects of differing rates of thermal transfer are shown (Fig. 58A). Next, M is made to assume finite positive values, and the effect of this (with the value of k held constant)

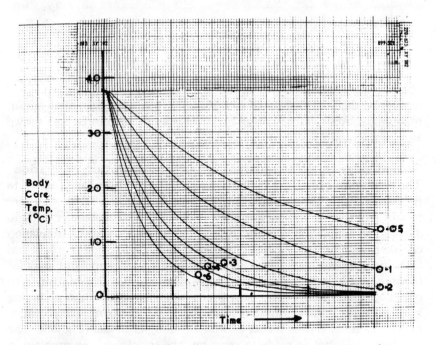

Fig. 58. Runs obtained from a simple two-compartment model of heat exchange under two sets of conditions:

(A). Rate of cooling of a body that has no internal source of heat, the lines corresponding to various arbitrary values of the thermal conduction factor. Environmental temperature on all runs was 0°C. (B), see overleaf.

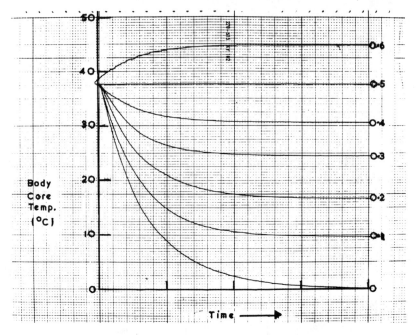

FIG. 58. (B). Rate of change of temperature of a body with a variable rate of internal heating, as shown by arbitrary values on each line; the thermal conduction factor was constant and the environmental temperature was 0°C.

on varying the final position of equilibrium shown (Fig. 58B). The output of amplifier A:01 (representing heat loss) can be monitored and shown to be equal and opposite to M at final equilibrium.

**Second stage in the simulation of body temperature regulation**
The next stage of the simulation is to join a second similar program to the first so that a three-compartment model of heat flow from body core to skin and then to the environment is obtained. Potentiometer P:02 in the original simulation is replaced by amplifier A:03, and the simulation can then monitor body core temperature and skin temperature; it has four independent variables (Fig. 59). The model simulates poikilo-thermic heat balance between the body core and the environment, with only heat losses due to convection, conduction and radiation occurring at the skin surface. A number of different runs, changing one potentio-meter at a time, can be made, as with the simpler model (Fig. 58). The computer can now be made to carry out the solution of the problem in rep-op mode, to show how blood flow (potentiometer, P:03) can be altered so as to maintain body temperature constant at its initial value over a relatively wide range of environmental temperature (potentio-meter, P:05), as long as the metabolic heat production and the skin-

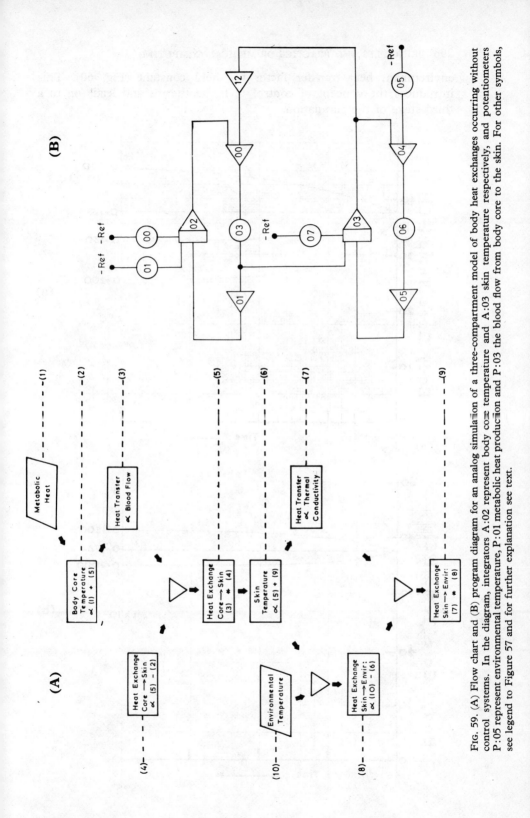

Fig. 59. (A) Flow chart and (B) program diagram for an analog simulation of a three-compartment model of body heat exchanges occurring without control systems. In the diagram, integrators A:02 represent body core temperature and A:03 skin temperature respectively, and potentiometers P:05 represent environmental temperature, P:01 metabolic heat production and P:03 the blood flow from body core to the skin. For other symbols, see legend to Figure 57 and for further explanation see text.

environment heat transfer factor are held constant (Fig. 60). This introduces the concept of control in homeotherms and leads on to a third stage of the simulation.

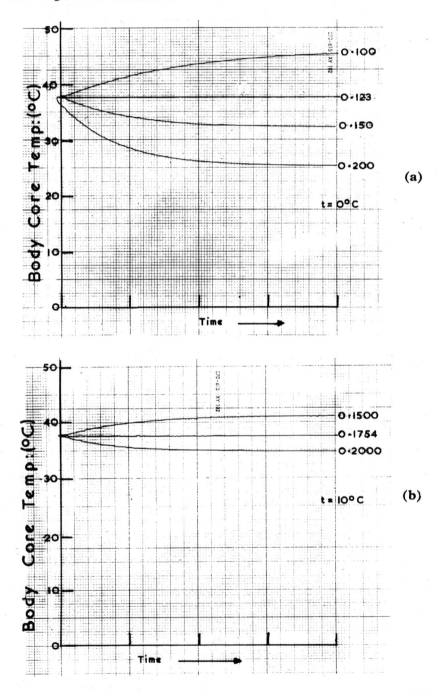

(a)

(b)

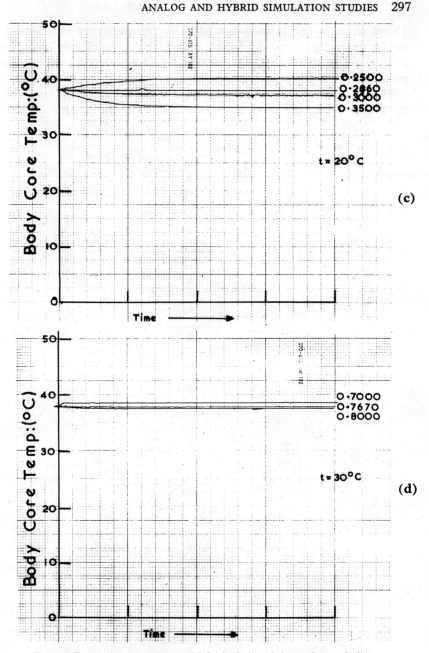

FIG. 60. Runs with an analog model for body heat balance, but excluding automatic control. This shows that, in the face of a varying environmental temperature, a rate of core to skin blood flow can be reached at which body core temperature can be maintained at 37°C. Runs were carried out with manual adjustment of the potentiometer (P:03, Fig. 59) which represents blood flow. Environmental temperatures (a), 0°C; (b), 10°C; (c), 20°C; and (d), 30°C. Note that, at low environmental temperatures, a small change in blood flow can produce a large change in heat balance. These traces were produced during an undergraduate teaching class.

## Third stage in the simulation of body temperature regulation

In this third stage, the only control introduced is one of skin blood flow. This assumes that control is exerted by monitoring an error signal generated by a difference between the body core temperature and the level of a cerebral thermostat, the type of control being one in which the magnitude of the response is determined by the magnitude of the

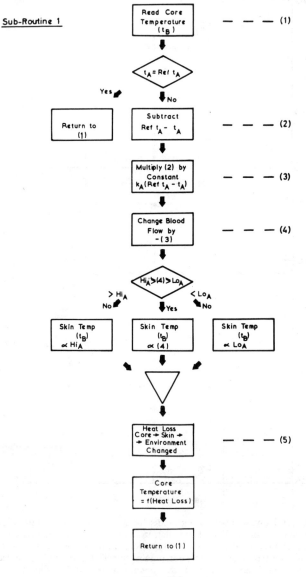

FIG. 61A

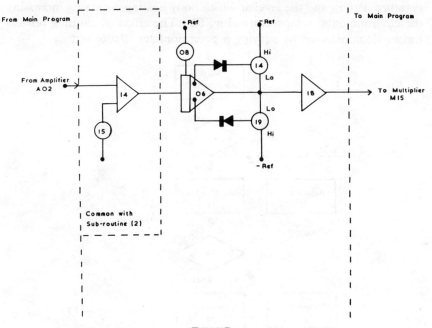

FIG. 61B

Fig. 61. (A) Flow chart and (B) program diagram for an analog simulation of the vasomotor control system for body temperature regulation. In the program diagram, amplifier A:14 represents the hypothalamic thermo-receptor area, and A:18 the core to skin blood flow. Integrator A:06 represents vasomotor control, with the accompanying diode circuits setting the high and the low limits. For other symbols, see legends to Figures 57 and 59, and for further explanation see text.

error. This is called positional feed-back, and the rate of correction error is monitored.

The concept of limits is also introduced at this stage, and requires the setting of maximum and minimum values for the blood flow. These steps are carried out (Fig. 61) by producing the error signal on an amplifier (A:14) placed between the core temperature (A:02) and a hypothalamic reference level (P:15), and using this error signal as the input to an integrator (A:06). Diode circuits are used to set high and low limits, and the output of the integrator (A:06) now represents the blood flow from body core to skin. In order to use this information about the blood flow, in place of one potentiometer (P:03) a multiplier (M:15) is substituted which has the analog of the temperature gradient (A:00) and negative blood flow (A:08) as its inputs.

The simulation can now be used to demonstrate vasomotor regulation in the maintenance of body temperature. The level at which body cooling will occur can be shown by reducing the environmental temperature (P:05), and the level at which body heating occurs by increasing the environmental temperature (Fig. 62). The effect of clothing on this can be demonstrated by varying a potentiometer (P:06) setting.

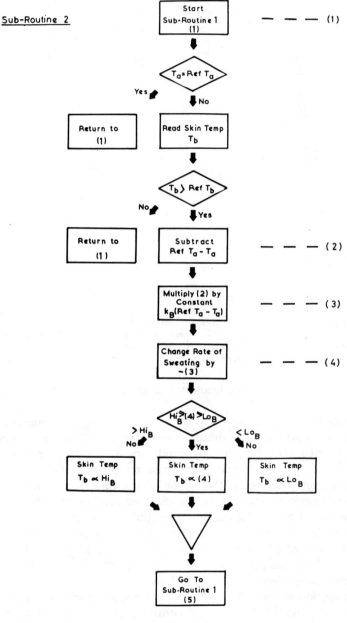

FIG. 62A

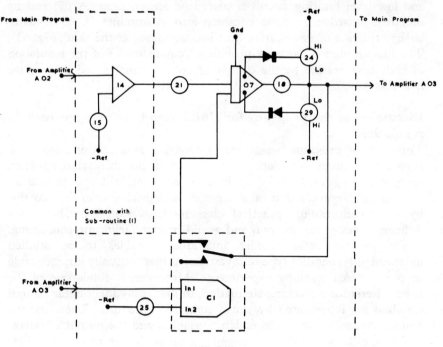

FIG. 62B

FIG. 62. (A) Flow chart and (B) program diagram for an analog simulation of the evaporative control system for body temperature regulation. In the program diagram, amplifier A:14 represents the hypothalamic thermo-receptor area and is shared with the vasomotor control system simulation. Comparator C:1 represents the skin thermoreceptors, which determine the temperature of the skin at which sweating begins. A control system with limits similar to those for vasomotor regulation (Fig. 61) is represented by integrator A:07 and the associated diode circuits. For other symbols, see legends to Figures 57, 59 and 61, and for further explanation see text.

## Fourth stage in the simulation of body temperature regulation

The fourth and final stage of the simulation involves adding the effect of an evaporative heat loss due to sweating. A further concept of control mechanisms is introduced here, namely a feed-back control that responds to an error signal, and that also has an on/off switch level below which it is inactive. When sweating occurs it is assumed that the amount is controlled by the hypothalamic thermostat, which again possesses both directional and positional feed-back. In this model the switching on and off is determined by the skin temperature, simulated by a comparator (C:1). The heat loss due to evaporation is simulated by an integrator (A:07) in which the input is an error signal multiplied by a constant, and where the mode varies between initial condition (no sweating) and operate (sweating), under the control of the comparator (C:1). A high and low level limiting circuit is placed on an amplifier (A:07) and its output is passed in a negative fashion into an amplifier (A:03) so as to change the rate of evaporative heat loss occurring at the skin (Fig. 63). The full simulation can now provide a demonstration of the regulation of body temperature by the control of both vasomotor and evaporative heat losses.

### Discussion of the program for simulating body temperature regulation

This type of program has several advantages as a teaching aid. The program is progressive and it is therefore possible, starting from elementary physics, to build up by a series of logical steps towards an approximate reproduction of a complex biological system. To do this by more conventional practical class methods would involve many different types of experiment, and would be extremely time-consuming.

The program also enables individual variables to be studied independently, another type of investigation that is usually impracticable in conventional teaching experiments. Moreover, it fulfils one of the basic criteria for a teaching simulation, in that easily identifiable natural variables are represented by single computing modules. These are the potentiometers for the independent variables, and the output of operational amplifiers for the dependent variables. These properties allow

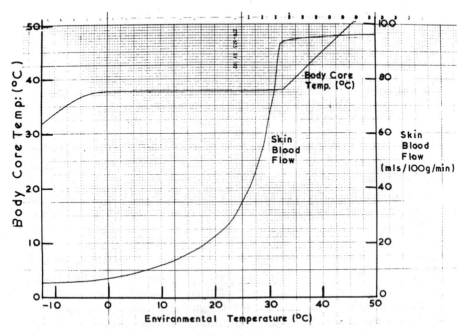

FIG. 63 A

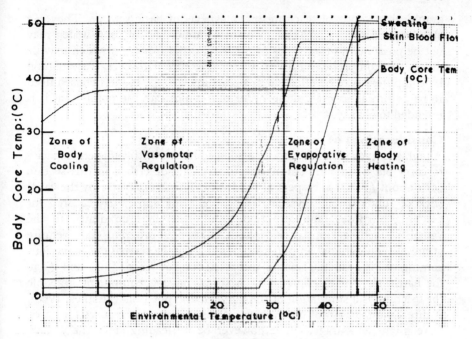

FIG. 63 B

FIG. 63. Runs with the full simulation firstly with vasomotor regulation alone (A), and secondly with both vasomotor regulation and sweating regulation (B). The purpose of these runs was to show how the body keeps in heat balance over a wide range of environmental temperatures. The models demonstrate that, only with the addition of evaporative regulation, can the body remain in thermal balance under conditions in which the environmental temperature approaches or exceeds the body core temperature. These traces were produced during an undergraduate teaching class.

many of the experimental observations on the simulation to be carried out by the student himself. The fact that the model may not be entirely accurate, and that many approximations to normal behaviour have been made, is relatively immaterial in the context of a teaching simulation. Several much more accurate models of body temperature regulation exist, but these are all complex and are for the most part unsuitable for teaching medical students since any teaching program should be capable of being fully understood by the student within the time available. The simulation described in this section is designed only to illustrate certain specific and fundamental principles in the control of body temperature. Once the student has gained an understanding of the principles demonstrated by the simulation, the more complex factors can readily be taught in a lecture or a small tutorial, and further reading is made easier.

Practical demonstrations or experiments based on simulations by analog computers, if well prepared and programmed, can provide simple graphical methods of teaching many aspects of basic science. They can also be used to demonstrate features of abnormal function which may not be possible in other types of practical experiment and which may be difficult to comprehend fully in a formal lecture. However, if simulation by computers is to be effective as a teaching aid, the models chosen need to be as simple as possible in order to demonstrate the points that it is intended to convey.

### Considerations of cost

A high accuracy general purpose analog computer with sufficient capacity to carry out a teaching simulation of the type described in this section costs about £5,000 in respect of hardware. This is expensive by the yardstick of funds usually available for purchasing apparatus required for teaching purposes, and attention should therefore be drawn to the valuable teaching simulations based on simpler programs that require at most 10 operational amplifiers and which can be carried out on various commercially available analog tutors costing between £100 and £150 for hardware. An example of such simple analog equipment available for teaching is a simulation of the nerve action potential (Hughes, 1968). A direct comparison of costs, such as this statement of figures for hardware might encourage, could however be misleading since the £5,000 equipment would be used as a service computer for much of the time and its great flexibility makes it a much more stimulating piece of teaching equipment. Under these circumstances, it is pertinent to ask how many students can be given practical instruction with an analog system such as the one we have been discussing. In our experience, although computer simulation can be used for demonstrations to groups of students up to 20 in number, it is more valuable as a method of teaching if the students get a period of 'hands-on' control of the computer. This demands that not more than six students should be working at any one time with a machine.

### Future developments in the use of simulation by computers for teaching purposes

Computer simulations can be used at all stages of the medical curriculum, but the available software is limited and future progress will mainly depend upon its development in a form suitable for teaching. Short-term developments are likely to make most use of small analog computers, since these have considerable advantages in terms of speed and ease of operation. Also, they depend on the use of programs in which easily recognisable physical or biological variables can be uniquely represented by a single potentiometer or by a single operational amplifier; this permits a high degree of manual control by the student. With a properly designed analog program, the student can readily devise and carry out his own 'experiments' on the model.

Digital computer simulations also have a place in teaching, particularly of the quantitative biological sciences such as biochemistry and biophysics. Again, however, special software is required so that the student can readily modify the programs. This has been partially achieved by the development of specialised simulation packages such as the IBM Continuous System Modelling Program, in which an essentially analog problem can be programmed for input to a digital computer.

Long-term teaching developments will probably be based on improvements in modelling programs for use with digital computers or with medium to large hybrid computers. With either of these configurations, it should be possible to simulate complex biomedical systems so as to reproduce the patterns of interaction of several body systems, both in health and in disease.

It seems inevitable that teaching simulations will eventually become an essential adjunct to traditional methods of laboratory and ward teaching. They are not subject to limitations upon the availability of suitable patients or of experimental preparations, and they permit a high level of participation by individual students. Furthermore each student can repeat an 'experiment' or an 'examination' as many times as seems necessary for understanding to be achieved. This subject is considered further in the next chapter.

## SIMULATIONS FOR RESEARCH PURPOSES

The main difficulty in developing research simulations is the formulation of a satisfactory definition of the system. This is essential if the equations that describe the problem are to be identified in a form such that they are adequate, not only to reproduce the already established behaviour of the system but also to predict unknown characteristics of the system, these predictions forming the basis of further experimental testing. The reason for this difficulty is that, in much mathematical modelling of biomedical systems, although certain portions of the system may be capable of simulation by equations referring to well defined physical systems (using equations in which only the optimisation of constants is required), in other portions of the simulation the equations are speculative.

It is in this speculative area that attempts can be made to extend knowledge. However, in this region there may be several equations that appear acceptable, any one of which might be able to be justified on theoretical grounds and which will, with optimisation of constants, reproduce the known behaviour of the system. Extrapolative simulations with these mathematical models permit conditions to be found in which differences in behaviour occur. On the basis of these critical conditions, key experiments can be designed to distinguish between the models. The point to be drawn from these statements is that computer simulations for research must proceed in parallel with experimental investigations, each complementary to the other in extending knowledge and suggesting further investigations, if they are to be anything other than games playing with numbers. It is nevertheless important to keep simulations as simple as is consistent with the immediate problem.

All the main types of computer have been used for research involving biomedical simulations, the most appropriate configuration depending on the specific requirements of the simulation. So as to illustrate points that are not considered in detail elsewhere in this book, we shall now describe the use of parallel hybrid computer simulation to study the biophysical problems presented by the mode of action of the heart as a pump (Taylor, 1971).

### The simulation of left ventricular contraction

Most mathematical models of the cardiovascular system have assumed that ventricular contraction can be represented by an instantaneous and synchronous change in compliance. However, the changes in muscle compliance are not instantaneous, since studies of the electrical (Scher and Young, 1956) and of the mechanical (Hider et al., 1965) activity of the ventricles have shown that ventricular contraction is serial rather then synchronous in nature. The question to be investigated was whether the degree of asynchrony of ventricular contraction was of functional significance. The problem to be solved by simulation required the devising of two models, in one of which the ventricle exhibited synchronous contraction, and in the other serial contraction. From these two models, a point of dissimilar behaviour had to be predicted that was capable of experimental study.

The main component of the simulation was the ventricle, so simplification of the input and output systems and valves could be used. Only the left heart and associated vascular beds were studied, and it was assumed that no change in atrial compliance occurred. The equations for this part of the simulation are based on those of Warner (1959). The model consists of four compartments—the pulmonary veins including the left atrium, the left ventricle, the arteries, and the peripheral vascular bed. The volume in each compartment was represented by:

$$V_{(T)} = V_{(0)} + \int_0^T (Q_1 - Q_2)\, dt \qquad \text{(Equation 15.6)}$$

where $V_{(T)}$ is the volume at time $T$; $V_{(0)}$ is the volume at zero time; $Q_1$ is the rate of inflow of blood; and $Q_2$ is the rate of outflow of blood.

The rates of flow of blood through the inflow and outflow valves were represented by the discontinuous equations:

$$Q = \frac{(P_1 - P_2)}{R} - \frac{Z}{R} \cdot \frac{dQ}{dt} \qquad \text{when } P_1 \geqslant P_2 \qquad \text{(Equation 15.7)}$$

$$\text{and } Q = O, \text{ when } P_1 < P_2 \qquad \text{(Equation 15.8)}$$

In Equations 15.7 and 15.8, Q is the rate of flow; $P_1$ is the pressure on the upstream side; $P_2$ is the pressure on the downstream side; R is the resistance to flow; and Z is the inertia of the blood.

A similar equation was used to describe the flow of blood from the arteries to the peripheral vascular bed, and the integrated blood flow in the peripheral vascular bed during one cardiac cycle was made equal to the inflow of blood into the pulmonary veins and left atrium, thus completing the flow loop.

The final equation in this part of the simulation related the pressure in the various compartments to the volume by means of the equation:

$$P = \frac{V^n}{C} \qquad \text{(Equation 15.9)}$$

where P is the pressure; V is the volume; C is the compliance; and n is a constant.

The various features of this problem, as represented in Equations 15.6 to 15.9, were all capable of a simple analog simulation, using established models and methods, but the speculative part of the simulation concerned the ventricle.

## The choice of model for ventricular contraction

The major difficulty with the ventricle has been how to determine the type of model to be used, since the cardiac ventricles are complex in shape and incapable of precise mathematical definition. On a superficial examination it might appear that a suitable simplification would be to regard the left ventricle as a muscular sphere, since this roughly describes its external appearance and as a sphere is capable of being expressed simply in mathematical terms. There are, however, functional deficiencies in accepting this model. During development, the heart starts as a muscular tube in which contraction passes from the proximal to the distal end and, although at later stages the tube becomes coiled and undergoes differential growth to assume its adult shape, it still retains many characteristics of the tube from which it originated embryologically (Hider *et al.*, 1965). A model based upon a serially contracting tube therefore seemed more appropriate and, rather than assume that changes in compliance occurred in stepwise fashion, a curved change in elastance (the reciprocal of compliance) was assumed having an equation of a general form:

$$E_t = E_0 + ae^{-b(\tau - t)^2} \qquad \text{(Equation 15.10)}$$

In this equation the symbols represent elastance (E), and the time in the cycle at which maximum contraction occurs ($\tau$), while a and b are constants.

It was assumed that the change in elastance started on the inner aspect of the muscular cylinder, at the proximal end, and that it was propagated radially at a velocity $V_S$ and longitudinally at a velocity $V_L$. It was then necessary to compute the changes in elastance which would occur in the tube, if all or part of it contracted in the manner postulated, a process which involved the solution of a complex multiple integral. The reason for the complexity of this integral derived from the fact that, at a given point in time, each part of the tube would be at a different stage of its mean contraction cycle, and the total elastance of the tube would be the spatial integral of all the contractile elements.

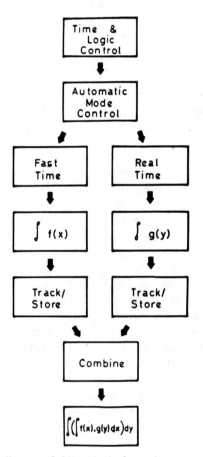

Fig. 64. Block diagram of the method of two-time computation using a parallel hybrid computer to solve a double integral in real time. The solution proceeds by steps under the control of the parallel logic, alternating between the fast time solution of $\int f(x)$ and the real time solution of $\int g(y)$. It is assumed that the value of $\int g(y)$ does not undergo significant change during the fast time updating of $\int f(x)$.

The technique used for the solution of the multiple integral made use of parallel hybrid computing methods. The technique adopted consisted basically of regarding the contractile tube as being composed of a series of cells, each taking a time $\Delta t$ to become activated, and therefore having dimensions of $(V_S . \Delta t)$ and $(V_L . \Delta t)$. The general equation for the solution of this was of the form:

$$\int (\int f(x) . g(t) \, dx) \, dt \qquad \text{(Equation 15.11)}$$

where $f(x)$ was the spatial function of the mass of muscle at the same stage of contraction at any time and $g(t)$ was the temporal function of the elastance with respect to time. Equation 15.11 can be solved by a technique known as two speed computation, in which the solution proceeds by discrete steps of $\Delta t$ (Fig. 64). At each step, the spatial

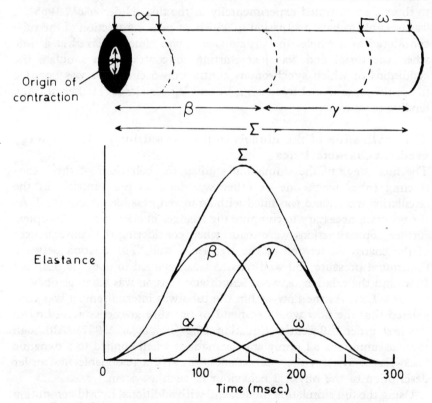

FIG. 65. Computer simulation of elastance changes in all parts of a muscular tube undergoing an asynchronous contraction that originates at the inner circumference at one end. Note that, by the time the distal end of the tube ($\omega$) has reached peak contraction, the proximal end ($\alpha$) is already fully relaxed. The computer model shows a good approximation to the contraction and relaxation sequence of the ventricular muscle observed in life (Hider *et al.*, 1965). (Reproduced by kind permission of the Editors of the *International Journal of Biomedical Computing*.)

integral of the mass of muscle at the same value of $\tau$ was first computed at a much accelerated rate (i.e. in fast time) and the result held in a track store. It could be assumed that during the period of this fast time computation the value of the complete function would not have changed significantly, and the fast time partial solution could therefore be used as a constant during a real time solution of the whole function over the time $\Delta t$. The whole stepwise process was then repeated, the switching between the fast and real time stages of the solution, and the advancement of t by small stages $\Delta t$, being under the control of parallel logic. By setting limits to zones of the model where elastance changes occurred, curves could be generated showing the total elastance changes produced when considering serial contraction of all or part of the tube (Fig. 65). These studies showed that, where the values of $V_S$ and $V_L$ corresponded to those demonstrated experimentally in the dog (Hider *et al.*, 1965), it was possible to have a situation in which, at peak contraction of the tube considered as a whole, the proximal end was almost relaxed at a time when the distal end was just starting to contract. To simulate the conditions in which synchronous contraction occurred, it was possible to use the same model by making $V_S$ and $V_L$ very large (mathematically, tending to infinity).

**The application of the models to the propulsion of fluid: energy gradient characteristics**

The final stage of the simulation studied the behaviour of these contracting tubes when one or other was used as the ventricle in the circulation model and was filled with an incompressible viscous fluid. As the program necessary to compute the changes in elastance was complex, further approximations were made when considering the consequences of the change in tension of the 'ventricle' wall. The relation between transmural pressure and wall tension was assumed to obey the Laplace Law, and the relation between length and tension was taken as obeying Hooke's Law. As the flow within the tube was intermittent, it was considered that the flow would respond to pressure gradients according to the first order differential Equation 15.3 (Fry *et al.*, 1957). Although these assumptions all imply approximations when applied to a dynamic visco-elastic system, they nevertheless do give a reasonable first order description of the physical behaviour of such a system.

Using the full simulation model, and with additional hybrid computing elements to provide the time control that gave the alternation of systole and diastole, the pressure and flow curves for the two types of model ventricle were produced. A significant difference occurred between the models. In the synchronously contracting ventricle, no energy gradient developed between the proximal and the distal portions until the onset of ejection. In the serially contracting ventricle, however, an energy gradient was present before the aortic valve opened. Following these simulation studies, the energy gradients between inflow and outflow portions of the left ventricle were studied experimentally in dogs and in sheep (Taylor, 1971) and an energy gradient was shown to occur before ejection; this gradient bore a close resemblance to the one predicted by the serially contracting model (Fig. 66). On the basis of these experiments

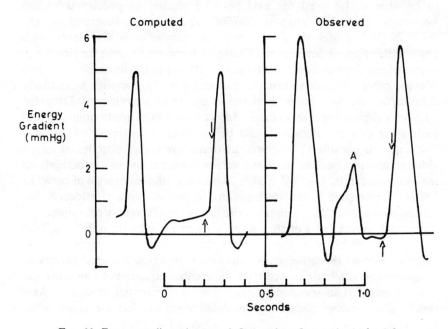

FIG. 66. Energy gradients between inflow and outflow regions of a left ventricle in a dog. Two tracings are shown:
1. The tracing initially *predicted* by the computer simulation for a serially contracting, valved cylindrical ventricle that has the inflow and outflow reservoir characteristics of the canine left atrium and systemic arteries.
2. The confirmation of the predicted tracing, as shown by *experimental* observations *in vivo* on the left ventricle of the dog. The arrows indicate when the mitral valve closed ( ↑ ) and when the aortic valve opened ( ↓ ). The letter 'A' identifies the wave due to atrial systole. (Reproduced by kind permission of the Editors of the *International Journal of Biomedical Computing*.)

it could be deduced that the serially contracting simulation provided the more correct model for describing the action of the ventricle. Whether the isovolumetric energy gradient is of any significance in achieving acceleration of the blood at the time of ejection cannot be predicted from the model used. The blood within the ventricles flows as stable expanding vortices (Bellhouse, 1970; Taylor and Wade, 1970), and a more complex model must be devised so as to take account of these flow characteristics before further predictive simulations can be carried out.

**Discussion of the simulation model of ventricular contraction**

This example of a simulation used for research purposes illustrates several important considerations, which apply whatever computer configuration is employed. As mentioned previously, the mathematical equations used to describe the system being modelled must do more than just reproduce the known behaviour—they must have sufficient theoretical justification to be able to be used for extrapolative studies to predict unknown behaviour, and thus suggest further experiments. Nevertheless, the mathematical model should be kept as simple as is consistent with reasonable physical description. The most important reason for simplicity in modelling derives from the fact that costs rise as the machine equations become more complex and increase in number. This applies particularly if multiple runs with different values of constants are required. Different parts of a simulation may demand different orders of approximation, and each stage of a simulation should be considered separately.

Even with considerable approximations, the errors introduced into a simulation may be less than the errors inherent in many methods of measurement in biomedical studies, where a confidence range of between 5 and 10 per cent is not uncommon. In the example considered, the critical section of the simulation was the serial change in compliance of the model 'ventricle'. For this, a fairly exact model with parallel hybrid computing capability was needed for the solution of a complex double integral. For all the other stages, however, it was considered justifiable to use simple algebraic or ordinary differential equations to describe the system, rather than some more exact partial differential equations. As a result, only analog computing modules were needed for these other stages.

## FUTURE DEVELOPMENTS

At present computer simulations are used widely in research and development work in the physical and engineering sciences, and a wide range of expert knowledge in their use and in the development of advanced software for computer simulation has already accumulated. The biological sciences are, by these standards, relatively far behind in the application of computer simulations. Future progress with these techniques as applied to research into biomedical problems will largely depend on taking full advantage of the developments which have already occurred in other sciences. The physical and engineering sciences use predominantly either hybrid or digital computers, employing specific modelling programs for the latter, and future software developments are likely to be principally with these techniques. It seems likely that, for a considerable time, computer techniques as such will continue to progress in advance of their application to biomedical problems. The factor limiting future advances in biomedical research making use of computer simulations will not so much be the lack of suitable software as limitations imposed by inadequate systems analysis and difficulties in the formulation of suitable mathematical models. For these difficulties to be overcome, co-operation will be needed on the one hand between the medical and the biological scientists, who have the problems, and the physical and engineering scientists who have the expert knowledge. The creation of inter-disciplinary teams will allow full advantage to be taken of existing computer techniques, so as to secure more rapid progress in biomedical research.

If simulation studies are used in association with other experimental methods, it seems likely that major advances will be possible in the understanding of the quantitative aspects of a wide variety of normal and abnormal body processes. The most important contributions from such a combined approach are likely to be in the study of dynamic systems. These would include many aspects of enzyme kinetics, of pharmaco-dynamics and of biorheology, as well as in the study of biological control systems and their breakdown under pathological conditions.

REFERENCES

DELLHOUSE, D. J. (1970). Fluid mechanics of a model mitral valve. *Journal of Physiology*, **207**, 72–73P.

FRY, D. C., NOBLE, F. W. & MALLOS, A. J. (1957). An electrical device for instantaneous computation of aortic blood velocity. *Circulation Research*, **5**, 75–78.

HIDER, C. F., TAYLOR, D. E. M. & WADE, J. D. (1965). The sequence of contraction of the right and left ventricles of the dog. *Quarterly Journal of Experimental Physiology*, **50**, 456–465.

HUGHES, A. (1968). Action potential simulated on an analog computer. *Journal of Physiology*, **198**, 83–84P.

SCHER, A. M. & YOUNG, A. C. (1956). The pathway of ventricular depolarisation in the dog. *Circulation Research*, **4**, 461–469.

TAYLOR, D. E. M. & WADE, J. D. (1970). The pattern of flow around the atrioventricular valves during diastolic ventricular filling. *Journal of Physiology*, **207**, 71–72P.

TAYLOR, D. E. M. (1971). Hybrid computer prediction of energy gradients within the left ventricle of the heart: with experimental confirmation. *International Journal of Biomedical Computing*. (To be published.)

WARNER, H. R. (1959). The use of an analog computer for analysis of control mechanisms in the circulation. *Proceedings of the Institute of Radio-engineers*, **47**, 1913–1916.

SUGGESTIONS FOR FURTHER READING

BAYLISS, L. E. (1956). *Living Control Systems*. London: Freeman.

CAMPBELL, E. J. M. & MATTHEWS, C. M. E. (1968). The use of computers to simulate the physiology of respiration. *British Medical Bulletin*, **24**, 249–252.

GREGORY, R. C. (1968). Models and the localisation of function in the C.N.S. In *Cybernetics. Key Papers*. Ed. Evans, C. R. & Robertson, A. D. J. London: Butterworth.

WARNER, H. R. (1965). Control of the circulation as studied with analog computer techniques. In *American Physiological Society, Handbook of Physiology*, Vol. **3**, Section II. Baltimore: Williams and Wilkins.

# CHAPTER SIXTEEN

# Teaching Clinical Diagnosis

## By F. T. de DOMBAL

## SUMMARY
POSSIBLE ways of using computers to assist in the teaching of clinical diagnosis are reviewed. The method of choice is considered to be by 'part-task' simulation, and the reasons for this selection are discussed. The problems which need to be overcome before computers should be widely used as aids to teaching about diagnosis include the delineation of a suitable role for the computer to play, the clarification of what is meant by 'diagnosis' (see also Chapter 9), and financial considerations.

## INTRODUCTION
TEACHING clinical diagnosis has never been a simple matter, but in the past we have been fortunate in Britain in many respects since the relative numbers of students, patients, and teachers have allowed the procedures involved in 'diagnosis' to be taught by example and by practice. It has been possible to demonstrate the diagnostic process to small groups of students, and then to give students opportunities to develop this knowledge by practising their newly acquired skills on patients. This situation is now changing since a need has been stated for a considerable increase in the output of medical graduates from the medical schools (Royal Commission on Medical Education, 1968).

Many short-term measures have been introduced, and several medical schools have declared an intention to increase their output in an attempt to bridge the gap between the current annual total of approximately 2,900 doctors and the estimated needs of 1980 for about 4,000 doctors each year. Problems are bound to arise as such rapidly increasing numbers of medical students come to be taught without corresponding alterations in the population of patients and teachers. Undesirable developments could include fewer opportunities for students to practise their diagnostic skills, and the degree of supervision and teaching available to students might be in danger of falling to unacceptably low levels. Furthermore, in some teaching hospitals, with their tendency towards increasing specialisation, the patients available to a student for 'diagnostic practice' may not be representative of the patients whom he is likely to encounter during most of his professional career.

There are at least partial answers to some of these problems, such as moving students into hitherto 'non-teaching' hospitals, but these fall outside the scope of this chapter. It is, however, clear that the conventional resources of teaching, particularly the staff, will find it increasingly difficult to deal with the expected rapidly expanding student population of this decade. Indeed, the Royal Commission Report (1968) quoted the University Grants Committee as stating that it could see 'no practical possibility of making more intensive use of the facilities already available'. Against this background can be seen a strong case for developing artificial systems for teaching clinical diagnosis, for it would seem reasonable to explore the possibility of supplementing conventional teaching resources by the use of modern educational technology, including teaching methods which involve the use of computers, particularly if conventional resources are unlikely to be able to keep pace with requirements.

## SOME POSSIBLE METHODS OF USING COMPUTERS TO TEACH DIAGNOSIS

### Computer-aided instruction and computer-managed instruction

Several classifications have been suggested for the various ways of using computers in an educational environment, but basically computers can be used in two different ways. In the first place, computers can be directly concerned with the conduct of specific teaching sessions, and interact directly with the student at this time; this method is most often called computer-aided instruction (C.A.I.), although it is also sometimes known as computer-aided learning (C.A.L.) or as computer-based learning (C.B.L.). In the other method of operation, computers can be used to analyse the student's performance, evaluate it, and suggest improvements; this form of usage is known as computer-managed instruction (C.M.I.).

Within the overall context of C.A.I., the student and the computer interact directly with each other and several possible ways of using the computer have been suggested; Stolurow (1965a, b) and Swets and Feurzig (1956) divided these into two main groups, the 'tutorial' and the 'Socratic' modes. In the tutorial mode, control of the lesson remains predominantly with the computer and the student works through a pre-set program under close control by the computer. By contrast, in the Socratic mode the type of teaching is oriented towards the student, the computer presenting the student with a problem for solution instead of providing a pre-set program; having presented the problem, the computer's main role may be to act as an information service, intervening in didactic fashion only when the student's performance falls short of pre-set requirements.

We prefer the Socratic or student-orientated teaching system since, in real life, clinical diagnosis is carried out by an individual and 'facts' pertaining to the diagnostic process are difficult to teach in didactic fashion because they themselves are still so poorly understood (Chapter 9). It would, therefore, seem reasonable to state that the degree of control exerted by a computer should be as small as possible, where a

# Program Dealing With On-Site Accident Handling
## Initial Sequence

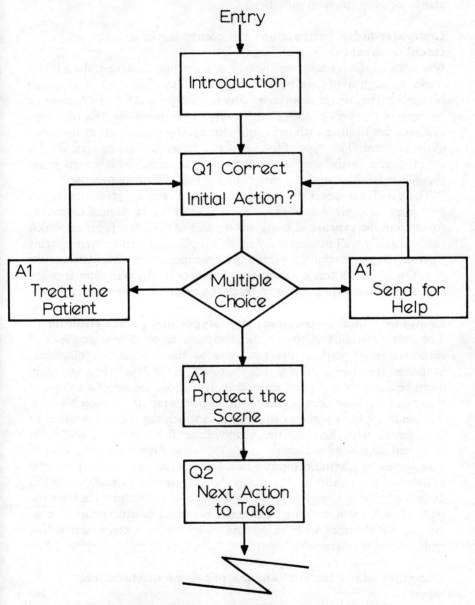

FIG. 67. Flow diagram to illustrate the initial steps in a branching program that deals with the handling of accidents at the site of the accident. The symbol Q1 refers to the first question, and A1 to the possible answers offered to the student. One answer allows him to move on to the next question (Q2).

computer-based system is used for teaching clinical diagnosis, so that the student will be encouraged as far as is practicable to think for himself and to develop his own initiative.

### Computer-aided instruction: the computer as a teaching machine

When the computer takes on the role of a teaching machine, the student works through a pre-set program, either of the linear or of a simple branching type, under close control by the computer. Figure 67 shows an example of this way of using computers, by outlining the first few steps in a program dealing with techniques for handling accidents at the scene of the accident. This type of use has some theoretical advantages, since it approximates to the sort of 'programmed learning' with which many people are familiar, and the programs are relatively easy to write.

The disadvantages of this method are, however, so great that it can have very little place in computer-based teaching of clinical diagnosis. Apart from the expense of using a computer to present a program which can be equally well presented by much simpler and well-proven systems such as certain 'teaching machine' programmes or scrambled textbooks (e.g. Owen, 1967), this close degree of control by the computer is probably out of place when trying to teach the diagnostic process.

### Computer-aided instruction: stereotypes and games situations

The next possibility is to use the computer to provide stereotypes of various diseases and to present these to the student for diagnosis. Students seem to enjoy this sort of approach, in our experience, but again it can be achieved easily and more cheaply without the use of a computer at all, and certainly does not merit an on-line computer approach as yet. The same applies to 'games situations' in which the student is asked to 'play games' with the computer. Although artificial, these are analogous to clinical diagnosis (de Dombal *et al.*, 1969a), and it is hoped that experience gained by playing computer-based games can subsequently be used to improve the quality of the student's performance in making clinical diagnoses. 'Game theory' may be a valuable tool in teaching students the types of task encountered in diagnosis, but there is little point in conducting these games with an on-line computer in a conversational or rapid response situation.

### Computer-aided instruction: the provision of statistical information

Another possible role for the computer is in the provision of statistical analyses relating to the diagnostic process in real time for the benefit of a student involved in a diagnostic problem; this requires the use of on-line facilities. In this example the student would be encouraged to enter details of a case-history, or any sub-set of attributes, into the computer and he would then be provided with a statistical analysis of these attributes by the computer. This approach is attractive to the computer programmer because it makes use of the calculating capabilities of the computer. However, the difficulties discussed in relation to Computer-aided Diagnosis (Chapter 9) apply with equal force here, and it is unlikely that the mere provision of statistical information will be of great value in the near future in the context of teaching about the diagnostic process.

**Computer-managed instruction: evaluation of the student and recording his performance**

There are two ways in which the computer can be used to manage instruction. First, it can be used to examine or otherwise formally evaluate the student. This is a controversial subject, and falls outside the limited scope of the present chapter. Stimulating and informative discussions of the problem can be found in papers by Anderson et al. (1968), Crow et al. (1969), and Dudley (1969).

On a less formal level, the computer can be used to record the performance of students, and to provide this record for retrospective analysis and discussion between the student and his teacher. In view of the current lack of knowledge concerning the diagnostic process, this discussive method would seem an acceptable way of using computers when teaching clinical diagnosis had has been employed in our own studies (p. 322).

## SIMULATION

At present simulation would appear to be the method of choice when teaching clinical diagnosis by artificial means—whether or not one is using a computer-based system. The concept of simulation is not a new one, although its use in the biomedical field has been somewhat limited until recently. Examples of the use of simulation in teaching diagnosis are provided in articles such as those by Feurzig et al. (1964), Heber (1968), Spivey (1969), and by Denson and Abramson (1969), and we have concentrated our attention on it also (de Dombal et al., 1969a, b, c).

Many attempts have been made to describe the concept of simulation, principally in relation to aerospace applications where simulators have been used since about 1910 (Ringham and Cutler, 1954). Precise description is difficult, however, since many facets are involved and different authors have placed varying emphasis upon these. Redgrave (1962), for instance, emphasised the fact that simulation transforms certain aspects of the real world out of their framework into a form more convenient for analysis, and Ruby et al. (1963) stressed that the process enables an investigator more easily to evaluate the performance of a system, or of its operators, under varying conditions. Westbrook (1961) went further when stating that the main purpose of simulation is to allow the experimenter to control the conditions under which a process takes place. More recently, several workers have attempted to combine the elements of previous definitions into a more comprehensive form, and one of the best of these definitions states that simulation is 'the art and science of representing the essential elements of a system (or process) out of their normal setting in such a manner that the representation is a valid analogue of the system (or process) under study' (Fraser, 1966).

## Planning a simulation

When planning a simulation, it is important to ask what sort of simulation is being attempted. Fraser (1966) emphasised the differences between 'whole-task' and 'part-task' simulation, and Urmer and Jones (1963) indicated that simulation should be based upon reliable and quantitative data obtained from existing performance achieved in a real-life situation, a point also stressed by Balogh and Purdum (1968). These authors were all concerned to draw attention to the ease of becoming involved in a 'simulation' study without having first given full consideration to all the factors involved in the analogous real-life situation, the danger of this approach being that the results obtained are not necessarily representative of those which would be observed in real-life. In other words, as Fraser (1966) pointed out, simulation procedures based upon guessed or extrapolated parameters may well be invalid in their practical application.

As far as teaching clinical diagnosis is concerned, it is necessary to decide whether to aim for a more ambitious form of 'whole-task' simulation, in which an attempt is made to reproduce a valid analogue of clinical diagnosis with as much realism and fidelity as possible. The alternative is to decide in favour of a less ambitious 'part-task' simulation in which the degree of realism and fidelity will be less, and only attempt to teach selected aspects of the diagnostic process. 'Whole-task' simulation requires a degree of understanding of the diagnostic process that does not yet exist, and a degree of capability of the computer in terms of realism that is beyond present-day techniques. In our studies, therefore, we have opted for a 'part-task' simulation, attempting to simulate and teach aspects such as certain techniques of patient interrogation rather than try to simulate the entire complex 'diagnostic process'. Our studies have been more directed towards research rather than to the routine training of medical students. The objectives of these operational and psychophysiological simulations are to study how the mechanical system is dealt with by its potential future users, and to examine the effects that the system has upon these users.

## A computer-based diagnostic simulator

The details of our work have already been reported (de Dombal et al., 1969, a, b, c) and this account will confine itself to discussing some of the main features of the work, and to commenting upon the difficulties of implementing a computer-based system. The Leeds version of a diagnostic simulator was first implemented in 1968, using an Elliott 903C computer (with 8K, 18-bit word store), a paper-tape punch, a paper-tape reader and an on-line teletype; later an experimental random access audio-visual display unit was added (de Dombal *et al.*, 1969b). This system has proved to be unacceptably slow in its response, and multi-access applications could not be implemented with this configuration. Recently, therefore, the Research Council's Computer Based Learning Unit in Leeds has begun to experiment with a Modular One computer (Computer Technology, Hemel Hempstead, Herts). However, since it seems highly unlikely at the present time that this form of simulation will be implemented for teaching purposes using this multi-access system, its use in a multi-access form will not be described here.

## Storage of clinical information

The information stored on computer file fell into the two broad categories of Patient Files and Ancillary Help Files. With the Patient Files, clinical information about one or a series of actual patients was stored, separate information files being set up to deal with the interview, the clinical examination, and special investigations performed on each patient. Within each information file, further subdivisions allowed the student to concentrate attention, for example, upon the presenting symptom, or upon the past medical history. In this way, the clinical interview could be subdivided along the lines indicated in Table XXVII. Within each information file, detailed structuring techniques allowed the student to obtain items of specific information, such as the site of pain or the duration of the presenting complaint, by asking for this information.

TABLE XXVII

Subdivision of clinical interview into separate information 'files'

CLINICAL INTERVIEW

| I Presenting symptom (pain) | II Other associated symptoms | III Previous medical history |
|---|---|---|
| (a) Site of onset | (a) Nausea | (a) Previous illnesses |
| (b) Site at present | (b) Vomiting | (b) Previous surgery |
| (c) Duration | (c) Bowel habit | (c) Family history |
| (d) Severity | (d) Appetite | (d) Drugs |
| (e) Progress | (e) Weight loss | (e) Allergies |
| etc. | etc. | etc. |

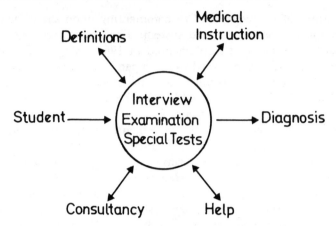

FIG. 68. Adaptation to simulation exercises in clinical diagnosis of the computer-aided learning system used in the Department of Surgery, University of Leeds. (Reproduced with permission of the Editor from de Dombal *et al.*, 1969a. *Lancet*, 1, 145–148.)

Ancillary help files (Fig. 68) of clinical data were provided so as to enable the inexperienced student to make his way through the diagnostic procedure. A file of definitions could be consulted if he was unsure of the meaning of any of the terms involved, and a 'consultancy' file aimed to provide consultative facilities in the sense that this file would explain the significance of any clinical attribute to the student. In addition, a medical instruction file was provided to assist the student who was unsure of how to set about the diagnostic process.

Experience with this system showed that, although the basic files of clinical information were reasonably satisfactory, the 'help' files were far from adequate. Sometimes a student would wish to apply directly for some specific piece of assistance; in this situation the 'help' files worked well. More often, however, the student merely came to a halt, unsure as to what came next, and unsure as to the sort of assistance he required. Accordingly, the basic system (Fig. 68) was adapted and a new 'help' file constructed, which seemed to give a more flexible and useful response to the student when in difficulties (Fig. 69).

### Performance by students with the Leeds Computer-aided Learning system

Using the system outlined in Figure 69, the student selects a 'patient' for diagnosis and obtains clinical information by means of questions to which the computer provides the answers. The student enters his questions on a teletype keyboard and, provided the questions have been considered relevant, the appropriate answers appear on the teletype or via a random access tape-recorder and visual projector unit (de Dombal *et al.*,

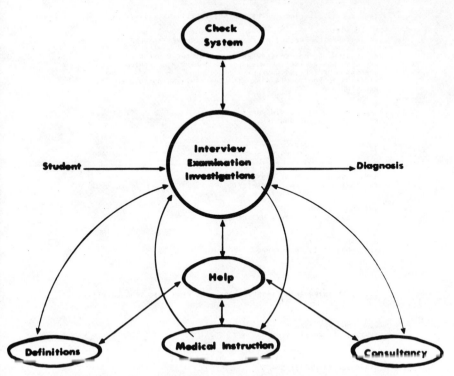

FIG. 69. Revision of the 'Help' file so as to ensure that students can either apply directly for specific help, or can merely type 'HELP'. In the latter case, the computer identifies the student's problem and then routes him directly to the appropriate 'Help' sequence.

1969b). A sample of the sort of 'conversation' which ensues is shown in Figure 70, in this simulation the 'patient' in this particular example being an imaginary sick astronaut (de Dombal, 1970).

The advantages of a 'student-orientated approach' have already been stressed (p. 316). In implementing this policy, we decided as a matter of principle to allow students freedom to interrogate the computer in any way they might choose. In its role as teacher, the computer was programmed so as to intervene only when a student's performance fell outside specified limits.

Three limitations were imposed upon the students. First, they were required to ask questions in such a way that the questions could have been understood by the 'patient' being interrogated. Second, they were required to ask certain key questions before moving on to another file, a 'key' question being defined as one that would have been asked by 75 per cent of the clinical teachers whose advice had been taken when programming the patient's case history for computer-aided learning purposes. Finally, each student was required to make a correct diagnosis. If

```
·················[TRANSCRIPT BEGINS]·························


    YOU ARE MEDICAL FLIGHT DIRECTOR ON THE CURRENT APOLLO 21
    MISSION .
    AT 124.6 HOURS GROUND ELAPSED TIME , AS THE COMMAND MODULE
    EMERGES FROM BEHIND THE MOON , THE COMMAND MODULE PILOT
    COMPLAINS OF FEELING UNWELL .
    IT IS UP TO YOU TO DIAGNOSE HIS COMPLAINT. GO AHEAD WHEN
    READY PLEASE .


    WHAT ARE YOU COMPLAINING OF ?
    DISCOMFORT IN THE ABDOMEN.


    WHEN DID THIS START ?
    IT BEGAN ABOUT 116 HOURS - ER THAT WOULD BE ABOUT 8 HOURS AGO.


    WHERE WAS THE PAIN AT FIRST ?
    IT STARTED RIGHT IN THE CENTER.


    WHERE IS IT NOW?
    AT THIS TIME IT IS OVER ON THE RIGHT .


    HOW BAD IS IT ?
    RIGHT NOW IT IS FAIRLY BAD.



    ········[ INTERVENING INTERVIEW DELETED FROM THIS TRANSCRIPT]····


    HAVE YOU FELT SICK ?
    THAT IS AFFIRMATIVE.


    ANY DIARRHOEA ?
    DIARRHOEA IS NEGATIVE .


    WHAT ABOUT THE PERIODS ?
    HAVE YOU GUYS GONE NUTS DOWN THERE?
    COMMENT:
            WE SHOULD PERHAPS HAVE STIPULATED THAT THE COMMAND
    MODULE PILOT WAS MALE BUT IT DIDNT SEEM NECESSARY.
    ANY MORE QUESTIONS?


    I WANT TO MAKE A DIAGNOSIS.
    FINE WHATS YOUR DIAGNOSIS PLEASE?


    ACUTE APPENDICITIS.
    VERY WELL. WHAT ARE YOU GOING TO RECOMMEND ?


    ETC ······· [TRANSCRIPT FINISHES]······················
```

FIG. 70. Extracts from a segment of printout from a computer-based diagnostic simulator used in 1970 in the Department of Surgery, University of Leeds. In this example the computer was simulating an interview with a sick crew member, a situation which students seem to find both interesting and instructive. (Reproduced with permission of the Editor from de Dombal, 1970. *Journal of the British Interplanetary Society*, **23**, 789–798.)

he failed to comply with any of these three requirements, the computer in its role as teacher intervened and suggested alternative ideas.

The computer has also been used to evaluate each student's performance, during the processes he adopted for collecting the clinical data, and in his attempts to diagnose the cause of each patient's symptoms. In assessing performance, the computer notes the accuracy of diagnosis since the actual diagnosis is already known from the case histories held on the computer's file—these mostly consist of surgical patients for whom the diagnosis had been established at operation. The computer also issues comments on the student's methods of data collection—printing this information out for subsequent examination and discussion between teacher and student. Control over a student's methods of collecting data can also be exerted in a real time mode by a computer connected on-line as he gathers his information. Experience gained so far indicates that the on-line mode works better with junior students, whereas retrospective assessment of a computer printout is the better method for more senior students.

## PROBLEMS ENCOUNTERED IN THE IMPLEMENTATION OF COMPUTER-AIDED LEARNING SYSTEMS
Large scale implementation of computer-based systems such as the one just described would seem to have certain advantages. We have found that students are more ready to challenge a 'computer-teacher' than its human counterpart, and frequently the ensuing discussion has revealed an underlying misconception with which the student had been struggling for some time, although reluctant to speak out during the more traditional bedside teaching sessions. There are, however, problems in implementing a computer-based system in practice, and these need to be discussed.

### The lack of information about diagnosis
The most serious problem we have encountered has been the realisation that much conventional teaching about diagnosis is based upon inadequate information. This subject has already been discussed (Chapter 9), but its implication in the present context is that no individual 'expert', no matter how experienced, should be allowed to act by himself as the ultimate authority.

The method we adopted to deal with this problem involved creating a panel of 'experts' in various subjects. We have so far concentrated our attention on surgical diagnosis, and the panel we set up consisted of a group of surgical teachers drawn from the University Department of Surgery in Leeds and from the National Health Service consultants working in several hospitals (some used for the teaching of medical students) in and close to Leeds. The use of a panel of 'experts' has proved much better than the usually didactic arrangements for pronouncing about diagnosis, but it has served to highlight the difficulties engendered by lack of information about the diagnostic process itself. As a result, the major portion of our effort is now being concentrated in this sphere, and we are attempting a 'task taxonomy' of the type described by Urmer and Jones (1963).

### Cost-effectiveness

This is another difficult problem. The high cost of implementing computer-dependent teaching systems can often be measured, at least in terms of hardware configurations, but their effectiveness is much harder to assess. When the effectiveness of an educational system is under scrutiny, a 'controlled trial to evaluate the system' is often suggested. In the present instance, however, it is difficult to see how such a trial can be 'controlled' and evaluated. It may be possible to show that the computer system teaches effectively, as measured by short-term tests of retention of facts, but its effectiveness needs also to be measured against bedside teaching. The reactions of students to the system should be taken into account, and many would say that they should weigh heavily in the balance. Many so-called 'evaluations' of teaching systems skirt round these considerations or avoid them altogether.

Despite these reservations, two points merit consideration, the first being the cost of software. One of the most worrying problems in recent years has been the increasing complexity and cost of the programming necessary for each new generation of computers if they are to be used at anywhere near peak efficiency. Fortunately, as far as the programs needed to simulate clinical diagnosis are concerned, although these programs are complex they can be standardised to a large extent. This means that, once a system is established, the cost of adding additional patients to the program library of patients is low. The hardware costs of the Elliott 903C system (de Dombal *et al.,* 1969b) were about £25,000, to which should be added the cost of about two man years of programming effort required to modify an already existing language for use in a medical application. Having absorbed these costs, however, further patients could be added to the file at about £1 per patient, although it is necessary to reiterate that the system has proved unsuitable for multi-access work and the Modular One system on which the Computer Based Learning Group are now working costs well over £50,000 for hardware alone.

The other point to stress, when it comes to evaluating a system, is that few workers so far have really asked themselves what their system is trying to accomplish in the field of education. In our own context—that of a busy clinical department—we believe that the primary objective of any system of simulation (whether or not it is computer-based) should be to undertake some task which cannot be accomplished by other methods of teaching. In this instance, the task for the computer is to present a series of 'patients' to the student so that he can himself practise privately certain specific aspects of his diagnostic technique. Thereafter, when he enters the real-life situation in the hospital wards and departments, he should know better the questions to ask, how to ask them, and what to look for when examining the patient. The computer, however, cannot teach him how to interview or examine the patient—this he can only find out for himself, at the bedside.

## FACTORS RELEVANT TO FUTURE DEVELOPMENTS

Several pointers towards possible future developments have emerged from studies already conducted. In the first place, any computer-based system that sets out to teach methods of clinical diagnosis must be 'student-orientated'. It must be predominantly controlled by the student, as otherwise there is a great risk of reducing his ability to take the initiative in a real-life situation.

Another facet which has emerged is what might be termed inter-disciplinary catalysis, and this has already had an important effect upon a number of medical students who have suddenly become interested in computers, as well as upon a number of students of mathematics who have suddenly become interested in clinical medicine.

Experience has shown next that 'part-task' simulation is all that can be attempted at the present time. Specific techniques for interrogating patients can be taught using a computer-based system, but only contact with living patients can teach a student how to establish rapport with, for instance, a frightened child or a deaf old man.

Finally, it would appear that the future place of computer-based systems for teaching about diagnosis is within an integrated curriculum that uses both live situations as well as other forms of simulation and 'games'. Obviously a wholly computer-educated student, with no 'live' experience, cannot be suddenly let loose on an unsuspecting public. However, specific aspects of the diagnostic process can probably be taught satisfactorily by a computer, acting as an adjunct to human teachers. In this supportive role, despite the expense and despite the many difficulties to be overcome before successful implementation, computers could well play an increasing part in medical education in the future.

## UNRESOLVED QUESTIONS

Two important questions are left entirely unresolved by the studies reported in this chapter. Firstly, is the computer a *sine qua non* as far as the simulation of clinical diagnosis is concerned? And secondly, if the computer is to be used, must this be in an on-line real time mode? It would obviously be a great advantage if a system of simulation could be developed which retained the benefits of our own computer-based system, but which at the same time avoided the expense and technical difficulties of using a computer in an on-line real time mode, as we initially tried to do. We have recently constructed a number of 'mark 2' simulators—some complex and some extremely simple—with a view to testing this hypothesis. It is our hope that we shall be able to report some additional information on this topic in the foreseeable future.

REFERENCES

ANDERSON, J., WOOD, H. & TOMLINSON, R. W. S. (1968). Examination marking by computer. *British Journal of Medical Education*, **2**, 210–212.

BALOGH, R. L. & PURDUM, D. L. (1968). *Computer Aided Instruction: Feasibility Study NASA Contractor Report CR 917*. Washington, DC.: NASA.

CROW, T. J., DIAMENT, M. L. & GOLDSMITH, R. (1969). On the evaluation of examination results by computer. *British Journal of Medical Education*, **3**, 232–236.

DE DOMBAL, F. T. (1970). Ground-based medical supervision of crew members during extended space missions. *Journal of the British Interplanetary Society*. **23**, 789–798.

DE DOMBAL, F. T., WOODS, P. A. & HARTLEY, J. R. (1969a). 'Digoxin': A computer based diagnostic game. *British Journal of Surgery*, **56**, 625–626.

DE DOMBAL, F. T., HARTLEY, J. R. & SLEEMAN, D. H. (1969b). A computer-assisted system for learning clinical diagnosis. *Lancet*, **1**, 145–148.

DE DOMBAL, F. T., HARTLEY, J. R. & SLEEMAN, D. H. (1969c). Teaching surgical diagnosis with the aid of a computer. *British Journal of Surgery*, **56**, 754–757.

DENSON, J. S. & ABRAMSON, S. (1969). A computer-controlled patient simulator. *Journal of the American Medical Association*, **208**, 504–508.

DUDLEY, H. A. F. (1969). Objects of objective tests: A theoretical and experimental analysis. *British Journal of Medical Education*, **3**, 155–159.

FEURZIG, W., MUNTER, P., SWETS, J. & BREEN, M. (1964). Computer-aided teaching in medical diagnosis. *Journal of Medical Education*, **39**, 746–754.

FRASER, T. M. (1966). *Philosophy of Simulation in a Man-machine Space Mission System*. National Aeronautics and Space Administration (NASA), SP–102. Washington DC.: NASA.

HEBER, A. J. (1968). A training model for endotracheal intubation in infants. *Anaesthesia*, **23**, 280–281.

OWEN, S. G. (1967). *Electrocardiography: A programmed text for self instruction in the principles of electrocardiography and the interpretation of cardiograms*. London: English University Press.

REDGRAVE, M. J. (1962). *Some Approaches to Simulation, Modelling and Gaming at S.D.C.* SDC–SP–721. Santa Monica, California: Systems Development Corporation (S.D.C.).

RINGHAM, G. B. & CUTLER, A. E. (1954). Flight simulators. *Journal of the Royal Aeronautical Society*, **59**, 153–159.

ROYAL COMMISSION ON MEDICAL EDUCATION 1965–68 (1968). *Report*. pp. 281 ff. London: Her Majesty's Stationery Office.

RUBY, W. J., JOCOY, E. H. & PELTON, F. M. (1963). Simulation for experimentation: A position paper. *Proceedings of the AIAA Simulation for Aerospace Flight Conference, Columbus, Ohio, 1963*. (Cited by Fraser, 1966.)

SPIVEY, B. E. (1969). Mannequin for practice of techniques and procedures. *Archives of Ophthalmology*, **82,** 487–488.

STOLUROW, L. (1965a). Model the master teacher, or master the teaching world. In *Learning and the Educational Process*, pp. 223–247. Chicago: McNally.

STOLUROW, L. (1965b). A model and cybernetic system for research on the teaching-learning process. *Programmed Learning and Educational Technology*, **2,** 138–157.

SWETS, J. A. & FEURZIG, W. (1956). Computer-aided instruction. *Science*, **150,** 572–576.

URMER, A. H. & JONES, E. R. (1963). Criteria for spacecraft simulation. *Proceedings of the AIAA Simulation for Aerospace Flight Conference, Columbus, Ohio, 1963.* (Cited by Fraser, 1966.)

WESTBROOK, C. B. (1961). *Simulation in Modern Aerospace Vehicle Design.* NATO Advisory Group for Aerospace Research and Development (AGARD) Report No. 366.

# CHAPTER SEVENTEEN

# Compartmental Analysis and Optimisation Procedures

## By J. H. OTTAWAY

### SUMMARY

THIS chapter briefly considers the mathematical background to compartmental analysis as applied to the metabolism of drugs and to isotopic tracer kinetics. Methods of obtaining the rates of transfer between different compartments from experimental data are discussed, with reference both to the use of analog computers and of digital optimisation programs. Some other uses of optimisation methods are reviewed.

### INTRODUCTION

The movement of chemical components of biological systems from one fluid space in the system to another can be studied by direct measurement of concentration changes or by the use of isotopic tracers, as can the metabolism of these components. Similarly, the distribution and metabolism of drugs can be investigated with the proviso that, unless the drug is isotopically labelled, its movement cannot be observed in the 'steady-state'—when its concentration for instance, in the plasma, is steady. The results of these experiments can be analysed and interpreted, for a wide range of chemical and biological systems, by simple assumptions drawn from chemical kinetics (see, for example, Solomon, 1953; Robertson, 1957; Atkins, 1969). The most important assumption is that the rate of diffusion or chemical change, per unit of distribution space, is proportional to the concentration of the chemical being observed; in this context, an isotopically labelled chemical is considered to be a separate species. The results of an individual experiment can then be generalised, by making an estimate of the proportionality constant (or 'rate constant') which links the rate of the reaction and the concentration of the reactants. Computers can be used in the estimation of these constants.

Digital computers have up till now played little part in compartmental analysis except in so far as the fitting of a straight line by least squares may be carried out by a computer program rather than by a desk-top calculating machine. Only one program designed for the task, SAAM 23 (p. 338), has ever been widely distributed, and examples of its use have been quoted by Berman (1969), but the program is now effectively unavailable in Britain. On the other hand, analog computation has been used very frequently (*see* Higinbotham *et al.*, 1963), and the author believes that this still represents the method of choice for a preliminary investigation of the theoretical aspects of such systems. Chapters 2 and 15 deal specifically with analog computers, and refer to their use as tools for solving systems of differential equations; analog computation will therefore not be discussed in detail here. However, attention is drawn to the book by Röpke and Riemann (1969); this describes a large number of model systems that are particularly relevant to pharmacological problems, together with the differential equations, patchboard configuration and specimen graphical output for each model.

The predominance of analog computers in the field of compartmental analysis is not likely to continue for much longer. In the last 10 years, much progress has been made with the mathematical technique of optimisation, which consists of the simultaneous fitting of a number of parameters to the numerical data associated with a particular equation. This technique depends on the successive testing of various values of the parameters until a 'best fit' is obtained. It can only be carried out with a digital computer, and indeed a fairly powerful central processing unit is required if results are to be obtained within a reasonable length of computing time. Optimisation is now beginning to be applied to biochemical problems (e.g. Kowalik and Morrison, 1968; Wieker et al., 1970) and, in particular, to compartmental analysis (Davis and Ottaway, 1971).

Optimisation is a very suitable technique to use for compartmental analysis because of its ability to estimate the values of several parameters simultaneously, and it is worth emphasising that only in very simple biological or medical systems is there only one rate constant to be estimated. The major emphasis in this chapter will therefore be upon digital methods of computation in analysing these metabolic problems, and above all on optimisation techniques. There are as yet few references to the use of optimisation in this field, and a single example, a problem of thyroxine metabolism, is therefore examined in some detail.

## COMPARTMENTAL ANALYSIS

### The theory of compartmental analysis

It is desirable first to consider the assumptions implicit in compartmental analysis, and the fundamental mathematical treatment which produces the equations that are commonly used. This account is necessarily abbreviated, and more rigorous expositions of the mathematical treatment have been published by Solomon (1949; 1953), Robertson (1962), Sheppard (1962), and by Hearon (1963). The underlying assumptions in compartmental analysis are well discussed by Reiner (1953).

A simple three-compartmental model (Fig. 71) will be considered. The mathematical treatment depends on the chemical concept that the rate of a reaction is proportional to the concentration (x) of the reactant, as expressed by the equation:

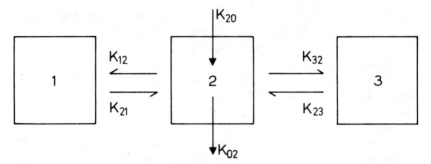

FIG. 71. A three-compartment mamillary tracer system. The central compartment is linked independently to each of the other compartments. The constants, K, are the first-order rate constants, the subscript notation indicating the inter-compartmental movements to which they relate (e.g. $K_{12}$ refers to the rate of movement from compartment 2 to compartment 1, and $K_{21}$ is the constant applicable to the movement in the opposite direction).

$$\frac{dx}{dt} = -kx \qquad \text{(Equation 17.1)}$$

In this equation, t represents time and k is a constant of proportionality, the first-order rate constant. The equation is not limited to chemical reactions, but can also apply to the transfer of substances from one organ to another within the body. The variable x in Equation 17.1 stands for the tracer, whether this be an isotope or not; when using this equation, it must be emphasised that no statement is being made about the nature of the reaction in which the unlabelled compound takes part, the so-called 'normal' reaction. Equation 17.1 implies that, when the tracer is present in low concentration relative to the concentration of the normal substrate and when there is no specific hindrance to the reaction or movement of the tracer (e.g. no 'isotopic effect' due to a difference in atomic mass), the rate of disappearance of the tracer will be determined by the competition between the normal substrate and the tracer, based on the relative numbers of molecules of each. In other words, the rate of disappearance of the tracer will depend on its specific activity, which is defined as the concentration of tracer per unit amount of unlabelled material.

Another assumption underlying the standard treatment of tracer kinetics is that the mixing of the tracer in all the compartments is continuous and is instantaneously complete. This is substantially true in many experimental situations, but it is nevertheless only an approximation. Mixing is never instantaneously complete and when tracers are injected into the bloodstream a finite time must elapse before the tracer becomes uniformly distributed throughout the circulation; the time is largely independent of the size of animal, being about 1.5 to 2 minutes.

Application of the principles underlying Equation 17.1 to the system shown in Figure 71 depends on the use of a conservation equation. Thus if $R_i$ is the total amount of tracer in compartment i, the conservation equation states that:

$$\frac{dR_i}{dt} = \sum k_u a_j - a_i \sum k_v \qquad \text{(Equation 17.2)}$$

where $\sum k_u a_j$ represents the sum of all the rates of influx of tracer with appropriate specific activities $a_j$ into compartment i, and $a_i \sum k_v$ is the sum of all the rates of efflux of tracer from compartment i, the specific activity of tracer in compartment i being $a_i$. In the system shown in Figure 71, Equation 17.2 becomes:

$$\frac{dR_1}{dt} = k_{12} a_2 - k_{21} a_1 \qquad \text{(Equation 17.3)}$$

Similar equations can be written for each of the other compartments. The various rate constants ($k_u$, etc., of which the dimensions are mass. $t^{-1}$) could be obtained from the system of equations corresponding to Equation 17.3 if all the rates of change $dR_i/dt$ could be estimated simultaneously and accurately. This is not normally possible, however, and the art of compartmental analysis lies in obtaining estimates of the individual constants ($k_{12}$, etc.) from less complete experimental observations such as the specific activity in one or more of the compartments at a number of observed times.

Integration of Equation 17.3 would eliminate the differential terms, but this cannot be done directly because there are two sets of variables, the 'R' variables and the 'a' variables. However, the total amount of tracer in a compartment (R) is equal to the total amount of chemical (P) in it, multiplied by the specific activity. For compartment 1 in Figure 71 this can be expressed by the equation:

$$R_1 = P_1 a_1 \qquad \text{(Equation 17.4).}$$

By means of equalities like this, the system of equations contained in Equation 17.3 can be turned into integrable equations either containing only terms in $R_i$ or only terms in $a_i$. There are advantages in using the former set of equations, and it should be noted that the expression $k_{21} a_1$, which appears in Equation 17.3, can be replaced by the equivalent expression $(k_{21}/P_1)R_1$, an instance of the general expression $(k_{ji}/P_i)R_i$. This is sometimes written as $\rho_i R_i$, the symbol $\rho_i$ having the dimensions of time$^{-1}$. The symbol $\rho$ is often called the fractional turnover rate, but confusion in nomenclature sometimes occurs and this is discussed by Atkins (1969, pp. 13 to 14).

The 'solution', or the integrated form, of the modified Equations 17.3 is a set of equations of the form:

$$R_i(k) = A_i e^{-\lambda_1 t} + B_i e^{-\lambda_2 t} + C_i e^{-\lambda_3 t} \qquad \text{(Equation 17.5).}$$

All the exponential terms become equal to unity in Equation 17.5 at zero time. Hence, at zero time $R_i(0)$, the amount of substance (tracer) in compartment i at the beginning of the experiment, is equal to $A_i + B_i + C_i$. This supplementary knowledge (the 'initial conditions') is essential if useful information is to be obtained from Equation 17.5, since $A_i$, $B_i$ and $C_i$, and $\lambda_1$, $\lambda_2$, and $\lambda_3$ are complex functions of the fractional turn-over rates and of the initial conditions. It is often insufficient simply to express experimental results in terms of $A_i$ and the various values for $\lambda$, difficult although this may be in itself. However, a direct algebraic attack on the complete form of Equation 17.5 (i.e. the equation containing all the various $\rho$ constants) is only possible in very simple cases, and it is the main purpose of this chapter to indicate how the use of a digital computer may enable the values for $\rho$ to be estimated, and from them the values for the different k and P constants, if desired.

Certain other experimental conditions have to be considered. It is possible, for instance, to introduce the tracer at a steady rate with the chemical input to the entire system (represented by $k_{20}$ in Fig. 71), rather than as a single injection into one compartment as has been assumed in the discussion so far. This technique implies that, after a long infusion when the exponential terms have become so small as to be negligible, the specific activity in each compartment will be the same as the specific activity of the tracer in the influx; usually the experimental results will only be valuable if they are collected well before this point is reached. An example of this approach is discussed by Reich (1968). Experiments involving steady rates of infusion require much more tracer than those in which the tracer is rapidly introduced into one compartment, and the consequent greater cost means that experiments of this kind are not often carried out. A situation in which the technique is useful, however, is when there is a second influx of unlabelled chemical into the system. If infusion is continued until the specific activities of the system are constant, and if the total mass of the system remains constant, consideration of the rates of transport of tracer into and out of the various compartments shows that it is possible to identify the compartment into which the second influx percolates, as well as the rate of influx. Differential equations need not be used for this type of investigation since all the computation can be done on a slide-rule; the technique is a variant of the isotope dilution method.

The normal chemical, or 'non-tracer', must obey a system of equations similar to those which describe the behaviour of the tracer. If the compartments are in a steady state, analysis of the total chemical flux merely reveals the obvious fact that the total influx equals the total efflux, and it is because this type of analysis is so uninformative that tracer experiments become necessary. However, when the system is not in a steady state chemically the situation is different as it is then necessary, in experiments with tracers, to measure the total pool size of each compartment at each time of sampling in order to calculate the values of $R_1$, etc., from the measurements of specific activity of the tracer. These measurements of chemical changes can then be used to construct a model to supplement the one representing the tracer fluxes; this further model is essential for providing enough information to solve the equations for the increased number of rate constants, since the influx and efflux for each compartment are no longer automatically equal to each other.

It is indeed possible to carry out compartmental analysis without a tracer, if the system is not in a steady state. Although this is very rarely attempted in complex systems, the widely used 'K' method of quantifying the response to a glucose tolerance test (Moorhouse et al., 1964) is a practical example of the method.

It may sometimes be possible to sample the tracer which has left the system, for instance as a metabolite in the urine, or as $CO_2$ in the expired air. In the model shown in Figure 71, the tracer is lost to the system from compartment 2, so the rate of loss from the system as a whole, following a single rapid dose of tracer, is given by the expression:

$$\frac{dR_T}{dt} = -k_{02}\, a_2 \qquad \text{(Equation 17.6)}.$$

It follows that the rate of increase of tracer in the 'sink' compartment $(R_S)$ is:

$$\frac{dR_S}{dt} = +k_{02}\, a_2 \qquad \text{(Equation 17.7)}.$$

It is, however, necessary to sound a warning about tracer experiments based on excretion studies. Although the major site of metabolism of the labelled compound may be an internal organ such as the liver, the metabolite can only reach the external measuring instruments after passing through the vascular system. The vascular system itself may form a multi-compartment system for the metabolite, however, especially with $CO_2$ (see Baker et al., 1961). If this occurs, the 'quick' and the 'slow' components deduced from the analysis of excretion curves may reflect nothing more than the complex distribution of the labelled metabolite between the blood and the extra-cellular fluids. This distribution may have to be studied separately, and this is always the case for tracers which are converted to labelled carbon dioxide.

## The analysis of experimental results

When it is possible to make observations only in one compartment, or in the 'sink', the standard method of approach is first to define numerically the exponential terms found in Equation 17.5. Unfortunately, this step in itself is difficult to do, partly because the exigencies of experiment usually prevent the experimenter from obtaining a set of data covering the whole range of the exponential decay curve. Instead, the 'tail' end is often cut off short but the graphical procedure and the linear regression computation, both of which are based on converting the data to logarithmic form, start from the data at the tail end of the curve. The exponential term with the longest decay time, which is presumed to be left exposed when the faster transients have died away, is fitted to the last few experimental points by eye or by least squares curve-fitting. At the point at which this computed line begins to diverge from the experimental curve, the calculated values for the slowest exponential term are subtracted from the experimental points, at each one of the earlier times at

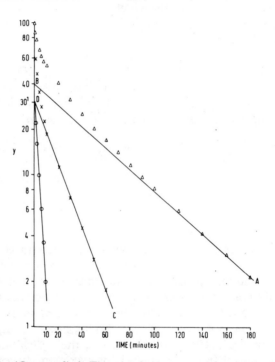

Fig. 72A. 'Curve-peeling'. The triangles represent values of the function $y = 30e^{-0.5t} + 30e^{-0.05t} + 40e^{-0.016t}$. At large values of 't' (t greater than 130 minutes) this function is approximated by $y = 40e^{-0.016t}$; it can be found graphically by drawing a line through the right-hand triangles and extrapolating the line to zero time (line AB).

At values of 't' less than 120 minutes line AB does not fit the triangles. If the differences between the values of 'y' given by the triangles and those given by the upper line (AB) are plotted on the graph, the points shown as crosses (x) represent the equation $y' = 30e^{-0.5t} + 30e^{-0.05t}$. By drawing a line through the crosses at large values of 't', and extrapolating, the term $30e^{-0.05t}$ may be established by means of the middle line (line CD). Finally, the difference between the values of y' given by line CD and by the crosses may be plotted (open circles), and thus give the value of the last term, $30e^{-0.5t}$, where the third line cuts the ordinate. Note that the scale on the ordinate is a double log-scale.

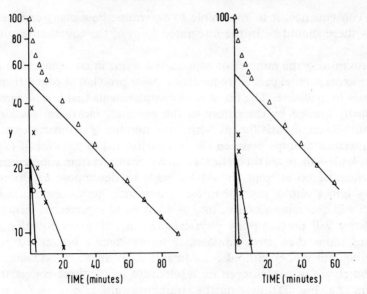

FIGS. 72B and C. The triangles plotted on these two graphs represent the same values of 'y' as those given in Figure 72A. Figures 72B and 72C show the progressive decrease in accuracy which is caused by extrapolating from earlier and earlier values of y. From Figure 72B, the value would be estimated to be;

$$\hat{y} = 28.5e^{-0.58t} + 21.5e^{-0.091t} + 50e^{-0.018t}$$

From Figure 72C it would be estimated to be:

$$\hat{y} = 23.5e^{-2.6t} + 22e^{-0.11t} + 55e^{-0.02t}.$$

which observations were made, to produce a new curve which is then analysed in the same way; this process is called 'curve-peeling'. It is easy to show, however, that it is possible to obtain estimates of the slowest exponential term which are far greater than the true values, unless the 'tail' is prolonged very considerably. This is demonstrated in Figure 72, which shows that an inaccuracy in the first estimation necessarily affects all the other estimates, and 'curve-peeling' has therefore come to be regarded with great suspicion as a method of analysing tracer data (*see* Ackerman *et al.*, 1967).

There is another more fundamental difficulty. The treatment outlined so far in this chapter has assumed that the experimenter has an unambiguous model of his system, and can therefore write down the corresponding equations and their solutions (e.g. Equations 17.2 and 17.5). This may not be the case, or the complete system may be very complex, and the experimenter cannot tell *a priori* which of the compartments may be combined, and which may be ignored, in order to produce a model of manageable size. Unless the number of the variables $R_i$, etc., and the relationships between the compartments are both known, a system of equations such as Equation 17.2 cannot be written.

As a consequence, it is impossible to determine how many exponential terms there should be in the integrated form of the equation, Equation 17.5.

Determining the number of exponential terms in an equation so as to fit the experimental data is frequently a major problem of compartmental analysis in medicine. The number of compartments that can be sampled is usually limited by the nature of the material, and there is seldom a sound theoretical basis for predicting the number of compartments, and the interrelationships between the compartments, in advance of experiment. Unless there are theoretical grounds, or results from supplementary experiments, no attempt should be made to decompose experimental curves into a sum of more than four exponential terms. Programs exist which will decompose a curve into as many as 51 exponential terms, but the latter will not have any physical meaning, since an equation containing more than two exponential terms cannot be related to an unambiguous model without considerable supplementary evidence. The correct choice of model, even for a relatively simple three-compartment system (e.g. Fig. 71), may not be straightforward.

## THE CONSTRUCTION OF MODELS

The term 'modelling' means basically the production of a system of interrelations such as that shown in Figure 71, and which can at least qualitatively account for the experimental results. A major part of the work involved in modelling can be accomplished by careful inspection of the experimental results, especially if it has been possible to sample more than one compartment. For example, if a decay curve crosses a 'rise-and-fall' curve at the maximum of this second curve, the precursor-product relationship of Zilversmit et al. (1943) almost certainly holds.

A computer program that would accept experimental results, test their fit to all possible model systems up to a certain level of complexity, and print out the system giving the 'best fit' to the data together with numerical estimates of the relevant constants, would be generally welcomed. Unfortunately, no program exists that has sufficient precision to discriminate between all the possible models which fit a limited set of data. Moreover, much of the information on which a model is based is not quantitative at all, but consists of constraints and limitations derived from other experiments and from results recorded in the literature. There is no method of providing all this information to the computer in such a way that it would take its proper place with the experimental data. There is, nevertheless, one program which attempts to provide a general modelling type of service. This is the Simulation, Analysis and Modelling Program (SAAM 23) (Berman and Weiss, 1967) developed by the Mathematical Research Branch of the National Institute of Health, Bethesda, Maryland. It has not proved particularly successful, unfortunately, and there are several reasons for this. It is a very large program and would require a lot of attention from specialist programmers to update it in response to changes in computer operating systems; this attention has not always been available. Its input requirements are inflexible, and at the same time obscurely documented, so that few people understand how to use the program. Its usefulness is also effectively limited to linear systems, i.e. systems having a constant size of compartment. The most limiting feature of all is that the iterative method for producing the best estimates of the parameters (p. 342) may fail to converge unless the program is provided with good initial estimates of the optimal values. However, these estimates can only be provided by another program or method, based on a model known in advance, so that in this sense SAAM 23 is unable to find the best model by a boot-strap approach. Nevertheless, when SAAM 23 can be made to work, it can provide much useful information including statistical estimates that are not at present available from any other source.

Since it is not yet possible to provide programs which will find the optimal model or 'best fit', the definition of modelling should be restricted to 'defining a compartmental system, by a mixture of logic and intuition, which will predict within reasonable limits the experimentally observed behaviour of the tracer'. It must be possible to derive from the experimental data estimates of constants which are compatible with the published values that relate to the problem under investigation. The most suitable model may be either compartmental or non-compartmental; non-compartmental models may be more satisfactory if mixing does not occur instantaneously (*see* Anderson *et al.*, 1967). It must be emphasised that methods of developing models and fitting data that may be helpful for compartmental models are not always suitable for non-compartmental models.

Two techniques will now be discussed which can serve as aids in the construction of compartmental models. The first of these involves analog computing, and the second is optimisation which is best carried out by digital computing methods.

## Analog computation in model construction

Analog computers are ideally suited for simulating the behaviour of systems of linear differential equations—steady-state compartmental models can be described by such systems (e.g. Equations 17.2 and 17.3), but there are disadvantages. Although the actual integration of the differential equations is almost instantaneous, patching and debugging the patched circuit can be tedious. Moreover, it is often forgotten that, every time a single parameter is changed, some or all of the others must be recalculated or the circuit will cease to represent a steady-state model. The more expensive analog computers may be provided with parallel logic, such as track-store and hold components; these enable values for parameters to be continuously adjusted until a pre-determined value of a variable (i.e. one corresponding to some experimental observation) is matched. It is also possible to use a hybrid computer in which a digital processing unit computes new parameter values, stores experimental data, and carries out the matching process (*see* Girling, 1969). However, for relatively simple models such as those likely to be encountered in compartmental analysis, and for retaining the maximum flexibility in searching among possible models, it is better to avoid the complexities of hybrid computers. Instead, matching of computer output to experimental data is essentially done by eye, using an X-Y plotter, which allows some of the difficulties of time-scaling to be avoided. It is usually obvious within about five attempts whether it is going to be possible to fit the output curves to the experimental data by reasonable adjustment of the parameters, and if this proves to be impossible then another model should be constructed.

Analog computation has limitations which chiefly depend on the relative size or 'scale' of the variables. The analogues to the variables are electrical voltages, and it would be unrealistic to expect operational amplifiers to have the same stability at, for example, loadings of 50 millivolts as at loadings of 50 volts. This type of disparity can largely be avoided by proper scaling, by adjusting amplifier gains or time constants, but these difficulties cannot always be overcome in biochemical problems. For instance, a relationship between a very small intracellular compartment, such as a substrate bound to an enzyme, and a much larger extracellular compartment may be under investigation, and scaling may be unable to overcome the effects of such disparities in size.

For those who do not have access to an analog computer, the IBM Continuous Simulation Modelling Program (CSMP) may prove an acceptable and helpful substitute. The connections between the variables and the initial conditions and parameter values are set out as they would be in an analog patching diagram (Chapter 2), so that familiarity with analog methods of computation is an advantage. It is preferable to use the interactive version of the CSMP program, if possible; in this version, analysis of the circuit logic as well as the results of the computations are issued as hard copy. The interactive version has been modified for use with an on-line console (time-sharing) system. The ICL 'Slang' package provides another digital computing method of solving differential equations that is more flexible than CSMP, but it is less related to analog computation.

## Optimisation in model construction

Optimisation may be defined as the process of determining the largest or smallest value of a mathematical function of one of several variables, and in some instances the values of the individual variables that are associated with the maximum or minimum. There are two kinds of optimisation, analytical and numerical, and this section will mainly be concerned with numerical optimisation.

Analytical optimisation is used when it is possible to specify a condition that must be met, in order that the optimum may occur, in such a way that an algebraic expression or set of expressions can be derived from which the values of the variables can then be calculated. For example, in fitting linear regression equations to data, it is usual to specify that the sum of the squares of the differences between the controlled variable (y) for each datum point and the corresponding value ($\hat{y}$) taken from the regression line should be a minimum. Many of the statistical procedures used to process experimental and field results are in fact analytical optimisations in this sense, although they are not usually called so. Most computer installations have a number of packages which carry out operations of this kind.

With numerical optimisation, no analytical condition can be specified. In this case the optimisation has to be done by a search procedure which yields a series of successive approximations to the optimum value. The search may be halted at any predetermined level of accuracy, and a digital computer can be programmed to carry out this sort of task very satisfactorily.

A simple example will be taken to illustrate numerical optimisation, namely the location of the square root of 13 by a direct search. In this method, the squares of 1, 2, 3 etc. might first be formed; this would quickly show that $\sqrt{13}$ lay between 3 and 4. Thereafter, the squares of 3.1, 3.2, . . . etc., might be formed, and this stage would show that $\sqrt{13}$ lay between 3.6 and 3.7, and so on. In each case the criterion of success being used is that the difference between the square of the number and 13 should be as small as possible, the search terminating when the accuracy reaches a pre-determined level. The process does not become faster as the accuracy of the calculation increases, and the convergence is therefore very slow.

This example illustrates the chief features of an optimisation method. Such simple techniques can be used when the objective function contains only a single variable, although it is usual to speed up the process by dividing each search field successively into larger and smaller fractions. Even with a computer, however, direct searches become completely uneconomic for more than two variables, remembering that only 100 steps for each of three variables means one million calculations.

It is possible instead to use formulae to find the square root of 13. In the first place, set $x_0 = G$, where G is an initial guess at the final answer. Then set

$$x_1 = G - \left(\frac{G^2 - 13}{2G}\right) \qquad \text{(Equation 17.8)}.$$

In Equation 17.8, $x_1$ is an improved estimate derived from the preceding estimated value, $G$. This process can be repeated, as follows:

$$x_2 = x_1 - \left(\frac{x_1^2 - 13}{2x_1}\right) \qquad \text{(Equation 17.9)}.$$

The process is halted at the 'i'th iteration if the absolute difference between $x_i^2$ and 13 is less than some previously agreed value, say 0.01. If $G$ were to be set at 1.0, this procedure would arrive at a value of 3.605 for $\sqrt{13}$ in four steps ($3.605^2 = 12.996$) and even if $G$ were initially to be set at the unlikely figure of 500, an acceptable answer would be produced in 10 stages.

This technique is clearly an immense advance on a direct search, and represents an example of an iterative method of optimisation, iteration being defined as a method of obtaining a new estimate $(x_{n+1})$ of the desired parameter by some calculation involving the previous one $(x_n)$. The formula used in Equations 17.8 and 17.9 represents a particular application of the Newton-Raphson method, one of the best known and most powerful of such iterative techniques. The Newton-Raphson formula is used to solve the equation $f(x) = 0$, and in the example already discussed

$$f(x) = x^2 - 13 \qquad \text{(Equation 17.10)}.$$

In the general expression of the formula, $f'(x_n)$ is the first derivative of $f(x_n)$ and the Newton-Raphson formula is then given by:

$$x_{n+1} = x_n - \frac{f(x_n)}{f'(x_n)} \qquad \text{(Equation 17.11)}.$$

The power of Equation 17.11 derives from the fact that it is quadratically convergent, which means in effect that the number of significant figures in the estimate doubles at each iterative step. This can be compared with the stepwise search described earlier, in which procedure each set of searches adds only one significant figure to the result. The Newton-Raphson formula is based on the Taylor series, and a good account of this important function together with a description of the basic theory and conditions for convergence is given by Noble (1964).

The Newton-Raphson method can be extended in its application to functions that contain more than one variable requiring to be optimised, but it does not provide a universal solution for all problems of numerical optimisation. For instance, the function to be optimised must be able to be differentiated to provide the denominator of the iterative expression; in some instances this may be impossible, or the resulting expression may be very difficult to evaluate. Frequently also, with more complex expressions, the Newton-Raphson formula may converge very slowly or even fail to converge unless a very good initial guess is provided, and the problem then arises as to where this good initial guess is to come from. For these and other reasons, much effort has been spent recently in developing improved methods of optimisation. About 20 procedures are widely used at the present time (Swann, 1969) and many computer installations possess some or all of these methods in their library of programs. Beveridge and Schechter (1970) give a comprehensive account of optimisation procedures and programs.

## AN EXAMPLE OF OPTIMISATION

This section describes the application of a modern method of optimisation, the method of Fletcher and Reeves (1964) to a particular problem in tracer kinetics. The problem chosen for consideration is the distribution of a single dose of radioactive thyroxine between perfusate, liver and bile during perfusion of the isolated rat liver (Hazelrig, 1964).

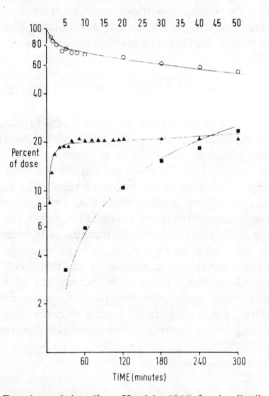

FIG. 73. Experimental data (from Hazelrig, 1964) for the distribution of thyroxine in the isolated perfused rat liver. The symbols denote the total radioactivity in the perfusate (O———O), the total radioactivity in the liver ( ▲——— ▲), and the total radioactivity in the bile ( ■——— ■). Note that the ordinate is on a double log-scale, from 1 to 100. (Based on data from Hazelrig, 1964.)

In this experiment it was possible to sample the radioactivity in the bile at intervals, and to estimate the total radioactivity in the liver by means of a suitable counter placed over the organ. The data are shown in Figure 73.

Estimates of the rate constants were made by a random search procedure (Ackerman *et al.*, 1967) and it was established that the data would be better fitted by the model shown in Figure 74 than by a simple three-compartment model. In this model $R_4$ is a miscellaneous compartment, the only justification for which was that it enabled a better fit to be obtained to the results. The external counter over the liver registered the sum of $R_2$ and $R_4$.

In a test of the optimisation program of Fletcher and Reeves (1964), four differential equations corresponding to the model shown in Figure 74 were integrated analytically. The resulting equations for the four variables $R_1$ to $R_4$, which formally resembled Equation 17.5 but which contained both the initial conditions and the fractional turnover rate constants, were inserted into a special subroutine. The experimental data were also read in, and the optimisation routine was asked to minimise the function

$$S = \sum \left[ \frac{(R_i) \ exp - (R_i) \ calc}{(R_i) \ exp} \right]^2 \qquad \text{(Equation 17.12)}$$

summed over all the experimental values of $R_i$, by varying the estimates for the rate constants; $(R_i)$ exp is the recorded or observed value and $(R_i)$ calc is the estimated value. It is necessary to use the sum of the squares of the *ratio* of the difference between the observed and calculated values, $(R_i)$ exp $- (R_i)$ calc, to the observed value, $(R_i)$ exp, because the absolute values for $R_1$ are much greater than for $R_3$, and would otherwise have completely outweighed them. The curves for $R_1$, $R_2 + R_4$, and $R_3$ corresponding to the optimal estimates of the rate constants are shown by the solid lines in Figure 73, and the time taken for the calculation was approximately one minute on an IBM 360/50 computer.

It is impossible to show graphically the rapidity of convergence of such a method when more than two parameters are involved, so the model of Figure 74 was simplified by using only the data for the radioactivity remaining in the perfusate. The equations then reduce to:

$$\left. \begin{array}{l} \dfrac{dR_1}{dt} = \rho_2 R_2 - \rho_1 R_1 \\[2ex] \dfrac{dR_2}{dt} = \rho_1 R_1 - (\rho_2 + \rho_3) R_2 \end{array} \right\} \qquad \text{(Equations 17.13)}.$$

In these equations $\rho_3$ is the total (fractional) rate of loss of radioactivity from compartment 2. In order to reduce the variables to two, use was made of the fact that in a steady state $k_{12}$ must be equal to $k_{21}$. From the

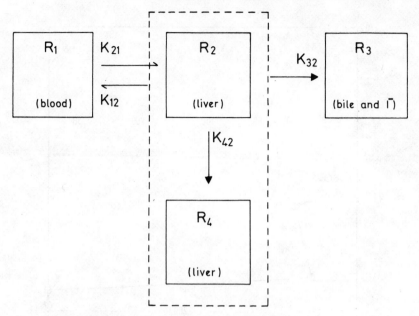

FIG. 74. The four-compartment mamillary model found to give a reasonable fit to the data presented in Figure 73. The external counter sampled the sum of the radioactivity for the two compartments shown inside the dotted lines.

definition of the values for $\rho$ (p. 333), namely that $\rho_1 = \dfrac{k_{21}}{P_1}$ and $\rho_2 = \dfrac{k_{12}}{P_2}$, it follows that:

$$\rho_1 = \frac{P_2}{P_1} \rho_2 \qquad \text{(Equation 17.14)}$$

There are good reasons for believing that $P_1 = 2 \times P_2$, and thus Equation 17.13 may be integrated in terms of the two parameters $\rho_1$ and $\rho_3$. Figure 75 shows the contour map obtained when the sum of squares for deviations of $R_1$ only are plotted against $\rho_1$ and $\rho_3$, the line showing that the optimum was reached in only seven steps. It is of interest to note that the values of $\rho_1$ and $\rho_3$ obtained were 0.103 and 0.010, compared with 0.227 and 0.047 yielded by the full procedure. This degree of agreement is not very good, and is almost entirely due to the fact that the complete data contained two more sets of observations ($R_2 + R_4$, and $R_3$) which helped to define the size of compartment 2 more rigorously. If the observations had been limited to the plasma compartment ($R_1$), no information about $k_{42}$ or about $k_{32}$ could have been obtained, nor could the existence of compartment 4 have been deduced. Optimisation cannot substitute for incompleteness of data, although it may enable the best use to be made of the data available.

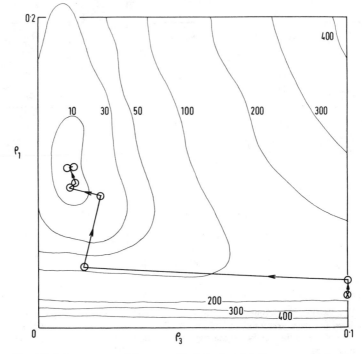

FIG. 75. A 'contour map' drawn to illustrate the simultaneous optimisation
of two parameters. The data used were those for compartment 1 (the blood)
in Figure 74, which are those of the top curve (○———○) in Figure 73.
The text explains how the four rate constants required in the model (Fig.
74) were reduced to two for purposes of this demonstration.

The possible values for the fractional turnover rates, $\rho_1$, and $\rho_3$, are
plotted on the axes of the contour map. The closed lines on the map join
points which all have a particular value for the sum of squares that is to be
minimised (the symbol S in Equation 17.12). The optimum values for the
constants correspond to a point, inside the smallest ellipse, that has the
lowest possible value of S for the values of $R_1$ used. The line shows the
intermediate estimates $\rho_1$ and $\rho_3$ made by the program, starting from the
initial guess that $\rho_1 = 0.02$ and $\rho_3 = 0.1$.

## DISCUSSION

Optimisation methods can be applied widely to problems of compartmental analysis, and to many systems of differential equations; they are
far superior to curve-peeling techniques. Analytical solutions can be
established for systems containing several differential equations with
constant coefficients, but if the number of variables exceeds three then
an eigenvalue/eigenvector program should be used to provide the
solution; this is available in most program libraries. If the compartments
are not in a steady state, the differential equations cannot be solved
analytically but must instead be integrated numerically (*see*, for example,
Knowles *et al.*, 1965). It is possible to obtain estimates of rate constants

even if data are only available for one compartment, a frequent situation in biomedical research, the chief limitation being the difficulty of defining unambiguously the compartmental system, and hence the system of differential equations.

It is not essential that systems requiring to be optimised should be expressed in the form of linear differential equations, whether integrated or not. For instance, the 'random walk' models for distribution of labelled calcium in the body, which lead to an equation containing power terms in 't' (Anderson *et al.*, 1967), or equations for the rate of enzyme catalysed reactions (e.g. Kowalik and Morrison, 1968; Wieker *et al.*, 1970), or equations derived from hypotheses of facilitated diffusion across cell membranes (Widdas, 1952), can all be treated by optimisation methods. The latter is only a technique for reducing to a minimum the difference between the experimental and the calculated results, for a given value of a controlled variable such as time.

Problems requiring optimisation for their solution arise, not only in the application of mathematics and physical methods of experiment to biomedicine, but in a wide range of economic and administrative matters. Examples include the planned maintenance and replacement of equipment to reduce operating costs; the control of idle time and queueing in out-patient clinics in order to economise on staffing or to minimise patient waiting time; and the planning and scheduling of efficient construction of new buildings or facilities. Before applying optimisation techniques to any of these problems, it is necessary to formulate a mathematical equation that describes the system under study, and for which a 'best' solution is required. If the variables of the system are not naturally numerical, relative numbers or weights may have to be allocated on an empirical basis in order to proceed. Beveridge and Schechter (1970) provide a thorough description of optimisation methods and, although their book is primarily written for chemical engineers, the importance of costs and profits in any field where questions of economics enter means that the book contains much that is relevant to many problems in medical administration.

REFERENCES

ACKERMAN, E., STRICKLAND, E. H., HAZELRIG, J. B. & GATEWOOD, L. C. (1967). Computers in biomathematical applications. *Clinical Pharmacology and Therapeutics*, **8**, 170–184.

ANDERSON, J., TOMLINSON, R. W. S., OSBORN, S. B. & WISE, M. E. (1967). Radiocalcium turnover in man. *Lancet*, **1**, 930–934.

ATKINS, G. L. (1969). *Multi-compartment Models for Biological Systems*. London: Methuen.

BAKER, N., SHIPLEY, R. A., CLARK, R. E., INCEFY, G. E. & SKINNER, S. S. (1961). C-14 studies in carbohydrate metabolism: V. Glucose metabolism in alloxan-diabetic rats. *American Journal of Physiology*, **200**, 863–870.

BERMAN, M. (1969). Kinetic modelling in physiology. In Computing techniques in biochemistry. Ed. Ottaway, J. H. *FEBS Letters*, 2 (Supplement), S56–S57.

BERMAN, M. & WEISS, M. F. (1967). *SAAM Manual*. U.S. Public Health Service Publication No. 1703. Washington, DC.: U.S. Government Printing Office.

BEVERIDGE, G. S. G. & SCHECHTER, R. S. (1970). *Optimization: Theory and Practice*. New York: McGraw-Hill.

DAVIS, R. H. & OTTAWAY, J. H. (1971). The application of optimization procedures to tracer kinetic data. *Mathematical Biosciences*. In preparation.

FLETCHER, R. & REEVES, C. M. (1964). Function minimization by conjugate gradients. *Computer Journal*, 7, 149–154.

GIRLING, B. (1969). An introduction to hybrid computers and their application to optimization problems. In Computing techniques in biochemistry. Ed Ottaway, J. H. *FEBS Letters*, 2 (Supplement), S58–S62.

HAZELRIG, J. B. (1964). The impact of high-speed automated computation on mathematical models. *Proceedings of the Staff Meetings of the Mayo Clinic*, 39, 841–848.

HEARON, J. Z. (1963). Theorems on linear systems. *Annals of the New York Academy of Sciences*, 108, (Article 1), 36–38.

HIGINBOTHAM, W. A., SUGARMAN, R. M., POTTER, D. W. & ROBERTSON, J. S. (1963). A direct analog computer for multi-compartment systems. *Annals of the New York Academy of Sciences*, 108, 117–121.

KNOWLES, G., DOWNING, A. L. & BARRETT, M. J. (1965). Determination of kinetic constants for nitrifying bacteria in mixed culture, with the aid of an electronic computer. *Journal of General Microbiology*, 38, 263–278.

KOWALIK, J. & MORRISON, J. F. (1968). Analysis of kinetic data for allosteric enzyme reactions as a non-linear regression problem. *Mathematical Biosciences*, 2, 57–69.

MOORHOUSE, J. A., GRAHAME, G. R. & ROSEN, N. J. (1964). Relationship between intravenous glucose tolerance and the fasting blood glucose level in healthy and in diabetic subjects. *Journal of Clinical Endocrinology*, 24, 145–159.

NOBLE, B. (1964). *Numerical Methods: 1. Iteration, Programming and Algebraic Equations*. University Mathematical Texts. Edinburgh: Oliver and Boyd.

REICH, J. G. (1968). Analogue computer analysis of tracer flow patterns through the glycolytic and related pathway in erythrocytes and other intact metabolic systems. *European Journal of Biochemistry*, 6, 395–403.

REINER, J. M. (1953). The study of metabolic turnover rates by means of isotopic tracers. *Archives of Biochemistry and Biophysics*, 46, 53–79.

ROBERTSON, J. S. (1957). Theory and use of tracers in determining transfer rates in biological systems. *Physiological Reviews*, 37, 133–154.

ROBERTSON, J. S. (1962). Mathematical treatment of uptake and release of indicator substances in relation to flow analysis in tissues and organs. *Handbook of Physiology*, Section 2, Vol. 1, pp. 617–644. Washington, DC.: American Physiological Society.

RÖPKE, H. & RIEMANN, J. (1969). *Analogcomputer in Chemie und Biologie*. Berlin: Springer.

SHEPPARD, C. W. (1962). *Basic Principles of the Tracer Method*. New York: Wiley.

SOLOMON, A. K. (1949). Equations for tracer experiments. *Journal of Clinical Investigation*, 28, 1297–1307.

SOLOMON, A. K. (1953). The kinetics of biological processes: Special problems connected with the use of tracers. *Advances in Biological and Medical Physics,* **3,** 65–97.

SWANN, W. H. (1969). A survey of non-linear optimization techniques. In Computing techniques in biochemistry. Ed. Ottaway, J. H. *FEBS Letters,* **2** (Supplement), S39–S55.

WIDDAS, W. F. (1952). Inability of diffusion to account for placental glucose transfer in the sheep and consideration of the kinetics of a possible carrier transfer. *Journal of Physiology,* **118,** 23–39.

WIEKER, H. J., JOHANNES, K. J. & HESS, B. (1970). A computing program for the determination of kinetic parameters from sigmoidal steady-state kinetics. *FEBS Letters,* **8,** 178.

ZILVERSMIT, D. B., ENTEMAN, C. & FISHLER, M. C. (1943). On the calculation of 'Turnover Time' and 'Turnover Rate' from experiments involving the use of labelling agents. *Journal of General Physiology,* **26,** 325–331.

GENERAL READING

GARFINKEL, D. & HEINMETS, F. (1969). Application of computers to the study of protein metabolism. In *Mammalian Protein Metabolism.* Ed. Munro, H. N. Vol. 3, pp. 253–324. New York: Academic Press.

HART, H. E. (Ed.), (1963). Multi-compartment analysis of tracer experiments. *Annals of the New York Academy of Sciences,* **108,** (Article 1), 1–338.

# CHAPTER EIGHTEEN

# Multiple Choice Questions and the Computer

## By B. P. MARMION and W. LUTZ

### SUMMARY

EXAMINATIONS are frequently used to help select candidates for admission to courses, as indicators of progress during the course, and as criteria of professional competence. There is a need to reassess the validity of some types of examinations and a need to automate at least part of the procedures, both in the setting and marking, in order to reduce the burden presently imposed by examinations.

This chapter considers the objectives and the types of multiple choice question (MCQ) tests. It discusses the construction, marking and analysis of MCQ papers and describes how, and to what extent, the processes can be assisted by a computer.

### INTRODUCTION

Every modern academic sensitive to educational fashion and student opinion knows that examinations are bad. They bedevil the syllabus; distort learning to a dull process of factual recall; cause anxiety and stress in the student; are subjective and unreliable in their scoring; and, finally, are unreliable predictors of future performance in the 'real' world outside the universities. In a thoughtful and amusing essay, Nisbet (1969) describes, in a cautionary, antithetic, fable, the long-awaited day in 1981 when these unsatisfactory yardsticks are finally abolished. By 1984, however, in response to proliferating private examinations and rising public clamour about nepotism and the insecurity from lack of generally defined standards, the authorities restore public examinations.

It seems, then, that universities, colleges of higher education and public bodies cannot avoid the task of measuring and ranking students in order of achievement, and of controlling standards. Apart from these functions, examinations can serve to orientate students to a defined set of educational objectives and, during a course, can provide both teacher and student with frequent monitoring of progress and of the efficiency of teaching methods.

### NEW METHODS OF EXAMINATION: RELIABILITY AND VALIDITY

In recent years there has been a welcome diversification of assessment techniques. For example, in-course assessment with various weightings, open book examinations, and distribution in advance of the bank of questions from which the final examination questions will be chosen have all been tried, as have long essay or other questions which may be answered in private during a period of about two weeks. There are also 'objective' examinations, in which the marks for every possible response that might be given by the candidate are determined before the examination. Multiple choice questions (MCQ) are the best known but not the only form of such objective examinations (Lennox and Wallace, 1970). Concurrently with the increasing use of these new objective tests, which are more reliable though not necessarily more valid, there has been an increasing scepticism about the reliability and validity of the familiar essay-type, short answer and oral examinations as currently practised (Bull, 1956; Hartog et al., 1936; McGuire, 1963). In the present context, reliability means the degree to which the examination provides consistent scores on repeated testing of the same students, and validity means the actual capacity for measuring what the method or procedure purports to measure—for instance, factual recall, comprehension, synthesis and evaluation, application etc. (see Hubbard and Clemans, 1961). While the reliability of essay-type examinations can be improved by the use of pre-agreed marking systems, and the marking of scripts by several examiners with consultation over discrepancies in marking (Lipton and Huxham, 1970), there remains the problem that a small number of essay questions has a large sampling error and can only cover a very limited area of a subject. Consequently candidates may, by chance alone, fare much worse or much better than their overall knowledge of the subject would justify. Similar problems of reliability may obtain with oral and practical examinations, but need not be discussed here (see Beard, 1969).

The use of multiple choice tests offers a level of reliability which cannot be matched by essay-type or short answer questions, but they do not automatically improve the validity. The purpose of this chapter is to consider types and objectives of multiple choice tests, their construction, what they may test, the methods of marking, and the analysis of their reliability.

## MULTIPLE CHOICE TESTS

These range from the familiar, simple, 'true-false' type of question (which is essentially a test of factual recall) through 'five choice completion', 'five choice association', 'excluded term' and 'relationship analysis'. This last group may be used to test cognitive abilities beyond the simple level of factual recall. Examples of these types of question, together with the directions for answering them, are illustrated in the Appendix (p. 371. See also Hubbard and Clemans, 1961).

The 'stem' in relation to which the different choices are offered in each of the questions may be a complete or an incomplete question or statement. Equally well it may be a clinical history, an anatomical diagram, a histological slide, an X-ray film, an ECG or EEG recording, a bacterial culture with a patient's history, histograms of the time- or age-prevalence of infectious diseases, and so on. The technique is highly versatile, and is particularly useful in practical examinations when these involve a large number of exhibits or 'spots'—three or more questions may be asked in relation to each exhibit, starting from the simple matter of identification and increasing rapidly in complexity to general and theoretical matters. With greater difficulty it is possible to devise a series of branching questions based, for example, on a clinical history. These may be arranged so that the answer to each question determines the choice of possibilities in the next questions, thereby allowing a serial decision-making process to be simulated (e.g. in relation to problems of patient management).

Multiple choice question techniques, particularly when these are rapidly marked and analysed by computer, are not necessarily restricted to formal, professional examinations. Instead, they may be used at any time by the student to monitor his own progress (*see* Harris, in Lennox and Lever, 1970), or to determine the effectiveness of teaching methods, sometimes with disconcerting results, by setting the same questions before and at the end of a course. Thus, in a recent study by Anderson *et al.* (1970), tests before and after an expensive, integrated topic teaching course showed a meagre 5 to 15 per cent improvement in the performance of students and no effect from attendance at lectures. Clearly any method is valuable which substitutes measurement, however broad, for the usual subjective and intuitive judgements of what a course ought to accomplish.

**The construction of a multiple choice examination**
The following stages may be recognised in the construction of an examination based on MCQ techniques:

1. Organisation of a pool of questions and determination of the reliability of the questions proposed;

2. Decisions on the weighting of marks and on the marking systems to be adopted;

3. Composition of the documents that are to be completed by the candidates;

4. Arrangements for the reading and scoring of answers for the analysis of results—this stage, in particular, should if possible make use of machine methods of marking and computer-dependent data processing;

5. Storage of the analyses of students' performance and of the results obtained for the various questions;

6. Arrangements for the retrieval of material from the records file for future examinations.

The first stage is probably best handled by a small group representing the different disciplines involved in the particular examination. For instance, when planning an examination in clinical pathology there should be at least one clinician and a representative from each of the branches of laboratory medicine included (e.g. clinical bacteriology, clinical chemistry). These individuals would probably solicit from their colleagues questions framed in several of the standard formats (p. 371) and then decide, as a group, on the most appropriate answer to each question in the light of current knowledge. They would also decide whether the stem of the question and the alternatives were clear, or were ambiguous in their meaning. It is important to note the use of the expression 'most appropriate answer', rather than the 'true' or the 'correct' answer, since decisions frequently cannot be absolute; rather, in many instances, it is a matter of the balance of probabilities.

The panel of question-setters should also attempt to decide whether the questions are mainly being set to test factual recall, when five choice completion questions would be particularly appropriate, or whether other cognitive skills can be brought into play such as relationship analysis. A balance needs to be struck between the types of question, so as to test different skills. However, the inclusion of a large number of different formats of question, although interesting as an exercise in technical virtuosity, can be confusing to the candidate and should be avoided.

The group of examiners should examine whether the inappropriate alternative answers, or distractors, are similar enough to the appropriate answer to make for real difficulty, or whether the distractors are patently so far removed in content from it that guessing alone will serve to identify the appropriate answer.

There are a number of other general criteria for construction of questions which should be satisfied, and these are discussed by Hubbard and Clemans (1961, pp. 44–45). Even when the examiners have refined the questions to their satisfaction, they still remain to be verified by use in an examination. On the first occasion they are used, the responses of the candidates to the questions should be analysed—and here computer analysis is almost indispensable—to see whether there is a smooth distribution of responses around the answer considered to be the most appropriate, or whether there is a bimodal response, with one maximum around the 'correct' answer and the other around a distractor. The latter pattern suggests that there may be an ambiguity in the wording, and draws attention to the need to review and modify the question.

### The assessment of questions: item difficulty
The first assessment of newly constructed MCQ should allow for the calibration of both their 'item difficulty' and their 'index of discriminatory power'. The former is a measure of the difficulty of an individual

question, as evidenced by the performance of the group of examinees:

$$\text{Fraction passing (C)} = \frac{\text{Number of correct responses to questions}}{\text{Total number of responses to item}} = \frac{R}{T}$$

(Equation 18.1).

According to Hubbard and Clemans (1961), determination of C values (called P values by Hubbard and Clemans) requires tests on a sample of 350 to 400 examinees. While a question with a C value of 0.50 gives maximum discrimination, the group setting the examination may wish to structure their examination with questions having a range of C values. Firstly, they may want to establish the amount of 'core' information that the great majority of candidates should have by means of questions having a low C value. Secondly, they may wish to include questions with higher C values that will spread candidates out in rank order, either at the top end of the distribution or around the (arbitrarily) chosen pass mark, or at both these points.

**The assessment of questions: the index of discriminating power**
Some approach to measuring the validity of questions may be made by comparing the score obtained with the questions when answered by the 'good' ('knowledgeable' or 'well qualified') students, with the scores obtained by the remaining candidates. The 'good' students are identified by other criteria such as different examination methods or by in-course assessment, etc. A commonly used index of discrimination, $\phi$, may be obtained by comparing the performance of the upper half of the group (i.e. the 'good' candidates) with the lower:

$$\phi = \frac{(P_u - P_l)}{2\sqrt{PQ}}$$

(Equation 18.2).

In this equation $P_u$ is the percentage of students passing the individual question amongst the 'upper' 50 per cent of students (i.e. the 'good' students as measured by the accepted criteria), $P_l$ is the percentage of students passing the same question amongst the remaining students (i.e. those students not designated as constituting the 'good' 50 per cent by the accepted criteria); P is the arithmetic average of $P_u$ and $P_l$ and Q equals $(1 - P)$.

In situations where independent criteria of assessment are not available, Equation 18.2 is still used but the definition of the upper 50 per cent of the students is replaced by those students scoring above the median mark of the MCQ examination. Using the MCQ examination itself to provide the dichotomy between 'good' students and the rest is not as satisfactory. Under these circumstances, the index merely indicates whether a particular question distinguishes between 'good' students and 'other' students in a manner consistent with the overall performance in the MCQ examination itself without however providing a convincing measure of validity of the individual question.

More complex methods of calculating discriminating power of items, such as the biserial correlation coefficient and the point biserial co-efficient, are discussed by Hubbard and Clemans (1961), and by Theobald (1964), and will be mentioned again later (p. 369). Once the questions have been calibrated, they may be recorded for future retrieval by type, by subject, and by origin together with their C and $\phi$ values, or other indices, on Cope Chat cards or in a computer file.

### Answer sheets and the marking of multiple choice questions

Manual marking of multiple choice question papers, with a mask or template covering all but the 'correct' answers is a familiar technique. It may be applied to marks made alongside questions as they are arranged on the examination paper or, preferably, to marks made on a single answer sheet which can then be kept separate from the examination paper proper. Even when an answer sheet is used which has been designed to be machine-readable, it is worth drawing it up so that arrangements can be made for it to be marked manually, if necessary, to allow for the possibility of crises due to machine failure. Manual marking of questions does not allow, at least with any ease, for the analysis of candidates' responses question by question, nor for the rapid calculation of statistical parameters of the population tested. A variant of simple manual marking, using feature cards and coincidence counting, has been described by Lever (in Lennox and Lever, 1970); this is said to be partly susceptible to computer analysis.

### Computer processing of MCQ examinations: the design of the answer sheet

The automation of the marking and analysis of MCQ examinations means that the students' returns must be set out in a simple and systematic way. There are many variations in the design of MCQ papers, and new designs will undoubtedly appear, but a few features are fairly common and merit discussion.

If candidates are required to mark the (one) most appropriate answer, and to leave the remaining alternatives blank, this may be done by filling or hatching a box, or by placing a cross, tick or line in a box opposite the question in the examination book or on a separate answer sheet (Figs. 76 and 77). A decision has to be reached whether the students' answers are to be made in the actual question book or not. If the book is used, there is little risk that it will be removed from the examination room. On the other hand, if the answers are on a separate card or sheet, then greater standardisation is possible and the same response card can be used without alteration at all MCQ examinations. Moreover the

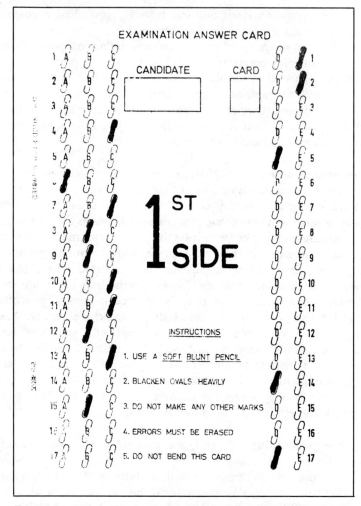

FIG. 76. Part of a mark sense card that has been used for entering answers to multiple choice questions. The numbered (horizontal) columns correspond to the questions and the lettered (vertical) rows to the possible answers. For question 1, in this examination, the candidate marked the answer as E and the mark sensing punch would later punch a rectangular hole to the left of the candidate's mark for this question. (Note that the question numbers on this card do not correspond to the questions discussed in the text of this chapter.)

material may be marked and manipulated with less effort. Books or answer sheets can be marked manually by the methods already described. For marking and analysis by computer, two main input methods are available, as follows:

1. The answer sheets or cards may be designed for use with a mark sense reader. In this instance, the responses of the candidates can be read

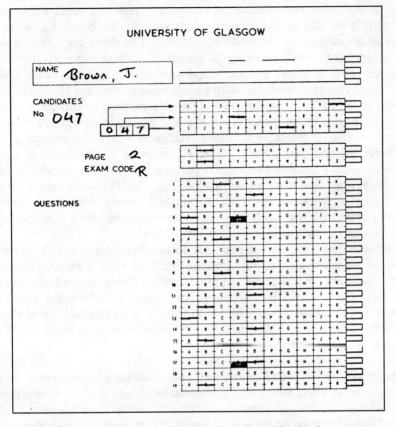

FIG. 77. Copy of a mark sense sheet that has been used for entering answers to multiple-choice questions. There was one answer to each question and the candidate marked answer C for question 1 in accordance with the marking instructions. (Note that the question numbers do not correspond to the questions discussed in the text of this chapter.) The candidate did not attempt question 3, and he changed his mind in respect of his answers to questions 4 and 17 where he deleted one of his answers (D in each case) by blocking in the lower half of the rectangle. A Lector machine reads this type of document and codes the column entries on to punched tape. (Figs. 76 and 77 reproduced with permission of the authors and the Editor from Lennox, B. and Wallace, A. C. 1970. *Scottish Medical Journal*, 15, 400–408).

immediately into the computer without further data preparation operations;

2. The answer sheets or cards may be transcribed on to punched cards or tape. This method requires some intermediate data preparation process before the data relating to the examination can be read into the computer. It is, therefore, a much slower and more error prone process. On the other hand, some safeguard is provided because the deck of cards can be run on a card sorter if the computer fails.

The punching and verification of cards or tape is a process that will usually delay the actual computer marking by 24 hours unless very special arrangements are made in advance. The delay may be reduced by arranging for each candidate to punch, directly or indirectly, his own answer card. A direct method employs the Port-a-Punch (IBM), the candidates using a small stylus to punch holes in the card (Diament and Goldsmith, 1970). One difficulty with this method would seem to be that, if the candidate makes a mistake and wishes to change his answer, it is presumably necessary for him to start a new card. An example of an indirect method uses a card of the Hollerith or 80-column type over-printed with a roughly rectangular pattern ('bones'); the candidate fills in the selected 'bone' with a soft pencil (Fig. 76). The cards are then read by a mark sense reader and a hole is punched corresponding to the pencil mark; after this the cards are read into the computer via a standard card reader (Harris and Buckley-Sharp, 1968).

Answer sheets can also be read in a document reader (e.g. ICL Lector) and the signals translated into punched cards or tape or entered directly into the computer. Recent simplification in the design of document readers (e.g. the MDR-2000 series developed by Motorola, Hitchin, Herts) should allow direct reading of cards, or of an equivalent area along the edge of an answer sheet, and thereby greatly speed up input of MCQ answer material into the computer.

## The marking of MCQ examinations: scoring procedures

A decision is often taken that all questions should consist of five parts and that only one of these five items is 'correct'. This convention simplifies the programming and the program preparations before the examination.

It is usual also to adopt a uniform scoring procedure, even though there is no compelling reason for introducing a standardised scoring procedure with MCQ examinations. The main advantage to be derived from such standardisation is that automated marking becomes simpler and quicker, even by computer, if this is done. Most users of MCQ examinations seem to have chosen one of three scoring systems, although occasionally other scoring systems or special marking conditions are imposed. The three commonly adopted systems award marks as follows:

1. One mark for a correct response, and zero for no response or for an incorrect response. This is often referred to as a 'no-penalty' system, because a student is not penalised if he guesses or responds incorrectly.

2. One mark for a correct response, zero for no response, and the loss of one mark for an incorrect response.

3. In questions permitting more than one correct response, $1/x$ is awarded for each correct answer, and $-1/y$ for each incorrect response, while zero marks are awarded if no response is made. In these expressions,

x denotes the number of correct and y the number of incorrect items in the question. This system has been used, for instance, for the MRCP examination (Owen *et al.*, 1967; Husak, 1968; Harden *et al.*, 1969).

Experience so far indicates that no great advantage, in terms of predictive ability, derives from using the more complex systems, as set out in the second and third alternatives above, when compared with the simple first alternative (Lennox and Lever, 1970). Similarly, we have found that the rank order is little affected.

Many academic computing departments in Britain have written general programs for the marking and analysis of MCQ papers. Among the more widely known are those used in Glasgow (Lennox and Wallace, 1970) and at the Middlesex Hospital (Harris and Buckley Sharp, 1968). These programs differ in their input facilities; in the constraints on the types of question acceptable to the program; in the method of scoring permitted; and they may also differ appreciably in the variety of tests and statistical calculations performed on the MCQ examination results. Despite these differences, MCQ marking and analysis programs overlap in many of their basic features. In the next section, the Edinburgh MCQ program which services MCQ examinations in clinical pathology, surgery and in medicine will be described using clinical pathology by way of illustration. The program is still evolving and no claim is made for its superiority over other systems of marking and analysis.

## THE EDINBURGH MCQ PROGRAM

The system developed at Edinburgh is shown in outline in Figure 78. It permits for each MCQ a variable number of parts (up to 10), a variable number of correct responses, and the possibility of varying the scoring system. This means that fractional or negative marking schemes may be used if considered desirable. The question paper may be divided into different subsections; this facilitates handling when several departments co-operate to set a single paper but still need separate sub-totals from the marking system.

The degree of flexibility available in the Edinburgh program involves a fairly substantial amount of preparatory work for each examination, as indicated in Figure 78, Stage I. The third and fourth stages rely on the following three general programs:

1. Input, checking and reading on to magnetic disc (Stage III(i) );
2. The marking program, including printing out of the results (Stages III(ii) and (iii));
3. The (optional) statistical analysis program (Stage IV).

These programs need setting for the number of candidates, the number of questions, the number of responses to each question, the scoring system, and for any constraints imposed upon the scoring. This entire specification must be ready before the examination can be marked. With so much detail necessary, a trial run on some 'dummy' returns is highly desirable to ensure the correct setting of parameter values.

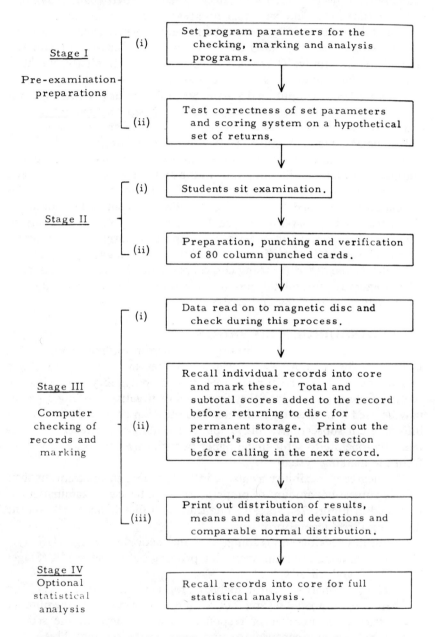

Stage I
Pre-examination preparations

(i) Set program parameters for the checking, marking and analysis programs.

(ii) Test correctness of set parameters and scoring system on a hypothetical set of returns.

Stage II

(i) Students sit examination.

(ii) Preparation, punching and verification of 80 column punched cards.

Stage III
Computer checking of records and marking

(i) Data read on to magnetic disc and check during this process.

(ii) Recall individual records into core and mark these. Total and subtotal scores added to the record before returning to disc for permanent storage. Print out the student's scores in each section before calling in the next record.

(iii) Print out distribution of results, means and standard deviations and comparable normal distribution.

Stage IV
Optional statistical analysis

Recall records into core for full statistical analysis.

FIG. 78. Flow chart of the MCQ computer marking and analysis program developed by the Department of Social Medicine, University of Edinburgh.

### Input procedures (Stage II, Fig. 78)

Little need be said about Stage II. The Edinburgh system relies on punched card input although it is hoped shortly to incorporate a document mark sense reader (Motorola 2000) for the direct entry of student returns with an increase of speed and elimination of errors arising during transcription or punching. At present, punching errors are reduced by the computer checks applied at Stage III and this feature will be retained even when a mark sense reader is used; some students will continue to give two or more answers to questions restricted to a single choice, and this must be taken into account at the marking stage. In practice, punching errors and student blunders (such as multiple responses), although troublesome, have not been numerous nor have they proved critical. This is because such errors involve the loss of only one mark, or at most only a small fraction of the total available marks, so do not affect the total score materially.

### Marking procedures (Stage III, Fig. 78)

The marking program operates by performing a simple procedure repeatedly. This is best described by considering a typical five-part question in which the possible responses are A, B, C, D and E (Example 1 in the Appendix, p. 372). For purposes of illustration, a marking scheme will be chosen in which $+1$ is awarded to the correct choice and zero to all incorrect responses.

The scoring system is stored in locations $S(A)$, $S(B)$, $S(C)$, $S(D)$ and $S(E)$, a distinct set of locations being allotted to each question. One of the locations holds a value of $+1$, for the correct response, but the values otherwise are zero; these stored values remain unaltered during the running of the program. Thus, for a question that has 'C' as the correct result, location $S(C)$ stores the value $+1$ but the other four locations ($S(A)$, $S(B)$, $S(D)$ and $S(E)$) contain zero.

In addition to the 'scoring locations', there are set aside a corresponding number of 'marking locations' $M(A)$, $M(B)$, $M(C)$, $M(D)$ and $M(E)$. These are initially all set to zero before marking of a question occurs. Thereafter, one or more of these marking locations changes its value to $+1$, depending upon the student's response to the question.

The operation of the system can now be considered in respect of the performance of two students. The first student marked the correct answer 'C' for this question whereas the second student indicated 'D'. The respective scores of these two students would be computed as follows:

*First student*: The program sets $M(C) = 1$, the other M values remaining set to zero. The score obtained for any question is given by the sum of the products of the values in the S and M locations, so that the following expressions hold:

$$\text{Score} = S(A)M(A) + S(B)M(B) + S(C)M(C) + S(D)M(D) + S(E)M(E)$$
$$= (0 \times 0) + (0 \times 0) + (1 \times 1) + (0 \times 0) + (0 \times 0)$$
$$= 1.$$

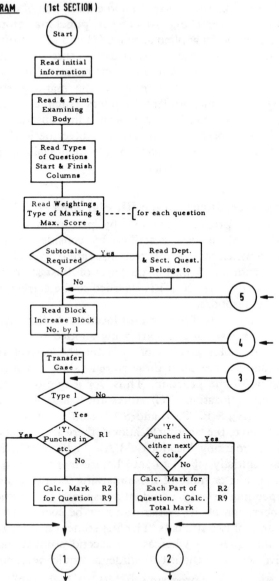

FIG. 79. Figures 79 and 80 should be studied in conjunction. They show the flow diagram of the computer marking program corresponding to Stages III (ii) and III (iii) in Figure 78.

*Second student*: His score is computed similarly. The program first sets $M(C) = 1$, while all the other M values remain set to zero. Thereafter:

$$\text{Score} = (0 \times 0) + (0 \times 0) + (1 \times 0) + (0 \times 1) + (0 \times 0)$$
$$= 0.$$

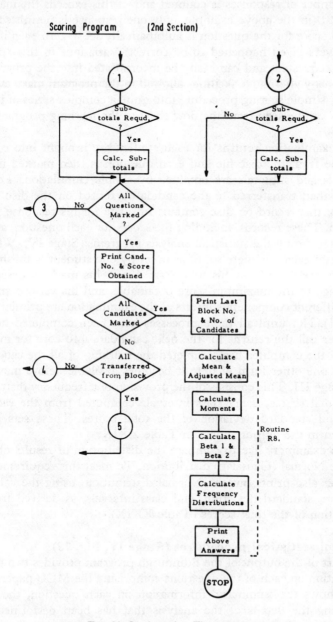

FIG. 80. See legend to Figure 79.

Because all the M locations are set to zero before the computer marks a question, a student who does not answer a question will be given zero by this procedure. In the case of student blunders involving multiple responses, special conditions have to be set. In the present system, the total number of responses is counted and, if this exceeds the maximum permitted (in the above example, only one response is permitted), then the final score for the question is automatically set to zero even if one of the answers given happened to be correct. Variations in this approach may be requested, and can easily be incorporated into the program.

The many alternative facilities allowed in the program make even this basically simple scoring procedure into quite a complex series of instructions, as can be seen from the flow chart of the marking program (Figs. 79 and 80).

The examination returns for each student are brought into core one at a time from the disc file and each question is then marked in turn; the totals and subtotals are obtained by simple cumulation. The total score is then transferred to the candidate's record on the disc file. In addition, this record on disc contains full data for his response to each question. These records, including the scores for each question, are used again later during the statistical analysis programs (Stage IV). When the marking of each complete set of answers by one student is finished, the student's serial number, his total (raw) score, his mark expressed as a percentage of the maximum score obtainable, and his various subtotals in the different component subjects of the examination are printed (Table XXVIII). Not until all these processes have been completed does the computer call the returns for the next candidate into core for marking.

When the computer has completed the marking of all the candidates' returns, one other form of output becomes available before moving on from Stage III. This consists of the provision of a frequency distribution of the total scores, using class intervals computed from the estimated mean and standard deviation of the total scores. These sets of data are given in the output shown in Table XXIX.

Some examiners like to compare the distribution of results observed with the Normal (Gaussian) distribution. To meet this requirement, the computer also prints out the Normal distribution, using the values for the mean, standard deviation, and class intervals, as derived from the distribution of the total scores (Table XXIX).

## Optional statistical procedures (Stage IV, Fig. 78)
This part of the output of the Edinburgh program provides two types of information on each of the questions comprising the MCQ paper. Table XXX shows the 'summary' information on each question, the legend explaining the details of the analysis that has been performed. This analysis has often been found to give the first indication that certain

TABLE XXVIII

RESULTS OF
CLINICAL PATHOLOGY EXAMINATION

INDIVIDUAL SCORES

MAX RAW SCORE = 120

| CANDIDATE NO. | RAW SCORE | ADJUSTED SCORE FROM 100 | SECT 1 | SECT 2 | SECT 3 | DEPT 1 | DEPT 2 | DEPT 3 |
|---|---|---|---|---|---|---|---|---|
| 1 | 91.000 | 75.833 | 38.00 | 25.00 | 31.00 | 32.00 | 28.00 | 31.00 |
| 2 | 62.000 | 51.667 | 2.00 | 22.00 | 15.00 | 33.00 | 9.00 | 20.00 |
| 3 | 85.000 | 70.833 | 3.00 | 24.00 | 24.00 | 20.00 | 27.00 | 24.00 |
| 4 | 74.000 | 61.667 | 3.00 | 23.00 | 24.00 | 20.00 | 30.00 | 24.00 |
| 5 | 73.000 | 60.833 | 3.00 | 20.00 | 18.00 | 22.00 | 26.00 | 25.00 |
| 6 | 69.000 | 57.500 | 3?.00 | 21.00 | 19.00 | 24.00 | 20.00 | 25.00 |
| 7 | 80.000 | 66.667 | 3.00 | 17.00 | 31.00 | 28.00 | 21.00 | 31.00 |
| 8 | 64.000 | 53.333 | 3?.00 | 22.00 | 13.00 | 21.00 | 24.00 | 19.00 |
| 9 | 87.000 | 72.500 | 3.00 | 26.00 | 28.00 | 27.00 | 30.00 | 30.00 |
| 10 | 72.000 | 60.000 | 3?.00 | 20.00 | 22.00 | 25.00 | 18.00 | 29.00 |
| 132 | 73.000 | 60.833 | 36.00 | 18.00 | 26.00 | 26.00 | 19.00 | 24.00 |
| 133 | 42.000 | 35.000 | 7?.00 | 11.00 | 11.00 | 16.00 | 13.00 | 13.00 |
| 134 | 83.000 | 69.167 | 7?.00 | 24.00 | 32.00 | 26.00 | 27.00 | 30.00 |
| 135 | 50.000 | 41.667 | 7?.00 | 17.00 | 9.00 | 20.00 | 11.00 | 19.00 |

LAST BLOCK WRITTEN TO = 90

NUMBER OF CANDIDATES = 134

Part of the output of individual scores and subtotals obtained by the 135 students who were entered for part of the Final M.B., Ch.B. Examination, University of Edinburgh.

Column 1 gives the student's serial number, column 2 his total score (maximum 120), and column 3 gives the conversion of this raw score to a percentage. Candidate 63 did not sit the examination, so that all the analyses have been based on 134 sets of results.

The section subtotals, given in Columns 4–6, refer to the three different groups of questions (e.g. True or False statements) used in this particular examination and give the marks obtained for each group. Columns 7 to 9 show the subtotals obtained on all the questions set for each of the three subjects by the departments involved (namely Bacteriology, Clinical Chemistry and Haematology).

The statement 'LAST BLOCK WRITTEN TO = 90 relates to storage information, and is only of interest to the programmer.

TABLE XXIX

| MEAN | 76.179 |
| --- | --- |
| ADJUSTED MEAN | 63.483 |

MOMENTS ABOUT MEAN

| 2ND MOMENT | 124.735 |
| --- | --- |
| 3RD MOMENT | -524.697 |
| 4TH MOMENT | 50556.991 |

| BETA 1 | 0.142 | BETA 1 IS 0 IF DISTRIBUTION IS SYMMETRICAL |
| --- | --- | --- |
| BETA 2 | 3.249 | BETA 2 IS 3 IF DISTRIBUTION IS NORMAL |

| INTERVAL | FREQUENCY | NORMAL FREQ. |
| --- | --- | --- |
| 42.674 | 1 | 0.181 |
| 45.466 | 0 | 0.218 |
| 48.258 | 1 | 0.433 |
| 51.050 | 2 | 0.805 |
| 53.842 | 1 | 1.411 |
| 56.634 | 2 | 2.320 |
| 59.426 | 2 | 3.583 |
| 62.219 | 7 | 5.206 |
| 65.011 | 8 | 7.102 |
| 67.803 | 2 | 9.108 |
| 70.595 | 12 | 10.977 |
| 73.387 | 13 | 12.428 |
| 76.179 | 12 | 13.227 |
| 78.971 | 12 | 13.227 |
| 81.763 | 16 | 12.428 |
| 84.555 | 11 | 10.977 |
| 87.348 | 14 | 9.108 |
| 90.140 | 8 | 7.102 |
| 92.932 | 3 | 5.206 |
| 95.724 | 4 | 3.583 |
| 98.516 | 0 | 2.320 |
| 101.308 | 1 | 1.411 |
| 104.100 | 2 | 0.805 |
| 106.892 | 0 | 0.433 |
| 109.684 | 0 | 0.218 |
| INFINITY | 0 | 0.181 |
| TOTAL | 134 | 134.000 |

STOPPED AT LINE 395

This is the form of computer output which follows immediately after the output shown in Table XXVIII. The 'MEAN' here refers to the total raw scores, while the 'ADJUSTED MEAN' refers to the mean percentage score (columns 2 and 3 respectively of Table XXVIII).

The variance (second moment about the mean) equals 124·735; this is followed by several estimates, including the BETA values, that are mainly of theoretical interest.

The frequency distribution of the total scores is shown in the first two columns. The corresponding Normal distribution (Mean = 76·179 and Variance = 124·735) is given in the third column.

The statement 'STOPPED AT LINE 395' indicates that the computer run ended correctly on the last instruction (line 395) of this program.

questions may not have been satisfactory in their present form and therefore require reconsideration. For instance, the mean score obtained for question 1 is 0·985, out of a maximum of 1; these data suggest that this question is too easy.

TABLE XXX

| MEAN | VARIANCE | STD. DEV. OF TOTAL SCORE |
| --- | --- | --- |
| 76.18 | 124.735 | 11.17 |

| QUESTION | MAX SCORE | MEAN | STD. DEV. | NO. NOT ATT. | PERCENT NOT ATT. | CORR. WITH TOTAL SCORE |
| --- | --- | --- | --- | --- | --- | --- |
| 1 | 1 | 0.985 | 0.122 | 0 | 0.0 | 0.04 |
| 2 | 1 | 0.588 | 0.494 | 20 | 14.9 | 0.24 |
| 3 | 1 | 0.910 | 0.288 | 1 | 0.7 | 0.03 |
| 4 | 1 | 0.910 | 0.287 | 0 | 0.0 | 0.21 |
| 5 | 1 | 0.848 | 0.360 | 2 | 1.5 | 0.38 |
| 6 | 1 | 0.695 | 0.462 | 3 | 2.2 | 0.14 |
| 7 | 1 | 0.800 | 0.402 | 4 | 3.0 | 0.09 |
| 8 | 1 | 0.797 | 0.404 | 55 | 41.0 | 0.13 |

The first part of the output from the optional statistical analysis on individual multiple choice questions. The first lines of output give the mean, variance and standard deviation of the total raw scores, followed by more detailed information on each question.

Columns 1 to 4 respectively give the question number, the maximum possible score for this question, the mean value scored (by all students) and the standard deviation of these scores. Columns 5 and 6 give the number and the percentage of candidates who did not attempt the question.

The final column gives the correlation coefficient between the student's score in this single question and his total score. In questions marked 1 or 0 only, care should be taken in interpreting both the standard deviation and the correlation coefficient.

Table XXXI shows the second form of output from the statistical analysis given during Stage IV (Fig. 78). This further analysis is more searching in its assessment of the suitability of individual questions, and of the various choices and distractors which together make up each question. The main objective of this analysis is similar to the one outlined for the index of discrimination (p. 354), except that candidates are divided by their total score into more than just two groups (the upper and the lower half) that occurs with the discrimination index. Up to eight divisions, by total score, are available, although these need not all be used. For instance only six divisions were used in the analysis displayed in Table XXXI as shown in the column headings ($0 < 50$, $50 < 60$, etc.); these intervals were chosen by the examiners and can be varied as requested, the choice being guided by the output of the distribution of scores given at Stage III (Table XXIX).

TABLE XXXI

SINGLE QUESTION STATISTICAL ASSESSMENT

```
| CI<X DENOTES A STUDENT TOTAL SCORE OF LESS THAN X |
| * DENOTES CORRECT RESPONSE                        |
```

QUESTION  1

| | TOTAL | EXAM | MARK | | | | | | | | |
|---|---|---|---|---|---|---|---|---|---|---|---|
| | 0< 50 | 50< 60 | 60< 70 | 70< 80 | 80< 90 | 90< 105 | TOTAL | | | | |
| NO. PASS | 2 | 7 | 25 | 43 | 41 | 14 | 132 | | | | |
| PERCENT PASS | 1.5 | 5.3 | 18.9 | 32.6 | 31.1 | 10.6 | | | NO. NOT ATT. | CORR WITH TOTAL SCORE | |
| NO.FAIL | 0 | 0 | 1 | 0 | 1 | 0 | 2 | | 0 | 0.04 | |
| PERCENT FAIL | 0.0 | 0.0 | 50.0 | 0.0 | 50.0 | 0.0 | | | | | |
| CI PERCENT PASS | 100.0 | 100.0 | 96.2 | 100.0 | 97.6 | 100.0 | | | | | |

| QUESTION PART | A | B | C | D* | E |
|---|---|---|---|---|---|
| RESPONSE | 0 | 0 | 1 | 132 | 1 |
| PERCENT | 0.0 | 0.0 | 0.7 | 98.5 | 0.7 |

QUESTION 46

| | TOTAL | EXAM | MARK | | | | | | | | |
|---|---|---|---|---|---|---|---|---|---|---|---|
| | 0< 50 | 50< 60 | 60< 70 | 70< 80 | 80< 90 | 90< 105 | TOTAL | | | | |
| NO. PASS | 1 | 2 | 10 | 27 | 29 | 13 | 82 | | | | |
| PERCENT PASS | 1.2 | 2.4 | 12.2 | 32.9 | 35.4 | 15.9 | | | NO. NOT ATT. | CORR WITH TOTAL SCORE | |
| NO.FAIL | 1 | 1 | 7 | 8 | 5 | 0 | 22 | | 30 | 0.26 | |
| PERCENT FAIL | 4.5 | 4.5 | 31.8 | 36.4 | 22.7 | 0.0 | | | | | |
| CI PERCENT PASS | 50.0 | 28.6 | 38.5 | 62.8 | 69.0 | 92.9 | | | | | |

| QUESTION PART | A | B | C | D | E* | F |
|---|---|---|---|---|---|---|
| RESPONSE | 5 | 2 | 0 | 1 | 82 | 14 |
| PERCENT | 4.8 | 1.9 | 0.0 | 1.0 | 78.8 | 13.5 |

This shows the computer output presenting a detailed analysis of the performance of students in Questions 1 and 46. For a fuller discussion of these data, see text.

Table XXXI shows the statistical assessment of two questions. With Question 1, 132 students out of 134 obtained full marks, and the distribution with respect to total score is given in the first row of the output; the corresponding percentages (out of the 132 correct answers) are given immediately below. All students attempted the question and the next two rows give the distribution and percentage (with respect to total score) of the two students who failed to obtain full marks in Question 1. The fifth line of output (CI PERCENT PASS) expresses the number of students with full marks for this question as a percentage of all students whose total score fell within each class interval (CI); this assessment would have included students who had not attempted the question. There is no discernible rise or trend in the percentages given in this fifth row of output in Question 1, another indication that this is not a satisfactory question. In an 'acceptable' question, this percentage should increase as the total score increases, but with some allowance for possible fluctuations in the overall trend due to the small numbers in each subgroup. The last three rows of output show the number of students choosing each of the possible responses. The letter marked automatically on the print out with an asterisk (D) is the correct response.

The verdict on Question 1 could be that it is far too easy, and that none of the distractors are worth retaining. On the other hand, the question could be rated as satisfactory, in that nearly all the class possessed the essential 'basic' or 'core' information which a student should have when faced with this question (p. 354, 372).

Another example is presented in Question 46 (Table XXXI). Here the immediate impression is gained that the question is more difficult, judging by the fact that 30 students (out of 134) did not attempt it. Alternatively, the question (p. 372) might be somewhat ambiguous. The progressive increase, with increase in total score, in the percentage of students with full marks seems satisfactory (CI PERCENT PASS), and the correlation with total score ($r = 0.26$) is at least significant. Nevertheless, the printout contains information which shows that this question (a six-part question with five distractors) needs revision, since at least three of the distractors (B, C and D) proved ineffective.

## Discussion of the Edinburgh MCQ program

The temptation to over-elaborate the statistical tests on the results has been resisted, in the belief that a few 'common sense' criteria are more easily understood by most examiners, and that these are effective in drawing attention to any major defects in the questions. If more involved computations should be desired, such as ordinary or point biserial r, these could easily be incorporated into the analysis. Various tests of reliability exist and these too can be incorporated. As indicated in Chapter 6, there is usually no programming problem in the incorporation of more advanced or mathematically more involved statistical procedures. However, the fundamental question is whether the examination results satisfy the various assumptions underlying the use of these statistical tests, and whether the results of these more involved tests permit interpretations that are helpful and meaningful to the examiner. Thus, even such a well known measure as the correlation coefficient may be difficult to interpret in this context, when the only marks awarded to a question are zero or $+1$, and when only a few students may fail to answer the question correctly, as should be the case with a question testing 'core' knowledge.

Further development and refinement of the existing programs has been postponed until a mark sense reader has been installed. The programs already offer a considerable degree of flexibility, permitting experimentation with varying types of questions and scoring systems. This flexibility does impose the tedious and repetitive process of setting parameters and requires rather longer computer run times than would a less versatile program, and computer operating time is expensive. When greater experience and confidence has been gained with MCQ examinations, it is likely that a standardised question format and marking procedure will evolve. It may then prove worthwhile to rewrite portions of the programs, to reduce both the amount of parameter setting and the length of each computer run.

## CONCLUSION

The speed, simplicity and reliability of MCQ techniques may reduce the frequency with which more traditional essay type questions are set. However, it is doubtful whether they will ever entirely replace essay questions. A major task is the preparation and maintenance of a bank of suitable, adequately tested and indexed multiple choice questions; these need to cover a sufficiently wide range of subjects and topics at various levels. Until a bank of valid questions has been prepared, the work entailed in setting MCQ examinations will continue to be very demanding. The speed and fascination of the technology of MCQ and the computer should not lead to a neglect of more important problems. These include attempting to define what each examination is trying to achieve, and research into the validity or reliability of the more difficult forms of examination such as the clinical or the long and searching oral examination.

ACKNOWLEDGEMENT

Much of the detailed programming of the Edinburgh MCQ program was initially undertaken by Mrs J. Wadsworth and later continued by Mrs J. Snashall. The authors gratefully acknowledge this help.

REFERENCES

ANDERSON, J., PETTINGALE, K. W. & TOMLINSON, R. W. S. (1970). Evaluation of topic teaching using computer marked objective tests. *British Journal of Medical Education*, 4, 216–218.

BEARD, R. M. (1969). A conspectus of research and development. In *Assessment of Undergraduate Performance*. Ed. Drever, J. pp. 34–43. Report of a university conference convened by the Committee of Vice-Chancellors and Principals and the Association of University Teachers, Spring 1969.

BULL, G. M. (1956). An examination of the final examination in medicine. *Lancet*, 2, 368–372.

DIAMENT, M. L. & GOLDSMITH, R. (1970). A simple automated method of marking multiple choice questionnaires using a computer. *British Journal of Medical Education*, **4,** 53–55.

HARDEN, R. McG., LEVER, R. & WILSON, G. M. (1969). Two systems of marking objective examination questions. *Lancet*, **1,** 40–42.

HARRIS, F. T. & BUCKLEY-SHARP, M. D. (1968). Automation of multiple-choice examination marking. *British Journal of Medical Education*, **2,** 48–54.

HARTOG, P., RHODES, E. C. & BURT, C. J. (1936). *The Marks of Examiners*. London: MacMillan.

HUBBARD, J. P. & CLEMANS, W. V. (1961). *Multiple Choice Examinations in Medicine*. Philadelphia: Lea & Febiger.

HUSAK, T. (1968). MCQ and the Membership. *Lancet*, **1,** 859.

LENNOX, B. & LEVER, R. (1970). Seminar on the machine marking of medical multiple-choice question papers. *British Journal of Medical Education*, **4,** 219–227.

LENNOX, B. & WALLACE, A. C. A. (1970). The use of computers in assessment of medical students. *Scottish Medical Journal*, **15,** 400–408.

LIPTON, A. & HUXHAM, G. J. (1970). Comparison of multiple-choice and essay testing in preclinical physiology. *British Journal of Medical Education*, **4,** 228–238.

McGUIRE, C. (1963). A process approach to the construction and analysis of medical examinations. *Journal of Medical Education*, **38,** 556–563.

NISBET, J. D. (1969). The need for universities to measure achievement. In *Assessment of Undergraduate Performance*, Ed. Drever, J, pp. 15–25, University Conference, Vice-Chancellors and the Association of University Teachers, Spring 1969.

OWEN, S. G., ROBSON, M. G., SANDERSON, P. H., SMART, G. A. & STOKES, J. F. (1967). Experience of multiple choice question examination for part I of the M.R.C.P. *Lancet*, **2,** 1034–1038.

THEOBALD, J. H. (1964). *An Introduction to the Principles of Classroom Testing*. Melbourne: Halls Book Store Pty. Ltd.

## Appendix

# THE STRUCTURE OF SOME OF THE COMMONLY USED FORMS OF MULTIPLE CHOICE QUESTIONS

The structure is best illustrated by giving specific examples, and some of the examples given here are considered in greater detail in the text of the main part of the chapter. The examples chosen have not been uniformly selected on the basis that they are 'good' questions, but rather to bring out points requiring discussion.

### Five choice completion

*Instructions.* The questions or incomplete statements in this section are all followed by five suggested answers or completions, each identified by a capital letter (A, B, C, D and E). Select the one letter which is most appropriate in each case. On the answer sheet, mark the letter that you have selected by means of a cross.

*Example* (Question 1: p. 368). Triple vaccine is used to immunise children against which of the following groups of diseases?
  A.  whooping cough, poliomyelitis, tetanus
  B.  whooping cough, measles, tetanus
  C.  diphtheria, poliomyelitis, tetanus
  D.  whooping cough, tetanus, diphtheria
  E.  poliomyelitis, whooping cough, diphtheria.

*Example Case history:* A young male aged 22 years developed a sore throat with fever, palatal petechiae and, within a week, extensive adenopathy. The spleen became palpable. A diagnosis of glandular fever was made. The three questions all relate to the same patient.
  1. The commonest single peripheral blood finding would be:
  A.  a polymorph leucocytosis
  B.  an increase in mononuclear cells
  C.  a rise in platelet count
  D.  a rise in erythrocyte sedimentation rate
  E.  a reticulocytosis.
  2. The single commonest biochemical finding would be:
  A.  a fall in plasma protein concentration
  B.  a rise in blood urea concentration
  C.  a rise in plasma protein concentration
  D.  a rise in serum alanine aminotransferase (glutamic pyruvic transaminase or GPT) activity
  E.  bilirubinuria.
  3. The single commonest serological finding would be:
  A.  a false positive Wassermann reaction
  B.  a rise in antistreptolysin-0 titre
  C.  a positive antinuclear factor (antibody) test
  D.  a positive cold agglutinin test
  E.  a positive heterophile sheep cell antibody test.

## Multiple choice association

*Instructions.* Each group of questions in this section consists of a list of between five and nine lettered combinations followed by a list of numbered words or phrases. For each numbered word or phrase select the lettered combination that most closely corresponds to it. On the answer sheet, mark the letter that you have selected by means of a cross.

*Notes:* (1) The same lettered combination may provide the best answer for more than one of the numbered words or phrases. (2) Not all the lettered combinations need have a numerical equivalent.

*Example* (including Question 46, p. 369)
  A.  Cold agglutinins
  B.  Purpura
  C.  Epstein-Barr virus
  D.  Abnormal haemoglobin
  E.  Leucoerythroblastic anaemia
  F.  Antiparietal cell antibody

44. Acute leukaemia
45. Primary atypical pneumonia
46. Metastatic carcinoma
47. Idiopathic thrombocytopenia
48. Sickle cell anaemia

## Excluded term

*Instructions.* Four of the five diseases or syndromes in the *numbered* list below are *lettered* functional disturbances. Select the one disease or syndrome which is the exception and the functional disturbance common to the remaining four.

*Example*

A. Decreased chloride concentration in CSF.
B. Mononuclear cell pleocytosis in CSF.
C. Unaltered glucose content in CSF.

1. Tuberculous meningitis.
2. Mumps meningoencephalitis.
3. Leptospiral meningitis.
4. ECHO 9 meningitis.
5. Coxsackie B meningitis.

## Relationship analysis

*Instructions.* Each question consists of a sentence with two parts; an assertion and a reason for the assertion. Select A if both assertion and reason are true statements and if the reason is a correct explanation of the assertion. Select B if both assertion and reason are true statements but the reason is not a correct explanation of the assertion. And, similarly, C if assertion is true but reason is false; D, if assertion is false but reason true; and, finally, E if both assertion and reason are false.

*Examples*

101. *Brucella abortus* grows in the bovine placenta
 *BECAUSE* The bovine placenta contains erythritol.
102. Children with the Bruton variety of hypogammaglobulinaemia recover normally from virus infections.
 *BECAUSE* antibodies are more important in recovery from bacterial infections than from viral infections.
103. Tetracycline is the antibiotic of choice for enterococcal endocarditis
 *BECAUSE* enterococci are sensitive to low concentrations of tetracycline.

# A System of Computer-based Records for University Students

## By A. S. DUNCAN and R. W. PRINCE

### SUMMARY

THIS chapter examines the implications of a computer-based system for maintaining records about students. It illustrates some of the advantages and problems of the scheme which has been adopted for use in the University of Edinburgh. The subject is considered under the three main headings of input to the computer, processing, and output of information from the computer.

### INTRODUCTION

There are four main areas of university administration in which computers can be used. These are for student records, for staff records, for buildings and physical plant, and for financial administration. Using a computer, it is possible to provide information of varying levels of sophistication for each of these areas, and Table XXXII outlines these. Only one area of the table will be examined in this chapter, this being a computer-based student records system which has been designed to provide retrieval statistics as a by-product. Some of the factors relevant to the design of such a system are considered from the standpoint of features desired by the university, by its students and by other legitimate users of the information. For the most part no particular distinction is drawn between medical students and students reading other subjects at the university since the broad principles of confidentiality and the nature of the information to be input are the same. There are some important differences, however, and these are discussed in the section on future developments.

Student records consist of the detailed information, both personal and academic, which can be related to an individual student. The term 'statistics' is used in this chapter in the sense of data relating to a group of students none of whom can be identified individually. It is the people who will make use of the records who mainly decide the nature and extent of the information to be recorded, and who as a result provide guidelines for the design of the record. Statistics, provided both on a regular basis and in relation to *ad hoc* enquiries, are needed by a university for internal use and by a number of other bodies. These include the University Grants Committee (U.G.C.), the Association of Commonwealth Universities, the Universities Central Council on Admissions (U.C.C.A.), the Committee of Vice-chancellors and Principals, the Local Government Education Authorities, and other bodies.

## TABLE XXXII

Areas of application of a computer to University administration
(Based on a table by Rourke and Brooks, 1967)

| Areas of application | Student records | Staff records | Buildings and physical plant | Financial administration |
|---|---|---|---|---|
| Record keeping procedures | Processing applications and admissions<br><br>Annual registration<br><br>Maintenance of current student records and records of graduates<br><br>Examination entry and recording | Personnel records of teaching and other staff | Inventory of teaching and other areas | Payroll and salaries<br><br>Payment of accounts |
| Management information | Analysis of student performance | Returns of academic staff<br><br>Analysis of teaching and of research by individuals | Utilisation of rooms<br><br>Allocation of classrooms for teaching and examination<br><br>Studies of building and maintenance costs | Analysis of departmental costs in relation to the teaching load |
| Examples of inter-relationships between areas of application | | Staff: student ratios<br>Teaching load on staff | | |

## INPUT: THE QUESTION OF CONFIDENTIALITY

A personal academic record is required by the university for each of its students in order to note and monitor progress during the university courses. It may also be used, with the student's permission, to help in the preparation of references for employment in later life. These records are usually held in the form of academic record cards, and the introduction of a computer-based system need not alter this procedure. To avoid the need for two separate records the computer can provide the conventional type of card as a hard copy by-product from the computer record. This hard copy offers the opportunity of adding to the record certain data which, as a result of policy decisions, the university may decide not to include in the input to the computer. This raises the question of confidentiality, a question which is so important in the whole field of student records that it merits detailed discussion.

### Confidentiality in student records systems

Like most thinking people, students have anxieties about confidential records, and particularly about records held on a computer file. They also have a fear, quite apart from the aspect of confidentiality, that they may lose the benefit of personal relationships with their academic advisors and become 'just another statistic'. This feeling can be mitigated by suitable design of the procedures, organisation and output to show that their problems have not been forgotten. Since input procedures are closely related to output characteristics in a computer-based system, these reservations of the interested parties have to be borne in mind when considering input. One organisational answer is to centralise the handling of machine-readable records, and to decentralise to Faculties and to individual university departments the responsibility for holding a computer-printed visual record to which confidential matter may be added without the need for the confidential material ever to have formed a part of the computer input.

A pre-requisite of any computer-based system of student records, for it to be acceptable nowadays, is that the students should know and should have agreed the categories of data that are to be included. If the record itself is to be made available on a console, or on a print-out to staff, difficulties will arise unless it can also be made available to the individual student at his own request. If two sets of data are kept—one to be available to the student himself and the other to be kept confidential— the suspicions of students will be aroused. This does not mean that no record of confidential information should be kept, and indeed it is in the students' interests that there should be files of confidential information, although such information need not be recorded on the computer-held records. Headmasters' reports and tutors' reports come into the category of confidential information; these would soon cease to have any value if the writers knew that their comments were going to be read by the persons referred to in the reports, or by others not immediately involved in decisions. It is only necessary to point out the importance attached to open testimonials, as compared with confidential references.

We believe, therefore, that it would be unwise to include in the computer input any information that should not be made available, on request, to the student himself. Examination grades would be included on the record but, in addition to headmasters' and tutors' reports, details of the student's personal medical history should be kept out of the program and handled, as at present, in a separate written record. If students are subjected to psychological tests of attitude or aptitude, the question arises as to whether the results of these tests should be added to their individual records. If this is to be done, the student's permission would be needed. If the tests have been designed to draw attention to students who are apparently particularly liable to academic failure, clearly this information would only be of any validity if used in conjunction with the rest of the academic record, and it would therefore best be handled if included within the input. Unless there are criteria of proven discriminating accuracy, however, there will be a danger of designating the wrong students as being at risk of failure, and this could possibly have serious adverse psychological effects.

## Medical records

The medical record also requires to be considered. If a routine or a selective medical examination is carried out at the time of entry to university or if, in special cases, information about the medical history is obtained, it is very easy to include specific items in the program. Medical data may be very important in the recognition of students who are academically at risk, as part of an 'early warning' system. However, we doubt whether this information should ever be included, and certainly it should not be included in the file of computer-held data without the explicit agreement of the student. We incline to the view that the medical record should probably always be kept entirely separate, whether or not it is held on a computer file, and we believe that at the most a marker should be placed in the main record to draw attention to the existence of possibly relevant information in the medical history, but without specifying the nature of this information. It would be relatively easy to record on computer file certain features such as the diagnosis and duration of any illness, and to update this information as occasion demands (p. 148). By itself, it is doubtful whether it would be economic to prepare and maintain such an abbreviated medical history for students at university, since they spend such a short part of their lives in this capacity. However, there might well be a particular value in relating the medical history of students to their academic performance, either as part of a research project into the performance of groups of students, or in the interests of an individual. It is probable that *ad hoc* programs would be better for both these purposes but, if medical records concerning students are to be held on computer file, then the format should as a matter of practical planning be made compatible with the main system of student records to allow for easy matching.

**The selection of input: data collection and preparation**

A wide range of information can theoretically be held on a records system concerned with students at university. The first problem, there-fore, is one of selecting what to include in the record. It is not possible, nor is it desirable, to hold in the computer's records all the information that is likely to be requested. Indeed, it is questionable whether it is the duty of the administrative staff at universities to collect any more information than represents the minimum needed to perform the job for which the system was set up. Because of this, although the system developed for the University of Edinburgh can be used to provide various statistics for research purposes, it has not been designed with the specific object of providing data for research workers.

A computer-based student records system for a university has to be designed to satisfy a range of demands for a variety of information; these may be received from users both inside and outside the university. To achieve this end, the system has to accept a range of data, and yet be able to adjust to changes over a period of time. The outcome is a com-promise between storing too much data and storing too little.

The main information held by the computer on its record is the detail supplied by each student on his registration or matriculation form (Fig. 81). This includes personal data, information about previous academic history and about the present course of study. The personal data consists of the student's name, sex, date of birth, home address and local address. The previous academic history contains the name of the last school attended, and details of the General Certificate of Education ('A' level) and Scottish Certificate of Education ('H' level) subjects passed, and the levels of performance attained. The data about the course that is being studied at university include the subject itself, the year of the course, an indication whether the subject is being studied on a full-time or a part-time basis and sometimes other details.

The design of the forms is a specialist function, and one which is important when planning data collection procedures. The usual method of collecting basic data in an educational institution is by requiring each student to complete an annual registration form. If this form is used for collecting information, it must ask for sufficient data and in enough detail to satisfy the demands of the users. Other important aspects in the design of the form are that it should be easy to complete, and able to be

# UNIVERSITY OF EDINBURGH

**Matriculation Form for First Degree and Certificate Courses**

**70**
─────
**71**

FACULTIES OF MEDICINE AND
VETERINARY MEDICINE

Before completing, please read the notes on the back page. Use **Block Letters** and where code numbers or letters have been provided ring the appropriate code.

1. Have you Matriculated at this University     Yes   1
   since October 1968?     No   2

2. Surname

3. Pre-names

4. Married women please state:
   (a) Maiden name
   (b) Is your husband a student     Yes   1
       at this University?     No   2

5. Sex     Male   1
       Female   2

6. Marital status     Single   1
       Married   2
       Widowed, Divorced   3

7. Date of birth     19
   (in figures)    day   month   year

8. Country of birth

9. Nationality

10. Home address
    Town
    County
    Country
    Tel. no.

11. **Term-time residence**—please ring appropriate code number; if you are living in University of Edinburgh accommodation select the name of the hall or student house from the list on page 4 and insert the code number below.

    **University Accommodation** (code from page 4)

    Lodgings (a) with some meals provided     21
          (b) rooms with cooking facilities     22
    Rented self-contained furnished flat or house     23
    At home with parent or guardian     31
    Own house (i.e. unfurnished, owned or rented)     35

    If you are not living in a named University Hall or Student House please give address:

    Tel. no.

12. Year of **first** entry to this University    19 ___
        year

13. Month and year of first entry to this course    19
        month    year

14. Are you matriculating for this course:
    For the first time  .  .  .   1
    To proceed to next year of course  .  .   2
    To repeat a previous year  .  .   3
    For examination and/or graduation without attendance this session  .  .  4

15. Ring year of course you will be in during this session.   1   2
    (NOT necessarily year of attendance)    3   4
         5   6

16. Is this the Final year of this course?     Yes   F
        No   X

17. Do your studies require attendance:
    Full-time for full session  .  .  .   1
    Part-time for full session  .  .  .   2
    Full-time for part session  .  .  .   3
    Part time for part session  .  .  .   4

18. (a) Please ring the code opposite the qualification for which you are registering
    M.B., Ch.B.  .  .  .   M B C 2 3
    B.Sc. (Med. Sci.) (Hons.) .  .   B S C 2 1
    B.D.S. .  .  .  .   B D S 2 3
    B.V.M.&.S. .  .  .   B V M 2 3
    Non-graduating (i.e. course not leading to a qualification of this University) .   N G R 5 3
    (b) Are you studying for a combined degree?    Yes   1
    (e.g. M.B. Ch.B./B.Sc. Med. Sci., (Hons.)    No   2

FIG. 81. The front page of the matriculation form completed by each undergraduate student on first entering the Faculties of Medicine and Veterinary Medicine, University of Edinburgh.

coded in large measure by the student himself choosing and ringing the appropriate answer in a set of alternative answers; furthermore, it should have a layout from which it is easy to transfer information on to punched cards or other input medium. Although certain aspects of the information to be recorded lend themselves to the use of document mark readers, the limitation of such machines in reading hand-written characters has up to the present discouraged their use in this field. However, improvements in design and reduction in cost of these document readers, as well as pressures arising from the increasing numbers of students, will lead to greater interest in this method of accelerating the processes of input preparation.

The matriculation forms used in Edinburgh University are of two types. There is a comprehensive form for students starting a new course of study (Fig. 81), and a short computer-printed form for students returning to the University to continue a course of study (Fig. 82). The first of these is completed entirely by the student, but the second is partly printed by the computer and then completed by the student. At the time of matriculation, calculations are made of fees chargeable; these are noted on the matriculation forms and by this means Fee Claims Forms for the Scottish Education Department and for English Local Education Authorities can later be printed by the computer. The matriculation forms are checked in the presence of the student as this has been found to eliminate the majority of discrepancies and queries which would otherwise appear at the later stage of coding the forms for input. After checking, the forms are coded, rechecked, and cards are then punched and verified before input to the computer. It is important both in a computer-held system and in a manual system of students' records to have an efficient method for dealing with amendments. Variations to records are of three main types. These are the addition of information to the record, the up-dating of information already held on the record, and the correction of an entry. A desirable feature in any amendment system is that the student should only be required to report a change once, and thereafter the system itself should disseminate the new information internally.

## PROCESSING DATA HELD ON STUDENTS' RECORDS

For several years before a computer was introduced for the handling of students' records, a small punched card data processing unit provided the basic statistics about student numbers. This unit was equipped with manual keypunching equipment, a verifier and card-sorter fitted with counting registers. This unit has now developed into a data-preparation unit, its equipment being supplemented by the addition of two automatic card punches, two verifiers, a reproducing punch and high-speed card sorter. The staff of the unit have been re-trained, and their number

**Re-matriculation form for students returning to continue a course.**

Fee Code    N

X-ray

(A)  Please CHECK the information given in Section I below.  If any changes or additions are necessary clearly PRINT the correct information above the appropriate box.

(B)  Complete Sections II and III on this page and the relevant parts of page 3 if you are a postgraduate.

(C)  Please copy your Enrolment number (shown opposite) on to your Fee Pass.

(D)  All students should sign page 3 and the card which you will receive with this form.

SCIENCE    UG

Enrol no.

68 109 98

## SECTION I  Personal Details

Surname

Pre-names

| 10 | 11 | 19 49 | M | S | |
|---|---|---|---|---|---|
| Day | Month | Year | Sex | Single/ | Maiden name (if married) |
| | Date of Birth | | | Married | |

### Permanent Home Address

INVERNESS—SHIRE

### Course Details

| B.SC. | H | CHEMISTRY | 2 | – |
|---|---|---|---|---|
| Qualification | H=Hons O=Ordinary | Subject of Study or Research Department | Year of Course | F=Final P=Practical |

| 19 68 | 10 19 68 | F | – | |
|---|---|---|---|---|
| Year of first entry to this University | Month and year of first entry to above course of study | F=Full-time R=Repeating year P=Part-time | | Staff status (where applicable) |

## SECTION II  Next of Kin

Name.................................................  Relationship.................................................

Address (in full) .................................................

................................................. Tel. no....................................

## SECTION III  Term-Time Residence

(a)  If you are living in University of Edinburgh accommodation select the name of the hall or student house from the list on page 2 and insert the code number in the boxes opposite.

(b)  If you are not living in a named University of Edinburgh hall or student house ring the appropriate code number and give address below.

University Accommodation (code from page 2)

Lodgings: *i.e.* with some meals provided  .    .    21
Flat: *i.e.* room(s) with cooking facilities  .    23
At home with parent or guardian  .    .    31
In your own house  .    .    .    .    25

Address .................................................

................................................. Tel. no....................................

FIG. 82. The front page of the re-matriculation form used by an undergraduate entering the second year of his course in the Faculty of Science, University of Edinburgh. The entries seen on this page have been printed by the computer.

increased from three to five to enable them to cope with the increased flow of data resulting from the wider scope of the new computer-based system. The computer used at present is an I.B.M. 360/50, situated at the Edinburgh Regional Computing Centre; this machine has a core store of 512 K bytes, and is provided with backing store of three disc drives, using replaceable disc packs, as well as three magnetic tape decks. Cards can be read in at 1,000 cards per minute or punched out at 300 cards per minute, using the extended Hollerith code on a combined card reader and punch. A line-printer with a line length of 132 characters and a printing speed of 955 lines per minute is available.

The I.B.M. 360/50 computer is operated under Operating System/360 (MFT II), normally with HASP II. The initials MFT II stand for Multiprogramming with a Fixed number of Tasks (Williams, 1970) and this system permits the simultaneous execution of a number of independent jobs. The program HASP (Houston Automatic Spooling System) is an I.B.M. program, permanently resident in core, which supplements the Operating System mainly by scheduling the input and output operations in an efficient manner. Student record programs are written in FORTRAN; subroutines written in I.B.M. assembler language are incorporated in certain programs in order to improve the speed of operation.

The input from the data processing office is in the form of either 80-column punched cards or magnetic tape, and jobs are run in batch-processing mode. Records are held in ascending sequential order on magnetic tape, each student being allocated a unique seven digit number on first entering the university. This number is used as a sort key, the first two digits reflecting the year of first entry to the university, the next four being allocated sequentially to new entrants, and the last digit being used as a check digit based upon the previous six digits. These numbers form the key to the students' records and are used in all computer-based transactions.

## OUTPUT FROM THE RECORDS SYSTEM

The output from a system of student records is usually in the form of printed lists or statistics. In some cases, both these aspects are present, since a printed list of names may be used to support the statistics.

The main lists employed in this university are lists of matriculated students and address lists. These are not produced at fixed and regular intervals, but are required more frequently during the first three months of each academic year and less often thereafter. Each month, lists of those students who have discontinued their studies are printed, for internal circulation to members of staff. Other lists regularly printed include the cumulative statistics of the numbers of students matriculated (e.g. Table XXXIII). Other lists produced at less frequent intervals

STATISTICS OF MATRICULATIONS FOR SESSION 1969-70: DATE 11TH SEPTEMBER, 1970

| FACULTY | FULL TIME | | PART TIME | | PG | TOTAL |
|---|---|---|---|---|---|---|
| | UG | PG | UG | PG | | |
| ARTS | 2415 | 218 | 16 | 69 | | 2718 |
| DIVINITY | 144 | 50 | 16 | 37 | | 247 |
| LAW | 463 | 15 | 37 | 6 | | 521 |
| MEDICINE | 870 | 95 | 1 | 353 | | 1319 |
| MED-DENT | 236 | 1 | 0 | 1 | | 238 |
| VET MED | 259 | 48 | 0 | 16 | | 323 |
| MUSIC | 61 | 2 | 0 | 6 | | 69 |
| SCIENCE | 2118 | 351 | 22 | 125 | | 2616 |
| SOC SC | 1427 | 408 | 10 | 95 | | 1940 |
| TOTAL | 7993 | 1188 | 102 | 708 | | 9991 |

EXCLUDED FROM ABOVE TABLE ARE 776 MATRICULATIONS FOR EXAMINATION, GRADUATION AND SUBMISSION FOR HIGHER DEGREES

Summarising list printed by the computer and giving a breakdown of the numbers of full-time and part-time students (UG = undergraduate; PG = postgraduate) matriculated in each Faculty on 11th September 1970. The listing excludes those students who have completed their work and have had to matriculate solely for the purpose of being examined or for attending a graduation.

include lists of students attending particular classes, lists of students for Directors of Studies, examination entry lists, the names of students from countries overseas, and a variety of statistical tabulations.

## BENEFITS OF THE COMPUTER-BASED RECORDS SYSTEM

The principal benefits to the University deriving from the computer-based student records system are two-fold. The first of these arises from the computer's need for rigid codes and definitions. The fact of having to decide on codes has the effect of encouraging all grades of staff to define their questions more clearly. Once the system has progressed beyond the basic level of data collection, therefore, it is able to play an increasingly important part in the production of a wide variety of statistics and tabulations. Since they employ consistent definitions, these statistics have the advantage of being reproducible at given dates, and over a period of time, thus enabling greater control to be gained over the planning of university expansion and development.

It can be seen from Table XXXII that, only when definitions have been agreed and code numbers devised for each of the four areas of university administration, does it become possible to calculate any of the more complex and useful ratios required by the university, such as the workload of teaching or the cost per student on a departmental basis. This requires careful design of the system in the initial stages, in order to work in the long-term towards the implementation of an integrated Management Information System. Eventually economies should be able to be effected and efficiency increased by linking the data-processing systems used in the universities with national services such as U.C.C.A. and with computer-based examination systems.

The other main benefit to the university is one which it can share with the students. This consists of bringing together the several aspects of data collection, thereby reducing the frequency with which information has to be requested. Much of the data need only be entered into the system once, although of necessity in a carefully defined format. The system for making amendments can also be designed to reduce the number of times that students have to be asked to report changes in information. Having once recorded the data on a computer file, there should be no need to ask students to have to repeat for input purposes identification information. All that is needed is for this to be printed out by the computer from its record and for the student to be asked to check the information and amend it if necessary. On these amendment forms data are printed out from an updated tape for all students expected to return to continue a course of study at the university during the next session, and the same tape can be used to print the identification data to be carried on each student's matriculation card.

Matriculation cards are produced each academic session and are used as evidence that a student has matriculated. With suitable embossing, the cards can be used to show membership of the University Library, the Athletic Club and of the Students' Union. They can also be embossed to indicate that a student has voted in the elections for the Rector or for membership of the Student Representative Council. In this way the computer can help the university by reducing the load of work involved in the input and validation of data about students, a load which reaches a climax at the start of each academic year. The system can also benefit students by reducing the extent to which they have to fill out forms.

It is difficult to analyse the benefits of a computer-based system in terms of cost. A straightforward comparison, based on numbers of staff employed, does not provide a valid criterion since the same work is not being done in each case. Before the computer-based system was introduced, three staff were employed in the data-processing unit in Edinburgh University for the production and maintenance of the punched cards held in respect of each student. These cards did not contain sufficient information to satisfy all queries, and staff in Faculty Offices and elsewhere were needed to produce more detailed statistics. With the introduction of the computer-based system, the data-processing unit was expanded to five staff, but these now deal with all aspects of data collection, preparation and the control of input. In addition two systems analysts or programmers have been employed to assist with the design of systems and to write, run and maintain the necessary programs. The main advantages lie in the improved service provided rather than in any reduction in cost. The computer system, now that it is operational, produces a wider range of tabulations and statistics more quickly and accurately and with greater flexibility. As Flynt (1963) says, 'We also expect the total costs to be less; but even if the new costs are somewhat greater than the old, the gains in speed, accuracy and flexibility would be well worth it'.

## FUTURE DEVELOPMENTS
### Applications for admission
Each year the University of Edinburgh Medical School is faced with the problem of selecting about 150 students from approximately 1800 applications. We have considered whether this process of selecting applicants merits some form of computer screening, but have decided against such a scheme. Other universities, faced with similar problems, may decide differently, the decision depending upon the numbers of applicants, the criteria for admission, the form in which the applications are made, and on the existence of a standard university course of study. In Britain, applications for admission are in an easily read, standard form and visual screening is probably as quick and efficient as any other procedure that can be devised. In addition, the translation of a headmaster's

report, or other subjective data, into a form of input suitable for statistical manipulation by a computer is not easy. However, if a more flexible type of medical curriculum were to be introduced, with more elective periods and optional components, as recommended by the Royal Commission on Medical Education (1968), or if the changing needs of the community were to call for the admission of students in proportion to a stated number of applicants each having different attributes for different types of medical practice, it would become much more difficult to handle applications for admission without the aid of a computer.

The production, by U.C.C.A., of its own computer print-outs and returns makes it unnecessary to attempt to combine a program dealing with applications for admission to university with the university's own program for student records, although compatibility between the programs should be ensured.

### Course planning

It seems doubtful whether the planning of courses with the aid of a computer will be either helpful or economic for medical schools in the foreseeable future. However, as an example of such a program, we would draw attention to the University of Purdue where each student selects options to be taken in his course, in consultation with his Director of Studies. The selections are then input to the computer, to ensure their compatibility with the overall timetable of the university, the availability of a place in the class, etc. Only six per cent of the students' selections were found to be impracticable (Blakesley, 1963).

### Grades obtained in coursework and in examinations and the follow-up of alumni

Records can be updated regularly by the addition of those grades relating to each student's performance that are selected by the academic authorities for inclusion in the computer-held record. Problems of confidentiality should not arise, because it is accepted on educational grounds that grades should be made known to the student, if performance in course work or examinations is given a grade. The program can weight the grades, average them, or convert them in any way that may be decided, such as by scaling or standardising methods of marking. The great advantage to be derived from including academic grades or marks in the record is that correlations with the performance of students before coming to university, or with their performance in other subjects at university, or with other attributes, becomes much more practicable.

There has been a great lack in the past of any practicable method of following the careers of graduates after they have left the university. With the introduction of computer-held records systems, however, archive files can be kept. Although it would be a formidable and expensive task, computer-printed routine circulars could be sent seeking such information as changes in address, alteration in occupation, etc. In addition, special questionnaires about career achievements, etc., could be added as research projects.

## Monitoring the efficacy of methods of teaching and learning

There is an increasing demand by university teachers for information about each student's record. As far as medical students are concerned, the mechanism for providing this has become more complicated with the extended use of increasing numbers of hospitals for teaching purposes, and the participation of many more teachers. It might seem easy with local consoles and printers to make such records available from a centrally based system. It is doubtful, however, whether such a procedure would be desirable either on confidentiality grounds, or in view of the possibility that it might make it more difficult to ensure the independent grading and assessment of students by separate teachers.

In terms of practical experience gained, with the increasing diversity of clinical attachments during the medical course, there have been complaints that some students never see certain basic fundamental clinical conditions whereas other students may have had to experience undue repetition of teaching in some instances. There would clearly be advantages if a teacher seeing students in a clinical attachment occurring late in the course were to know what his students, who may have been in different groups on previous occasions, had already seen. It is entirely practicable for each student to update his own record of clinical experience gained, probably kept as a subsidiary separate record, by adding coded information daily or weekly as to what he has seen and done. When required later in the course, a printout could be given in relation to each student for his new teacher to determine where deficiencies existed and to remedy these.

Following qualification as a doctor, the Royal Commission's Report (1968) envisages further periods of general and then more specialised training in the profession of medicine. At this stage of each doctor's career, computers could have at least two important applications. In the first place, by extending the records of assessment from the undergraduate medical curriculum on into the period of continuing postgraduate education, this could well improve the choice of eventual career by linking the academic records to the results of aptitude and attitude tests. Secondly, computer-held records could help in the preparation and planning of appointments sequences in hospitals, in community medical care or in research, as well as other appointments to suit the aspirations and needs of individual graduates. The acceptability of potential applicants to the doctors who might be responsible for their training will also be an important part of planning.

A simple example of computer-based arrangements for the selection of appointments is provided by the Pre-Registration Appointments Matching Scheme (P.R.A.M.S.) which has been in operation in Edinburgh since 1967. In this, both the applicant and the consultant have the opportunity to express their preferences in rank order (Doig and Munday, 1969). A slightly different scheme has been in operation in Newcastle (Leishman and Ryan, 1970), and other regions in Britain are adopting this practice. Experience in the United States has shown that a national scheme is entirely practicable, but it does involve standardisation in the dates when appointments commence, and there is inevitably a loss of personal contact between potential employer and employee to an extent that might not be generally acceptable.

## CONCLUSIONS

The introduction of a computer-based system for student records into a university requires a knowledge of the capabilities of computers, but it also needs to take into account economic and organisational factors, and a consideration of human relationships (Mumford and Ward, 1968). The logic of the computer system tends to cut across existing departmental functions and barriers, and time must be taken over the necessary re-examination of the organisational structure. With suitable design of the system, the introduction of a computer can offer the practical advantages of flexibility in the handling of the data, the ability to calculate correlations and a variety of ratios. It is unlikely in the short-term to reduce overall costs, but this may occur in the longer term.

A properly designed computer system should reduce the number of repetitive form-filling and copying tasks required for the preparation and maintenance of the records system. Provided the need for confidentiality is observed, the use of a computer can also improve communications within the university, and thus be operated to the general benefit of both staff and students.

REFERENCES

BLAKESLEY, J. F. (1963). Computer scheduling at Purdue University; Mimeo, April 30th, 1963. Also Computer drop and hold operations; Mimeo, April 29th, 1964.

DOIG, A. & MUNDAY, G. (1969). A co-ordinated scheme for the allocation of pre-registration house-officer posts. *Lancet*, **1**, 1250–1252.

FLYNT, R. C. M. (1963). The role of data processing. *Higher Education*, **20**, 7–10.

LEISHMAN, A. G. & RYAN, R. P. (1970). Appointment of provisionally registered house-officers by computer match. *Lancet*, **2**, 459–461.

MUMFORD, E. & WARD, T. B. (1968). *Computers: Planning for People.* London: Batsford.

ROURKE, F. E. & BROOKS, G. E. (1967). Computers and university administration. In *Administrative Science Quarterly*, pp. 575–600. Cornell University, Ithaca, New York: The Graduate School of Business and Public Administration.

ROYAL COMMISSION ON MEDICAL EDUCATION, 1965–68 (1968). *Report* pp. 85–120. London: Her Majesty's Stationery Office.

WILLIAMS, P. E. (1970). *A Guide to the Use of the I.B.M. 360/50 at the Edinburgh Regional Computing Centre (ERCC).* Available from the ERCC.

# Future Developments and Outstanding Problems

# CHAPTER TWENTY

# Computer Systems for Hospitals and Communities: A Forecast of Future Developments

## By G. E. THOMAS and C. NICHOLAS

## SUMMARY
THIS chapter attempts to forecast, on the basis of the present position in business and in medical computing, the trend of likely developments in the next 10 to 20 years. The possibilities of bringing together some of the computing activities described in the earlier chapters are examined, and some of the fundamental difficulties highlighted. The considerations that should govern the development of medical computing are indicated. Finally, a few developments which might make a radical difference to the general field of medical computing are discussed.

## INTRODUCTION
Hospitals and other communal health services now operate as complex organisations in which there have evolved a variety of information and control systems that interact to provide a main end-product, namely patient care. This care needs to be of a high quality, sensitive, efficient and economical. In earlier chapters a number of existing computer applications have been described, and limited forecasts have been made of developments relating to these specific topics. In this chapter we seek to make more general forecasts, on the basis of existing applications of computers both in the business field and in medicine, and on the basis of technologically feasible developments, as to how the present applications of computers in medicine might be expected to coalesce and contribute to an integrated medical information system in ways which might improve the central objective, the quality of patient care.

The impact of the new technologies of computers and telecommunications on the design and operation of such complex operations as placing a man on the moon are evident to the public at large. The exploitation of these developments in local and more personal situations is limited, at this time, to relatively simple operations such as the reservation of hotel beds and airline seats, or the rapid determination of the identity of the owner of a motor vehicle. While no standard information system using computers and telecommunication facilities has been developed for health service use, several exploratory hospital and community health service computer projects have been undertaken in recent years. As the results of this exploratory work and of discrete routine applications

become available, it is necessary to distinguish what are the main characteristics of the various information systems and how these impact on the
different categories of health service staff. Baruch (1968) conducted an
excellent analysis of this nature, and in this chapter we use his framework to study the way in which medical information systems have grown
and are likely to continue growing.

## CATEGORIES OF HEALTH STAFF CONCERNED WITH INFORMATION HANDLING AND A CATALOGUE OF INFORMATION SYSTEM CHARACTERISTICS

Baruch (1968) defined three categories of staff involved in any communal health service: (1) staff concerned with the administration of the
health service; (2) staff directly involved in patient care; and (3) staff
concerned with research and education. In addition, he categorised six
characteristics of a medical information system, on the following lines:

1. High access speed; a system designed to respond to a command or
enquiry within a few seconds, with a low probability that response will
be long delayed (i.e. for hours).

2. High content reliability; a system with negligible probability either
of recording data with an undetected content of errors, or of the subsequent corruption of this data.

3. Record continuity; the ability to store and extend records over a
long time, if necessary providing lifetime records for large populations.

4. Bulk processing ability; the capacity to process large collections of
data for accounting or statistical purposes.

5. Ease of modification; the ability to modify programs and the format
of data files in the light of experience.

6. Training ease; the ability, with minimal effort, to teach the user how
to benefit from the system.

These six characteristics of information systems have each featured in
varying degree in the specific computer applications described in earlier
chapters, and their impact on each of the three categories of staff can be
separately discerned. In the hospital or in a community health organisation of the future, information and control has to pass effectively between,
and to be exercised over, each category of staff. Eventually, we believe
that there will need to be continuous routes for data through a network
of computers and communication systems. Each of the six system
characteristics will be supported in varying degrees at different parts of
the network. At this time, however, the network assembly process is only
beginning and, before we consider the systems of the future, we can profit
by examining how our current computer and telecommunication systems
are applied, which categories of staff they serve, and what balance of
system characteristics has been developed to meet the needs of present
day users.

## Bulk processing facilities

The administrator and the research worker engaged in any communal health service has learned how to collect, file and analyse data on a wide variety of record systems. Following Liebnitz's invention of the mechanical calculator came Hollerith's introduction of the punched card, and these inventions still feature significantly in the systems of administering medical resources and in research calculations. In the last 20 years, the business machine industry has flourished with the introduction of electronic computers. The computer manufacturers have identified basic administrative functions such as the payment of wages, the preparation of invoices, the scheduling of complex productive processes, the maintenance of share registers and the calculation of sales statistics as amenable to solution on their equipment.

Many of the basic needs for processing data in business also find application in the medical field, in hospital and regional health service administration, where standard equipment and procedures have been applied typically within the administrative unit that serves a regional grouping of hospitals. In the U.S.A. the privately financed foundations and clinics require tighter financial controls than those of a state supported system, and bulk data processing installations now feature as an integral part of the private institution's operation.

The research worker and statistician has until recently found the computing tools and procedures of his business orientated colleagues incompatible with his analytical requirements. Typically, the research statistician is interested in a comprehensive examination of data over a period of years, with discontinuities and trends being detected by substantial amounts of computation. The administrator is interested in small amounts of computation and sequential processes, such as the regular payment of wages and the detection of out-of-limit occurrences such as over-expenditure against budgeted projects. This mixture of requirements is recognised by the business machine manufacturer and, in the third generation of computers, reasonable efficiency of operation for both categories of user has been achieved on the same design of computer.

The input/output characteristics of the present day bulk processing computer installation are still largely dictated by the operations relevant to the use of punched card equipment, as developed over 30 years ago. Punched cards are still by far the commonest method of data input, with the majority of data being transcribed from manuscript by data preparation staff associated with the processing installation. The introduction of mark and character sensitive reading mechanisms will, in certain applications, permit data to be entered directly by the human originator into the computer. Perhaps for the next decade, however, we can anticipate a continuing need for the intermediary process of manual data preparation. On the output side, administrative reports and invoices flood from high-speed printing mechanisms designed to accommodate a wide variety of pre-printed and multi-copy stationery. In intensive reporting situations, such as the social security data processing centres in Britain, batteries of high-speed printers are supplemented by fast microfilm printers, and the subsequent handling and packaging of individual notifications are extensively automated. In this flow of paper, the relatively short records which derive from scientific calculations are in danger of being lost, or delayed unduly by the complicated scheduling requirements of the administrative work load. The technology of the bulk processors now on the market will, however, permit simultaneous execution of several job streams, and the software in control of the processing schedule can ensure that several input and output stations can be in use, both local to the processor and remotely. It is therefore possible on a sufficiently large installation to maintain at least two streams of work, one to satisfy administrative functions, the other the needs of the scientist.

While the arithmetic and input/output functions of the modern computer can readily accommodate both administrative and scientific processes, the programming and record handling procedures of the two populations of users are barely compatible. In practice, the degree of success that has been achieved to date in providing a harmonious environment for both the administrative and the scientific user, on the same bulk processing installation, is largely a function of the degree of independence of the management of the installation from the respective management hierarchies of the two other functions. For historical reasons, many health service bulk processing installations are the direct responsibility of the treasurer or secretary of the respective health service board. The scientific and teaching applications are frequently stimulated by proximity to university and other research organisations with scientifically orientated installations. It is only at a relatively advanced stage of evolution of the bulk processing facilities, in any individual health service community, that the generality of the services needed is recognised and particular measures taken by management to overcome earlier specialisation.

It has been suggested (Ockenden and Bodenham, 1970) that information processing officers should be appointed with status comparable to other senior health service officers such as the secretary, treasurer or senior administrative medical officer of a regional hospital board. The appointment of competent staff at this level should, it is hoped, result in the more effective use of bulk processing installations by both administrators and scientists engaged in health service work. However, this common computing system environment would not attract the physician or nurse directly involved in patient care, the third category of health service staff with whom we are concerned. The services so far described are remote from the ward and the practice, and we have to consider now which of the remaining five system characteristics have to be exercised before the vital field of patient care can benefit directly from the computer.

## Fast access to the computing function: (a) information handling

Computing systems outside the health services have made progress towards high speed accessibility in the last 10 years, in certain special situations. An airline's economy is crucially dependent on the proportion of the seating capacity which is occupied on each of its scheduled flights. A bank can only fully invest its cash resources if it possesses a round-the-clock knowledge of the deposit and withdrawal position at each of its branches. To meet these particular situations on an internationally reproducible basis, millions of pounds' worth of development activity has been committed by the business machine manufacturers and the industries in question. As a result, the major airlines now conduct their seat reservation procedures on a complex of computers and tele-communication channels. Airline clerks at the major cities of the world can interrogate the booking lists of each scheduled flight for their air-line; these lists have been generated and updated on the storage mechan-ism of their company's seat reservation computer. The input/output process is typically conducted via a keyboard and a television tube display of alphabetic and numeric characters, connected by a telephone circuit to the centrally located computer. A major airline can afford to spend sums in excess of £30,000,000 on the provision of this new and expensive collection of telecommunication and computing equipment if, as a result, the utilisation of its equally expensive and rapidly depreciating fleet of aircraft can be improved. The banks are now inheriting the role of innovator and designer for high speed access systems from the airlines and, in Britain, networks of terminals are extending to cover branches throughout the country. The massive costs need to be recovered through the extra investment income open to a bank which now has complete precision in the daily calculation of its assets. It is possible to demonstrate benefits deriving from such large computer installations on financial grounds, in the business field, but this is much more difficult to show in a non-profit making organisation such as the National Health Service.

As the scale of these high access speed applications extends, so does the quantity of components manufactured, with a consequent fall in component costs. The necessary input/output terminals still need to fall in cost from their present level (over £1,000) to more nearly that of the domestic television receiver (about £100), however, before they can substitute for the telephone handset that constitutes the principal communication terminal in the modern hospital.

The general practitioner or the physician in hospital is in contact each day with a succession of distinct or separate medical occurrences. To deal competently with each, he requires rapid access to the recent medical history of the patient. The conversion of the records of a patient in hospital, as they develop day by day, on to punched cards, and the subsequent collection and validation of these records on magnetic tape at a data processing centre, may be a necessary requirement for the purposes of long-term development and control of the hospital system. However, this process is slow, depending on the extent to which clinical as well as administrative details are recorded, and the information may not be retrievable in time for the next ward visit. Handwritten documents and charts, therefore, have to remain in the hospital ward and in the general practitioner's surgery, unless computer systems with much higher speed of remote and multiple access, in conversational mode, can be developed for medical use.

Telecommunication facilities are still largely designed on the basis of speech communication so that digital transmission involves conversion processes at each end of the link to the computer, with a consequent increase in cost. A computer serving as the hub of a network of remote terminals in a hospital, or terminals distributed among a number of general practitioners' surgeries, is bound to be large. The computers and storage mechanisms at present employed (mostly in business operations) at the hub of a network of remote terminals are expensive and are still, in most cases, designed for conventional bulk processing operations; they revert to these functions at night, or when the access requirements are otherwise substantially reduced. To reduce the costs of the computing system to an acceptable level, numerous attempts have been made to organise the work of the central computers so that, even during temporary lulls in the interrogation process, they can be productively engaged in background calculations.

The technology of high speed access systems has been in a marked state of flux for several years. While this continues, the necessary cost reductions cannot be expected to materialise and there will, therefore, be a delay before these systems become generally available in the health service. At first, only a select group can expect to experience the provision of high speed access systems in the patient care environment of a ward or a general practice. In Britain, experimental installations are being developed at King's College Hospital and, for general practice, in the Guys-Essex (Thamesmead) project. The difficulties should not be underestimated, as the reports by Opit and Woodroffe (1970a, b) show, but progress can be anticipated and a regular study of the literature will be required in this field.

## Fast access to the computing function: (b) patient care

The standard information handling operations of patient care, as carried out in the hospital ward or out-patient department and in a general practice, may not be available economically on a central computer for another decade. However, the number of specialised situations is increasing where a small computer, coupled with suitable sensors, can undertake a very intimate degree of individual or group patient care. At present, such systems are mainly used for monitoring various physiological signals and giving warnings when the signals move outside pre-set limits. The next critical stage comes when the computer itself initiates action to deal with the abnormal condition in the patient, at which stage a closed-loop control system involving the patient, but not a member of the patient-care team, would have been set up. Initially it will probably be necessary for the computer to alert the nursing staff that it is having to deal with an out-of-limits condition, but this will probably only be a temporary phase. Closed-loop systems are being investigated but are still largely at the experimental stage (p. 266). The widespread introduction of these computer-controlled aids to patient care will depend on the speed with which we can isolate and then concentrate development on the most effective applications.

## Ease of modification

Recent developments in micro-electronics will stimulate attempts to identify worthwhile applications of special purpose computers. The highly complex electronic configurations needed within a computer can now be produced very cheaply and within a very small total volume of equipment. Tooling costs are high, however, and massive production quantities are required; the manufacturers of the large scale integrated circuits, which are the product of this new technology, will only invite those designs which are guaranteed a large market. This large market can now be envisaged, with the prospect of tailor-made electronic computing systems coming increasingly to the aid of doctors immediately concerned with patient care. It is, therefore, appropriate to consider the characteristic of the system having most significance to research and education for a health service serving the whole community. Baruch (1968) places greatest weight on the need to ensure ease of modification, and we support his view.

The first decade of significant electronic computer manufacture (1945–1955) was distinguished by the number of machines designed and marketed; each had a different structure, and primitive programming aids which required an intimate knowledge of the basic processes of the machine itself. The second decade (1955–1965) saw the introduction of high level programming languages, in which problems could be formulated in large measure independently of the functions of the machine. At the same time the manufacturers gradually recognised the need for a greater degree of internal management of the resources of the computer system, and operating systems were provided to control the use of program and data files, the diagnostic facilities and accounting procedures. It was in this decade that a significant degree of use of computers commenced in the health service.

Now, in the third decade (1965–1975), there exist users of computers who have established that the standardised languages and file handling systems provided by the computer manufacturers are not necessarily appropriate to their particular requirements. The manufacturers recognised this position in 1969, when new purchasing arrangements were introduced so that extensions to the repertoire of software available from a manufacturer could be separately purchased. While this exploration of language and file structure by research and educational users is desirable, the constant redevelopment of the compilers and operating system routines consequent on a change in the equipment or its technology is not economic or practical. There is, therefore, a need to provide either a standard specification for the equipment, or to devise some intermediate facility which will disguise changes in the equipment from the compilers and operating systems.

The international computer manufacturers are likely, in our opinion, either to have permitted their equipment designs to have converged by 1975, or to have stabilised on individual designs which will not thereafter be subject to change for the subsequent 10 to 20 year period. The user who is content to work within such a standardised design will be free to commission the special software needed for his modified language requirements. There remains, however, the group of users who will expect their total computing environment to contain special equipment, such as that mentioned in the previous section; some of this would, of necessity, fail to conform to any rigid equipment specification. The users of computers, both for research and education in medicine, are therefore seeking methods now to provide the new language and file manipulation features which they require in such a way that complete re-design and development will not be needed when they translate their ideas and operational situations to machines of different design or manufacture.

One method in use in various research centres is to write new compilers or operating system components entirely in a high level systems writer's language, so that movement from one machine design to another only requires, in the first instance, the preparation of a compiler for the systems writer's language. The application of this technique in Edinburgh has supported the movement of applications and system programs across computers as diverse as the Ferranti ATLAS, English Electric KDF9, IBM 360/50, IBM 360/67, ICL System 4-50, ICL System 4-75, PDP 8/L and PDP 15. The opportunity, for example, to test text editing procedures on a large central machine with comprehensive diagnostic facilities, and then to implement the same procedure rapidly on a small dedicated installation, is most valuable. This type of flexibility is unlikely to be achieved entirely within the computing provisions of a health service community. It is more likely to occur where there is overlap between medical and university populations, as occurs in the medical faculty of a large university.

Each category of computer user in the health service has now been related to that specific computer system characteristic which predominates in his present day practice of computing. It remains to examine how the characteristics of record continuity, training ease, and high content reliability (Baruch, 1968) influence each category of user.

## Record continuity

The significance of continuity of records to the worker who needs to span complete life histories is self-evident; genetic studies provide a typical example. The administrator, wrestling with the problem of the movement of patients and potential patients from one part of the country to another, is having constantly to enlarge the population area served by his records repository. In Britain, the social security records for the entire population are held at Newcastle-on-Tyne, and regional centres refer to this centre whenever a transaction with an individual's record is required.

The collection of comprehensive records for individual patients in machine readable form is a very sporadic activity, dependent on the procedures of individual areas of application. Primary data on the occupation of beds, hospital inventories, etc., are collected relatively consistently. In the area of direct care, as mentioned earlier, machine readable records are rarely generated at the moment, and the problems of continuity are necessarily deferred until the high speed access systems of the future become commonplace.

## Training ease

Administrative staff will generally be involved in a constant process of re-education and development, as they progress through the various levels of management responsibility. The training consequent on the introduction of computer-based information systems should, therefore, come as a natural extension of their normal training programme. This is particularly the case where the computing system is dedicated to bulk processing operations, where the rhythm of the work still follows the pattern of conventional manual systems. When data collection methods advance to the extent that entry to the computer system is made from the patient's bed, from the casualty department reception counter, from the dispensary, or from the laboratory, then conventional rhythms will disappear and the administrators who use data collected in this way will need to re-think their own procedures. Fortunately the time-scale for designing, implementing and introducing into service systems of this nature is spread over several years, during which period training courses and simulation exercises can ensure adequate preparation for the administrative staff concerned.

The educationalist or research worker may not require for his own benefit computer systems to which he can readily re-adjust after change, but if he is to influence his students and the staff whom he wishes to see apply his ideas, then the ease of their learning processes must receive attention.

When staff concerned with direct patient care become significantly involved with a computer information system, a major factor in the overall effectiveness of the new system will be the ease with which staff and patients can be trained in its use. The terminal equipment that is being developed now for clerks in airline seat reservation offices and in the branch offices of the banks will need further development before a nurse or a ward sister will be able to command the necessary fluency and confidence of operation. The physician, both specialist and general practitioner, will be even more demanding in his requirements for equipment and systems, in order that any departure from his current practice or particular set of medical objectives may be rapidly understood.

## High content reliability

The administrator is vitally concerned with the accuracy of records, both in respect of finance and patients, in the sense that an accumulation of errors will prejudice his control of the complete situation (e.g. overexpenditure against budget or under-employment of existing hospital facilities). The bulk processing computer systems have gradually evolved over the last 20 years a variety of checking procedures which are applied at each stage of processing. The validation of manually collected data requires a highly systematic sequence of tests to be applied, and there must be provision for the re-submission of corrected data. Any changes that are made to the records or files held by the computer need to be checked, and copies of the active files have to be secured at regular intervals so that the data can be reconstructed in the event of system or human error.

Patient care procedures require high reliability in those aspects of instrumentation, record keeping and computation which could influence the medical treatment and welfare of the individual. The computer, instrumentation and communication systems that are now in regular use in the aero-space industries for the control of aircraft and space vehicles have improved the reliability of components and systems to levels approaching those needed for use in the immediate care of patients. Duplication of equipment does not necessarily provide the additional reliability needed, in that procedures and equipment that effect the substitution of standby equipment or allow comparison of separately computed data are themselves subject to breakdown. The only satisfactory long-term solution requires an increase in the basic reliability of individual components and a reduction in the number of components. While these developments in technology proceed, it is as well to limit the complexity of systems applied directly to the care of patients, or to insist on a significant degree of human supervision, until an adequate measure of system reliability has been obtained.

The needs of the administrator and of staff directly involved in patient care for reliability of equipment should ensure that the research worker and educationalist are adequately served. Where a system is being extended or modified in pursuit of a research objective, some reduction in reliability is almost inevitable. If the research is successful, then re-establishment of reliability is necessary before it can be translated into a productive situation; this commitment should be recognised and, where possible, measured in the assessment of the research work.

## SUMMARY OF THE PRESENT SCENE

So far, in this chapter, we have suggested that the administrative departments of the health services are at present effectively employing bulk processing installations to mechanise their existing clerical procedures, whereas staff concerned directly with patient care, in hospitals and laboratories, are cautiously experimenting with computing systems having high access speeds, the majority of these systems being dedicated to limited tasks. Research workers and teachers are aware of the need to modify and develop the characteristics of systems available to them from the business machine and scientific instrument manufacturers, and a variety of studies are being pursued in this connection.

Interaction between each of these sectors of administration, hospital service work, and research and teaching is limited. Inherent in the technology on which each development is based, however, is the feasibility of transferring and sharing data between one system and another. An analogous situation exists in the large process industries where the sales, accounting and personnel functions employ an increasingly integrated set of procedures on centralised business-orientated computing systems whereas, in the research laboratories and production processes, special purpose dedicated computing installations operate largely independently of the central administrative system.

Computing equipment is expensive and ready made procedures and computer programs which would permit the rapid exploitation of the investment are scarce. The British Medical Association (BMA) in 1969 estimated that a large computer installation serving a large hospital group (e.g. £400,000 for the central hardware) might cost between £1,000,000 and £2,000,000 over a period extending from two years before installation to five years afterwards. Eventual running costs were estimated in the region of 4 per cent of the annual budget of the hospital group being served.

The evaluation of benefits available from the use of computer systems is of vital importance if the health agencies are to govern their computing developments. The categories of benefit have been defined (BMA, 1969) as follows:

1. Direct cost savings over existing operations;

2. Improved quality of work, fewer errors, improved legibility, comprehensiveness, etc.;

3. Time saving so that specialist staff can operate more productively;

4. Presentation of summaries, reports and evaluation of work done in time to influence further work.

Ways of attaching a real financial and medical value to these benefits in specific applications are primitive, however, and the following general statement also comes from the BMA (1969) report:

'We predict that within our time horizon the most hopeful prospects arise from the simpler rather than the more ambitious applications, particularly in laboratory automation and reporting, listing and transfer functions between branches of the health service, simple clerical replacements and scheduling schemes in all branches of the service, and in the development of service evaluation methods based upon simple data capture and record linkage operations'.

This prediction, if followed, should lead to a programme of development evolving around specific applications in which it is hoped that benefits will be measured with increasing accuracy. The rate of provision of effective computing facilities would then largely depend on the scale of finance apportioned from the health service budget, and on the discernment of the control agencies which allocate funds for the various development studies. The evolutionary approach will probably prevail for medical computing developments in Britain in the foreseeable future and, with an increasing commitment of suitably trained medical and information analysts, respectable progress should be maintained. In the 10 to 20 year time-scale which would span any significant consolidation of the type of medical computing facilities we have discussed, several new technological and sociological revolutions can be expected. In the remaining sections we outline three major developments which could have an impact on the methods presently conceived for handling information in the health service.

## SOME AREAS OF DEVELOPMENT IN INFORMATION HANDLING

### Pattern recognition

The activities in the medical environment falling into this broad classification are wide-ranging. They include the actual processing of symptoms and physical signs so as to yield a treatment, the analysis of EEG signals, and the identification of chromosomes. Work on these problems may be radically affected by the development of a new type of computer, specifically a computer in which numerous logical tests are made on the data simultaneously. This kind of approach, particularly when linked to some sort of adaptive learning process, would appear very promising; it would be similar to the human process of visual identification of images. The possibility of building such computers has become much more feasible with the ability to build into single electronic components complete adaptive logic networks.

## Identification of the individual and his location
In several chapters the difficulty of uniquely defining individual patients has been mentioned. Similarly, in a large hospital, there exists the problem of determining the precise location both of the patient and of the staff involved in his care at any time. Until these problems are solved, much information may be unnecessarily delayed in transit, or cannot be made available on demand at sufficient speed, or may possess an unacceptably high error content.

The nearest solution to this problem at present in use is the system in which individuals are issued with portable radio receivers responding to broadcast signals in a code particular to individual receivers. If the recipient is co-operative and free from other commitments, when his receiver responds to a signal he will proceed to the nearest telephone and be given a verbal message. In a 20-year time-scale, we can envisage dramatic reductions in the size and cost of these personal radio beacons, and the adaptation of private telecommunication networks in which present day handsets are replaced by more elaborate units capable of sensing the proximity of a person equipped with a radio beacon for which a broadcast appeal has been issued. A hospital equipped with a telecommunications network of this kind would have the opportunity of interconnecting its computer system to a message collection and distribution system that could greatly improve the access to staff and patients. Verbal messages of today could more readily be replaced in the future by visual messages displayed in transient form on video displays and retrievable from the memory systems of the telecommunication network. The recipient could nominate the messages for subsequent use in the overall information system, if he wished to do so.

Telephone codes that are entirely numeric provide every telephone subscriber with a unique numeric label. Through the use of minute micro-electronic labels, capable of responding to local high energy interrogations, it will be possible to provide an individual with an electronic copy of his telephone number or national health service code, or some other unique number. The size of these labels could be made sufficiently small as to permit their being implanted in, for instance, the little finger of either hand by a procedure similar to the simple process of vaccination. This idea may sound futuristic, but the identity of an individual equipped in this way could be reliably determined by submitting either or both of his little fingers to electro-magnetic interrogation. The identity code of a patient requiring a period of intensive medical care could then be transferred to a personal beacon of the type described previously and effective communication maintained between him and his doctors through the telecommunication network of the hospital.

These projected developments may appear far-fetched and irrelevant to present day hospital practice, but they represent entirely reasonable applications of the still relatively untapped field of micro-electronic technology. They could significantly affect the pattern of evolution in information systems on which plans for hospitals are currently being based.

### The growth of the computing/communication utilities

The majority of hospitals now depend on the national grid for their main source of electricity, with standby facilities provided specially for the most exposed situations (e.g. in operating theatres and in intensive care units). The economics of scale dictated the disposition of very large electricity generating stations at a limited number of sites, with distribution organised through a complex network of power lines and substations to individual consumers. There is no inherent similarity between the technologies of electrical power and electronic information processing, but already there are indications of the growth of industries devoted to the electronic processing of information for subscribers who have relinquished their original independent provisions. These developments have become possible as the facilities to communicate with remote computing installations have improved and the needs of certain communities of users have become sufficiently proscribed as to merit their provision on a large scale by an independent agency.

The Department of Health and Social Security already operates a number of large computing installations in England and Wales, particularly in connection with the administration on a national basis of social security benefits. These centres will undoubtedly expand and might reasonably be expected to provide a more economic method of handling some of the routine bulk processing tasks of the various health areas as these tasks become standardised on a national basis. External to the Health departments, the Post Office Corporation is also expanding its network of general purpose computing installations. The new Corporation is busily planning a major new data oriented transmission network which, in 20 years' time, will link 80 cities in Britain with facilities capable of transmitting data at speeds in excess of the transfer rates of the magnetic tape mechanisms that are now in regular use for holding data files in the individual health area computing centres. When the communications network and the computers are combined, the Post Office Corporation will possess the largest single computing resource in the country, and should be well placed to inherit from government-financed departments their responsibility for standardised computation and file keeping.

The general practitioner of the future may depend increasingly on computers for his immediate needs in respect of information processing. It seems likely that these needs will be met via the telephone system, through which he should be able to communicate either with a standardised information system provided by the Post Office Corporation or, when in need of specialist assistance, with an appropriate hospital-based or 'consultant' system. The hospital, as a unit designed to render specialist medical care, will undoubtedly retain control of its own internal information system. However, this might best be refined to deal largely with the critical aspects of medical treatment, thereby leaving the longer term management and analytical functions to devolve on the background computing facilities provided elsewhere.

REFERENCES

BARUCH, J. J. (1968). The generalised medical information facility. In *I.F.I.P.* (*International Federation for Information Processing*) *Congress Proceedings, Edinburgh – August, 1968*. Vol. 1, pp. 19–23. Amsterdam: North Holland Publishing Company.

BRITISH MEDICAL ASSOCIATION (1969). *Planning Unit Report No. 3: Computers in Medicine*. London: British Medical Association.

OCKENDEN, J. M. & BODENHAM, K. E. (1970). *Focus on Medical Computer Development*, pp. 70–84. London: Oxford University Press.

OPIT, L. J. & WOODROFFE, F. J. (1970a). Computer-held clinical record system – I; Description of system. *British Medical Journal*, **4**, 76–79.

OPIT, L. J. & WOODROFFE, F. J. (1970b). Computer-held clinical record system – II, Assessment. *British Medical Journal*, **4**, 80–82.

GENERAL READING

*Science Journal*, (1970). Special issue: Computers in the Seventies. Vol. **6**, 3–104.

# Epilogue: Some Outstanding Problems

## By W. LUTZ and L. G. WHITBY

## SUMMARY

THIS closing chapter discusses some general problems relating to finance, staffing, and questions of confidentiality, each and all of which require decisions in respect of policy as such decisions will seriously influence developments in the field of medical computing. The view is put forward that many applications of computer technology to the medical field are still at an experimental stage, and the need to conduct a planned programme of further experiment, with financial support assured, is strongly advocated.

## INTRODUCTION

The introduction of computers into medical work, both administrative and clinical, is just one aspect of medicine getting to grips with the scientific revolution. Computer Science and Statistics were among the subjects listed by the Report (the Zuckerman Report) on the Hospital Scientific and Technical Services (1968) as part of the initial basis of the newly structured Hospital Scientific Service proposed in the Report. The consequences of mechanisation and automation of some processes in the health services have been critically examined by several committees and *ad hoc* working parties set up to advise the government.

Hitherto the health services have been labour intensive, one of the principal exceptions to this generalisation being the scientific laboratory services. In planning for the introduction of computers, there are opportunities to substitute an intensive capital investment process at least in part for the further development of a labour intensive process. There has quite rightly been some hesitation about launching into widespread capital investment in computers, because of a desire to be certain that they will fulfil the tasks required of them and will do so at an economic rate. Procedures of cost evaluation and cost-benefit analysis are still relatively rudimentary in medicine, however, and some experiments in the field of medical computing have been rendered necessary by the increasing difficulty of recruiting and retaining sufficient staff to maintain and develop the health services.

The introduction of automation has major implications for the health service as a whole. An indication of these was given in the Zuckerman Report (1968) and detailed consideration of the effects on planning in one specific area was given in a further report from the Department of Health and Social Security (1970) on the hospital laboratory services. The implications of a capital intensive process include the need to use expensive equipment as intensively as possible if its purchase is to be justified. With laboratory services this implies the need to consider centralisation of services, whenever practicable, and the same arguments can in large part be transferred to the field of computers provided for health service use.

Among the reasons for considering automation and centralisation of laboratory services have been shortages of trained staff. This also applies to computer applications in the health services, but staff shortages have different implications in the computer field. While computer applications to health service work remain to a considerable extent unproven, on a cost-effectiveness basis, it is essential to encourage experiments, and to base these on staff capable of conducting such essential exploratory work. Only in this way can working guidelines for the long-term use of computers in medicine be gained (Ockenden and Bodenham, 1970). Nevertheless, encouragement of local enthusiasm and expert knowledge with the provision of the necessary finance for computer hardware, software and supporting staff should not be made uncritically. Projects need to be defined, with objectives clearly stated and a time-scale mapped out with, as far as practicable, methods available for assessing in due course whether the objectives have been achieved.

## COMPUTER DEVELOPMENTS
### The appraisal of proposals
This chapter discusses some general aspects of medical computing, selected partly because they are causing wide concern and partly because the problems relating to them have not yet evoked any clear decisions on policy. Technical innovations may give rise to marked changes in administrative arrangements or in social conditions of a nature not always clearly foreseen at the time the innovation was first contemplated. Equally, policies that ignore, misunderstand or overplay the technical developments of the day, are in danger of proving costly and disappointing mistakes. Computers are no exception to these statements, since their introduction to the medical field has already given rise to problems that, once recognised, have called for policy decisions involving financial, organisational and even political aspects over and above purely technical considerations. Medical records systems provide a good example—many of the technical problems relating to computer-stored and processed medical records are already resolved and the large-scale application of computers in this field now awaits financial support and organisational reform as well as the development of receptive attitudes among staff working in the health services.

Within the limitations imposed by the financial allocations to the

National Health Service, the extent to which computers are to be introduced depends upon considerations which attempt to weigh the benefits to be anticipated from introducing computers against the advantages to be gained from deploying these same resources in other ways. The rate of introduction of new developments depends on the finance available for such developments, and in this connection it is worth recalling that Britain spends a smaller proportion of its gross national product on its health services than many other 'developed' countries. On the basis of present knowledge, and bearing in mind the need for a largely experimental approach, subjective judgement is bound to play a large part in formulating medical computer policies. Nevertheless, in respect of many proposed computer applications, certain questions can be asked:

1. Is the system proposed sufficiently flexible in its concept as to be capable of responding to change, to new developments and to expansion in the use made of the health services over a period of five years, 10 years or perhaps even longer?

2. Will the computer system be placed in a working situation that will be capable of staffing and running the facilities at high efficiency, and will this situation be capable of adaptation to changes likely to occur in the next five years?

3. What benefits possibly attributable to the introduction of computing into a specific area of medical application will be measurable in monetary terms, or as improvements in the quality of the service or in the welfare of patients, and will the anticipated benefits be commensurate with the cost of computer developments when expressed in these terms?

4. Is the application proposed likely to affect the traditional methods of work and work relationships within the relevant areas of medical practice and, if so, has consideration been given as to how to forestall or overcome resistance to change so that co-operation can be gained sufficiently rapidly as to make the investment worthwhile?

### Batch mode, on-line and interactive computing
The application of these criteria leads to the conclusion that the widespread adoption of computers suitable only for operation in batch mode is likely to prove costly because the hardware is unlikely to be fully utilised in a single hospital. Such installations are also likely to prove inflexible, since it is difficult to extend the hardware and the software of a system that operates exclusively in batch mode so as to meet the growing demand for on-line and interactive extensions. Another reason for inflexibility lies in the fact that batch mode installations do not require staff of as high a calibre as more advanced systems, so any upgrading or extension to the basic batch mode system is likely to be hampered by lack of the right kind of staff and by the absence of computing experience among the clinicians and nurses in the hospital—computers operating in

batch mode are usually remote from these important categories of staff.

The application of these same criteria is also liable to lead to the rejection of large centrally situated hospital computers provided with immediate on-line or interactive extensions to wards and laboratories. So far, the benefits that can be shown to derive from inter-ward and inter-departmental connections are minute in relation to the cost of providing such computer-based facilities, nor is such provision often justified in terms of the speed of the activities which take place within the hospital system. For example, ordering a prescription through a computer-dependent communications system has only a small effect upon the time taken for the drug to reach the patient, if account is also taken of the time required to dispense and to deliver the prescription. Furthermore, experience to date suggests that a fully interactive system requires the recording and reporting of information about patients in a manner that is not yet acceptable to the majority of clinical and nursing staff, resulting in the under-utilisation or even rejection of the computer equipment.

Interactive computing has not yet fulfilled its early promise. With some applications, sufficient progress has been made for on-line software to be sold with the medium-sized and large computers. In addition, some commercial firms, offering interactive console facilities and selling computer time on their own computers, provide time-sharing services and are operating profitably. The success of on-line computing largely depends on the kind of work submitted, in this respect on-line programming and editing with on-line computational (mathematical) work perhaps being the most successful. The development of programs in this way is especially worthwhile, and seems to have increased the productivity of programmers as much as threefold. In addition to running tested programs on-line, it is feasible to use the same programs for work in batch mode, which suggests that on-line VDU's or teletypes should initially be placed in those laboratories and hospital-based departments, especially university departments, where computational work and some program development is already occurring.

On-line file handling applications in medicine are at present restricted to the accessing of limited amounts of stored data (e.g. general practice records where selected components of the record are held, and the file contains only a few thousand cases); to limited file-manipulating facilities; and to situations where the volume of data per case is severely limited and highly structured (e.g. the National Insurance computer system). The evidence suggests that full on-line file handling systems in medical practice will be very expensive, and further technical developments and the writing of improved software are both needed in this field. Queueing presents a major problem. For instance, the on-line initiation of a high priority search of a computer file lasting several hours may be difficult to justify when batch processing could do the same job much more cheaply at off-peak hours, returning the same output the next morning. Nevertheless, limited on-line transfer of data direct from the hospital records office, with the ability to check such data rapidly, promises to be rewarding even at this stage, and any experience that can be gained should allow technical advances to be incorporated more readily. For the present, the 'immediate' recall of a patient's record file must be regarded as impracticable since insufficient benefit is derived in return for the cost and complexity of the system.

Batch mode installations have severe limitations according to the questions posed (p. 410), and on-line interactive systems have not yet justified themselves economically. If computing is to be introduced into medical practice to any significant extent in the near future, this will probably be on the basis of computer systems serving several hospitals on a regional basis. These installations would initially and basically offer batch mode services to surrounding hospitals, including the smaller hospitals, with on-line facilities limited initially to the records offices and on a pilot basis to a few selected wards and laboratories. These central services could be augmented by dedicated computers (e.g. in clinical chemistry laboratories and in X-ray departments), not connected to the central installation until experience and confidence led naturally to such on-line extensions. The cost of such a regionally organised system would be competitive since a single large computer with fully utilised hardware is more economic than a multiplicity of smaller machines sited in individual hospitals. Flexibility would be retained because a mixed system of this type could be designed and staffed so as to permit progressive extensions to its on-line facilities. In this way, experience of more complex computing facilities would be gained progressively and co-operation of various grades of staff obtained during the initial period when the central batch mode computer and the local dedicated computers together satisfied the needs of most of the already proven applications.

### Staffing considerations

The installation of computers to serve medical applications cannot be considered without reference to the staff required to develop and to run the systems. There is generally no problem over recruiting junior staff, but senior staff in all grades (hardware, software and systems personnel) are at a premium. Ockenden and Bodenham (1970) stressed the need for the health services to offer computer staff prospects of a worthwhile career, both in respect of salaries and job satisfaction, if recruitment and retention of good quality staff are to be achieved. A new structure of salaries and conditions of work may need to be set up to cater for the computing branch of the health services, if only to compete satisfactorily with industry. As far as career prospects within the health service are concerned, a regional computing centre should be in a much better position than a relatively small installation serving a single hospital, since the larger regional system should be able to offer a wider range of experience, including interactive on-line work, and a graded career structure within its own organisation. Retention of high calibre staff depends as much on job satisfaction as on salary. Here again a regional medical computing organisation has advantages over a number of smaller separate installations, since the needs of the various hospitals served from the centre will probably not be identical. This means that there will be a greater likelihood of constant development and maintenance of programs, a wider range of problems to be solved, and the possibility of engaging in a variety of statistical and operational research studies.

## PRIVACY AND CONFIDENTIALITY

We have discussed some of the problems of how, in general, to select computer installations for health service work, leaving out of this discussion the special purpose machines, often dedicated black-boxes, where analog techniques excel. We have also referred to problems of staffing the operation of such equipment, and mentioned the thorny subject of how to finance work which is still largely in the developmental stages when deficiencies still so clearly exist elsewhere within the health services. We now briefly consider questions of confidentiality, a problem which has been mentioned in earlier chapters, and one which must be solved before computing systems can become generally acceptable both to the medical profession and their patients. Uninformed publicity, sometimes misleading, on the 'data bank society' has helped to foster misunderstandings, and could seriously delay the wider introduction of computing techniques in important fields such as medical records and patient care.

Problems of privacy and confidentiality are not new but little attention was paid to them prior to the introduction of computers; special aspects relate to confidentiality in medicine. The computer potentially aggravates the problems of confidentiality in at least three ways:

1. The volume of material recorded on individuals could increase, and the nature of computer technology means that it will be more readily stored and retrieved.

2. Record linkage techniques operated in association with computer-held files mean that it will be possible to collect scattered reports into a single comprehensive file to an extent inconceivable prior to the introduction of electronic data processing.

3. Unless special precautions are taken, an unknown number of unauthorised persons may become capable of accessing these computer-held records.

Several safeguards have been advocated to guard against unauthorised access. These include legal safeguards, both in respect of writing to and reading from personal files, and the coding of the data stored on computer files so that unauthorised access still requires the deciphering of any information retrieved. A further but different type of safeguard proposed has been that everyone should have the legal right of access to their own personal file, to verify the contents and to allow for the possibility of an appeal in cases of dispute over the correctness of the data held on the file.

Confidentiality is essentially a legal and political problem, and controls can be imposed by any society determined to do so. It is worth pointing out, however, that technical security in terms of the physical prevention of unauthorised access to stored information is much better with a properly designed system of computer-held files than it could ever be without the assistance of electronic data processing. Reference need only be made to the methods still commonly used for handling and storing medical records in hospitals and general practitioners' surgeries, etc. where a variety of non-medical personnel, often in quite junior grades, have ready access to written records concerning patients.

Policy decisions are needed in respect of the rights of access to medical records. Proposals so far mostly favour the keeping of such records entirely under separate medical control even to the extent of storing medical records solely at N.H.S. computer installations to which only designated N.H.S. personnel would have access. Suitable code restrictions could restrict the access of consultants and of general practitioners to the records of their own patients only. For research purposes, other methods of search could allow access to all records on an impersonal basis, coding restrictions ensuring that access for statistical and similar research investigations was unable to retrieve information such as the name and address of individual patients unless appropriate permission had been granted.

## CONCLUSIONS
### Computer expansion and financial support
This chapter has discussed some general problems—finance, staff and questions of confidentiality—each and all of which could seriously influence developments in the field of medical computing. Decisions on policy are needed now, and a deliberate programme embarked upon to attempt the progressive implementation of this policy. An experimental situation still exists in many areas of application of computers to medicine, and experiments to some extent must involve financial risks. Failure to devote money to necessary experiments could seriously delay the likelihood that medicine in this country will profit in the foreseeable future from advances in computer technology. We conclude that the government should now declare its intention to finance further experi-

ments in this field, and make the arrangements necessary to guarantee the implementation of its programme of work.

Although we stress the need for a declaration of intent, and the earmarking of a budget to implement a programme of experiments, these statements must be coupled with a caveat that the programme should not be so rigid as to prevent variation in the light of further experience gained before its completion—there is a need for a built-in system of periodical reviews. This call for some element of flexibility is needed if only to take account of technical advances which are still occurring, both in respect of computers and their peripheral equipment, since the rapidity of these advances has in the past sometimes rendered installations obsolete before provision had been made for their replacement.

Another lesson that can be learned from the past, and which is relevant to any attempt at estimating the financial requirements for implementing a policy, is the unfortunate fact that most estimates of computer costs and requirements have undervalued the price of software, underestimated the level of expertise required to write this software, and failed to recognise the amount of effort required to maintain this software over several years' operation during which unsuspected errors may be revealed or modifications become necessary. There is also a general tendency seriously to underestimate the time taken to produce proven software and to overestimate the efficiency with which the finished product will run; in practice it is often found to require far more computer time than was originally allowed for, and computer time is expensive.

## Changing attitudes

Finally, we draw attention to our belief that the changing attitudes of the younger generation towards computers is not always fully appreciated. The rapid introduction of programming courses, often with on-line facilities, into the schools and the increasing likelihood that most undergraduates will at least attend computer appreciation courses means that the general level of computer awareness is increasing among the younger members of society. This growing awareness, familiarity and understanding of computers will express itself in a demand for more computer facilities. In the medical field, young doctors, nurses and social workers will come to prefer working in an environment that provides computing facilities, whether locally or through a regional computing centre, and the lack of a basic computer service in a hospital could be regarded in 1980 as representing inadequate facilities, not only for the doctors but also for the patients.

REFERENCES

OCKENDEN, J. M. & BODENHAM, K. E. (1970). *Focus on Medical Computer Development*, pp. 64–87. London: Oxford University Press.

REPORT (1968). *Hospital Scientific and Technical Services.* London: Her Majesty's Stationery Office.

REPORT HM(70)50 (1970). *Hospital Laboratory Services.* London: Department of Health and Social Security.

# Index

(*Note :* Most of the technical computer terms are described in the Glossary, and are not specifically indexed here).